DATE DUE

DEMCO 38-296

CONTEMPORARY MUSICIANS

Explore your options!
Gale databases offered in
a variety of formats

DISKETTE/MAGNETIC TAPE

Many Gale databases are available on diskette or magnetic tape, allowing systemwide access to your most-used information sources through existing computer systems. Data can be delivered on a variety of mediums (DOS formatted diskette, 9-track tape, 8mm data tape) and in industry-standard formats (comma-delimited, tagged, fixed-field). Retrieval software is also available with many of Gale's databases that allows you to search, display, print and download the data

ONLINE

For your convenience, many Gale databases are available through popular online services, including DIALOG, NEXIS (Mead Data Central), Data-Star, Orbit, Questel, OCLC, I/Plus and HRIN.

CD-ROM

A variety of Gale titles is available on CD-ROM, offering maximum flexibility and powerful search software.

The information in this Gale publication is also available in some or all of the formats described here. Your Customer Service Representative will be happy to fill you in.

For information, call

GALE

ISSN 1044-2197

CONTEMPORARY MUSICIANS

PROFILES OF THE PEOPLE IN MUSIC

SUZANNE M. BOURGOIN,
Editor

VOLUME 14
Includes Cumulative Indexes

 Gale Research Inc.

An International Thomson Publishing Company

I(T)P

NEW YORK • LONDON • BONN • BOSTON • DETROIT • MADRID
MELBOURNE • MEXICO CITY • PARIS • SINGAPORE • TOKYO
TORONTO • WASHINGTON • ALBANY NY • BELMONT CA • CINCINNATI OH

STAFF

Suzanne M. Bourgoin, *Editor*

Brian Escamilla, Geri J. Speace, *Associate Editors*

Paul E. Anderson, Robin Armstrong, Barbara Carlisle Bigelow, Carol Brennan, Matthew Brown, Susan Windisch Brown, John Cohassey, Ed Decker, Stewart Francke, Alan Glenn, Simon Glickman, Anne Janette Johnson, Lazae Laspina, Ondine E. Le Blanc, L. Mpho Mabunda, Emily J. McMurray, Sarah Messer, Diane Moroff, John Morrow, Nicholas Patti, Debra Power, Joseph M. Reiner, Joanna Rubiner, Julia M. Rubiner, Susan Salter, Pamela L. Shelton, Sonya Shelton, B. Kimberly Taylor, Thaddeus Wawro, *Contributing Editors*

Neil E. Walker, *Managing Editor*

Marlene Lasky, *Permissions Manager*
Margaret A. Chamberlain, Linda M. Pugliese, *Permissions Specialists*
Susan Brohman, Diane Cooper, Maria Franklin, Pamela A. Hayes, Arlene Johnson, Josephine M. Keene, Michael Lonoconus, Maureen Puhl, Shalice Shah, Kimberly F. Smilay, Barbara A. Wallace, *Permissions Associates*
Edna Hedblad, Tyra Y. Phillips, *Permissions Assistants*

Mary Beth Trimper, *Production Director*
Shanna Philpott Heilveil, *Production Assistant*
Cynthia Baldwin, *Product Design Manager*
Barbara J. Yarrow, *Graphic Services Supervisor*
Todd Nessel, *MacIntosh Artist*
Willie Mathis, *Camera Operator*

Cover illustration by John Kleber

∞™ This book is printed on acid-free paper that meets the minimum requirements of American National Standard for Information Sciences— Permanence Paper for Printed Library Materials, ANSI Z39.48-1984.

♲ This book is printed on recycled paper that meets Environmental Protection Agency Standards.

ISBN 0-8103-5738-0
ISSN 1044-2197

10 9 8 7 6 5 4 3 2 1

I(T)P™ Gale Research Inc., an International Thomson Publishing Company.
ITP logo is a trademark under license.

Contents

Introduction ix

Cumulative Subject Index 273

Cumulative Musicians Index 293

Introduction

Fills the Information Gap on Today's Musicians

Contemporary Musicians profiles the colorful personalities in the music industry who create or influence the music we hear today. Prior to *Contemporary Musicians,* no quality reference series provided comprehensive information on such a wide range of artists despite keen and ongoing public interest. To find biographical and critical coverage, an information seeker had little choice but to wade through the offerings of the popular press, scan television "infotainment" programs, and search for the occasional published biography or exposé. *Contemporary Musicians* is designed to serve that information seeker, providing in one ongoing source in-depth coverage of the important names on the modern music scene in a format that is both informative and entertaining. Students, researchers, and casual browsers alike can use *Contemporary Musicians* to meet their needs for personal information about music figures; find a selected discography of a musician's recordings; and uncover an insightful essay offering biographical and critical information.

Provides Broad Coverage

Single-volume biographical sources on musicians are limited in scope, often focusing on a handful of performers from a specific musical genre or era. In contrast, *Contemporary Musicians* offers researchers and music devotees a comprehensive, informative, and entertaining alternative. *Contemporary Musicians* is published twice yearly, with each volume providing information on more than 80 musical artists and record-industry luminaries from all the genres that form the broad spectrum of contemporary music—pop, rock, jazz, blues, country, New Age, folk, rhythm and blues, gospel, bluegrass, rap, and reggae, to name a few—as well as selected classical artists who have achieved "crossover" success with the general public. *Contemporary Musicians* will also occasionally include profiles of influential nonperforming members of the music community, including producers, promoters, and record company executives. Additionally, beginning with *Contemporary Musicians 11,* each volume features new profiles of a selection of previous *Contemporary Musicians* listees who remain of interest to today's readers and who have been active enough to require completely revised entries.

Includes Popular Features

In *Contemporary Musicians* you'll find popular features that users value:

- **Easy-to-locate data sections:** Vital personal statistics, chronological career summaries, listings of major awards, and mailing addresses, when available, are prominently displayed in a clearly marked box on the second page of each entry.

- **Biographical/critical essays:** Colorful and informative essays trace each subject's personal and professional life, offer representative examples of critical response to the artist's work, and provide entertaining personal sidelights.

- **Selected discographies:** Each entry provides a comprehensive listing of the artist's major recorded works.

- **Photographs:** Most entries include portraits of the subject profiled.

- **Sources for additional information:** This invaluable feature directs the user to selected books, magazines, and newspapers where more information can be obtained.

Helpful Indexes Make It Easy to Find the Information You Need

Each volume of *Contemporary Musicians* features a cumulative Musicians Index, listing names of individual performers and musical groups, and a cumulative Subject Index, which provides the user with a breakdown by primary musical instruments played and by musical genre.

Available in Electronic Formats

Diskette/Magnetic Tape. *Contemporary Musicians* is available for licensing on magnetic tape or diskette in a fielded format. Either the complete database or a custom selection of entries may be ordered. The database is available for internal data processing and nonpublishing purposes only. For more information, call (800) 877-GALE.

Online. *Contemporary Musicians* is available online through Mead Data Central's NEXIS Service in the NEXIS, PEOPLE and SPORTS Libraries in the GALBIO file.

We Welcome Your Suggestions

The editors welcome your comments and suggestions for enhancing and improving *Contemporary Musicians*. If you would like to suggest subjects for inclusion, please submit these names to the editors. Mail comments or suggestions to:

The Editor
Contemporary Musicians
Gale Research Inc.
835 Penobscot Bldg.
Detroit, MI 48226-4094
Phone: (800) 347-4253
Fax: (313) 961-6599

CONTEMPORARY MUSICIANS

Arthur Alexander

Singer, songwriter

When rhythm and blues singer-songwriter Arthur Alexander died on June 9, 1993, he was in the midst of a triumphant comeback. He had just appeared at the Los Angeles Summerlights Festival and was about to complete a national tour of summer music festivals to promote his first new album in 20 years, *Lonely Just Like Me.* He was also set to promote his 1960s and 1970s hits, which were reissued in 1993 by Razor & Tie Records as *The Ultimate Arthur Alexander.*

Alexander's return to fame followed a fall into obscurity after a final album for Warner Brothers in 1972 and 1975's pop hit "Every Day I Have to Cry Some." Although the Beatles, the Rolling Stones, the Who, Bob Dylan, and Ry Cooder had all covered his original compositions, and despite his own repeated success on the charts, Alexander remained underpaid for his music. So he dropped out and began driving a bus in Cleveland, Ohio, for a local social service organization. It was not until his friends—who had cut R&B recordings with him in the 1960s in Muscle Shoals, Alabama—tracked him down in 1991 that Alexander began performing again.

After meeting with Elektra's senior director of product development, Danny Kahn, following an appearance at New York's Bottom Line in September of 1991, Alexander agreed to go back to the recording studio. At that time the singer remembered and praised the ongoing support of his listeners and found himself inspired again and back on track. "The fans always was great," he told Chris Morris of *Billboard* in 1993. "It just made me want to do more just to please 'em, because they were the ones that kept my stuff alive.... It makes me want to come back, and give it another shot."

Combined Country and Soul

Born on May 10, 1940, in Florence, Alabama, and raised in Sheffield, Alabama, during the 1940s and 1950s by a father who was himself a semiprofessional musician, Alexander grew up in a segregated South with exposure to both white and black sounds. Alexander's father abandoned his own interest in music when he discovered Arthur's interest. "He gave up something he loved to steer me right," Alexander was quoted as saying in *Pulse!* "I was an avid radio man. I kept the radio on. And it only played white singers. Red Foley, Patti Page, stuff like that. The only black singers I heard was in church or up and down the street. Not until I was 10 or so did I hear professional black singers, and even then, it was when they would bring black movies to town."

Born May 10, 1940, in Florence, AL; died of respiratory and heart failure, June 9, 1993, in Nashville, TN; father was a guitarist; married twice; three children.

Sang in and led teenage gospel group the Heartstrings in Alabama, beginning in 1953; sang rock and roll on regional television in Alabama, late 1950s; recorded first song, "Sally Sue Brown" (later covered by Bob Dylan), on Judd label, Memphis, TN, 1961; released first album, *You Better Move On,* Fame Studios, 1962; toured extensively, 1960s; dropped out of music business, 1975; returned with concerts in Alabama; New York City; Austin, Texas; and Los Angeles, 1991-93.

Awards: Inducted into Alabama Music Hall of Fame, 1991.

In his own songs, Alexander combined the influences of country and soul. "There's a bluesy sadness to much of his work, but the steel guitar and twang make it distinctly country," Robert Gordon wrote in *Pulse!* With a singing voice described by Gordon as "full and smooth" and revealing "no rough edges," Alexander became a central force in developing southern R&B from the early 1960s to the early 1970s.

Led 1960s Southern R&B

Although he achieved his first Top 40 hit song in 1962 with "You Better Move On," Alexander had gained early experience singing gospel and rock and roll locally. As an older teen in the late 1950s, he led the teenage gospel group the Heartstrings and appeared singing rock on a regional television show. He began writing songs then but did not achieve success until his 1962 hit. His song "Sally Sue Brown," for example, came out earlier on the Memphis, Tennessee, Judd label and earned little notice; the tune, however, was rerecorded to broader recognition on *Lonely Just Like Me* for Elektra/Nonesuch in 1993.

Mark Coleman of *Rolling Stone* credited Alexander's 1962 hit with ushering in the long chart run of Rick Hall's Fame Studios in Muscle Shoals, Alabama. "When [popular television dance show host] Dick Clark said he was interested in that record," Alexander recalled to Coleman, "I knew I was *bona fide.* My first check off the record was about $1,700—more money than I'd ever seen in my life. But then the publishing rights got away from me—went to this guy in Nashville,

and from that day on I never saw a dime." Alexander nonetheless continued singing and writing and working with a number of musicians to bring noteriety to Fame Studios through their songs on the Dot label. He would maintain his ties with those musicians throughout his life.

Influenced the Beatles

By 1975, however, Alexander's difficult financial straits caught up with him. "I had so many disappointments about getting paid," Alexander told Gordon of *Pulse!* "The money was always short and if you didn't have a chart record, you couldn't even work. But I had big records and I still never got paid for them." Alexander explained his break from his career to *Rolling Stone's* Coleman: "In '76 I was through forever. After I remade 'Everyday I Have to Cry' for Buddah in 1975—a Top 50 record, *didn't get a dime*—I went back to Alabama, rejoined the church and started working with the young people in Sunday school." Two years later he moved to Cleveland to be with his future second wife and their daughter. Soon after arriving in Cleveland, he stopped playing in local clubs and in 1981 became a bus driver for Cleveland's Center for Human Services.

Meanwhile Alexander's influence continued to be felt internationally. Providing important early album cuts for the Beatles, who covered "Anna," and the Rolling Stones, who remade "You Better Move On," Alexander was a central figure in defining British rock in the 1960s. In a 1987 *Billboard* article, Paul McCartney said, "If the Beatles ever wanted a sound, it was R&B. We wanted to be like Arthur Alexander." In the same article, Rolling Stones guitarist Keith Richards related, "When the Beatles and the Stones got their first chances to record, one did 'Anna,' and the other did 'You Better Move On.' That should tell you enough!"

Later, the Who covered Alexander's song "Soldier of Love," Bob Dylan remade "Sally Sue Brown," and Ry Cooder put out "Go Home, Girl." While he wished he could have enjoyed more direct recognition for his songs, Alexander appreciated the exposure. "Every artist wants to think they can sell a million records," he expressed in *Rolling Stone.* "But some artists are geared to be suppliers. Though I wasn't getting paid, the Beatles and the Stones kept my songs in front of a big audience."

Alexander's own career was far from over, however. In Cleveland in 1991 he received a call from Fame's Rick Hall. Hall convinced Alexander to play at the Alabama Music Hall of Fame, into which Alexander was eventually inducted. At a later appearance at the Helen Keller Festival, held at the blind educator's hometown of

Tuscumbia, Alabama, Alexander's fellow ex-Muscle Shoals singer and songwriter friend Donnie Fritts asked him to perform six songs at the songwriters night In Their Own Words in September of 1991 at New York's Bottom Line. There Alexander met Elektra's senior director of product development, Danny Kahn, who introduced the idea of recording for Elektra's American Explorer series.

The American Explorer series was meant to present classics of American music. Kahn noted in *Billboard,* "A lot of people have tried to capture this same feel, but these are the same people who created the music.... This is a real thought-out document of what their music means to them." Alexander's 1993 album, *Lonely Just Like Me,* features 12 songs, including "striking new originals" and "a handful of remakes," according to Rob O'Connor of *Musician.*

Songs Tell Stories

Keeping with his trademark style on *Lonely Just Like Me,* Alexander spins yarns of doomed relationships and troubled lives. "I like story lines," he told Robert Gordon of *Pulse!* "Roy Rogers, Rex Allen, Louis Jordan—they all told stories." Alexander's stories arose from some connection to his own life. "Most of these songs were fashioned from an era when I was lonely, but now I'm not lonely," he continued. "I've got four grandkids, a passel of children, and I'm surrounded by kids every day."

Alexander considered his new recording opportunity with Elektra a second chance—and one he took altogether seriously. "When I cut records earlier," he divulged in *Rolling Stone,* "I'd have to rest for about a week before I cut the final vocals. This time I was in strong voice all the way through. Yeah, I stopped drinking and carousing, got myself cleaned out and got back to my basic roots. I guess God said, 'I got to give him another blessing and see what he does with it.'"

Alexander embraced that opportunity with an enthusiasm tempered by caution. Despite the new recording, for example, by April of 1993 he had not yet quit his day job. Still, before he died he had planned to perform in showcases in New York City and Los Angeles with fellow American Explorer musician Sid Selvidge during the summer. In addition, Jimmie Dale Gilmore, who hosted an appearance by Alexander in Austin, Texas, in

March of 1993, expressed an interest in bringing Alexander with him on the road.

Just after the Austin concert with Gilmore, Alexander once again expressed his heartfelt appreciation for his audience. After he died on June 9, 1993, *Arthur Alexander: The Ultimate Arthur Alexander* was released. *Billboard* described the LP, a collection of reissues of his classic 1960s hits, as a "monument to a singular talent."

Selected discography

Singles

"Sally Sue Brown," Judd, 1961.
"Every Day I Have to Cry," Buddah, 1975.
"Sharon and I Together," Buddah.

Albums

You Better Move On, Fame Studios, 1962.
Arthur Alexander (includes "Rainbow Road"), Warner Bros., 1972.
Lonely Just Like Me (includes "All the Time," "I Believe in Miracles," "Go Home Girl," and "Sally Sue Brown"), Elektra/Nonesuch, 1993.
Arthur Alexander: The Ultimate Arthur Alexander (includes "Anna [Go To Him]," "You Better Move On," "Go Home Girl," and "Every Day I Have to Cry Some"), Razor & Tie, 1993.

Alexander's songs have been recorded by such artists as the Beatles, the Rolling Stones, the Who, Ry Cooder, Bob Dylan, Elvis Presley, and Otis Redding.

Sources

Billboard, April 10, 1993; June 19, 1993; August 14, 1993.
Musician, June 1993.
New York Times, June 11, 1993.
Pulse!, July 1993.
Rolling Stone, August 5, 1993.
Spin, August 1993.
Village Voice, July 6, 1993.

—*Nicholas Patti*

Aphex Twin

Ambient music pioneer

Photograph by Joseph Cultice, © 1994 Sire Records Company

Along with a handful of other musicians, Richard James, better known as Aphex Twin, has developed a new kind of music and a new kind of performance. Samples of this completely electronic, elegiac variety of rave and techno matched the sales of rock albums in Europe in 1994. In the United States, the music began gaining its first broad exposure and popularity that same year, when Aphex Twin released his second volume of ambient sound sculptures, *Selected Ambient Works Volume II,* to acclaim on the Sire/Warner Bros. label.

Considered descendants of 1970s "progressive" rock acts Pink Floyd and Tangerine Dream, Aphex Twin and fellow ambient musicians Brian Eno, Orb, and Orbital altered their performance and marketing approaches as well; emphasizing the music over their own celebrity stardom, they perform by mixing their music and others' live as DJs in the shadows of their sequencers on stage. The dancers and the rest of the audience—rather than the artists—take the limelight.

Ambient music emerged from the underground rave scene in the early 1990s. James got his start in the music industry around the same time, having emerged from his parents' garage in Cornwall, England, where legend has it he began fiddling with synthesizers and recreating the sounds in his head all night—every night—since age 12.

Explosive Performances

Richard James debuted as Aphex Twin in early 1992 at the Tressor Club in Berlin; since 1991 he could be found deejaying in London raves and recording for a number of small independent labels under a variety of pseudonyms. His floating melodies and dark, screeching soul-searches found their first audience in exhausted dancers in U.K. West Country raves. This crowd made his 1992 *Didgeridoo* album—released on the Belgium techno label R&S—a hit in Britain. The single "Analogue Bubblebath" led to a follow-up, U.K. Independent Top Ten double album of pure ambient music. Titled *Selected Ambient Works 85-92,* it was issued by the same label later in the year.

Aphex Twin's fast rise to mainstream prominence has not been without its wrinkles, however. First there was the small explosion during one of his concerts in Germany. "The only big problem I've had was when I electrocuted myself in front of 17,000 mad Germans at the Mayday techno festival," he told Matt Bright of *Melody Maker.* "I put my finger on a live terminal.... My finger just started to sizzle when it blew. I was thrown off the keyboard and all the power for the rave went down."

Born Richard James, August 18, 1971, in Cornwall, England. *Education:* Studied electronics at college in London, c. 1991.

Began sampling sounds and deejaying at raves in Cornwall, c. 1986; developed first hit, "Didgeridoo," in Cornwall raves, c. 1990; moved to London, deejayed, and recorded singles—including ambient hit "Analogue Bubblebath"—as Aphex Twin and AFX for Mighty Force Records, 1991; debuted as Aphex Twin at Tressor Club, Berlin, January 1992; recorded *Didgeridoo* for Belgium label, R&S, early 1992; as Caustic Window, started own label, Rephlex, and recorded "Joyrex J4" and "Joyrex J5," 1992; as Aphex Twin, recorded double-album *Selected Ambient Works 85-92,* late 1992; as Polygon Window, signed to British independent label, Warp Records, and recorded *Surfing on Sine Waves* and *Quoth,* both 1993; as Aphex Twin, recorded EP *Phlegm,* 1993; signed to Sire Records/Warner Bros., mid-1993; embarked on first U.S. tour, late 1993; released *Selected Ambient Works Volume II,* Sire, early 1994. Remixed songs for Curve, Jesus Jones, and others, c. 1991—.

Addresses: *Record company*—Sire Records/Warner Bros., 75 Rockefeller Plaza, New York, NY 10019.

Aphex Twin usually does not involve himself so explosively in his concerts, though, and he has actually received criticism for his mediocre stage presence. Reviewing James's performance as "lacklustre" at the Midi Circus of underground dance acts in Britain in the summer of 1993, a *Melody Maker* contributor wrote, "[For] all the talk of ambient swirls, quiet genius and off-kilter imagination, he's ultimately pretty dreary.... The rock gig thing being what it is, everyone resolutely faces the stage, when they'd perhaps be better off with their backs to it." With dazzling high-tech and high-cost visuals, *Melody Maker* mused, Aphex Twin at Midi "would be redefining the stadium experience." Without those visuals, however, his show appeared a dud.

Aphex Twin staunchly defended his mode of performance against such criticism. "So?," he asked *Melody Maker* in response to the critique. "I don't want people to stand there staring at me. I want them to dance. What's so good about a guy bouncing around with a guitar? I'm too busy to bounce around. I usually forget that I'm doing a gig. It's as if I'm at home."

Reviewing the largest techno concert in New York ever in late 1993, *Village Voice* music writer Frank Owen maligned Aphex Twin's performance on similar grounds, and with a similar response from the musician. Asked whether he had intended an anti-performance, Aphex Twin answered, "Yeah, if you mean I don't ponce about onstage like some d—-head rock star. I leave that type of thing to Moby." A rising ambient-techno star from the United States, Moby embraces the rock-style celebrity performance, aiming for "techno's answer to [U2's] Bono—a rave version of the rock and roll messiah." The *Voice* considered Moby "clearly the hit of the evening with the [New York] audience." Still, Aphex Twin finally represented for the newspaper "the artistic future of techno."

The History of Ambient Music

The split in ambient-techno is only one of many that have afflicted techno since it grew in popularity. Aphex Twin has been at the center of a deeper shift in audience, while techno has splintered into two major factions. Rave, which first became a movement in the late 1980s in Britain, divided in much the same way as acid rock had in the late sixties and early seventies and as punk had earlier in the eighties. One strand of rave became hardcore—"'ardkore" in Britain—with a beat increasing to as high as 200 per minute. This strand appealed to "working class young people who live for the weekend," according to the *New York Times,* and followed in the tradition of heavy metal devotees in the seventies, and skins and "oi" punk rockers earlier in the eighties.

Meanwhile, another strand slowed down the music and often dispensed with beat altogether. This variation was alternately called ambient, the dominant term—as well as progressive, post-rave, chill-out, techno purism, the New Electronica, intelligent techno, and electronic listening music. Aphex Twin and other ambient musicians have appealed largely to older ravers, characterized as more middle- than working-class, and non-ravers such as indie-rock fans, music theory connoisseurs, and so-called "aging hippies."

Obsessed With Music From an Early Age

Richard James followed a circuitous route through early musical isolation and later rave deejaying before becoming the leading ambient musician Aphex Twin. James, who was born in 1971, came from the remote coastal region of Cornwall, England, where his father worked in the mining industry. His exposure was limited to his sister's records, including those of Echo & the

Bunnymen, Kraftwerk, John Peel, and not much else. A few days after being introduced to the piano at age 12 by his parents, James decided he preferred playing the strings directly on the inside rather than through the keyboard on the outside. He then scavenged for other one-of-a-kind instruments, learned the rudiments of electronics in school, and began composing various sounds he imagined—sometimes even while asleep. It was then, so the story goes, that he began sleeping only two to three hours each night.

James also began deejaying in the Cornwall area's local raves when he was in his late teens. Recording his own tracks furiously as well, he left numerous tapes with friends, who would later cull many of these for his first collection. His first hit, the single "Didgeridoo," was conceived as a piece that would help the listener wind down from a night of heavy rave dancing.

A Link to the Classics

In 1991 James moved to London and recorded a number of samples under a variety of names, including Aphex Twin, AFX, Caustic Window, and Polygon Window. With *Selected Ambient Works 85-92,* recorded as Aphex Twin for release by R&S in 1992, and *Surfing on Sine Waves,* recorded as Polygon Window for release by the fiercely independent British label Warp Records in January of 1993, James established his audience and his prominence. His 1994 album, *Selected Ambient Works Volume II,* creates "eerie sound-paintings," according to the *New York Times;* the tracks on the release have been described as "spooky" and "textured" by *Rolling Stone* and as "deeply unsettling" by the *Metro Times.*

Ambient music carries on a fairly new tradition within classical music, and Aphex Twin brings his own edge to this tradition. *Billboard* cited Brian Eno's 1978 album *Music for Airports,* the theories of John Cage, and the minimalist composers Steve Reich, Philip Glass, and Terry Riley as the predecessors of ambient. When two musicians—Alex Patterson of Orb and Jimmy Cauty, formerly of Orb and KLF—combined this environ-centered classical music in 1988 and 1989 with the popular acid-house music of Detroit and Chicago, they invented the "ambient house" genre. While ambient house declined in popularity, Aphex Twin found a growing audience by pushing the bounds of the genre with his sometimes disturbing, sometimes funky compositions.

Perhaps because of ambient's roots in contemporary classical music, Simon Reynolds of the *New York Times* deemed Aphex Twin a pioneer in the classical as well as the ambient-techno field. "While a horde of Aphex imitators have reduced ambient to little more than a soothing soundbath for the stressed-out, Mr. James has opened up a new frontier for techno," Reynolds began. "At times, he's making what sounds like classical music for the next millennium."

Meanwhile, a number of diverse bands have invited him to remix their songs. The band Curve acknowledged seeking out his influence for their own work: "What seems to be special is the way he hears sound," bandmember Dean Garcia was quoted as saying in *Melody Maker.* "Have you heard what he did with our track 'Falling Free'? He's taken one little bit of it—we can't work out where he got it from—and made it into this kind of choral thing. It's really spaced-out and very, very sparse, very womb-like: it's actually inspired us in the way we work, and sparked off other ideas." James has also made samples of sides by Curve, Jesus Jones, St. Etienne, PCP, and Meat Beat Manifesto, among others.

Despite his status as a leader of ambient, Aphex Twin creates a sound that remains difficult to classify. "Richard's music isn't easy to pigeonhole," Matt Bright wrote in *Melody Maker.* "One minute he's crafting something which Eno or Philip Glass would be proud of, the next he's making enough racket to give Butthole Surfers a migraine.... Aphex Twin is the Midi Circus' trapeze artist." Bright concluded that the artist's sound is best described as having a texture to it: "He doesn't so much make tracks as sculptures. It's as if the melodies and the beats have a physical presence." Aphex Twin reportedly beamed in response: "That's exactly it! I mean, some of the tracks I've recorded for 'Ambient Works 2' consist of just one sound. I'm trying to make music which surrounds you, which fills the room."

Selected discography

Singles

(As Caustic Window) "Joyrex J4," Rephlex (self-owned), 1992.
(As Caustic Window) "Joyrex J5," Rephlex, 1992.
(As AFX and Aphex Twin) "Analogue Bubblebath," Mighty Force Records, 1991.

Albums

Didgeridoo (includes "Analogue Bubblebath"), R&S, 1992.
Selected Ambient Works 85-92, R&S, 1992.
(As Polygon Window) *Surfing on Sine Waves,* Warp, 1993.
(As Polygon Window) *Quoth,* Warp, 1993.
Phlegm (EP), R&S, 1993.
Selected Ambient Works Volume II, Sire/Warner Bros., 1994.

Sources

Billboard, July 23, 1994.
Chicago Tribune, November 5, 1993.
Details, May 1994.
Melody Maker, January 30, 1993; June 19, 1993.
Metro Times (Detroit), May 11, 1994.
New York Times, March 13, 1994.
Rolling Stone, June 30, 1994.
Village Voice, November 9, 1993.

Additional information for this profile was obtained from biographical notes provided by Formula Artist Development & Public Relations, January 1994.

—Nicholas Patti

Arrested Development

Rap group

In a profile of Arrested Development for *Musican* magazine, Jon Young mused, "Rarely have morality and killer beats been paired more effectively." Just when hip-hop seemed inextricably bound up in the "gangsta" aesthetic, the group appeared with its hopeful message, Afrocentric politics, and distinctive, earthy sound. First capturing listeners with their reflective single "Tennessee," they racked up sales and awards, endured the inevitable backlash, and prepared to weather the storms of the music industry. "We try to make people aware of issues they may not be aware of," the group's leader, Speech, told *Billboard*. "Also, we attempt to make fly music that might expand what hip-hop is all about."

Though the band originated in the southern United States—and gained considerable attention for its rural southern style—Speech did not. He was born Todd Thomas in Milwaukee, Wisconsin, in 1968, the very year that civil rights trailblazer Martin Luther King, Jr., was assassinated. Thomas's parents divorced, and he ended up in the custody of his mother, who ran a newspa-

Photograph by Jeffrey Scales, © 1994 EMI Records Group

For the Record . . .

Members include **Ajile** (joined group 1994), dancer; **Kwesi Asuo** (joined group 1994), DJ; **Rasa Don** (born Donald Jones), percussionist; **Montsho Eshe,** dancer; **Dionne Farris** (left group 1993), singer; **Foley** (joined group 1994), bassist; **Headliner** (born Timothy Barnwell, c. 1968, in Savannah, GA), DJ and rapper; **Nadirah** (joined group 1994), singer; **Baba Oje** (born c. 1930), spiritual adviser and performer; **Speech** (born Todd Thomas in 1968 in Milwaukee, WI), singer, rapper, and songwriter; **Aerle Taree** (born Taree Jones, c. 1974), dancer.

Performing and recording group formed by Speech and Headliner, 1988—. With other members, group signed with Chrysalis Records, 1991, and released debut album *3 Years, 5 Months and 2 Days in the Life of...,* 1992; contributed song "Revolution" to *Malcolm X* film soundtrack, 1993; appeared on Lollapalooza Tour, 1993; guests at U.S. presidential inaugural festivities, Washington, DC, 1993; appeared on MTV *Unplugged* and released recording of performance, 1993; toured with En Vogue, 1993; performed in South Africa, 1994.

Awards: Quadruple-platinum award for debut album, 1993; Grammy awards for best new artist and best rap album, 1993; Soul Train Music Award, 1993; Best Rap Video of the Year, MTV, 1993; named Band of the Year by *Rolling Stone,* 1993; Album of the Year honors from *Musician* and the *Village Voice,* 1993.

Addresses: *Record company*—Chrysalis Records/ERG, 1290 Avenue of the Americas, New York, NY 10104. *Management*—Bart Phillips, Entertainment Resources International, 9380 SW 72nd St. Suite B-220, Miami, FL 33173. *Life Music Foundation*—c/o *Milwaukee Community Journal,* 3612 Martin Luther King, Jr. Dr., Milwaukee, WI 53212.

per, the *Milwaukee Community Journal;* years later he would write a column for the paper titled "20th Century African."

Thomas's mother took him and his brother Terry on trips to Africa, though at the time this ancestral journey had little impact on him. During the summers of his youth, however, he visited his paternal grandmother in Ripley, Tennessee. His experiences there—picking crops, exploring—proved deeply resonant. "Up North I was playing with video games," Speech was quoted as saying in *Vibe.* "Down South I had the grass and the fields." As he explained to Touré of the *Source,* "The rural South is a place where a lot of the African traditions are still here in their rawest form from when our ancestors were here as slaves."

"Rebel" Inspired Reflection

Thomas headed South in 1987, chasing his vision. "I wasn't too good a student in high school, so regular college wasn't really an option," he told Young. "But my mother wanted me to have some kind of higher education, and you have to respect your parents! I studied music at the Art Institute of Atlanta because it didn't have strict academic criteria and I became a great student." It was there that he met Timothy Barnwell, a Georgia native who would later call himself Headliner and serve as Arrested Development's DJ. Danyel Smith of *Vibe* cited Barnwell's recollection of their acquaintance: "Once I met Speech, my outlook on life totally changed in an instant." Todd Thomas explained the derivation of his own stage name to the *Source:* "I was a DJ back in Milwaukee and they used to call me 'Peach' because I'm light-skinned," and added, "When I started rhyming more, I put an 'S' to it so it had more sense than 'Peach.'"

Speech and Headliner formed a rap group heavily influenced by the prevailing "gangsta" style. "We knew we wanted to be in rap and that was the stuff that was really catching on," Speech recounted in the *Musician* interview with Young. "But after a while it didn't feel right. We realized it wasn't just about making money, it was about expressing inner feelings, and we had a lot more to say than 'bitch' and 'ho.'" Part of this realization came from hearing "Rebel Without a Pause" and other politically charged rap songs by the innovative group Public Enemy, which galvanized the two aspiring rap artists to pursue something deeper. "My parents had been involved in the civil-rights struggle," Speech told Keith Moerer of *Request,* "but 'Rebel Without a Pause' put it in more youthful terms, put it with a bass sound and screeching noise and a hard rap, and it sort of got through my thick skull. It opened a new world to me in a five-minute period."

Long Wait Provided Debut Album Title

Speech and Headliner began to put their vision of "Life Music" together, predicated on spirituality and the regeneration of the black community. They received counsel from Baba Oje, an elder statesman of Afrocentrism whom they met on the Art Institute campus and who became the group's "spiritual adviser." They were then joined by Speech's cousin Montsho Eshe, a teenaged dancer who lent a striking visual component to their live appearances. They next met drummer Rasa Don and his fiancée, singer Dionne Farris, both of whom went backstage after an early performance and ended up joining the fledgling band. Arrested Development takes its name from the historic plight of black people: "We saw the state of the black community as being in a state of arrested development," Speech informed Touré. "So we wanted to constantly remind ourselves of what we wanted to get beyond".

> ### "Arrested Development is the further evolution of rap."
> ### —Spike Lee

It took a long time for Arrested Development to negotiate a record deal. Originally set to release a single, the group recorded an album's worth of material before signing with Chrysalis Records. Indeed, the amount of time consumed by the process—from formation to contract—is reflected in the record's title. *3 Years, 5 Months and 2 Days in the Life of...* hit the stores in 1992. With its exuberant grooves, blues and upbeat funk samples, and overall celebratory vibe, the record fulfilled its claim of being "Life Music." Yet it took two deaths within a few days of each other in 1991—of Speech's grandmother and his brother Terry—to provoke the spiritual and emotional voyage that resulted in the release's hit single "Tennessee."

Became Unwilling Symbols

Ancestral landscapes serve as the basis for the impassioned exploration of identity and purpose in "Tennessee." The song uses a sample from funk-rock pioneer Prince's "Alphabet St." as a point of departure, incorporating a loping groove, Farris's athletic, soulful wailing, and mournful group chanting—along with Speech's pained but ever-hopeful narrative. In the words of a *Spin* writer, the rapper "let something larger than him speak through him, and, like all true visions of the divine mystery, the style of its arrival was ... inexplicably strange."

MTV picked up the starkly beautiful black-and-white video for "Tennessee," and soon the group had a strong following. The singles "People Everyday" and "Mr. Wendal" followed; the former features the chorus of Sly & the Family Stone's late-1960s anthem "Everyday People" and tells of Speech's confrontation with a rude self-proclaimed "nigga," while the latter praises the wisdom of a homeless man he'd met. Soon the album

went platinum; the band scored two Grammy awards—including the first-ever best new artist trophy awarded a rap group—as well as a Soul Train Music Award, an MTV nod for best rap video, honors from the National Association for the Advancement of Colored People (NAACP), and Band of the Year kudos from *Rolling Stone*.

Arrested Development joined the alternative-rock festival Lollapalooza in 1993: "We want the brothers and the sisters from the 'hood to come out and see us," proclaimed Speech in *Us*. The group also put out an *Unplugged* album from a live MTV appearance and contributed the song "Revolution" to the soundtrack of maverick filmmaker Spike Lee's *Malcolm X;* Lee had offered to direct one of their videos, but they turned him down. "Arrested Development is the total package—the look, the roots, the music, the live drummer," Lee remarked in *Vibe*. "And I think it's the further evolution of rap."

Politics and Business

Indeed, Arrested Development's celebration in the mainstream press as "anti-gangsta" led to something of a backlash from hardcore rappers and their supporters, who seemed to suspect the group of exploiting the white establishment's fantasies of happy, peace-loving blacks. What often got lost in such claims was Arrested Development's espousal of revolution. "We're not trying to be an opposite voice [to hardcore], just another voice," Speech insisted in the *Musician* interview. "Instead of being seen as part of the pie—one perspective on black reality—some people in the media tried to use Arrested Development as their voice and say, 'This is the way hip-hop needs to be.' We never took the stance that our form of hip-hop was the only form of hip-hop."

Perhaps the greatest honor awarded the group was the chance to play at the celebration marking black South African hero Nelson Mandela's 1994 election as the first president in the nation's post-apartheid era. Their appearance there—and at U.S. President Bill Clinton's inaugural festivities in January of 1993—suggested that in the minds of many, Arrested Development represented hope for the future and had become a musical symbol for positive, peaceful change.

But the tremendous success and visibility brought dissention and difficulties. Speech had acquired a reputation for being domineering; after an alleged altercation during the group's tour with soul-pop divas En Vogue, Farris departed, though she'd always been touted as a guest artist and was busily pursuing a solo career. Other personnel changes ensued, and Headliner was

---

moved from DJ to co-rapper, his place at the turntables taken by new member Kwesi Asuo. Stalwart jazz and funk bassist Foley also joined the lineup, as did singer Nadirah and dancer Ajile.

Despite Speech's claims to the contrary, some industry observers feel that Headliner was pushed aside in the shuffle. "It's very sad," the latter lamented in *Vibe.* "This business has no avenue for feelings. It's money, money, money, money. Let's make money. If you're not making money, let's move on. It's a band, but it's really a business at this point."

And business called. Arrested Development's sophomore album *Zingalamaduni*— named after a Swahili word meaning "a beehive of culture"—appeared in mid-1994. As Speech explained in *Billboard,* the title was chosen to celebrate the group's philosophy about its increased use of samples. "Every time you sample notes," he claimed, "you're also sampling the spirit of whomever you're sampling." The album failed to take off as its predecessor had, due in part to the even greater stranglehold of gangsta rap and Arrested Development's lack of novelty.

Reviews of *Zingalamaduni* were mixed: *Rolling Stone* declared that the band "ecstatically combine group dynamics and solo rebel spirit" and awarded the album four stars, and *Entertainment Weekly*'s Greg Sandow called the record "as appealing—and artistically deep— as any pop album you're likely to hear." *Spin,* meanwhile, was more ambivalent, and *Entertainment Weekly* writer Michael Walker, endeavoring a few weeks after the magazine's favorable review to explain the album's lack of immediate success, lamented Arrested Development's tendency to "shove peace, love, and understanding (and a nearly unpronounceable album title) [down their] audience's throat."

But even in the face of a possible sophomore slump, Arrested Development appeared ready for the long haul. Speech bought a house in Georgia (satisfying the need for land he had sung about in songs like "Ache'n

for Acres"), looked forward to the birth of his child, and continued to write his column for his mother's paper, which also serves as the base for the group's Life Music Foundation. He was emphatic in a *Musician* interview: "We're gonna be around for 10 or 12 years, at least," he declared. "In that time I feel confident that we'll be able to do all the things we want to do. Someday we'd like people to be able to look back at 12 different albums and say 'Dang, they did some fly stuff.'"

Selected discography

On Chrysalis

3 Years, 5 Months and 2 Days in the Life of... (includes "Tennessee," "People Everyday," and "Mr. Wendal"), 1992.
Unplugged, 1993.
(Contributors) *Malcolm X* (soundtrack; appear on "Revolution"), Qwest, 1993.
Zingalamaduni (includes "Ache'n for Acres"), 1994.

Sources

Billboard, April 23, 1994.
Black Beat, June 1994.
Ebony, November 1993.
Entertainment Weekly, August 14, 1992; December 25, 1992; June 17, 1994; July 29, 1994.
Metro Times (Detroit), July 20, 1994.
Musician, November 1992; June 1994.
People, August 17, 1992.
Request, December 1992.
Rolling Stone, January 7, 1993; June 30, 1994.
Source, September 1992.
Spin, July 1992; December 1992; January 1993; July 1994.
Time, August 17, 1992; August 8, 1994.
Us, August 1993.
Vibe, August 1994.
Wall Street Journal, October 8, 1992.

—*Simon Glickman*

Janet Baker

Opera singer

Mezzo-soprano Janet Baker's early interest in music was so keen that before she received her first piano as a young teenager, she often listened to the radio and "played" a large Victorian sideboard in her parents' house. Thus the English singing sensation Dame Janet Baker—she was named commander of the Order of the British Empire in 1970 and dame commander six years later—began her training.

Prior to her retirement in 1982, Baker was an acclaimed master of both opera and lieder (nineteenth-century German art songs for vocals and piano) for more than 30 years. Her singing talent was first recognized back in the early 1950s, when she was barely 20 years old. She won various local competitions in northern England, and her choral singing was praised in the Yorkshire press. The daughter of an engineer, she enjoyed a middle-class upbringing and a supportive family circle. When she quit her full-time London bank job to pursue her training—not knowing what the result would be—her family helped her out financially.

Baker began singing at weddings and funerals while working part-time as a receptionist. She auditioned for the BBC in 1955 and was soon singing on the radio. English citizens wrote fan letters comparing her to British singing star Kathleen Ferrier. Indeed, Baker took second place at the Kathleen Ferrier Prize competition the following year, at age 23. According to Alan Blyth in *Janet Baker,* one of the judges, Lord Harewood, recalled Baker's voice as "very well contained, very beautiful ... the timbre it is now in embryo, cool and collected." Lord Harewood looked back on the decision not to award her first place with regret, although he noted it did not seem to have hurt her subsequent career, an understatement to say the least.

In 1957 Baker made an operatic appearance as Roza in the Bedrich Smetana composition *The Secret.* An *Opera* magazine reviewer called her work "outstanding," and the London *Times* and *Guardian* were similarly impressed. Nonetheless, Baker was still an apprentice. She took master classes in London with the well-known Lotte Lehmann and studied English and French songs with Meriel St. Clair. "Meriel used to say that however hard I was trying I was looking like a lump of pudding," Baker recalled in Alan Blyth's 1973 biography *Janet Baker.* She found that making the move from a "student and an executant into a performer" was quite difficult. "The real step is taken by something psychological inside yourself," Baker concluded.

Around the time of her appearance in *The Secret,* Baker married James Keith Shelley, who eventually became her business manager. The couple decided against

Donald Cooper/Photostage, London

For the Record . . .

Born Janet Abbott Baker, August 21, 1933, in Hatfield, Yorkshire, England; daughter of Robert Abbott and May (Pollard) Baker; married James Keith Shelley, December, 1956. *Education:* Studied under Helene Isepp, Meriel St. Clair, and Lotte Lehmann, early to mid-1950s.

Classical and operatic singer. Worked as a clerk in a bank in Leeds and London, England, c. 1950; began professional career in the mid-1950s; sang frequently on the BBC; appeared as Roza in Smetana's opera *The Secret,* 1957; made U.S. debut in 1966; subsequent opera work limited to three main companies in Great Britain: the English Opera Company, the Scottish Opera, and Covent Garden; retired in 1982. Principal appearances included roles in Hector Berlioz's *Les Troyens,* Gaetano Donizetti's *Mary Stuart,* and Christoph Gluck's *Orfeo.*

Awards: Honorary doctorate from University of Birmingham, 1968; named commander of the Order of the British Empire, 1970, and dame commander, 1976.

included what he considered an even rarer ability: that of communicating serenity and repose.

Baker made her debut in the United States in 1966, performing on both coasts and dazzling New York critics as Smeton in *Anna Bolena* at Carnegie Hall. Towards the end of the decade, in 1968, she recorded an album titled *A Tribute to Gerald Moore;* over the years, pianist Moore had accompanied Baker on various recordings and in recital.

During the 1970s, Baker worked primarily with three opera companies: the English Opera Company, the Scottish Opera (Glyndebourne), and London's prestigious Covent Garden. In 1982 she published a journal of her professional life recorded during the previous season, a book called *Full Circle.* Invited by Covent Garden to perform the title role in *Alceste*—an important part early in her career—she also reprised several other key roles that season, performing in Italian composer Gaetano Donizetti's *Mary Stuart* with the English Opera Company and at the Glyndebourne Festival in a staging of Christoph Gluck's *Orfeo.* With this, the singer felt a "full circle" had been reached. She announced her retirement from stage work in 1982.

Baker's memoir closes with a touching description of her final stage opera performance on a summer's evening that year: The chorus of *Orfeo* presented her with an engraved lyre, a reference to the golden lyre that accompanied her character in the opera on a trip to the underworld. Baker regarded the gift as a symbol of her leaving the stage to younger singers. The cycle of music would continue, but the memento lyre would remain with her as a reminder of the music world and its abiding affection for her.

having children because of the travel involved in Baker's career. She began a recital tour of England while singing frequently on the BBC and developing a stellar reputation for her interpretation of the works of eighteenth-century German composer Johann Sebastian Bach. Winning the Queen's Prize in 1959, Baker also sang in a London performance of Bach's 1727 composition *St. Matthew Passion.*

An incredible professional experience came the year after Baker's 1962 debut with the English Opera Group in Suffolk. Looking back in her 1982 memoir *Full Circle,* Baker wrote about her work with Benjamin Britten and Peter Pears—the two men who she feels ended England's long-standing reputation as "an unmusical nation." She explained that in performing roles like Polly in Britten's *Beggar's Opera*—under the intense gaze of both Britten and Pears—a singer underwent a "sacred fire" and emerged changed, in her case achieving the rank of an internationally renowned star.

In the mid-1960s, Lord Harewood, the erring judge who had awarded Baker second place in the Ferrier Prize competition, became a devoted admirer and noted that Baker's singing style had freed up. Her emotional investment—she became known for her impressive handling of dramatic roles such as that of Dido in French composer Hector Berlioz's opera *Les Troyens*—now

Selected discography

A Midsummer Night's Dream, Angel, 1961.
Elgar: *The Dream of Gerontius,* Angel, 1964.
Lieder Recital, Saga, 1965.
A Pageant of English Song, Angel, 1967.
A Tribute to Gerald Moore, Angel, 1968.
A Schubert Evening, His Master's Voice, 1970.
Owen Wingrave, London, 1970.
La Calisto, Argo, 1971.
Donizetti: *Mary Stuart,* Angel, 1983.
Gluck: *Orfeo* (a recording of her final stage appearance), RCA, 1983.
Mahler's Songs of Youth, RCA, 1985.
Berlioz: *Les nuits d'ete,* Virgin Classics, 1991.

A video recording of Baker in concert, *Christmas at Ripon Cathedral,* was released by Home Vision in 1987.

Sources

Books

Baker, Janet, *Full Circle,* MacRae, 1982.
Blyth, Alan, *Janet Baker,* Drake, 1973.
International Dictionary of Opera, Gale, 1993.

Periodicals

New York Times, December 18, 1966, p. 19.
Opera News, July 1977.
Rolling Stone, November 16, 1978.
Stereo Review, June 1983.
Time, September 21, 1970, p. 68.

—Joseph M. Reiner

Frank Black

Singer, songwriter

After several years as Black Francis, leader of alternative rock icons the Pixies, musician Charles Thompson underwent another name change. Choosing the relatively spare Frank Black as his new moniker, he embarked on a solo career that allows him to indulge his eclectic pop sensibility unhindered by a band format. Having received mixed reviews and only minor airplay for his 1993 debut effort, he returned the next year with a solid collection that reflected a "rigorously inventive swirl" of styles, according to the *Los Angeles Times*.

While his fascination with surrealism and science fiction and his penchant for psychotic noisemaking—a mainstay of his work with the Pixies—remained very much in place, the emphasis on these elements in the 1994 release *Teenager of the Year* was augmented by greater attention to songcraft and tunefulness, not to mention new concerns, like the future history of Southern California. "To me music is artificial," he mused in a *Details* interview. "It's a thing we stick in a machine and use electricity to run at a certain speed. It's an artificial experience."

Raised on Pop Music

Charles Michael Kitteridge Thompson IV was born in 1965 in Long Beach, California, and raised in Boston. He was heavily influenced by the music of the '60s, '70s, and '80s. "I was a member of the Boston Folk Song Society," he admitted in *Details*. "I traveled from school to school in the area with my song teacher, playing guitar, leading other children in [American folk legend] Woody Guthrie songs. That's the kind of child I was." He grew up infatuated with Cuba—thanks to his grandmother's recollections of the place—and pop music. "The Beach Boys were one of the first bands I really got into," he told *Option*. Among his other wholesome musical interests were "of course, the Beatles. Oh yeah, and surf music—I love surf music."

In his teens, however, as he noted in *Musician,* "the most influential band on me was [new-wave pop hitmakers] the Cars. And I didn't even know it! I don't own the Cars' albums, but remember how their first hit singles had that muffled guitar riff? Dun-dun-dun-dun ... all of a sudden it was okay to muffle your hands on the strings and just pluck some stupid guitar riff. I learned how to do that and it was like, 'Oh my God, I sound like the Cars!' You can't imagine how many [Cars leader] Ric Ocasek impersonations I wrote when I was 16!" Though it would seem a long way from Cars hits like "Just What I Needed" and upbeat beach music to the scorching absurdism of the Pixies, Thompson's tunefulness shines through on even their harshest work.

For the Record...

Born Charles Michael Kitteridge Thompson IV, 1965, in Boston, MA. *Education:* Attended University of Massachusetts, c. 1980s.

Recording and performing artist, 1986—. Formed group the Pixies with Joey Santiago, Kim Deal, and Davis Lovering, using stage name Black Francis, beginning 1986; signed with 4AD Records and released EP *Come On Pilgrim,* 1987; released Elektra debut *Doolittle,* 1989; contributed to Leonard Cohen tribute album *I'm Your Fan,* 1991; composed score for television special *America Laughs,* 1992; group dissolved, 1992. Adopted stage name Frank Black and released solo debut *Frank Black,* 4AD/Elektra, 1993; released limited-edition EP through Hello Recording Club, 1993.

Addresses: *Record company*—Elektra Entertainment, 75 Rockefeller Plaza, New York, NY 10019; or 345 North Maple Dr., Suite 123, Beverly Hills, CA 90210.

But Thompson didn't form his band right away. In fact, he first immersed himself in academic pursuits, attending the University of Massachusetts and even spending a term studying anthropology and Spanish in Puerto Rico through an exchange program. Ultimately, though, he grew tired of the academic world. "It was interesting," he explained to *Option*'s Mark Kemp. "Y'know what I mean? But I wanted to be in a band. I just saw all of these other bands doing this shit and figured if they could do it, I could do it, too." This was the spirit of punk rock. In *Musician* he claimed, "Part of the beauty of the guitar is that it's somewhat easy, accessible. Everyone knows a couple chords, and if you don't, you can learn a couple chords quickly."

Formed the Pixies

Soon he was out of school, living in Boston, and forming his group. He first recruited friend and novice guitarist Joey Santiago; then, through an ad, they found bassist Kim Deal, who in turn brought in drummer David Lovering. Formed in 1986, the Pixies had a deal with adventuresome British independent label 4AD and a release—the EP *Come On Pilgrim*—by 1987. Thompson had adopted the cryptic stage name Black Francis. "I always liked sort of funny, corny, pompous stage names, like Iggy Pop and Billy Idol," he told Chris Mundy of *Rolling Stone,* "so I wanted one. My father suggested Black Francis; it's an old family name."

Francis noted in *Musician* that his mysterious lyrics—evident in the Pixies' first release—"start out as gibberish and sometimes I add meaning. For the most part, though, they're from the [early 1970s glam-rock sensations] T. Rex school of poetry. You know, just baloney. I'm trying to come up with something that sounds good, rather than content."

Meanwhile, the Pixies gained an underground following that worshipped Black Francis as a genius. In a *Musician* dialogue with fellow post-punk songwriter Bob Mould, he admitted to the peculiarity of standing onstage before the genuflecting mosh-pit crowd: "I think, 'I'm just a fat dude with a guitar and I don't want to be here.'" For their first full-length recording, the band worked with producer Steve Albini, an underground icon who gave their chaotic sound an appropriate sonic heft. The result, *Surfer Rosa,* was, as Kemp opined nearly four years after its release, "the most beguiling Pixies record."

Group Split After Underground Success

The band's breakthrough came with *Doolittle,* their debut release for major label Elektra, which by then distributed 4AD. Celebrated mainstream producer Gil Norton helmed the project; Black Francis told Mundy that the album "is him trying to make us, shall I say commercial, and us fighting to remain somewhat grungy." It was a productive tension, however, as *Doolittle* yielded the college radio hits "This Monkey's Gone to Heaven" and—arguably the Pixies' most melodic, radio-friendly song—"Here Comes Your Man." The group was firmly established on the alternative-rock scene, though it soon had competition from Deal's side project, the Breeders.

The Pixies honed their distinctive fusion of punk rock, power pop, surf, and salsa music on their albums *Bossanova* and *Trompe le Monde,* but the spark and group spirit that animated them in the early days was gone; Black Francis had moved to Los Angeles with his girlfriend, and only touring and recording brought the band together. In 1993, after months of rumors on the underground grapevine, they officially announced their breakup. "I was hoping I could keep it a simple sabbatical or vacation, which is how we left it at the end of our last tour," he confessed in *Details.* "O.K., not 'we'; I admit I just sort of said, 'We're gonna take a year off, O.K.?' Just dropped the bomb like that. You get sick of it. You really love it while you're doing it, but I've heard those songs more times than our biggest fan. I don't need to hear them anymore." He had, in the meanwhile, begun hatching plans for a solo project and was at work on a television score.

Partly to clear away the Pixies associations for his new solo project—and partly due to his aforementioned fondness for stage names—Black Francis became Frank Black. "I think that in the case of Black Francis, it never really worked," he stated in an interview with *Rolling Stone's* Elysa Gardner. "I was constantly referred to by journalists and record-company people by various combinations of the stage name and Charles Thompson: Black Thompson, Francis Thompson, Charles Francis Thompson, Black Angel—I just got sick of it. I wanted something a little more swift, a little more to the point, a little more workingman."

Collaborating with Eric Drew Feldman, a former member of Captain Beefheart's Magic Band, he set about recording *Frank Black*. "I have to say that seventy-five to eighty percent of that record was done through the computer," he informed Gardner. "I would write basic songs with basic arrangements and show them to Mr. Feldman, who would then input the music in his computer and elaborate on the arrangements."

The album's leadoff single, "Los Angeles"—pronounced with a hard "g," as in days of old—and a cover version of the Beach Boys' "Hang Onto Your Ego" received some modest rotation, but critics found the album uneven. *Entertainment Weekly* complained about the production and fervently hoped for a Pixies reunion once "Black gets this fling out of his system." *Rolling Stone*, meanwhile, admired its dissimilarities from his old band's work: "It's funnier, more musically whimsical and varied, looser in spirit." Ultimately, noted reviewer Christian Wright, "it sounds like Frank Black's having a good time." *Spin*, meanwhile, sniffed that "it takes more than a new name to redefine yourself."

Refined Style with *Teenager*

"I can't attach much nostalgia to my music," Frank Black insisted in an interview with Ann Powers of *Musician*. "If it becomes precious, making it gets weird. I'll start thinking about what the lyrics mean and how they connect to my soul and ah ... forget it. I don't want music to be that serious." He elaborated on his "goal" in the *Detroit Free Press*, stating that he aims "to fill up 35-45 minutes of blank tape with pure entertainment and call it an album." Yet the small audience that heard his limited-edition EP for the Hello Recording Club—established by friend and They Might Be Giants member John Flansburgh—found a new seriousness, not to mention gentleness, in Frank Black. The CD's four minimalist songs—including blueprints of tunes he would flesh out on his next record and a tender rendition of the romantic 1950s classic "Duke of Earl"—suggested a refined sense of purpose and an even more focused melodicism.

This emphasis was confirmed with the release of 1994's *Teenager of the Year,* an album allegedly named for a title Thompson once held. According to *Musician's* Chuck Crisafulli, "The big difference this time is in the songs," an eclectic batch held together by "off-the-cuff wit and warmth"; the album, Crisafulli concluded, "would have sounded great back in '78 blasting out of a Dodge Dart's FM radio, but it happens to sound great this year, too." *Rolling Stone* reviewer Al Weisel called it "an epic collection of ... powerful songs that often equals—if not surpasses—[Black's] best work with the Pixies." *Teenager* earned an "A-" from *Entertainment Weekly* and began making its way up the college and alternative charts thanks to the infectious single "Headache."

Frank Black and his band joined punk idols the Ramones—whom he'd saluted on the first solo album's "I Heard Ramona Sing"—on tour. He also penned the publicity bio accompanying *Teenager,* as he had done for the previous record. "I declare to all of you," he wrote at the end of a fancifully cryptic narrative uniting the themes of the album's songs, "to look up and behold that pie in the sky. Hope you enjoy the record."

Selected discography

With the Pixies

Come On Pilgrim, 4AD, 1987.
Surfer Rosa, 4AD, 1988.
Doolittle (includes "Here Comes Your Man" and "This Monkey's Gone to Heaven"), 4AD/Elektra, 1989.
Bossanova, 4AD/Elektra, 1990.
Trompe le Monde, 4AD/Elektra, 1991.
(Contributors) *I'm Your Fan: The Songs of Leonard Cohen* (appear on "I Can't Forget"), Atlantic, 1991.

Solo; as Frank Black

Frank Black (includes "Los Angeles," "Hang On to Your Ego," and "I Heard Ramona Sing"), 4AD/Elektra, 1993.
Frank Black (limited edition EP; includes "Duke of Earl"), Hello Recording Club, November 1993.
Teenager of the Year (includes "Headache"), 4AD/Elektra, 1994.

Sources

Details, April 1993.
Detroit Free Press, June 11, 1993.
Entertainment Weekly, March 19, 1993; June 3, 1994.
Guitar Player, April 1991; October 1993.
Los Angeles Times, June 5, 1994.

Melody Maker, March 19, 1988; April 1, 1989.

Musician, April 1988; December 1990; February 1992; June 1994.

Option, January 1991.

Pulse!, April 1993.

Rolling Stone, March 23, 1989; February 4, 1993; March 18, 1993; April 1, 1993; August 25, 1994; November 17, 1994.

Spin, December 1991; January 1992; November 1992; April 1993; May 1993; July 1994.

Additional information for this profile was obtained from Elektra Entertainment publicity materials, 1994.

—Simon Glickman

Paul Bley

Pianist, keyboardist, composer

Courtesy of IAI Records

In 1953 Paul Bley played with jazz legend Charlie Parker at the Chez Paree in Montreal. In 1975 he participated in a joint reading-recital performance at New York University's Loeb Student Center onstage with avant-garde poet William Burroughs. In 1992 and 1994 he continued to push the frontiers of jazz at the Montreal Jazz Festival, playing alongside old friends such as John Scofield and Gary Peacock and on the same bill as world beat musicians Gonzalo Rubalcaba from Cuba and King Sunny Ade from Nigeria.

Bley has long been at the center of a number of cutting-edge movements in jazz piano. He played with Charles Mingus and Charlie Parker, with Ornette Coleman, Don Cherry, and Sonny Rollins, with Bill Evans and Cecil Taylor, and—from the late 1980s to the mid-1990s—with Paul Motian on drums, Charlie Haden and Steve Swallow on bass, Jimmy Giuffre on clarinet and saxophone, and Bill Frisell on electric guitar. "Like Keith Jarrett, Thelonious Monk, Bill Evans, and Cecil Taylor, Bley is a unique musician, and like these pianists he has discovered and energetically cultivated his own musical vision, informed by an exacting sense of inner logic," wrote Jon Balleras for *Down Beat* in 1985. "It's this internal rightness of conviction that marks Bley as a major artist."

Born in Montreal on November 10, 1932, Bley began the study of violin at age five and piano at eight. At 11 he was awarded a "junior diploma" from McGill Conservatory; years later, in 1949, Bley appeared at the Alberta Lounge in place of Oscar Peterson with the Peterson trio's bassist and drummer. A Montreal pianist seven years older than Bley, Peterson had left the group for a shot at fame in New York. Bley, who was known as "Buzzy" Bley around Montreal then, impressed the elder musicians. "That was my first really serious jazz gig," he was quoted as saying in *Boogie, Pete & the Senator.*

From Juilliard to Prominence at 21

Shortly thereafter, Bley moved to New York, studying composition and conducting at the Juilliard School of Music and meeting up there with Art Blakey and bassist Charles Mingus, with whom he would make his first record. While still at Juilliard, Bley started the Montreal Jazz Workshop; he invited Charlie Parker to Montreal and shared the stage with him during Parker's February 5, 1953, performance on CBFT-TV's "Jazz Workshop."

In 1958 Bley left New York for Los Angeles with his future wife, composer Carla Borg, drummer Lenni McBrowne, and bassist Hal Gaylor. Charlie Haden replaced Gaylor

For the Record . . .

Born November 10, 1932, in Montreal, Quebec, Canada; married Carla Borg (divorced); married Annette Peacock (divorced). *Education:* McGill Conservatory, junior diploma, c. 1943; graduated from Juilliard School of Music, 1953.

First played professionally as "Buzzy" Bley at Alberta Lounge, following Montreal pianist Oscar Peterson in trio, 1949; brought Charlie Parker to Montreal for "Jazz Workshop," 1953; joined horn player Ornette Coleman onstage in Los Angeles, 1958; played in trio led by Jimmy Giuffre, early 1960s; played across Canada, the United States, and Europe, beginning in 1960s; with Pat Metheny, pioneered early electric piano and jazz synthesizers, early 1970s; headed own label, Improvising Artists Inc. (IAI), 1976-80; reunited with old partners, including Giuffre, Steve Swallow, Paul Motian, Gary Peacock, and others, late 1980s-mid-1990s.

Addresses: *Record company*—IAI Records, P.O. Box 4, Cherry Valley, NY 13320.

---

on the bass, David Pike joined the group, and they released an album on GNP Crescendo. Soon a new drummer, Billy Higgins, entered the fray, and the trio worked at the Hillcrest in Los Angeles. The group then hired horn players Ornette Coleman and Don Cherry—at a time when both were grossly unpopular because of their innovative playing styles. Coleman had been exploring microtonality, those pitches between the traditional notes of the horn. Shortly after hiring Coleman, Bley and the band lost their jobs to an unappreciative audience.

The group soon broke up, and Bley sat in with a number of bands in Los Angeles, where he was offered numerous positions. Based on this success, Bley and Borg decided to try sitting in with bands in New York; along the way they stopped at the Lennox School of Music in Massachusetts, where they saw Coleman again. Bley also met bassist Steve Swallow, with whom he would work as a duo over the next two years.

Altered Concept of Jazz Trio

From a shared concert at the Lennox School of Music, the seeds of a pathbreaking trio—including Bley, Swallow, and multi-reedman and composer Jimmy Giuffre—were planted. These three performers played together through the early 1960s. Art Lange of *Down Beat* described the band, headed by Giuffre, as "the freshest, the freest, and the most sublime" of Giuffre's bands to that time. "So just as Coleman's music challenged the validity of the pianist as accompanist, Giuffre's music challenged the validity of the drum/bass format as a rhythm machine," Bley told Lange. "We found that one of the ways to get out of a particular era in music that has us locked in is to change the instrumentation."

Breaking new ground with Giuffre and Swallow in the early 1960s led Bley to form his own trios for the Savoy and ECM labels. The 1963 album *Footloose,* recorded with Swallow and guitarist Pete LaRoca for Savoy, represented a landmark step forward for Bley.

In retrospect Bley considered *Footloose* to be his first truly significant recording: it demonstrates his emphasis on process instead of structure in improvisation and elaborates on his restrained, deliberate, personal approach. During the rest of the 1960s, Bley reexamined rhythm, harmony, form, and tempo in his playing and paved the way for other innovative players such as Keith Jarrett and Bill Frisell.

Founded Own Label, Experimented with Form

Early synthesizers became available by the beginning of the 1970s, altering the sound of jazz piano. Bley pioneered some of these explorations. Around this time, he played with Bruce Ditmas on drums, a fledgling Pat Metheny on guitar, and Jaco Pastorius on bass. The 1993 release *Jaco,* recorded two decades earlier with Metheny and Pastorius, was hailed by Josef Woodard of *Down Beat* as "a raw-nerved, fascinating document, both of Bley's foray into electronic jazz and as a crude archival snapshot of future jazz legends."

In 1976 Bley's lifelong struggle between artistic freedom and commercial viability led him to found his own label, Improvising Artists Inc. (IAI), to promote experimental jazz. Although the label folded four years later, many of the recordings—such as his solo album *Alone Again* and a 1964 quartet reissue, *Turning Point,* with Jimmy Giuffre—remain available.

The 1980s and 1990s proved to be a long period of consolidation for Bley, during which he revisited and reinterpreted some of his earlier musical forms. Specifically, he returned to standards and experimented with a unique approach to bebop. A number of his albums from throughout his career were reissued on compact disc in the early 1990s. In addition, Bley reunited with his old musical comrades, including Giuffre, Motian, and Haden.

In 1991 Bley, Giuffre, and Swallow came together once again—25 years after their first encounter—to record *The Life of a Trio: Saturday and Sunday.* A *New York Times* reviewer asserted, "Thoughtful, exacting jazz of this sort has been too long ignored." Likewise, Lange commented in *Down Beat:* "Over the course of these 28 solos, duos, and trios, a sense of warmth and intimacy is maintained; dynamics are usually restrained, there's a delicacy of interaction, and sheer lyricism is the foremost concern. Like so many Monet canvasses, the impressionistic blue hues are tinged with mystery, with melancholy, but also with joy and a deeper understanding of human complexities. Beautiful."

The following year, *Memoirs,* a collaborative effort featuring Bley, Motian, and Haden, was released. "*Memoirs* serves as a tidy summation of Bley's gifts as an individual and a musical conversationalist," noted Woodard. "Motian is roughly to the drums what Bley is to the piano, capable of sculpting icy, paradoxical emotions; on a moment's notice, they can venture 'out' where tonal centers and rhythmic pulses are not invited." Francis Davis of the *Village Voice* cited "Latin Genetics" and "Monk's Dream" on *Memoirs* as evidence that Bley was Ornette Coleman's "cagiest reinterpreter." Bley also released a CD in tribute to each of his former wives, Carla Borg (Bley) and Annette Peacock.

Some music critics contend that Bley has never completely won the recognition due his playing. Still, his lifelong mission to reinvigorate jazz by stretching its limits have brought him lasting distinction. In the midst of his reunion recordings and reissues in the early 1990s, Bley was quoted in *Down Beat* as describing his ongoing purpose: "If I thought for a moment that there was nothing new to be done, whether it was playing a tune in a different way or taking [Austrian composer Arnold] Schoenberg's atonality as a premise for a project, then I would happily retire to the country and enjoy the company of my children and come out only for those events that were really useful."

Selected discography

(With Charles Mingus and Art Blakey) *Introducing Paul Bley,* Original Jazz Classics, 1953.
(With Mingus) *Mingus,* Candid, 1960.
Footloose, Savoy, 1962, later released as *The Floater Syndrome,* Vogue.
With Gary Peacock, ECM, 1963.
Ballads, ECM, 1967.
Open, To Love, ECM, 1972.
(With Jimmy Giuffre) *Quiet Song,* IAI, 1974.
Alone Again, IAI, 1974.

(With Charlie Parker) *On the Road* (recorded 1953), Jazz Showcase, 1975.
Turning Point (recorded 1964, 1968, and 1976), IAI, 1976.
Tears, Owl, 1983.
Tango Palace, Soul Note, 1983.
Fragments, ECM, 1986.
Notes, Soul Note, 1987.
Bebop, Steeplechase, 1989.
Rejoicing, Steeplechase, 1989.
(With Giuffre and Steve Swallow) *The Life of a Trio: Saturday and Sunday,* Owl, 1989.
(With Franz Koglmann) *12 (+6) in a Row,* hat ART, 1990.
Japan Suite (recorded 1976), IAI, 1992.
Memoirs (includes "Latin Genetics" and "Monk's Dream"), Soul Note, 1992.
(With Gary Peacock and Koglmann) *Annette,* hat ART, 1992.
Blues for Red, Red, 1992.
(With Giuffre) *Flight, Bremen 1961* (recorded 1961), hat ART, 1993.
(With Jaco Pastorius and Pat Metheny) *Jaco* (recorded 1974), IAI, 1993.
Axis (recorded c. 1977), IAI, 1993.
Plays Carla Bley, Steeplechase, 1993.

Sources

Books

Encyclopedia of Music in Canada, edited by Helmut Kallman and others, University of Toronto Press, 1992.
Lord, Tom, *The Jazz Discography,* Volume 2, Lord Music Reference Inc., 1992.
Lyons, Len, *The Great Jazz Pianists: Speaking of Their Lives and Music,* Quill, 1983.
Lyons, Len, and Don Perlo, *Jazz Portraits: The Lives and Music of the Jazz Masters,* Morrow, 1989.
Miller, Mark, *Boogie, Pete & the Senator: Canadian Musicians in Jazz—The Eighties,* Nightwood Editions, 1987.
Miller, Mark, *Cool Blues: Charlie Parker in Canada, 1953,* Nightwood Editions, 1989.

Periodicals

Billboard, November 23, 1991.
Chicago Tribune, July 11, 1994.
Down Beat, November 1985; October 1988; November 1991; August 1992; October 1992; December 1992; June 1993; October 1993.
New York Times, March 24, 1975; May 19, 1991.
Village Voice, June 30, 1992.

—*Nicholas Patti*

Blondie

Rock band

Blondie formed in New York during the vital transitional period between glitter rock and punk, powered by an eclectic combination of musical styles, tongue-in-cheek attitude, and the frosty, intelligent glamour of frontwoman Deborah Harry. After building a reputation within the "New Wave" rock underground, the band crossed over with their triumphant disco-era single "Heart of Glass" and enjoyed a brief reign on the charts before a variety of factors sabotaged their momentum. They broke up in 1982.

Harry—after nursing partner and bandmate Chris Stein back to health from a devastating illness—pursued a solo recording career and film acting; the group's influence, meanwhile, persisted in much of the indie rock of the 1990s. Andrew Mueller of *Melody Maker* may have been in a hyperbolic mood when he dubbed them "history's greatest pop band and, let's face it, possibly history's greatest *thing,*" but he no doubt reflected the general sentiment of many who enjoy smart, well-crafted pop.

AP/Wide World Photos

Members included **Clem Burke** (born November 24, 1955, in New York; joined group c. 1975), drums; **Jimmy Destri** (born April 13, 1954), keyboards; **Nigel Harrison** (joined group 1978), bass; **Deborah Harry** (born July 1, c. 1945, in Miami, FL), vocals; **Frank Infante** (joined group 1977), guitar, bass; **Billy O'Connor** (left group 1975), drums; **Fred Smith** (left group 1975), bass; **Chris Stein** (born January 5, 1950, in Brooklyn, NY), guitar, vocals; **Gary Valentine** (band-member 1975-77), bass.

Group formed c. 1974, in New York City; signed with Private Stock label and released debut *Blondie,* 1976; signed to Chrysalis Records, 1977, and released *Parallel Lines,* 1978; contributed to *Roadie* and *American Gigolo* film soundtracks, 1980; group disbanded, 1982.

Harry released solo debut *Koo Koo,* 1981; Stein launched own label, Animal Records, 1982, before being stricken with *pemphigus vulgaris;* Destri released solo album *Heart on the Wall,* 1982; Harry and Stein co-authored book *Making Tracks: The Rise of Blondie,* 1982; Harry appeared in films *Union City,* 1979, *Videodrome,* 1982, and *Hairspray,* 1988, in stage production *Teaneck Tanzi: The Venus Flytrap,* 1983, and in television program *Mother Goose Rock 'n' Rhyme,* 1989; Stein wrote music for cable television program *Fifteen Minutes* and material for Harry's 1986 album *Rockbird;* Harry dueted with Iggy Pop on *Red, Hot + Blue* anthology, 1990; Burke played drums with Eurythmics, Dramarama, and others; Harry was sued for song-publishing income by former manager Peter Leeds, 1993.

Awards: Platinum awards for albums *Parallel Lines,* 1979, *Eat to the Beat,* 1980, and *Autoamerican,* 1981, and for single "Call Me," 1980.

New York in the early 1970s became something of a hotbed for offbeat rock, thanks in large part to adventurous clubs like CBGB and Max's Kansas City; Harry had worked as a waitress at the latter. It soon became clear that the old rules of rock were changing. As the glam-rock practiced by groups like the New York Dolls lost its luster, something new began to take shape: a scavenging, garage-band ethic, heavy on attitude and confrontation. It would be a few years before anyone called it "punk." The Ramones had yet to codify their pummel-ling three-chord formula, and British impresario Malcolm MacLaren had yet to assemble the media-ready supernova known as the Sex Pistols—and subsequently take credit for inventing punk rock. In the interim, there existed no "alternative" formula, so bands like Blondie simply made a musical collage of their disparate passions.

Girl-Group Beginnings

The earliest incarnation of Blondie, a campy girl group known as The Stilettoes, featured Harry—a former Playboy bunny and 1960s scenemaker who had sung with the short-lived folk-rock outfit Wind in the Willows—along with two female backup singers, Fred Smith on bass, drummer Billy O'Connor, and Chris Stein, a guitarist who joined the band after seeing an early show. He and Harry connected immediately, as he told Kurt Loder in a profile published in *Bat Chain Puller:* "I was totally taken with her, and did the best I could to win her over." After he joined the group, the pair became romantically involved. The band endured numerous personnel changes, the most important of which involved the replacement of O'Connor and Smith with Clem Burke and his friend Gary Valentine. Burke, who was still in his teens when he joined the group, shared Harry and Stein's adoration of 1960s girl groups like the Shangri-Las; his propulsive drumming was a crucial component of their energetic sound.

After experimenting with various name changes, Harry came up with Blondie, and it stuck. "I would walk down Houston Street and all these truck drivers were always yelling out, 'Hey, Blondie!'" she told Loder. "So I said, shit, that's great, you know? *Poi-fect!*" It was 1975, and the punk scene was still in an embryonic stage of development; Blondie continued playing tiny clubs for virtually nothing. Yet 1960s enthusiast and record-collector magazine editor Alan Betrock took the group under his wing and set them up in a low-budget studio to record some demos.

Distinctive Brew

Blondie soldiered on and added keyboardist Jimmy Destri, who played the very retro-sounding Farfisa organ. The group lived together in a loft across from CBGB and spent most of their time refining their unusual approach. Surfy guitars, British-Invasion pop melodies, girl-group vocals, and monster-movie camp meshed into a sensibility that borrowed punk's tough attitude but preserved the romanticism of classic pop. According to most critics, though, even this distinctive brew might have vanished into cultdom had it not been for Harry.

Her profoundly glamorous appearance aside, she sang with a rough-hewn authority and radiated a charisma at once steely, ironic, sexy, sentimental, and playful.

After meeting producer Richard Gottehrer—a veteran of 1960s rock who had produced the Ramones' debut—Blondie found themselves recording a single, originally called "Sex Offender" but changed to "X Offender" to avoid controversy. The band recorded their self-titled debut album in 1976 for the Private Stock label but later signed with Chrysalis, which reissued the record. They then embarked on a national tour with proto-punk rocker Iggy Pop.

> One critic may have been in a hyperbolic mood when he dubbed Blondie "history's greatest pop band and, let's face it, possibly history's greatest thing," but he no doubt reflected the general sentiment of many who enjoy smart, well-crafted pop.

Blondie followed up with 1977's *Plastic Letters,* dubbed "half-great" by Loder, featuring Frank Infante on bass (for the exiting Valentine) as well as on rhythm guitar. It was an especially tumultuous time for the band. "It seemed like I spent half my time either trying to keep certain people in the group or trying to convince Debbie and Chris to get other ones in," Burke told Loder. "Somebody was always on the outs with somebody else." Nigel Harrison took over the bassist position in 1978, and Infante moved to full-time guitar. Two singles from the album reached the U.K. Top Ten, but the group had already begun working with then-hot producer Mike Chapman on their next album, *Parallel Lines.* Released in 1978, this third outing featured a revised version of a song on the early demos—first known as "The Disco Song," then "Once I Had a Love," and finally "Heart of Glass."

In his list of the Top Ten albums of 1978, *New York Times* critic John Rockwell lauded *Parallel Lines* as Blondie's best so far. "Deborah Harry's singing continues to improve, and the band's blend of progressive experimentation and popsy appeal works better here than ever before," he wrote. "A really delightful disk, and it's surprising that it didn't do a bit better commercially." Of course, it did later: "Heart of Glass" became an international smash, and *Parallel Lines* went platinum. The album later yielded another hit, "One Way or Another." After toiling in obscurity for years, the members of Blondie were rock stars, and Harry's near-ubiquity in jeans ads and elsewhere necessitated the promotional slogan "Blondie Is a Group."

Eat to the Beat, the group's 1979 release, yielded the hit "Dreaming." But even as they highlighted their power-pop leanings, Blondie continued to dabble in dance music, scoring another smash with "Call Me," a song from the *American Gigolo* film soundtrack that paired Harry's lyrics with music by disco svengali Giorgio Moroder. Next came *Autoamerican,* which sported "Rapture," an exercise in rap when the genre was in its infancy. It is a tribute to the musical instincts of Harry and Stein that they so cannily pursued a form that few in the music world took seriously; the song sat atop the charts for two weeks and—along with the sprightly calypso-reggae cover "The Tide Is High"—helped the album go platinum.

The End of the Line

By 1981 the group had lost cohesion. Harry had already recorded a solo album when Blondie reunited to record *The Hunter,* which Donald Clarke, in his *Penguin Encyclopedia of Popular Music,* deemed "a sad parody of former glories." It did yield a moderately successful single, "Island of Lost Souls," and thus necessitated a tour; this venture proved disastrous as Chris Stein had by then come down with a rare and debilitating illness called *pemphigus vulgaris.* "We'd see Chris come off-stage and go directly to oxygen," Destri related in the interview with Loder; this undignified spectacle convinced the group to pack it in, and much of Stein and Harry's money went to pay his substantial medical bills.

Harry pursued acting and periodic music projects but spent the bulk of the mid-1980s nursing Stein back to health; she has also had to deal with substantial litigation over profits generated by the group. Although she released a number of solo albums in ensuing years, critics have generally dismissed them as pale when compared to her best work with the band. Only "French Kissin' in the USA," a collaboration with Stein from her 1986 effort *Rockbird,* generated any chart action. Destri, meanwhile, moved into record production after releasing a 1982 solo album; Burke played drums for Eurythmics and, later, for indie rockers Dramarama.

Yet the intervening years have also seen a number of compilations and the spilling of considerable ink regarding Blondie's sainted place in power pop history. As producer Dan Loggins put it in the notes to the collection he compiled entitled *Blonde and Beyond,* the band "crafted three minute pop gems; timeless and contradictory symbols of their own era." Paul Mathur of *Melody Maker* proclaimed, "For more of us than would perhaps care to admit, Deborah Harry's music has been a mark against which all other pop is judged."

Harry herself, according to *Rolling Stone,* was at her peak "the ultimate urban babe: streetwise, glamorous, tough, very cool." Her influence on the scores of woman-led and all-female indie rock bands—notably the celebrated "Riot Grrrl" groups—became a favorite topic for her champions in the rock press. But regardless of Harry's status as an icon, Blondie's place in posterity is assured, thanks to a solid—and strikingly versatile—body of work.

Selected discography

On Chrysalis, except where noted

Blondie (includes "X Offender"), Private Stock, 1976, reissued, Chrysalis, 1977.

Plastic Letters, Private Stock, 1977, reissued, Chrysalis, 1977.

Parallel Lines (includes "Heart of Glass" and "One Way or Another"), 1978.

Eat to the Beat (includes "Dreaming"), 1979.

(Contributors) *Roadie* (film soundtrack; featured on "Ring of Fire"), 1980.

Autoamerican (includes "Rapture" and "The Tide Is High"), 1980.

(Contributors) *American Gigolo* (film soundtrack; featured on "Call Me"), 1980.

The Best of Blondie, 1981.

The Hunter (includes "Island of Lost Souls"), 1982.

Once More into the Bleach, 1988.

The Complete Picture: The Very Best of Deborah Harry and Blondie, 1991.

Blonde and Beyond, 1993.

The Ultimate Collection, 1994.

Atomic (12-inch dance remix), 1995.

Solo recordings by Deborah Harry

Koo Koo, 1981.

Rockbird (includes "French Kissin' in the USA"), Geffen, 1986.

Def, Dumb and Blonde, Geffen, 1989.

(With Iggy Pop) "Well Did You Evah," *Red, Hot + Blue,* Chrysalis, 1990.

Debravation, Sire/Reprise, 1993.

Solo recordings by Jimmy Destri

Heart on the Wall, 1982.

Sources

Books

Clarke, Donald, *Penguin Encyclopedia of Popular Music,* Viking, 1989.

Encyclopedia of Rock, edited by Phil Hardy and Dave Laing, Schirmer Books, 1988.

Harry, Deborah, and Chris Stein, *Making Tracks: The Rise of Blondie,* 1982.

Loder, Kurt, *Bat Chain Puller: Rock & Roll in the Age of Celebrity,* St. Martin's, 1990.

Rees, Dafydd, and Luke Crampton, *Rock Movers & Shakers,* ABC-CLIO, 1991.

Stambler, Irwin, *Encyclopedia of Pop, Rock & Soul,* St. Martin's, 1989.

Periodicals

Melody Maker, March 9, 1991; July 10, 1993.

New York Times, December 22, 1978.

Rolling Stone, April 15, 1993; October 14, 1993.

Additional information for this profile was obtained from the liner notes to *Blonde and Beyond,* Chrysalis, 1993.

—*Simon Glickman*

Luka Bloom

Singer, songwriter, guitarist

Not just another Irish musician to hit it big in the United States, Luka Bloom has been transforming what folk music means with his rhythm-heavy, hip-hop way of playing guitar. "May more strummers and hummers pick up the gauntlet this feisty artist has thrown down," wrote Ann Powers in a *New York Times* review of a solo performance at the Bottom Line in New York. As of early 1995, Bloom had three albums to his credit, the first of which was compared by Paul Evans of *Rolling Stone* to acclaimed artist Van Morrison's *Astral Weeks.*

In 1994's *Turf,* Bloom slowed his strumming somewhat and emphasized his ballads. Critics were divided over the strength of the ballads—"warm and full," according to Thom Jurek of the Detroit *Metro Times;* "narcissistic," according to Geoffrey Himes of the *Washington Post*— but Bloom's shows continued to rivet audiences. In fact, his electric performances across the United States had attracted a following even before he recorded his first album in 1990. Since then, his many shows in pubs, clubs, and large halls across Europe and the States have helped him maintain a live feel in his records and, more importantly, ensured an enthusiastic reception from listeners.

A Long Trek on the Road to Success

For some time into his musical career, Bloom failed to find his signature sound; success evaded him. He did not catch on with American audiences until he was in his early thirties. Born Barry Moore in the small Irish town of Newbridge, County Kildare (30 miles south of Dublin), he is the younger brother of folksinging legend and celebrity Christy Moore. Playing in the shadow of his brother's popularity, Bloom performed in Dublin pubs for eight years through the mid-1980s without finding broader acceptance. "People had gotten used to seeing me as a struggling contemporary folk singer/songwriter guy," he told Edward Guthmann of the *San Francisco Chronicle.* "It was boring for them, and it was boring for me. I needed a kick in the ass, really."

The problems with Bloom's early career ran far deeper than being eclipsed by the fame of his older brother, however. Some critics have speculated that Bloom himself had not yet opened up in his music—personally and artistically—as he would later in the United States. After dropping out of college in the mid-1970s, the singer played in folk clubs around Europe as Barry Moore and even recorded three albums, which are no longer available. He finger-picked on his guitar until a chronic tendinitis forced him to start strumming toward the mid-1980s. Following a brief stint as the head of a

Photograph by Frank Ockenfels, © 1994 Reprise Records

rock band called Red Square—inspired by the groups Simple Minds and U2—he returned to solo work.

Around the same time, Bloom realized he had a drinking problem and decided it was time to quit. "Drinking did not stimulate my songwriting, did not stimulate my imagination," he told *Rolling Stone.* "[It] completely deadened and depressed everything I wanted to do, and thank God it did. I probably wouldn't be alive today if I had had some success." In 1987 Bloom recognized his stagnation and decided on a radical change. "I said, 'Okay, I'm thirty-two years old, I'm going to change my name, and I'm going to go to America, and I'm going to stay there until something happens,'" he recounted in an interview with Michael Azerrad for *Rolling Stone.* Leaving behind a longtime lover and a young son from a previous marriage, Bloom moved on to Washington, D.C., with his guitar and only $200 to start off.

New Name for a Burgeoning Career

On the flight over to the United States, Moore invented his new stage name. He wanted something "as pretentious as Iggy Pop or Bono or Sting ... that would stick in people's minds," he noted in the *San Francisco Chronicle.* He took "Luka" from folksinger Suzanne Vega's song and "Bloom" from the seminal twentieth-century novel *Ulysses* by Irish writer James Joyce. The new name freed him in his art as well. "When I worked under my own name," he told Azerrad, "I was a very self-conscious performer, a very self-conscious writer and a very self-conscious individual generally. In taking on

this mask of Luka Bloom, it became possible for me to expose myself in all sorts of ways."

Soon after Bloom landed in the States he was playing in a Georgetown University pub, where he quickly built a following. His mix of rock, contemporary folk, and Irish mysticism—along with his intense guitar playing and haunting voice—quickly attracted listeners in New York and Boston as well as D.C. Soon he was touring the country as an opening act for both the Pogues and Hothouse Flowers and making a mark with his shows from Philadelphia to San Francisco. With some showcase performances under his belt, he signed with the Reprise imprint of Warner Bros. Records and set to work on his 1990 U.S. debut, *Riverside.*

Joined "Folk Vanguard"

Inspired by the pared-down sound of Michelle Shocked on *The Texas Campfire Tapes* and the Cowboy Junkies on *The Trinity Session,* Bloom chose an approach that featured a single microphone and no overdubs. He played and sang and stomped around the studio as if in concert; other musicians contributed minimal backing later on instruments ranging from the electric guitar to the Iranian finger drum. His "sharp lament" on a father's death in "The Man Is Alive" and his forlorn love ballads "Gone to Pablo" and "This Is for Life" succeeded particularly well, according to *Rolling Stone's* Evans, who concluded that Bloom was "able and worthy" of what he had targeted—"the folk vanguard" of Vega, Shocked, and Tracy Chapman.

Later Bloom remained rooted in a rhythmic style but grew more reflective in his lyrics. His cover of L.L. Cool J.'s rap song "I Need Love"—his first single from 1992's *Acoustic Motorbike*—was acclaimed as "surprisingly effective" in *Billboard.* Several reviewers agreed, however, that some of Bloom's lyrics did not equal the power of his music.

In his 1994 release, *Turf,* Bloom grew even more searching and somber, although he still aimed to maintain the high-energy feel of his live performances. Living back in Dublin, the singer unveiled most of his songs in shows there over the summer of 1993 and honed them on tour in Europe in the fall. "The Fertile Rock" incorporated a live sing-along from the Tivoli club in Utrecht, Holland; "Diamond Mountain," a reference to a place in historic Connemara in Ireland (where the album cover art was photographed), was intended to evoke the spirit and feeling of Bloom's homeland.

Bloom received mixed reviews for *Turf.* "Even when he sings about the plight of aborigines in Australia or blacks in America, he seems to be talking to himself in a humorless, private meditation," Himes wrote in the *Washington Post*. "The droning low notes and heavily echoed vocals reinforce the sense of a man locked in his own bedroom." In sharp contrast, Jurek of the *Metro Times* expressed a different view: "The disc's sound is warm and full despite the lack of other instruments, and the songwriting is top-notch. This is easily Bloom's best effort and shows him coming into his own as both an artist and a storyteller."

Having stretched the bounds of folk with his racy strumming and rhythm experiments on his first two albums, Bloom had continued to express his own passions on his third. In addition, he maintained a steady schedule of live performances, mounting a promotional tour for *Turf* in the summer of 1994. He explained his love for playing live to Azerrad: "Life is not a sterile business. Life is blood and guts and shit and heartbreak, and it's f——ed up, and it's a mess. I think you can articulate that better sweating in a club with a wooden instrument in your hand."

Selected discography

Riverside (includes "The Man Is Alive," "This Is for Life," and "Gone to Pablo"), Reprise, 1990.
Acoustic Motorbike (includes "I Need Love"), Reprise, 1992.
Turf (includes "The Fertile Rock" and "Diamond Mountain"), Reprise, 1994.

Sources

Atlanta Journal and Constitution, April 18, 1992.
Billboard, February 15, 1992; July 2, 1994.
Metro Times (Detroit), July 6, 1994; July 13, 1994.
New York Times, February 22, 1993.
Rolling Stone, March 8, 1990; February 6, 1992; April 1, 1993.
San Francisco Chronicle, April 29, 1990.
Washington Post, July 8, 1994.

Additional information for this profile was obtained from Reprise Records publicity materials, 1994.

—*Nicholas Patti*

The Brand New Heavies

Acid jazz band

During a run of wildly successful shows in New York with their new lead singer, N'Dea Davenport, the Brand New Heavies broke onto the scene as bold jazz-funk innovators in late 1991 and early 1992. They soon began to play their music as live accompaniment to the rhymes of rappers like Grand Puba, Masta Ace, and the Black Sheep. Such live collaboration led to their second album, 1992's *Heavy Rhyme Experience: Volume I.*

Meanwhile, cuts from the Brand New Heavies' debut album from 1991, *The Brand New Heavies,* found an audience over the airwaves and rose in the rhythm-and-blues and pop charts in both the U.S. and their native U.K. Their third album, *Brother Sister,* released in 1994, offered a mix of their newfound jazz hip-hop pace and the 1970s-style funk and soul reminiscent of their first record. Before they began "setting the pace," as described in *Rolling Stone* in 1994, however, the Brand New Heavies had to overcome an initially unreceptive audience in their native U.K.

Photograph by Michael LaVine, courtesy of EastWest Records America

For the Record . . .

Members include **Simon Bartholomew,** guitar; **N'Dea Davenport** (from Atlanta; began singing, 1991, made full band member, 1994), lead vocals; **Jan Kincaid,** drums, keyboards; and **Andrew Levy,** bass.

Band formed in London informally, late 1970s, formally, 1985; released debut album, *Brand New Heavies,* 1991; toured U.S., 1991-92; "Dream Come True" hit U.K. Top 20, 1992; recorded album *Heavy Rhyme Experience: Volume I,* with East Coast rappers Main Source, Gang Starr, Grand Puba, and Kool G Rap, L.A.'s Pharcyde, and others, 1992.

Addresses: *Record company*—EastWest Records America, 75 Rockefeller Plaza, New York, NY 10019.

The Brand New Heavies came out of the "Rare Groove" scene in the U.K. in 1985 to playing soul and dance music. Ian Gittins of *Melody Maker* described the three original members—Jan Kincaid on keyboards and drums, Andrew Levy on bass, and Simon Bartholomew on guitar—as "three old muckers from art college." The spiritual root of their music derives from 1970s funk and soul masters such as James Brown, Earth, Wind and Fire, Chic, and others. In fact, the three high-school friends started playing together in the late 1970s, but didn't become more serious until the mid-1980s. When Gittins suggested the three had a sound similar to 1970s television cop shows, they cheered. "Yeah, the music to something like 'Starsky and Hutch' was brilliant," Levy asserted. "Or the first 'Death Wish' film. It was the standard thing then. Now everything's gone Housey [keyboard-driven, beat-heavy dance music]."

Early on, the Heavies helped establish a new label called Acid Jazz. "When we first started, we were the only real band on the Acid Jazz label," drummer Kincaid told Marisa Fox of *Raygun* in 1994. He continued, "There was a techno DJ, and the label was based out of one room. We launched that label." Since then the group has influenced a score of new groups and labels, including Mo' Wax and Talkin' Loud.

When the Brand New Heavies released their debut album, and before they signed on N'Dea Davenport as lead singer, the group found at best a reluctant reception in the U.K. Gittins described it thus: "[Their] killer fusion of freeform jazz, heavy-duty funk and rave euphoria was greeted by the British public with earth-shattering indifference." Rather than merely accepting

their lot or remaking themselves to fit dominant U.K. taste, however, the band shored up their sound and took it to the United States.

First, the Brand New Heavies hooked up with Atlanta-born N'Dea Davenport, former backup singer for Young MC and Madonna. "When I was on my own, I was always looking for another sound, the sound that the boys—the Heavies—had," Davenport was quoted as saying in *Vibe* in 1994. "I was just a little ol' backup singer, singing behind Madonna and a bunch of other people. I was supposed to be the third girl in the Blond Ambition tour, but something told me not to go. I didn't. I heard the Heavies. I moved to London. They accepted me. That was it." Matt Dike and Michael Ross of the Delicious Vinyl imprint at Atlantic Records had heard both Davenport and the Heavies and suggested the match.

In London, Davenport and the Heavies joined together and departed for a debut tour of the U.S. Soon the songs from their debut album made the charts on both sides of the Atlantic. Their single, "Never Stop," became the first by an English group to make the U.S. rhythm and blues Top Ten since Soul II Soul. Likewise, "Dream Come True" made the U.K. Top 20. Gittins called "Dream Come True" an "upfront, untroubled soul smooch which provides a fine platform for N'dea's vocal prowess." Still, the hit was simpler and more commercial than the album, which Gittins characterized as "past-midnight, darkly serene, an intricate jazz-tranquility dotted with pockets of intriguing funk turbulence."

While playing for the first time in New York at S.O.B.s in early 1991, the Heavies combined with rappers MC Search and Q-Tip, who jumped onstage during the Heavies' encore and improvised to their music for a thrilled audience. The Heavies' second album, *Heavy Rhyme Experience,* featured "the current cream of the East Coast hip-hop crop," according to *Reflex.* Still, the album failed to garner altogether positive reviews.

Frank Owen of *Vibe* pointed out that the idea of combining rap with live music and not merely sampled sounds dated to 1982 to Grandmaster Flash and the Furious Five's album *The Message.* While he credited *Heavy Rhyme Experience* as the most ambitious such attempt to date in 1992, he also reported that, unlike the live mixing, the record was compiled by combining various tracks: The instrumentals came first, followed by the rappers' vocals, and finally, additional bass and guitar lines.

The difficulty of recapturing the live feel in the recorded product continued to haunt the Brand New Heavies in their third album, *Brother Sister.* Marie Elsie St. Leger noted that drawback in *Rolling Stone,* but excused

Davenport's singing from the critique. "She has a quality not found in R&B vocalists since the height of disco: looseness," St. Leger wrote. "Vocalists of that era—from Gloria Gaynor to Donna Summer—could make you believe that those screeching high notes were nothin' but a thang. Davenport, of course, doesn't screech; she sings sexily, without coyness.... She is as fluid as the band is tight, as blase as the players are intent." With the aid of Davenport's vocals, *Brother Sister* finally succeeds, according to St. Leger.

When the Heavies were finishing *Heavy Rhyme Experience* with a number of rappers, Davenport collaborated with Guru, an old friend of hers, to record another jazz hip-hop album, *Jazzmatazz*. Reported in 1994 to have been named an official member of the Heavies, Davenport considered both *Heavy Rhyme* and *Jazzmatazz* to be "side projects, not really reflective of what we're about as the Brand New Heavies," she told *Raygun*. *Brother Sister* approaches the sound of their first album, solid funk and soul with a fusion jazz twist.

What the Brand New Heavies are really about, however, is experimentation and the generation of a new sound. From their debut album, which *Rolling Stone* praised for "[setting] a standard that was hard for imitators to meet," through their 1994 recording, the Heavies continued to develop their particular style. Although other bands have picked up on their funk and soul combination, the Heavies are not worried about losing their distinct identity. "We don't really sound like anybody else," Kincaid told Fox of *Raygun* in 1994. "I mean, we're constantly changing anyway, so it would be hard for a band to keep up with us even if they wanted to."

Selected discography

The Brand New Heavies (includes "Never Stop" and "Dream Come True"), Delicious Vinyl, 1991.
(With Grand Puba, Masta Ace, the Black Sheep, and others) *Heavy Rhyme Experience: Volume I,* Delicious Vinyl, 1992.
Brother Sister (includes "Have a Good Time," "Dream on Dreamer," "Mind Trips," and "Forever"), EastWest, 1994.

Sources

Melody Maker, March 7, 1992.
Raygun, April 1994.
Reflex, issue 29.
Rolling Stone, September 17, 1992; April 7, 1994.
Vibe, fall 1992; May 1994.

—*Nicholas Patti*

Marty Brown

Singer, songwriter

Photograph by Dean Dixon, courtesy of MCA Records, Nashville

A small-town Kentucky singer-songwriter who actually slept in the alleys of Nashville until he was "discovered" in 1991, Marty Brown records his own down-home songs in a voice that has drawn comparisons to the legendary Hank Williams, Sr., and country pioneer Jimmie Rodgers. At a time when the country music industry has attempted to lure new listeners by offering rock- and pop-flavored artists, Brown has made no concessions in his traditional music. Instead, he has taken his particular sound to the people who appreciate it most, performing live at small venues throughout the South and Midwest. *Dallas Morning News* music critic Michael Corcoran wrote: "Make no mistake about it.... The pride of Maceo, Kentucky, is one heck of a country singer.... Brown sings like he's on a front porch at the end of six miles of dirt road. He's the real thing."

The story of Marty Brown's climb to success is one of the most notable in recent memory. The young artist has estimated that he made more than 100 trips from his small Kentucky hometown to Nashville's fabled Music Row before any industry executives agreed to listen to him. "Used to be that country music did nothing more than make me a good mechanic," Brown told the *Lexington Herald-Leader*. "I'm used to driving $200 cars and then working on them myself." Now, thanks to exposure on the CBS television show *48 Hours* and articles in the pages of *People* magazine, Brown has found a national audience, released three albums with MCA Records, and received effusive reviews in the *Washington Post* and *Rolling Stone*. "What's happening now is simply wild," he told the *Lexington Herald-Leader*. "It's more than I ever dreamed of."

Hank Williams and the Everly Brothers

Marty Brown was born and raised in the tiny hamlet of Maceo, Kentucky (pronounced "*May*-see-o," population 500). One of six children of a factory worker and a homemaker, he was surrounded by a variety of musical influences. His parents liked traditional country music and early Elvis Presley tunes; his older brother preferred hard rock. From infancy, Brown was completely devoted to country music himself. He learned how to play his father's guitar at the age of nine and began composing his own songs in his teens. "Country music that's good country music—it don't never die," Brown told the *Los Angeles Times*. "That's what I chose to listen to: early Johnny Cash, early Elvis Presley, Hank Sr., George Jones, Merle Haggard, and my biggest influence, [pop duo] the Everly Brothers."

Brown would shut himself in the bathroom to tape-record songs he had written. He was convinced that they were as good as any he heard on the radio and that, with proper instrumental backup, he could perform them and become a star. By the time he graduated from high school, he had consigned dozens of original songs to tape. "I used to cry myself to sleep at night wanting this to happen to me," he told the *Philadelphia Inquirer.* "I think if the Lord sees you want something bad enough, He's going to reach down and He's going to help you achieve it. But you have to really prove yourself first."

The trips to Nashville began. Brown, who was supporting a wife and two young children on what he could earn as a plumber's assistant and part-time mechanic, spent his spare time knocking on doors in Nashville, trying to get an agent, a recording contract, or even a dependable performing gig. No one was interested. At home in Kentucky he entered a talent show sponsored by the Everly Brothers—and lost. Time after time Brown found himself penniless and ignored, sleeping in Nashville's alleys while waiting for his mother to come drive him home to Kentucky. "Man, I'd come back from those failed trips [to Nashville] like a dog with a tail between his legs," Brown recalled in the *Lexington Herald-Leader.* "I'd throw that old guitar down that night and say I'd never mess with it again. But in the morning, I'd be up writing a new song again."

A Dream Came True

After one particular day of pavement-pounding in Nashville, Brown was ready to give up completely. Trudging down the sidewalk, he saw the words "Trust Jesus" scrawled on the sidewalk in front of a firm that represents songwriters. "I looked up at the sky and just took me a deep breath and I went in there," Brown told *USA Today.* An agent listened to him perform eight songs and agreed to try to find him a recording contract. Then, in a bizarre twist of fate, Brown found himself the subject of a CBS-TV news documentary on country music that was broadcast on *48 Hours,* a popular newsmagazine anchored by Dan Rather. The show gave Brown ample room to demonstrate not only his songwriting talent but also his engaging, down-home personality. After the show aired, Nashville's biggest record companies engaged in a bidding war to sign the would-be country star.

Brown's debut album, *High and Dry,* was released in 1991. Almost immediately the artist encountered the problem that has plagued him ever since—many radio stations in large markets would not play his singles; ironically, Marty Brown—with his hillbilly vocals and catchy laments about lost love—is considered "too country" for modern country radio. None of the singles from his first three albums managed to break the top 40 on the country charts.

Taking His Music to the People

Brown still managed to find his audience, however. *High and Dry* has sold more than 100,000 copies. As Corcoran noted in the *Dallas Morning News:* "The only way to hear Brown's music is to buy it, and fans of real country music are doing that so often that he may become the first album-oriented country artist since Boxcar Willie." However, in a review of Brown's third LP, *Cryin', Lovin', Leavin',* in *Country Music,* Rich Kienzle asserted, "It would be an opportune time for Brown to hit the radio since this ... is his best album ever," and added, "Brown's ballads remain achingly intense and direct, with the pure, old-fashioned moralism of a weathered 'Jesus Saves' sign along a rural highway." Kienzle remarked that with the debut of a classic country station in Nashville, Brown may have a chance at airplay alongside staple original country artists including Johnny Cash and Loretta Lynn.

Brown has augmented his recording with a touring schedule that includes—along with the obligatory state fairs—live performances at Wal-Mart stores, especially in the South. Brown began his Wal-Mart appearances the year after his first album was released and has continued to do them ever since. Typically, the shows, which are underwritten by MCA Records, are performed in a store aisle with modest amplification and a stage about a foot high. Fans give Brown homemade cookies, jam, and fishing lures. "I wanted a tour like this to hit these small, out-of-the-way towns," Brown told the *Lexington Herald-Leader.* "Coming from a town like Maceo, I know that you don't get to see anything exciting come into town very much. I think it's also a neat way to get out in front of ordinary people who would ordinarily never get to see you."

"Ordinary" may be a defining word for Marty Brown. His songs are heartfelt without resorting to cliche, his soulful voice echoes the Hank Williams tradition, and his easygoing personality has not been altered by his brush with fame. "My music is quite real to me," Brown told the *Lexington Herald-Leader.* "That's why I think real people will relate to it. I've experienced that stuff. That's been my way of dealing with life." Asked what kept him going through all the years of rejection, Brown told *USA Today:* "I didn't want to turn 50 and look at these songs in a drawer and say, 'I wonder what would have happened if I had tried.'"

Selected discography

High and Dry, MCA, 1991.
Blue Kentucky Skies, MCA, 1993.
Cryin', Lovin', Leavin', MCA, 1994.

Sources

Chicago Tribune, October 17, 1991.
Country Music, July/August 1994.
Dallas Morning News, March 2, 1992.
Lexington Herald-Leader, October 20, 1991; September 4, 1992; March 19, 1993; June 4, 1993; April 30, 1994.
Los Angeles Times, March 18, 1992.
People, November 18, 1991.
Philadelphia Inquirer, August 11, 1993.
Rolling Stone, November 14, 1991.
State (Columbia, SC), June 25, 1993.
USA Today, September 24, 1991.

—Anne Janette Johnson

Tony Brown

Record company executive, producer

Courtesy of MCA Records

In 1978, when Tony Brown left his keyboards behind and joined the artists and repertoire (A&R) ranks at RCA, few would have suspected that within 15 years he would assume the presidency of MCA/Nashville. But with Brown's on-the-road experience and many hours spent in the recording studio, he had his hand firmly on the pulse of the average country music listener. Lyle Lovett, Vince Gill, and Trisha Yearwood are only a few of the many artists he discovered—and all three have helped country music rise to unprecedented popularity during the 1990s. Brown's understanding of the traditional country sound, combined with the pop influences of the present, have made him a significant force in determining the future of the Nashville recording industry.

Brown was raised in Greensboro, North Carolina, and grew up in a family heavily influenced by gospel music. He took to the piano as a child and played in his family's gospel group; when he went on the road as a professional musician, one of his first jobs was as keyboard accompanist for the then-gospel sounds of the Oak Ridge Boys. Over time, Brown's musical tastes broadened beyond the restrictions of gospel. He worked for a while with the Sweet Inspirations Band; then, in 1975, he played with the Stamps Quartet, a career move that allowed him an incredible opportunity: the Stamps were hired as backup vocalists by none other than Elvis Presley, and Brown was able to perform onstage in Las Vegas with the King himself. After Presley's tragic death in 1977, Brown signed on with country-folksinger Emmylou Harris and performed with her Hot Band, a stop along the road to success for such high-caliber, innovative musicians as guitarists Ricky Skaggs, Rodney Crowell, Albert Lee, and Vince Gill.

During the year that followed, Brown began to reconsider his role in the music business; he decided to try his hand at other facets of the recording industry. In 1978 he accepted a leadership role in the A&R department of Los Angeles-based Free Flight Records, a pop subsidiary of RCA. (A&R representatives are responsible for recruiting and nurturing talent at the record label.) When the label was discontinued two years later, he was given the option to remain in California or to transfer to RCA's Nashville office. The choice was easy: Brown's roots were in country music, so he returned to Tennessee, where he signed such talented acts as Alabama and Debra Allen to the RCA label.

After a year in Music City, Brown decided to return to the studio as a musician. Along with Gill and bass player Emory Gordy, Jr., he played keyboards with the Cherry Bombs, the backup band for Roseanne Cash and Rodney Crowell, who were married at the time. Working

For the Record . . .

Born c. 1947 in Greensboro, NC. Keyboardist for the Oak Ridge Boys and Sweet Inspirations; keyboardist for Stamps Quartet, Las Vegas, NV, 1975-77; member of Emmylou Harris's Hot Band, 1977-78; head of Artists & Repertoire (A&R), Free Flight Records (an RCA subsidiary), Los Angeles, CA, 1978-80; worked in RCA's A&R department, Nashville, TN, 1980 and 1983; keyboardist for the Cherry Bombs, c. 1980-83; joined MCA/Nashville's in-house A&R department, 1984, became executive vice-president and head of A&R, then served as president of MCA/Nashville, 1993—. Has produced records for artists including Jimmy Buffett, Vince Gill, Wynonna, the Mavericks, McBride & the Ride, Reba McEntire, George Strait, and Steve Wariner.

Awards: Country Music Association (CMA) Award for production on single of the year, 1991, for Vince Gill's "When I Call Your Name"; producer of the year, *Billboard,* 1990, 1991, 1992, and 1993.

Addresses: *Record company*—MCA/Nashville, 60 Music Sq. E., Nashville, TN 37293.

full-time with such musical talent sparked Brown's interest in the production end of the industry. Calling upon his extensive background knowledge of gospel music, he worked with gospel artist Shirley Caesar on three albums that would culminate in Caesar's winning the 1984 Grammy Award for best female gospel/soul performance.

From RCA to MCA/Nashville

After proving his skills as a producer, Brown returned to RCA later in 1983. That same year he produced Steve Wariner's hit single "Midnight Fire." Then, shortly after signing former bandmate Gill to RCA, rival MCA/Nashville made Brown an offer he couldn't refuse: he joined the label in 1984. "I wanted to produce," he noted in an MCA profile. "MCA was then reorganizing, starting an in-house A&R department with in-house production. In hindsight, it was a good move on my part."

If it was a good move for Brown, it was certainly one for MCA/Nashville. The list of stars he has signed to the label reads like a who's who of "Young Country": Rodney Crowell, Marty Brown, Lyle Lovett, Nanci Griffith, Marty Stuart, the Mavericks, Tracy Byrd, Trisha Yearwood, Mark Chesnutt, and Gill—whom he wooed from

RCA in 1989. And Brown has produced top-selling albums like Reba McEntire's *Rumor Has It; I Still Believe in You* by Gill; Wynonna's self-titled solo debut; Patty Loveless's *Honky Tonk Angel;* Marty Stuart's *This One's Gonna Hurt You;* and western swing master George Strait's *Pure Country.*

But Brown wasn't always such a strong force in the country music industry. As Peter Cronin noted in *Billboard,* "The Nashville powers that be had Brown pegged as a bit too edgy for the mainstream" in his early days with MCA. Brown drew folksinger and songwriter Nanci Griffith to MCA in 1987 and produced *Lone Star State of Mind,* an album that would become her biggest country hit. Lyle Lovett was another of Brown's finds; the idiosyncratic musician's self-titled debut was produced on MCA's Curb label in 1986. And songwriter-guitarist Steve Earle was signed by Brown in 1986; their work together on that year's *Guitar Town* introduced one of the most exciting new Nashville-based talents of the decade. While each of these releases proved to be a watershed for the respective performers' careers, they showed little, if any, movement on the all-important sales charts for MCA.

Making an Impact on Country Music

Brown, however, remained confident that his musical tastes reflected those of the record-buying public, particularly the country radio audience. "I really, really thought I could make an impact on country radio with those artists. I didn't end up making an impact on country radio, but I did make an impact on country music." Artists like Lovett, Griffith, and Earle helped blur the distinctions between country music and the genres of jazz, folk, and rock—and paved the way for an influx of new styles into the country music mix. Finally, Brown's first big commercial production—Rodney Crowell's *Diamonds and Dirt* in 1988—led to a succession of top-selling records that made the producer a key player in Music City circles.

After five singles from *Diamonds and Dirt* charted, more successes were quick to follow. Country crossover artist Lovett's 1989 effort, the Tony Brown-produced *Lyle Lovett and His Large Band,* received that year's Grammy Award for best vocal performance by a male country artist; Brown's production of Gill's "When I Call Your Name" won the Grammy Award for song of the year in 1990, and together the Gill/Brown duo took the same award the following year for "I Still Believe in You."

In addition to expanding the boundaries of country music, Brown bucked the conventional wisdom that women buy records mainly by male artists who wear hats and look cute. Vocalist Wynonna—a member of the Judds until her mother, Naomi, retired from the duo because of health problems—made her debut album as a solo act with Brown's capable production. Against industry tradition, *Wynonna* went double-platinum in 1993. The huge success of that album came on the heels of Brown's third "producer of the year" award from *Billboard;* these back-to-back successes propelled him up another rung of the industry ladder.

Named President of MCA/Nashville

In a contract maneuver that was preceded by a great deal of speculation in the music industry, Brown replaced Bruce Hinton as president of MCA/Nashville in 1993. While noting that Brown had been unhappy with his existing MCA contract, attorney James Mason told *Billboard* that the producer "wasn't looking to leave the place where he's been that successful." Brown welcomed his additional responsibilities but made it clear that he would not leave the studio, explaining to *Billboard's* Debbie Holley: "I'm not going to turn into such an administrative person that I will dilute my creative position."

Many music critics agree that there is no overall "Tony Brown Sound." The reason may be that Brown enters the recording studio confident in the instincts of the musicians he is producing. During studio sessions, he is noted for his light touch—his ability to give his artists the reins while offering subtle guidance. "For me, producing is a feel thing, and it's contributing to what's happening in the room," Brown told Cronin. "Country music is not a producer's forum like pop music is. Country is an artist's forum."

Respect and appreciation for a musical artist as just that—an artist—have earned Brown a reputation as both a sound judge and a prudent creative force in the country music arena. In 1994, with numerous gold, platinum, and multiplatinum albums to his credit, Brown was honored with a Grammy nomination for producer of the year, the first time a member of the country music recording industry had been in contention for that award since 1979.

Sources

Billboard, January 30, 1993; February 6, 1993; June 11, 1994.
Entertainment Weekly, March 20, 1992; October 30, 1992; March 4, 1994.
GQ, May 1993.
Stereo Review, June 1994.

Additional information for this profile was provided by MCA publicity materials.

—*Pamela L. Shelton*

Tim Buckley

Singer, songwriter

In a 1974 *Sounds* interview quoted by his friend and collaborator Lee Underwood in *Down Beat,* Tim Buckley mused, "Sometimes you're writing, and you know you're just *not* going to fit in. But you do it because it's your heart and your soul, and you gotta say it. It's the foremost thing in your mind.... It's hard to play the kind of music that musicians like to play and that the audiences like to hear, too." Such was the central dilemma of Buckley's professional life, for his audience's admiration of his earlier, more straightforward work limited the commercial possibilities of the experimental and deeply heartfelt creations he fashioned later on.

Signed as a "folk" artist in the mid-1960s, Buckley was an uncompromising, eternally restless songwriter who melded jazz, pop, and avant-garde musics into a signature sound that showcased his virtuosic, unearthly voice. A five-star 1971 *Down Beat* review of *Starsailor*—arguably Buckley's most powerful personal statement—proclaimed that "far too few (if any) pop artists exhibit such expressive control of the resonance and general tone of the voice as does Buckley." Sadly, he suffered a string of commercial setbacks and died of a drug overdose at age 28; only in the late 1980s and early 1990s were his works re-released and his prodigious talents reassessed.

A Teenaged Overachiever

Born in Washington, D.C., Tim Buckley moved with his family to Southern California when he was 12. He spent much of his adolescence experimenting with his voice, struggling to reach the highest and lowest imaginable notes. "So I practiced, and I screamed and I practiced some more," he recalled in an interview cited by Underwood, "until I finally ended up with a five- to five-and-a-half-octave range."

Enamored of folk and country music, he studied banjo and played in a band with friends like Dan Gordon. "I would love to say our roots were [country pioneer] Hank Williams," Gordon said in a conversation with Scott Isler of *Musician,* "but it's just not true. It's all [1950s-1960s folk band] the Kingston Trio." Nonetheless, even as Buckley played in Top 40 bands like the Bohemians, he also explored the anti-establishment beatnik fringes with Harlequins 3 and found himself powerfully drawn to modern jazz luminaries like Miles Davis, John Coltrane, and Charles Mingus.

After being introduced to Herb Cohen, who managed Frank Zappa's anarchistic rock experimentalists the Mothers of Invention, among other acts, Buckley began to perform more intensively. He eloped with high school

MICHAEL OCHS ARCHIVES/Venice, CA

For the Record . . .

Born Timothy Charles Buckley III, February 14, 1947, in Washington, DC; died of a drug overdose, June 28, 1975, in Los Angeles, CA; married Mary Guibert, c. 1965 (divorced 1968); married Judy Henske, 1970; children: (first marriage) Jeffrey Scott; (second marriage) Taylor. *Education:* Attended college briefly.

Performing and recording artist, mid-1960s-1975. Signed to Elektra Records and released debut album *Tim Buckley,* 1966; produced 1970 album *Blue Afternoon* for Straight Records; signed to Warner Bros. and released *Starsailor,* 1971; recorded *Sefronia* for DiscReet, 1973.

the Beatles' landmark *Sgt. Pepper's Lonely Hearts Club Band*—the beginning of the rock album as "art"—and influential recordings by singer-songwriter Bob Dylan, rock guitarist Jimi Hendrix, and an array of psychedelic bands from San Francisco, the creative ante had been upped markedly.

Buckley, undaunted, became more adventuresome; his *Goodbye and Hello,* Isler wrote in *Musician,* "sounds as if all concerned were inspired by *Sgt. Pepper* to create their own overarching statement on pop culture." With its anti-war sentiments and romantic ballads, it presented Buckley as just the sort of sensitive young troubadour the hippie culture was beginning to demand. "Once I Was," his most enduring "folk" performance, helped make the album his most successful. In addition to developing his striking vocals, Buckley had begun to write lyrics; Beckett, who had contributed to *Goodbye and Hello,* was fading from the scene.

Experimentation and Frustration

Buckley was idolized by many young fans, but Underwood claimed that the singer "resented being set up as a rock 'n' roll savior, insisting that people should learn how to do their own living instead of propping musicians up as 'easy gods' who did the living for them." Buckley was similarly disgusted by the music business, never understanding the market-based concerns of the labels for which he recorded.

At a time when blues-rock guitar was all the rage, Buckley championed jazz; the influence of bop and post-bop styles would appear on his next album, 1968's *Happy/Sad.* With only Buckley's voice and guitar accompanied by vibes, string bass, and congas—Underwood was ousted temporarily due to his excessive drinking—the album eschewed the sonic overkill of mainstream pop for a meditative, nuanced quality. *Happy/Sad* featured a number of Buckley's most highly regarded compositions, notably "Buzzin' Fly" and "Gypsy Woman," and the album marked a quantum leap for him as composer, singer, and lyricist.

All the words to each cut on *Happy/Sad* were Buckley's, and the jazzy textures complemented them ideally. Isler called *Happy/Sad* "a fully realized work" and reminded readers that its creator was a mere 21 years of age at the time of its completion. Buckley subsequently toured the United Kingdom, and his debut concert there was recorded, but it was not released for 22 years.

By the late 1960s, Buckley had reached his commercial peak. Ever trying new avenues, he served as producer on his next album, *Blue Afternoon,* which is generally

sweetheart Mary Guibert and enrolled in college. Buckley was forced to grow up quickly, attempting to juggle his education with his marriage while building a music career—all before the age of 20. The marriage was rocky, and he and Guibert lived together only sporadically. He dropped out of college before completing his first year and played in L.A. nightspots like the Troubadour as well as far-flung coffee houses and other venues amenable to folk music. Cohen introduced Buckley's distinctive sound to Elektra Records founder Jac Holzman, who told Isler in *Musician:* "I loved the writing, I loved the approach, and I loved the fact that he had both folk roots and rock 'n' roll aspirations."

Thanks to Cohen's involvement, Buckley landed gigs at a Greenwich Village club, the Night Owl, and there he met and began collaborating with guitarist-keyboardist Lee Underwood. The musician became one of Buckley's most devoted sidemen and a virtual disciple of his artistic fervor. Playing songs he wrote with poet friend Larry Beckett, Buckley formed a band consisting of Underwood on lead guitar and Jim Fielder on bass.

Elektra released his debut album, *Tim Buckley,* in 1966; Holzman told Isler that the record "had an air of stridency about it. [Buckley] wasn't really comfortable in his own musical skin." Even so, it introduced the young singer's powerful voice and won some critical praise. That year also saw Guibert give birth to the couple's son, Jeffrey, but she and Tim had already agreed to divorce. Jeff Buckley would himself later emerge as a rock singer-songwriter and struggle to distinguish his work—and his powerfully familiar voice—from the work of the father he met only once.

The year between Buckley's first and second albums proved to be a transitional period for pop music. With

considered to have been made too quickly and without adequate care. The singer-songwriter next embarked on a more obscure path; the first result was *Lorca*, named after a Spanish poet and sporting irregular time signatures and some of his most avant-garde singing. The album, Isler commented in *Musician*, "exploded with musical daring."

Dropped by Elektra, Buckley moved to Warner Bros., which in 1971 released *Starsailor*. The album—in part a collaborative effort that reunited him with Beckett—is regarded as the ultimate expression of Buckley's passionate experimentation. In addition to lavishing praise on Buckley as a "consummate vocal technician," *Down Beat* deemed him "a sincerely eclectic and compassionate artist who, as the adage speaks, must be heard to be believed." The album's track "Song to the Siren"— written with Beckett years before—was later covered by the British act This Mortal Coil and then used in a television ad in the United Kingdom.

Posthumous Revaluation

But critical adoration didn't equal album sales. Fans were often bemused by Buckley's refusal to perform old favorites live; an often-cited anecdote has an audience member calling out, "How about 'Buzzin' Fly'?," to which the singer responded, "How about horseshit." His incantatory, often dissonant vocal excursions tended to leave crowds—like the one observed by Michael Cuscuna of *Rolling Stone*—"baffled and dismayed." Persuaded to do an album in the blues-rock idiom, Buckley recorded 1972's *Greetings from L.A.*, which consisted of songs too raunchy for the radio and most record buyers of the time; though it flopped commercially, the album seems truer to the spirit of blues music to many listeners than does most of the work by Buckley's rock contemporaries.

Buckley had gone through periods of intense depression and drug and alcohol abuse—particularly after the commercial failure of *Starsailor*—but he soldiered on, playing gigs, recording a few more rather anticlimactic albums, and writing a semi-autobiographical screenplay. In 1975, at the home of his friend Richard Keeling, he snorted what he thought was cocaine but was in reality a heroin-morphine mix; this, combined with alcohol already in his system, did him in. Ironically, Buckley is said to have kicked his heroin habit prior to the incident; his system was therefore rendered particularly vulnerable to the effects of the drugs.

Buckley died on June 28, 1975, "in debt, owning only his guitar and his amp," Underwood noted. Years later

Melody Maker lamented that "his death was premature, pathetic, a terrible waste. But those who have heard him will never forget him." Keeling was charged with murder for supplying the illegal substances and ended up serving four months in prison for involuntary manslaughter.

The ensuing years have seen a continuing reassessment of Buckley's music, a process that has been aided by the release of his work on CD. Along with the studio albums, Buckley enthusiasts can now enjoy a number of seminal live recordings—notably a 1968 London performance issued in 1990 as *Dream Letter*, which *Folk Roots* magazine declared the "timeless art of a genuine genius." *Rolling Stone* hailed the re-release of Buckley's albums and pronounced his catalog "a poignant example of how far one songwriter was willing to go in search of a greater, purer form of musical expression."

Selected discography

Tim Buckley, Elektra, 1966.
Goodbye and Hello (includes "Once I Was"), Elektra, 1967.
Happy/Sad (includes "Buzzin' Fly" and "Gypsy Woman"), Elektra, 1968.
Blue Afternoon, Straight, 1970.
Lorca, Elektra, 1970.
Starsailor (includes "Song to the Siren"), Warner Bros., 1971.
Greetings from L.A., Warner Bros., 1972.
Sefronia, DiscReet, 1973.
Look at the Fool, DiscReet, 1974.
Dream Letter: Live in London, 1968, Bizarre/Straight, 1990.
Live at the Troubadour, Bizarre/Straight, 1994.

Sources

Books

Rees, Dafydd, and Luke Crampton, *Rock Movers & Shakers*, Billboard, 1991.

Periodicals

Chicago Tribune, July 28, 1994.
Down Beat, March 4, 1971; June 16, 1977.
Folk Roots, May 1990; October 1990.
Melody Maker, January 31, 1987; October 24, 1987.
Musician, July 1991.
Rolling Stone, April 2, 1970; August 14, 1975; December 14, 1989; December 13, 1990.

—*Simon Glickman*

Eric Burdon

Singer, songwriter

Sometimes referred to as a "black singer trapped inside a white skin," Eric Burdon achieved international fame by belting out bluesy rock numbers with the Animals in the mid-1960s. His raw, hard-edged vocals were a key ingredient in a number of hits for the band in their native United Kingdom and abroad. After the original Animals disbanded, Burdon made his mark as a vocalist with the black band War.

While growing up in Newcastle upon Tyne, a port city just south of England's border with Scotland, Burdon had no burning desire to be a singer. His first exposure to the music that would hook him came at about age 12, when a merchant seaman who lived in his building let him listen to records he had brought home from the United States. Burdon became a lover of rhythm and blues after listening to recordings of Fats Domino, Bill Doggett, and other black artists—works that couldn't be obtained in England at the time. Thinking he didn't have the skills to play an instrument, Burdon concentrated on developing his voice.

At the Newcastle College of Art, where he studied graphics and photography, Burdon further developed his interest in blues artists and formed a band. At the time, his only interest in music was as a diversion. After leaving school, however, he began performing for money because he couldn't find a job in television as a set designer or art director. In 1962 Burdon found work as a lead singer with the Alan Price Combo, which took in about 30 shillings (a little over $4) a week for each musician. The group changed its name to the Animals, began to develop a following as regulars at the Club A Go-Go in Newcastle, and by 1963 were landing gigs in other English cities. Members of the Animals included Burdon on vocals, Chas Chandler on bass guitar, John Steel on drums (succeeded by Barry Jenkins), Price on organ (later replaced by Dave Rowberry), and Hilton Valentine on lead guitar.

Animals Became Worldwide Sensation

Soon the group recorded a demo for local fans; the tape was taken to London by their manager and found its way to producer Mickie Most, who then came up to watch them perform. Most saw the group's potential, brought them to London, and signed them to a recording contract. In London, the Animals performed regularly at the Scene Club and continued to build up their audience.

The Animals recorded a cover of Bob Dylan's "Baby Let Me Take You Home," which made it onto the charts in April of 1964, and earned the group a slot on a Chuck Berry Tour in the United Kingdom. They then hit Number

For the Record . . .

Born May 11, 1941 (one source says April 5, 1941), in Newcastle upon Tyne, England; immigrated to the United States, mid-1960s; returned to England, 1983. *Education:* Attended Newcastle College of Art.

Vocalist with Alan Price Combo, a band that later became the Animals, beginning in 1962; signed contract with manager-producer Mickie Most and moved to London, 1964; recorded cover of Bob Dylan's "Baby Let Me Take You Home" with the Animals for first charted single, 1964; recorded first Number One hit, "House of the Rising Sun," with the Animals, 1964; moved to California and formed the New Animals, 1966; announced retirement, 1968; regrouped original Animals for Christmas concert in Newcastle, 1969; became front man for War, 1970; cut album with Jimmy Witherspoon, 1971; formed Fire Dept. with German musicians; appeared in several European movies, late 1970s; starred in and wrote soundtrack for German film *Comeback,* 1981; resettled in London, 1983; wrote autobiography *I Used to Be an Animal, but I'm All Right Now,* 1986.

Addresses: *Record company*—Raven, P.O. Box 26811, Richmond, VA 23261.

One later in 1964 with their version of the traditional ballad "House of the Rising Sun"—and for the next two years were one of the hottest acts in the world. Vital to the group's success was Burdon's gift for vocals; his powerful, unrefined sound placed the Animals in a class with the Beatles and the Rolling Stones for a time during the mid-1960s.

In 1965, after turning out hits such as "Don't Let Me Be Misunderstood" and "We Gotta Get Out of This Place," the Animals suffered a creative blow with the departure of keyboardist Price, whose subtle arrangements and organ playing helped give the group its distinctive sound. Meanwhile, Burdon was causing dissension in the band with his rowdiness, heavy drinking, and purported use of LSD. After greatly reducing their number of concert dates, the group disbanded in 1966. Burdon recorded a solo album in early 1967 with New York studio musicians, then took a sabbatical from music. He claimed to be working on a novel and pursuing film projects with a rock-music theme.

Saying that he preferred a warm climate, Burdon decided to move to California. He settled first in Los Angeles because it offered the latest recording technology and

was the heart of the movie industry. In time, he moved on to San Francisco, where he formed the New Animals with Vic Briggs on guitar, John Wieder on guitar and violin, Danny McCullough on bass, and former Animals drummer Jenkins. The group later featured Andy Summers, who eventually became the guitarist for the Police.

In the late 1960s, living in the U.S. capital of "flower power," Burdon attempted to transform himself from streetwise tough-guy to hippie leader. His music shifted along with him, from an emphasis on tough R&B to the increasingly popular acid rock. He signed his new group to a contract with MGM and released four albums, including the double album *Love Is.* Burdon's New Animals placed singles on the charts with "Good Times" and "San Francisco Nights" in 1967, "Sky Pilot" in 1968, and "Ring of Fire" in 1969.

Revived Career with Soul-Funk Band War

After the demise of the New Animals, Burdon stationed himself in Los Angeles and was often seen with guitar virtuoso Jimi Hendrix on the rock circuit there. When Hendrix died of a drug overdose, rumors about Burdon's own drug problems proliferated. He stated he was retiring from music, but in 1969 producers Jerry Goldstein and Steve Gold urged him to get involved with another band.

They connected him with members of Nite Shift, which featured six black musicians and a highly regarded Danish harmonica player named Lee Oskar. Burdon first went into the studio with the group, then toured with them as Eric Burdon and War. Their first album together, *Eric Burdon Declares "War,"* was very successful and remained on the charts for much of 1970. Burdon's funky vocals on "Spill the Wine" brought the single to Number Three on the U.S. charts. The singer soon found himself back in the limelight, and the group was invited to make guest television appearances on the *David Frost* and *Ed Sullivan* shows. In August of 1970, Eric Burdon and War performed in Britain.

Burdon's assumption of a black persona with War incited some race-related controversy, especially with the release of the less-than-tactfully-titled *Black Man's Burdon* in December of 1970. Despite his musical success with the group, Burdon and War parted ways in less than a year.

The vocalist revealed that his interest in the blues was as strong as ever when he teamed up with blues legend Jimmy Witherspoon on *Guilty!* in 1971. Burdon went back to perform in Britain in 1973, then shifted gears away from black music in 1974 to record two heavy rock albums with his Eric Burdon Band. He released a reunion album with the original Animals in 1977, then put together the band Fire Dept. with German musicians for one album, *Last Drive,* released in 1980. Burdon further cashed in on his enduring popularity with German audiences by appearing in the German film *Comeback* in 1982, which also featured his original soundtrack. Comparisons could not be avoided of Burdon's own life to the movie, which was about the downfall of an aging rock star.

Reflected on Career

When a re-release of "House of the Rising Sun" became a hit in 1982, Burdon and the original Animals went on a six-week tour of the United States. By this time more than 40 years old, Burdon still managed to capture all the raw power of the hit songs that had sealed the group's fame in the mid-1960s.

Despite his frenzied stage performances over the years, Burdon wrote in his 1986 autobiography *I Used to Be an Animal, but I'm All Right Now* that he had always hated touring and being in the public eye. The memoir traces Burdon's life from his working-class origins, through the development of his musical interests in the blues, and recounts the ultimate turmoil of touring: Burdon reveals that he was repulsed by the invasions of privacy he suffered in the United States during his first visit there—but enthralled by seeing his heroes James Brown and B. B. King at the Apollo Theater in Harlem. He also laments that his manager had lost the Animals millions of dollars in shady tax deals. In her review of the book for the *New York Times Book Review,* Andrea Barnet commented: "Taken as social history, [Burdon's] auto-biography stands as a vivid record of what has now become pop mythology."

Various contractual and personal problems made Burdon's output erratic during the 1970s and 1980s, but the staying power of Animals material was confirmed by the 1991 *Roadrunners* CD, a collection of live recordings from Burdon's music files. In a *Rolling Stone* review, David Fricke noted that the collection "vividly captures the punky stage intensity of the band's mongrel acid-R&B sound."

Considered by some observers to be music's greatest white blues vocalist, Eric Burdon also revealed an ability during his career to achieve success in a variety of genres ranging from blues-tinged rock to psychedelia to funk. The multifaceted singer's erratic career shifts and often self-defeating lifestyle caused his popularity to wax and wane over the years. However, he is un-equivocally credited with providing the penetrating energy that propelled the Animals to superstardom in the 1960s.

Selected discography

Singles; with the Animals

"House of the Rising Sun," 1964.
"Don't Let Me Be Misunderstood," 1965.
"We Gotta Get Out of This Place," 1965.
"It's My Life," 1965.

Singles; with the New Animals

"San Francisco Nights," 1967.
"Sky Pilot," 1968.
"Ring of Fire," 1969.

Singles; with War

"Spill the Wine," 1970.

Albums; with the Animals

The Animals (with Eric Burdon), MGM, 1964.
Animal Tracks, MGM, 1965.
Animalism, MGM, 1966.
The Best of Eric Burdon and the Animals, MGM, 1967.
Before We Were So Rudely Interrupted, Jet, 1977.

Albums; with the New Animals

Winds of Change, MGM, 1967.
Every One of Us, MGM, 1968.
Love Is, MGM, 1968.
Roadrunners (a compilation of live recordings from the late 1960s), Raven, 1991.

Solo albums

Eric Is Here, MGM, 1967.
Survivor, Polydor, 1978.
Black and White Blues, MCA, 1979.
I Used to Be an Animal, Striped Horse, 1988.

Albums; with War

Eric Burdon Declares "War," MGM, 1970.
Black Man's Burdon, MGM, 1970.
Love Is All Around (recorded 1970), ABC, 1976.

Albums; with the Eric Burdon Band

Sun Secrets, Capitol, 1974.

Stop!, Capitol, 1975.

Other albums

(With Jimmy Witherspoon) *Guilty!,* MGM, 1971.
(With Fire Dept.) *Last Drive,* 1980.
Comeback (soundtrack), 1982.

Sources

Books

Burdon, Eric, *I Used to Be an Animal, but I'm All Right Now,* originally published in 1986, Faber, 1987.
The Guinness Encyclopedia of Popular Music, Volume 3, edited by Colin Larkin, Guinness Publishing, 1992.
The Harmony Illustrated Encyclopedia of Rock, Harmony Books, 1988.

Helander, Brock, *The Rock Who's Who: A Complete Guide to the Great Artists and Albums of 30 Years from Rockabilly to New Wave,* Schirmer Books, 1982.
Kent, Jeff, *The Last Poet: The Story of Eric Burdon,* Witan Books, 1989.
The Penguin Encyclopedia of Popular Music, edited by Donald Clarke, Viking, 1989.
The Rolling Stone Encyclopedia of Rock & Roll, edited by Jon Pareles and Patricia Romanowski, Rolling Stone Press/ Summit Books, 1983.
Stambler, Irwin, *Encyclopedia of Pop, Rock & Soul,* St. Martin's, 1989.

Periodicals

New York Times Book Review, May 3, 1987.
Rolling Stone, October 27, 1983; March 21, 1991.
Stereo Review, December 1988.

—Ed Decker

Frank Cappelli

Children's entertainer

Courtesy of The Brad Simon Organization, Inc.

According to an article in *Parents* magazine, "With Frank Cappelli, you swing, you sway, and you learn where the fork goes ('To the left of the plate, to the left, my friend')." Therein lay the key reasons why children's musician Frank Cappelli has gotten so popular recently: his engaging personality and very singable songs gently instruct while they entertain. More importantly, the simple sophistication of his music charms toddlers but rarely annoys their parents, as is so often the complaint about music for the smaller set. Cappelli's ability to walk that fine line—and a great deal of luck—has pushed him to the top of his field in a very short time.

Born on August 17, 1952, in Utica, New York, Cappelli moved with his family to Mount Lebanon, Pennsylvania, when he was four. As a sixth grader he decided to take up the guitar, and it was only then that he learned he could actually sing. He eventually performed George Gershwin tunes with a group around the Pittsburgh area. Although Cappelli adored performing, his parents encouraged him to go to college in order to have something to fall back on. He graduated from West Chester State College qualified to teach music to children. It was the student teaching necessary for this degree that made it clear his greatest talent lay in singing for children.

Discovered His Gift

In the mid-1970s Cappelli worked as a substitute teacher in the tough schools of South Philadelphia. "The thing that saved me was, I would bring my guitar," he told Maryland's *Frederick News-Post*. "I found I could sing to kids and get their undivided attention," he further explained in *Billboard*. "Then I realized I could also teach them with music and started writing little songs." Cappelli discovered, however, that singing professionally paid better than teaching. He would perform songs with friends in coffeehouses and folk clubs in Philadelphia and Atlantic City, New Jersey, and substitute teach on occasion during the day.

In 1977 Cappelli moved back to Pittsburgh and met his future wife, Patty, a waitress in one of the clubs where he performed. Together they formed the first singing telegram company in Pittsburgh, but after four very successful years, their idea had stirred up so much competition that they decided to sell the company in 1982.

With their two young children, the Cappellis moved to Denver, Colorado, taking jobs at a lumber company. While they gained a degree-full of business experience, they missed home. Frank had moved to Denver to break into the music industry, but as he told Frances Borsodi

Born August 17, 1952, in Utica, NY; son of Emilio Frank (in sales) and Caroline (Gitto) Cappelli; married Patty Broderick, 1978; children: Giuseppi, Caroline, Timmy, and Frankie, Jr. *Education:* Graduated from West Chester State College.

Began singing for children as a substitute teacher, mid-1970s; started first singing telegram company in Pittsburgh, PA, 1977-82; worked in sales for a lumber wholesaler, Denver, CO, c. 1982-88; began record label, Peanut Heaven, and released first four albums, 1988; signed with A&M Records, 1989; A&M released all four Peanut Heaven cassettes; *Cappelli & Company* aired on WTAE-TV in Pittsburgh and was syndicated to five major Midwest cities, 1990-93; *Cappelli & Company* aired on cable station Nickelodeon, 1993.

Awards: Achievement in Children's Television Award, Action for Children's Television, for *Cappelli & Company,* 1990; Pennsylvania Association of Broadcasters Award for Best Children's Program in Pennsylvania for *Cappelli & Company,* 1990, 1991, 1992, and 1993; Parent's Choice Gold Award for *All Aboard the Train,* 1990, and for *Pass the Coconut,* 1991; Emmy awards, Mid-Atlantic Chapter of the National Academy of Television Arts & Sciences, for outstanding children's programming/series for *Cappelli & Company,* 1990 and 1992; Gabriel Award for Outstanding Achievement in Children's Programming for *Cappelli & Company,* 1990 and 1993.

Addresses: *Publicity*—Peanut Heaven, 717 N. Meadowcroft Ave., Pittsburgh, PA 15216. *Management*—The Brad Simon Organization, Inc., 122 E. 57th St., New York, NY 10022.

Zajac in the Pittsburgh *Herald Standard,* "I didn't put value on the fact that in Pittsburgh people knew me so they would come to see me. In Denver, they didn't know me." Now a family of five, they went home.

The Cappellis had not lost the love of running their own business, though, and all arrows pointed to Frank's singing ability. In 1988, with the financial support of an attorney friend and business partners, the Cappellis started their own record label, Peanut Heaven. They recorded and released four albums: *Look Both Ways, You Wanna Be a Duck?, On Vacation,* and *Good.* They

took care of the publicity and distribution and eventually got National Record Mart to stock the albums in their Pittsburgh stores. It was an executive of those stores who introduced the Cappellis to A&M Records.

An A&M representative went to see Cappelli play two West Virginian dates in 1989. The first concert was a smash, but the second—in a run-down mall in a rural town—was a disaster; nobody even knew Cappelli was coming. He apologized to the A&M rep and played his set anyway. The second show sold the representative on Cappelli. Frank recalled to the *Herald Standard's* Zajac, "[The A&M rep] said, 'You can make magic. Once you started singing, people forgot they were in a boarded-up mall.'" In July of 1989 Cappelli signed a worldwide promotion and distribution contract with A&M Records, and in October of the same year A&M released all four of the existing Peanut Heaven children's cassettes.

Connected With Little People

Luck and talent continued to pay off when, having just pitched a show and been rejected by a local radio station, Cappelli ran into the program director of WTAE-TV, which shared a lobby with the rejecting radio station. From 1990 to 1993, 65 episodes of *Cappelli & Company* were taped at WTAE-TV, the Pittsburgh-based ABC network affiliate. The show featured an audience of 40 to 50 children between the ages of three to seven. They sat with Cappelli on a simple stage set while he talked and sang, brought on educational guests, and played music videos of his own songs. "I think young children like my show because it provides them with a safe place to go," Cappelli reflected to Zajac in the *Herald Standard.* "They feel comfortable. And I believe they like watching other children.... They're not talked down to. They're treated like people. And there's something in my personality: I connect with little people."

In addition to his audio cassettes, Cappelli released two video cassettes in 1990: *All Aboard the Train and Other Favorites*—which won the 1990 Parent's Choice Foundation Gold Award—and *Slap Me Five.* Both releases are samplers of *Cappelli & Company.* Reviewing the tapes for *Billboard,* Moira McCormick voted *All Aboard* "the more engrossing of the two, especially for preschoolers.... But the songs [on both tapes] are uniformly catchy and fun to sing—and as a result, rate very low on the parental-irritation meter.... A pair of winners." *TV Guide,* voting them two of the "Best in Home Video," found "Cappelli's magic ... in his varied delivery, using styles as diverse as reggae and polka, opera and rock and roll, and his songs are lively, imaginative and memorable."

In June of 1991 A&M released the audio cassette *Pass the Coconut*. *Parenting* magazine gave it an "A" and felt that "Cappelli's great stew of instruments ... and musical styles ... mesh seamlessly with lyrics that are playful, pleasantly simple, and even mildly educational." *Pass the Coconut* won the 1991 Parent's Choice Foundation's Gold Award, the citation for which declared Cappelli "a witty, fun-loving delight who lets his imagination run free. The result is an enchanting, entertaining mix of off-beat songs in a variety of pop styles.... A clever collection."

Cappelli & Company Went National

On April 5, 1993, *Cappelli & Company,* which had earned several Emmy awards from the Mid-Atlantic chapter of the National Academy of Television Arts & Sciences, and which had been syndicated to stations in Boston, Baltimore, Kansas City, Milwaukee, and Dayton, went national as all 65 episodes were purchased by Nickelodeon, the Children's Cable Network. It would now broadcast into 57 million homes. *TV Guide* voted it one of "Pre-School's Best Bets" in their special parents' guide: "Decent, fatherly Frank Cappelli simply looks like a dad you can trust. The show is informative, patient, and simple without ever slipping into a patronizing tone. As for the music, the performers are all engaging, and the tunes are sing-along accessible without being cloying."

Billboard emphasized, "Few artists have Cappelli's songwriting skills. Whether writing cautionary tunes about brushing your teeth and crossing the street or simply fun numbers about trains and fruits, Cappelli finds a melody that's hard to shake. It doesn't hurt, too, that he's hammy enough to deliver in broad, winning strokes."

In September of 1993 A & M released *Take a Seat*. Once again critics marveled at Cappelli's gift for making everyday events in a kid's life into wonderful musical experiences. *Parents* summed it up: "Mostly he teaches (by example) that it's pure joy to fill up your lungs, open your mouth and sing."

Although in the mid-1990s *Cappelli & Company* was no longer in production, the Cappellis were still hard at work developing new projects. Frank was at work on a new series entitled *People, Places and Things,* which he planned to host. Devised as a tool for classroom teachers, the programs use music, story, song, and location documentaries to enhance a new approach to teaching reading—the Whole Language Learning process.

Television aside, Frank Cappelli is at his best when performing for children. His trademark "sing-and-dance-alongs" always generate enthusiastic participation from concert goers. Whether alone on stage or with a symphony orchestra backing him up, Cappelli wanders throughout the crowd, his acoustic guitar unplugged and uninhibiting, charming the socks off his younger audienatice as well as the bigger folks, their parents.

Selected discography

On A&M Records

Look Both Ways, 1989.
You Wanna Be a Duck?, 1989.
On Vacation, 1989.
Good, 1989.
Pass the Coconut, 1991.
Take a Seat, 1993.

Also released videos *All Aboard the Train* and *Slap Me Five,* both 1990.

Sources

Billboard, July 14, 1990; August 10, 1991; November 28, 1992.
Entertainment Weekly, December 3, 1993.
Frederick News-Post (MD), March 18, 1994.
Herald-Standard (Pittsburgh, PA), February 20, 1994.
Parenting, June/July 1992.
Parents, November 1993.
People, March 5, 1990.
Saturday Evening Post, January/February 1993.
School Library Journal, October 1990; February 1994.
TV Guide, March 2, 1991; October 30, 1993.
Update: The Campaign for QED (newsletter of WQED-TV, Pittsburgh, PA), June 1994.
Video, November 1990.

Additional information for this profile was obtained from Peanut Heaven publicity materials, 1994.

—*Joanna Rubiner*

Ron Carter

Bassist

Photograph by William Claxton, courtesy of Capitol Records

As a Michigan teenager studying classical music, Ron Carter abandoned cello training and switched to double bass. Following a mere half year of intensive work, he managed to win a scholarship to the prestigious Eastman School of Music in New York. Carter had planned on a classical music career, only vaguely aware of jazz, but in 1958 a conductor visiting the school, Leopold Stokowski of the Houston Symphony, admired his work. However, Stokowski readily admitted that the South, at least, wasn't ready for black musicians in their orchestras. Hearing this, Carter abruptly realized that racism had permeated the entire U.S. orchestral world—a state of affairs that, he would note in the late 1980s, really hadn't changed much.

Carter finished his Eastman studies in 1959 and took off for the New York jazz scene. He immediately secured a gig with the well-known Chico Hamilton Quintet, featuring saxophonist Eric Dolphy. The group cut a record for Warner Bros. that was deemed too experimental and never released. After several months of touring, Carter settled down in New York for further training at the Manhattan School of Music.

For the next few years Carter did session work with a great number of musicians, including Cannonball Adderley, Randy Weston, and Jaki Byard. He also earned a master's degree in music. But it was not until 1963 that Carter garnered national—and even international—attention, when he began his five-year stint with the now-legendary Miles Davis Quintet. With Carter on bass, a 17-year-old Tony Williams drumming, and Herbie Hancock playing piano, the quintet possessed "what has been called perhaps the greatest jazz-time-playing rhythm section ever," according to *Jazz—The Essential Companion.*

Acoustic Preference

If not for his commitment to acoustic bass, Carter might have remained with this extraordinary group for several more years. In 1968 the Davis quintet completed an important album, *Filles de Kilimanjaro,* which hinted at an abandonment of past practice: Davis required Carter to play an electric bass in the performance. This electrification was a step toward Davis's famous 1969 jazz-rock fusion release *Bitches Brew.* Carter apparently wanted no part of the fusion trend and in 1968 departed the group.

Not long after this, in a 1972 *Down Beat* interview with bass master Richard Davis, Carter explained his attachment to the acoustic bass: he said he feels it has a unique sound, one that the electric bass could never

For the Record...

Born May 4, 1937, in Ferndale, MI. *Education:* Received bachelor's degree from the Eastman School of Music, 1959; further study at the Manhattan School of Music.

Bass player, music teacher, recording artist. Trained from youth as a classical musician but pursued career in jazz. Moved to New York City, early 1960s, and began playing with Chico Hamilton, Eric Dolphy, and others; joined the Miles Davis Quintet, 1963; played with Herbie Hancock, Sonny Rollins, and others, beginning in the 1970s; signed with Milestone Records, late 1970s; began teaching music at the City College of the City University of New York, 1980s.

Awards: Grammy Award for best individual or group jazz instrumental performance, 1995, for *A Tribute to Miles.*

Addresses: *Record company*—Blue Note, 810 Seventh Ave., New York, NY 10019.

In the early 1970s Carter worked with various artists, including immortal songstress Lena Horne during her New York appearances, flutist Hubert Laws, and jazz guitarist George Benson. He also recorded with Art Farmer, saxophonist Joe Henderson, Horace Silver, and others. Later in the 1970s Carter was signed by the Milestone label, which issued many of his records, including 1977's *Piccolo,* featuring the bassist's early efforts at piccolo playing; *1+3,* a live Tokyo album from 1978—essentially a Miles Davis Quintet rhythm section reunion with Tony Williams and Herbie Hancock; and *Patrao,* recorded two years later with Chet Baker.

The Davis rhythm section reunion played for some time under the name VSOP and, along with Hancock and Williams, included saxophonist Wayne Shorter and trumpeter Freddie Hubbard. Two albums and a worldwide tour later, Carter was with another outfit, this one led by tenor sax player Sonny Rollins. He further built his list of all-star associations with the Rollins group, since it afforded him the opportunity to play with pianist McCoy Tyner. In 1981 some VSOP members regrouped as the Hancock Quartet, featuring the addition of trumpeter Wynton Marsalis; this new quartet embarked on an international tour and released a double album. Later in the 1980s, jazz saxophonist Branford Marsalis, future bandleader for *The Tonight Show with Jay Leno,* appeared for a time in the Hancock Quartet.

replace. Even hard-boiled session men prone to seeing the giant instrument as an antique enjoyed it when Carter showed up with his 70-year-old instrument. (He once boasted that his favorite bass had a sound that rivaled an antique one he owned made in 1734.) Nonetheless, Carter admitted that he always allocated the electric bass an hour or so of practice time a week in order to remain versatile.

"Things Are All Backwards"

Record-industry racism and a lack of commercial interest in jazz have concerned Ron Carter his whole career. In the *Down Beat* interview with Davis, Carter railed against suggestions that jazz help sell itself by going pop. "Why should jazz groups play the Beatles' music?" he demanded. "Why not propagate ... Herbie Hancock's music ... or Thad Jones' music. Why propagate music that was stolen from us anyway?" Carter also decried the music business claim that jazz doesn't sell; record company executives, he argued, make no effort to sell it. "They spent $80,000 or so for a sign on Broadway for a rock group that can't play, so why can't they spend a third of that for a group that can play—and make some money while they're at it. Things are all backwards."

Interest in Classical Music Resurfaced

Around the same time, Carter began a serious teaching career at City College of the City University of New York, handling practical courses as well as an authoritative examination of post-World War II jazz history. Carter's music also appeared on film soundtracks, one ambitious project being Bertrand Tavernier's 1988 motion picture *Beatrice.* The music for this film was made using only medieval instruments, including the vielle, sackbutt, hurdy gurdy, and string bass. The project required intense research and challenged Carter's limits.

The *Beatrice* film score project resurrected Carter's lifelong interest in classical music, an echo of boyhood training. In the late 1980s he voiced a desire to compose for string orchestras and quartets. Having already successfully recorded Bach cello music on Nippon/Polydor, Carter worked through the early 1990s on an album eventually released as *Ron Carter Meets Bach.* The classical music world resisted the project, however; after major classical labels rejected *Bach,* it wound up on the jazz label Blue Note. Hearing the finished album, a *Musician* magazine contributor hailed "the autumnal richness of the low-end colors [and] the surprising malleability of [Carter's] dancing, singing bass parts."

Not all listeners shared the *Musician* reviewer's enthusiasm. Kevin Whitehead, a National Public Radio (NPR) jazz critic, wrote in the pages of *Pulse!* that the album might be classified as comedy; he further lamented an inappropriate jazz trill, out-of-tune playing, and multi-tracking that seemed to emphasize a lack of time sense. Still, the album was generally well reviewed, at least in jazz publications. The Bach album reflects Carter's willingness to venture beyond safe country—that country being jazz of the last several decades. After appearing on over 1,000 albums and authoring multiple volumes on jazz-craft, teaching, and playing around the world, Ron Carter has built his own kingdom in the music world.

Selected discography

My Funny Valentine, CBS, 1964.
Miles Smiles, CBS, 1966.
Filles de Kilimanjaro, Columbia, 1968.

VSOP Live under the Sky, CBS, 1977.
Piccolo, Milestone, 1977.
1+3, Milestone, 1978.
Patrao, Milestone, 1980.
Herbie Hancock Quartet, CBS, 1981.
Etudes, Elektra Musician, 1983.
Ron Carter Meets Bach, Blue Note, 1993.

Sources

Books

Jazz—The Essential Companion, edited by Ian Carr, Prentice Hall, 1988.

Periodicals

Down Beat, May 11, 1972.
Musician, February 1988; February 1993.
Pulse!, June 1993.

—*Joseph M. Reiner*

The Church

Rock band

Critics' descriptions of the Church's sound have varied with the band's ever-changing albums, but the Church's distinctive style and ambience remain a constant. The group was formed in Sydney, Australia, in 1980 and over the years has garnered international attention. "Once upon a time," singer Steve Kilbey recalled in *Raygun,* "we were four young fellows starting a band in Sydney in 1980, and we all ate the same things, and looked the same way, and wore the same clothes."

Those four young fellows—Kilbey, guitarists Marty Willson-Piper and Peter Koppes, and drummer Richard Ploog—made up the Church's original lineup. The year following their formation, the band released *Of Skins and Heart,* their debut album on Australia's Parlophone Records, featuring the single "The Unguarded Moment." In 1982 they landed a deal in the United States with Capitol Records and released *The Church,* which included most of the cuts from their first Australian release plus three other songs from a double-45 single.

Courtesy of Arista Records

For the Record . . .

Members include **Jay Dee Daugherty** (member 1988-93), drums; **Steve Kilbey,** vocals, bass guitar; **Peter Koppes** (left group 1993), guitar; **Richard Ploog** (member 1980-88), drums; **Marty Willson-Piper,** guitar.

Band formed in Sydney, Australia, 1980; released first album, *Of Skin and Heart,* in Australia on Parlophone Records, 1981; released self-titled debut album in U.S., Capitol, 1982; recorded for Carrere Records in Australia, 1982-83, and Warner Bros. in the United States, 1984-86; signed with Arista Records, 1987. Marty Willson-Piper and Steve Kilbey released first album as a duo, 1994.

Addresses: *Record company*—Arista Records, Inc., 6 West 57th St., New York, NY 10019.

The Church didn't make any more records for Capitol after their self-titled U.S. debut; instead they continued to produce albums in Australia, including 1982's *Blurred Crusade,* with critically acclaimed tunes like "I'm Almost with You" and "Come Up and See Me," and 1983's *Seance,* featuring the tracks "Travel by Thought," "Fly," and "Dropping Names." Then, in 1984, the Church signed a deal with Warner Bros. and released their next album in the United States, *Remote Luxury.* With "Constant in Opal," the hit single and video from the album, they started developing a dedicated cult following in the States.

Changes Brought Hit Album

That same year, the band went into the studio with producer Peter Walsh to record *Heyday,* which landed in record stores two years later. The Church moved toward stronger and catchier melodies with songs like "Tristesse" and "Myrrh." After recording the album, guitarist Marty Willson-Piper decided to leave Australia and move to Stockholm, Sweden.

Though the Church's following had built steadily, they had yet to attain hit status or gain widespread recognition in the United States. They opted to switch record labels once again and in 1987 inked a deal with Arista. In the meantime, Kilbey, Willson-Piper, and Koppes each signed solo deals with Rykodisc and began working on their own material.

Determined to promote the Church, Arista suggested producers Greg Ladanyi and Waddy Wachtel work with them on their next album. A year later, *Starfish* got them the attention they were waiting for. "*Starfish* is the best in a long line of great Church hymnals," wrote a *Rolling Stone* contributor, "thanks to the band's refined studio poise and a bumper crop of jangle-and-strum jewels like 'Blood Money,' 'Reptile,' and Marty Willson-Piper's 'Spark.'" In addition, their hit single "Under the Milky Way" received significant radio airplay, and the Church made their first major tour of the United States. Arista re-released the band's entire back catalog that same year, and the band developed a whole new fan base.

Chemistry Created Simple Pleasures

After their tour, the Church went back into the studio to work on their next album, *Gold Afternoon Fix.* When they finished recording, they booted drummer Richard Ploog out of the band and recruited Jay Dee Daugherty to replace him. *Gold Afternoon Fix,* released in 1990, featured the singles "Metropolis" and "You're Still Beautiful" but failed to live up to the popularity of *Starfish.* However, the band's goals don't necessarily include getting the top spots on the charts. "I feel that it's really important to just write songs without worrying whether it's going to be a hit or not," Willson-Piper noted in the band's Arista Records press biography. Chris Mundy, writing in *Rolling Stone,* described *Gold Afternoon Fix* as "the Church's invitation to visit its murky, ethereal world. It's an invitation that should not be refused."

As a conceptual lyric writer, Kilbey has often been asked to define the songs on the Church's albums, and *Gold Afternoon Fix* stimulated the question with cuts like "Pharaoh," "Terra Nova Cain," and "Russian Autumn Heart." "Simple pleasure is the most important thing," Kilbey stated in *Musician.* "The sun shining on an open field on a nice day is more important than the Pythagorean [theorem of right triangles]. The sun shining on an open field means more than the collected works of Western literature over the last 10,000 years.... You don't eat pizza and then go back to the chef and say, 'But what did this pizza *mean*?' Do you? Why can't music be like that?"

More than any other ingredient, the chemistry existing between bandmembers sparked the Church's creative output. Kilbey, Willson-Piper, and Koppes all had their solo projects to express their individual creativity, so when the band came together, they concentrated on unifying their ideas. In 1992 they produced *Priest=Aura,* featuring the single "Ripple." "It was the classic, introspective, ambiguous Church album," Willson-Piper said in the *Boston Phoenix*. Moving away from the more commercially oriented sound of their last two albums, the Church seemed to head in a darker direction with *Priest=Aura*. "Set against this elegant soundscape, not so quiet storms add a glint of savagery, bringing moments of drama and beauty to stately songs," proclaimed Ira Robbins in a *Rolling Stone* review of the album.

Foursome Reduced to Duo

The Church toured the world once again, with a last stop on their home turf in Australia. Just hours before their tour of Australia began, Koppes announced his intentions to leave the band after 13 years. He agreed to finish the tour but quit as soon as they completed their last set. Kilbey and Willson-Piper dismissed Jay Dee Daugherty not long after Koppes's departure. "We weren't sure if the band was going to exist anymore," Willson-Piper said in the band's press biography. "I figured we would just know if and when the time was right to get back into the studio."

In the middle of 1993, Willson-Piper left his home in Stockholm to join Kilbey in Australia, and the two of them started working on the next Church album. "Originally, we were worried about the chemistry being different after all that time together as a four-man band," Willson-Piper explained in their press biography. "So we just started messing about together in the studio. Once we recorded ["Lost My Touch"], we knew everything was going to fall into place." *Sometime Anywhere*—written, recorded, and mixed in two months during the summer of 1993 and released in 1994—became the first Church album produced by the two remaining members.

"Two Places at Once," the first single from the album, reflects a true collaborative effort by Willson-Piper and Kilbey. After they had cowritten the music for the song, they each penned separate lyrics. When they came back together, the members of the duo found that they had completely different concepts of what they thought the song was about. They decided to combine the two sets of lyrics—with each member singing his own version—until the end of the song, when the two blend together seamlessly. *Pulse!* contributor Scott Schinder considered the material on *Sometime Anywhere* "denser, darker territory" than the band's earlier releases, and Brian Q. Newcomb commented in a *Riverfront Times* review of the album: "It delivers not only impressive sounds, but also compositional substance and lyrics

filled with irony, intelligence, and charm." It seems that in its new incarnation, the Church was still aiming to deliver "contemporary, intelligent rock."

Selected discography

Of Skins and Heart, Parlophone, 1981, reissued, Arista, 1988.
The Church, Capitol, 1982.
The Blurred Crusade, Carrere, 1982, reissued, Arista, 1988.
Seance, Carrere, 1983, reissued, Arista, 1988.
Remote Luxury, Warner Bros., 1984, reissued, Arista, 1988.
Heyday, Warner Bros., 1986, reissued, Arista, 1988.
Starfish, Arista, 1988.
Gold Afternoon Fix, Arista, 1990.
Priest=Aura, Arista, 1992.
Sometime Anywhere, Arista, 1994.

Sources

Books

The Trouser Press Record Guide, edited by Ira A. Robbins, Collier Books, 1991.

Periodicals

Alternative Press, July 1994.
Billboard, November 10, 1984; March 5, 1988; April 23, 1988.
Boston Phoenix, May 20, 1994.
Flagpole, May 11, 1994.
Honey, May 1994.
Melody Maker, February 13, 1982; July 10, 1982; August 7, 1982; December 15, 1984; April 6, 1985; May 31, 1986; March 12, 1988; March 19, 1988; April 23, 1988; March 24, 1990; May 19, 1990.
Musician, October 1988, September 1990.
Pulse!, July 1994.
Raygun, June 1994.
Riverfront Times, June 1, 1994.
Rolling Stone, April 21, 1988; May 19, 1988; December 15, 1988; May 17, 1990; April 16, 1992.
Scene, May 19, 1994.
Variety, June 22, 1988; June 20, 1990.

Additional information for this profile was obtained from Arista Records publicity materials, 1994.

—Sonya Shelton

Perry Como

Singer

Courtesy of RCA Records

In 1958 Perry Como received the first gold disc ever awarded by the Recording Industry Association of America for his ballad "Catch a Falling Star." Como's star itself has never really fallen. Even grey-haired and grandfatherly, Como remained a popular middle-of-the-road vocalist throughout the 1960s and 1970s. However, Perry Como's biggest decade was half a century ago—during the 1940s. In 1946, for example, some four million Como records were pressed during *one week*. Ten years later, 11 of his singles had sold over a million copies each.

Born Pierino Como in 1913, the singer was one of 13 children of a Roman Catholic family. He started working early in life, owning his own barbershop by age 14 in his hometown of Canonsburg, Pennsylvania. At his father's urging, he completed high school in 1929 before settling into his role as Canonsburg's premier barber. In 1934, after marrying his school sweetheart, Roselle Beline, Como auditioned for a spot in the Freddie Carlone Orchestra. He spent the next few years touring the Midwest with the band for $28 a week. By 1937 he had joined the Ted Weems Band, which recorded on the Decca label.

Como considered his touring experience an invaluable tool in the development of his industry professionalism and his early calm in the face of fame. In a 1957 *Down Beat* profile, he explained how difficult it was to acquire a businesslike demeanor and sense of style, commenting, "A couple of records can't give it to you." Without road work, he continued, "too many kids hit big and then have nothing. I hate to see that happen to anyone."

A Natural Appeal

The Weems band broke up in 1942 due to World War II, and Como headed back to Canonsburg, intending to resume the quiet life of a hometown barber. However, CBS interfered in the form of a $100-a-week radio show offer. The following year RCA Victor signed him up, and there was no more talk of barbering. Over the next 14 years, Como landed 42 Top 10 hits; only crooner Bing Crosby proved more popular during this time.

The good-natured Como appealed to young and old audiences alike, and this helped account for his success. He never abandoned singing material suitable for family listening—even when doing Vegas acts in the 1970s. However, Como's mild music and trademark relaxed manner did not appeal to all. One *Time* magazine writer noted that the singer sometimes gave the impression he was "made of sponge rubber with a core of [the sedative] Seconal."

For the Record . . .

Born Pierino Como, May 18, 1913, in Canonsburg, PA; son of Pietro (a mill hand) and Lucille Como; married Roselle Beline, 1933; children: Ronald, David (adopted), Teri (adopted).

Barber, late 1920s-early 1930s; started touring as a big-band vocalist with Freddie Carlone and Ted Weems, mid-1930s; signed by RCA Victor, 1943; radio and club singer throughout the 1940s; by the end of the 1950s, had 42 Top Ten hits on the *Billboard* charts; host of Saturday night variety show on NBC-TV, 1955-63; headlined in Las Vegas with Ray Charles, Tony Bennett, and Dean Martin, 1970s; retrospective CD released by RCA, 1993.

Selected awards: Named top-selling male singer in a *Billboard* poll, 1946; Emmy awards for most outstanding television personality, 1956 and 1957; Grammy Award for best vocal performance, male, 1958, for "Catch a Falling Star"; Special Award of Merit, American Music Awards, 1979; Kennedy Center Honors, 1987; named knight of the Equestrian Order of the Holy Sepulchre of Jerusalem.

Addresses: *Record company*—RCA Records, 1540 Broadway, New York, NY 10036.

Along with his singing success on radio and across the club and theater circuits, Como attracted attention in Hollywood. He appeared in a trio of films during the mid-1940s for Twentieth Century Fox, all of which co-starred flamboyant dancer Carmen Miranda. Miranda proved more memorable than Como in these efforts, although his song in *Doll Face,* "Hubba Hubba Hubba," was a hit.

"Ed Sullivan With Talent"

In 1955 Como took a whack at television, hosting NBC's *Perry Como Show,* a Saturday night variety hour. (Some critics called Como an "Ed Sullivan with talent.") Playing up his "Mr. Nice Guy" image, numerous magazine stories of the day described the star relaxing in front of the television, stretched out on the couch and munching a piece of fruit. The first year out, Como's TV show won an Emmy and the Peabody, Christopher, and Golden Mike awards.

Como's easygoing manner carried over into the studio. In recording a song, Como told *Down Beat,* "I like to do

about half a dozen takes.... Then we pick the best one and that's it." The singer added, "I don't work at home at all. Once you know a song too well, you start to fool around with it. At the session, when the band's working on the arrangement, I learn the tune right there." Yet recording engineers and others working with him classified Como as a perfectionist. "Perry knows what he can do," noted one collaborator in the same article. "He saves it up and gives it to you. He knows when he's done it that you've got his best. You don't see it in his face or his manner—it comes from inside. He gives you all he's got and that's it."

Como's television variety show lasted until 1963, when he finally said goodbye to "the kids"—as he referred to members of his cast, notably the Ray Charles singers. By this time, the entertainment industry had started to change, and Como was beginning to seem old-fashioned. The singer went into semi-exile, although he continued to record and do TV specials, his Christmas program being something of an institution.

But in 1970 Perry Como donned the stage tux once again in a summertime show in Vegas that broke a 25-year, self-imposed ban on live performances. With him was his old pal, pianist-singer Ray Charles. Como's material consisted of tunes like "If I Could Read Your Mind," and "It's Impossible," the latter hitting gold.

More Road Work

As he approached his sixtieth birthday, Como headed out on an international tour; he continued to find success making live appearances for the next decade. Como's 1976 tour of Australia was standing room only, and at the time one RCA executive crowed that the whole Como catalogue was "moving out fabulously." The previous year, a K-tel record promotion in England had secured the singer five weeks of Number One U.K. charting.

In 1993 a three-CD compilation set, *Yesterday & Today—A Celebration in Song,* appeared on Como's lifelong label, RCA. The package included his last recording, "Wind Beneath My Wings," from 1987, as well as two duets from the 1950s with Eddie Fisher ("Watermelon Weather" and "Maybe") and older material not reissued since first appearing on 78s. "Perry Como is a cultural icon," stated the publicity material accompanying the release, "and it is only right that his talent should be celebrated in a boxed set as extensive as this." A curious note was sounded in this post-heyday compilation history when in 1994 a Rhino Records CD appeared called *The Beat Generation.* This CD included spoken-word performances by such standard avant-garde types as Jack Kerouac and William Burroughs. But, nestled bizarrely among such unusual fare came the voice of Perry Como, singing the song "Like Young."

Musing over his varied successes in an interview with Alan Ebert for *Good Housekeeping,* Como concluded, "For the amount of talent I had—and I couldn't dance, act, or tell a joke—I enjoyed a tremendous career."

Selected discography

Till the End of Time (recorded 1945), RCA, 1948.
I Believe, RCA, 1954.
So Smooth, RCA, 1955.
Hits from Broadway Shows, RCA, 1956.
Merry Christmas Music, RCA, 1957.
Saturday Night With Mr. C., RCA, 1958.
Como Swings, RCA, 1959.
Season's Greetings, RCA, 1959.
Sing to Me, Mr. C., RCA, 1961.
By Request, RCA, 1962.
Mr. President (features the music of Irving Berlin), Columbia, 1962.
It's Impossible, RCA, 1970.

Yesterday & Today—A Celebration in Song, RCA, 1993.
(With others) *The Beat Generation* (appears on "Like Young"), Rhino Records, 1994.

Sources

Books

Penguin Encyclopedia of Popular Music, edited by Donald Clarke, Viking, 1989.

Periodicals

Billboard, September 19, 1970; November 4, 1972; May 15, 1976.
Down Beat, May 16-30, 1957.
Good Housekeeping, January 1991.
Look, November 28, 1944.
Time, March 18, 1946; December 19, 1955; March 16, 1959.

Additional information for this profile was obtained from RCA publicity materials.

—*Joseph M. Reiner*

Stewart Copeland

Composer, percussionist

Courtesy of I.R.S. Records

Amultitude of musicians have been hailed as "experimentalists," but perhaps no one has been more deserving of the label than Stewart Copeland. His many achievements include forming the enormously successful pop supergroup the Police, scoring numerous films, and composing operas. The versatile artist's works range from punk/new wave hit songs that topped the charts in the 1980s to esoteric soundtracks for television and film.

The diversity of Copeland's repertoire springs from his multicultural childhood spent in such exotic locales as Egypt, Syria, and Lebanon. His father, Miles Copeland II, who helped develop the infrastructure of the Central Intelligence Agency (CIA), was the organization's head of operations in the Middle East. Stewart, the youngest of four children, was ushered into the music world while living in Beirut; his brother Ian started drumming for a band in one of the local gangs. Stewart became fascinated with percussion, and his father bought him a drum kit. One night, at an American beach club, the young Copeland performed for the first time as a substitute drummer for one of the bands.

In 1966 the political situation in Beirut changed dramatically, and the family was given 15 days to leave the country. They fled to England, where Stewart attended the prestigious Millfield school in Somerset. In 1971 he returned to the United States and entered the University of California at Berkeley, but because of his inability to transcribe music, he was denied acceptance to the music program.

The Police Penetrated Punk Scene

It was not until the end of Copeland's first year in college that an opportunity to work in the music industry was presented by his brothers Miles and Ian. While Stewart was spending his days in classrooms, Miles had maneuvered himself into the world of rock promotion, marketing groups like the Climax Blues Band and Wishbone Ash. Miles and his assistant, Ian, asked Stewart to help manage and promote several bands. Always in search of a new challenge, he headed immediately to England.

Copeland's first real break came in 1974 when one of Miles Copeland's groups, Curved Air, needed a new drummer. Stewart naturally volunteered. Essentially a live band, they toured constantly, but incompatibilities with producers, lack of material, and debts to record companies led to their eventual stagnation. After a performance one night in December of 1975, however, Copeland attended a late set by a local band in Newcastle called Last Exit, whose singer/songwriter/bassist had curiously named himself "Sting." Sting, born Gordon Sumner, had struggled through the ranks to help form Last Exit, and when Copeland saw the band they had just signed a contract with Virgin Records and were on the brink of fame.

The ultimate demise of Curved Air came in 1977, and Stewart, who had aligned himself with the punk movement, was eager to form a band. He already had a name—the Police—and now all he needed were the faces. Since Last Exit had recently disbanded, Stewart contacted Sting and arranged for a meeting. With the addition of Andy Summers, former guitarist for Soft Machine and Eric Burdon and the Animals, the Police were born. With Miles Copeland's support, the bleached-blond trio began to record, promote, and perform at a fast pace in an attempt to penetrate the punk market.

"Went Berserk" With the Police

Copeland decided he had found his true calling with the Police, stating in *The Police,* a chronicle of the band's formation: "I think I was able to use more of my talent with the Police than I was with Curved Air. In Curved Air I had to keep laying back. With the Police I went berserk; I played like a madman." The Police's first album, *Outlandos D'Amour,* was recorded in 1978, and with Miles's management and A&M Records behind them, they released their first single, "Roxanne." However, the single and its follow-up, "Can't Stand Losing You," were

met with dismal noninterest, so the band headed to the United States for a grueling, whirlwind tour that started with a concert at the legendary punk birthplace CBGB's the very night their plane touched American soil.

The Police returned to England, released *Regatta de Blanc,* and embarked upon the rest of their fast and furious career, selling over five million singles and two million albums in 1979 alone. The group's singular combination of Sting's harsh lyrics, Summer's textured guitar-playing, and Copeland's driving rhythm created a power trio supergroup that defied categorization. Called anything from punk to reggae to new wave, the Police sound quickly became the boilerplate for struggling new artists.

Became a Prolific Composer

In the late 1970s Copeland took a short respite from the Police and assumed the personality of Klark Kent, whose single "Don't Care" made a brief appearance on the charts. The collector's album that followed, released on the obscure Kryptonite pseudo-label, was distributed by A&M, pressed on green vinyl, and packaged in a die-cut double K cover. Copeland claimed he was not connected to Kent, a supposed native of the Welsh fishing village Llandyckkk, but the vocals, attitude, and such lyrics as "Don't care if you really wanna hang around/ Don't care cause I am the neatest thing in town/ If you don't like my arrogance you can suck my socks," were pure Copeland.

An unprecedented 19-country Police world tour, a sell-out concert in New York City's Madison Square Garden, and a third album, *Zenyatta Mondatta,* followed in 1980 and 1981. The introspective and moody *Ghost in the Machine,* released in 1981, topped the U.S. and U.K. charts at Number Two, and 1983's *Synchronicity,* along with the monster hit single "Every Breath You Take," reached Number One. The Police soon realized, however, that at the height of their career the energy was gone. Oddly enough, Sting predicted the breakup in a 1981 interview with *Rolling Stone* when he said: "I don't think we'll be relevant in two years. I think we will have said all we have to say within four, maybe five albums." Indeed, after four platinum albums and nine singles in the Top 40, the Police disbanded, and the band's members pursued solo careers.

The multitalented Copeland was not idle for long. In 1983 he composed the soundtrack for Francis Ford Coppola's teen angst film *Rumblefish,* which earned him a Golden Globe Award nomination. The following year he directed *So What?*—a 35-minute movie comparing the punk scene of 1977 to that of 1982—and also traveled to Africa to participate in the documentary *The Rhythmatist*, a chronicle of the music from Tanzania, Zaire, Kenya, Burundi, and the Congo. A solo album, also titled *The Rhythmatist*, showcases the music explored in the documentary.

Copeland also ventured into the realm of television, penning the themes for George Lucas's *Droids* and *Ewoks* Saturday morning cartoons and composing the music for *The Equalizer*, an Emmy Award-winning television show that subsequently spawned 1988's *The Equalizer and Other Cliff Hangers*, an instrumental album composed and performed entirely by Copeland.

Copeland's earlier success with the film score *Rumblefish* earned him the attention of Hollywood, and he was asked to compose music for a string of motion pictures, including Oliver Stone's *Wall Street* and *Talk Radio* and John Hughes's *She's Having a Baby*. In 1994 he wrote the blues-influenced score for *Fresh*, the critically acclaimed film about a young boy's struggle to survive in New York City's gang underworld.

Expanded Repertoire to Include Opera

Copeland also experienced heightened interest in other forms of music, and he conquered yet another musical form: the opera. Having already composed a 20-minute ballet version of *King Lear* for a San Francisco troupe in 1986, he wrote his first full-blown production in 1989, the three-hour *Holy Blood and the Crescent Moon*. The piece was selected to open the Cleveland Opera's 14th season and was later performed by the Fort Worth Opera in Texas. The performance was met with a negative reaction for Copeland's lack of experience and praise for what he accomplished as an "untrained rock musician." One critic writing in the *Christian Century* called *Holy Blood* "one of the most significant moral statements to come from the arts community in many years."

As for Copeland himself, he told *Musical America*, "I thought opera was a guy ... with his chest pumped out making a loud noise. I had no idea what kind of a door was being opened to me. Opera is the ultimate art form. There's nothing that can freeze your blood like the combination of drama and music." The genre had captured Copeland's interest, and he later composed *Horse Opera* (1993) for British television, and the mini-opera *Cask of Amontillado* (1994), based on the Edgar Allan Poe short story of the same title.

Copeland also ventured back into the world of popular music in 1989 when he formed the group Animal Logic with bassist Stanley Clarke and singer Deborah Hol-

land, ultimately releasing two self-titled albums. In 1994 he launched an innovative tour with a sampling of percussion groups from countries around the world, including Zaire, Spain, and West Africa.

Stewart Copeland is no stranger to the challenges of composition, and whether he writes a libretto or a film score, he incorporates his experiences with music in all of its varied forms. As a percussionist, he tunes himself into the rhythm of the world's music and finds the inherent beat in his subject, then, in writing music he draws on the full range of musical styles to produce a distinctive sound.

Selected scores

Film

Rumblefish, 1984.
Out of Bounds, 1986.
She's Having a Baby, 1986.
Wall Street, 1987.
Talk Radio, 1988.
See No Evil, Hear No Evil, 1989.
The First Power, 1990.
Men at Work, 1990.
Hidden Agenda, 1990.
Taking Care of Business, 1990.
Riff Raff, 1991.
Highlander II, 1991.
Wide Sargasso Sea, 1993.
Raining Stones, 1993.
Decadence, 1993.
Fresh, 1994.
Surviving the Game, 1994.
Rapa Nui, 1994.
Silent Fall, 1994.
Fresh, 1994.

Television

The Ewoks, 1985.
Droids, 1985.
The Equalizer, 1986.
After Midnight, 1989.
TV 101, 1990.
Seconds Out, 1992.
Fugitive Among Us, 1992.
Afterburn, 1992.
Babylon 5, 1993.

Selected discography

(As Klark Kent) *Music Madness From the Kinetic Kid*, I.R.S., 1978.

The Rhythmatist, A&M, 1985.
The Equalizer and Other Cliff Hangers, I.R.S., 1988, reissued, 1993.

With Curved Air

Live, BTM.
Air Borne, BTM.
Midnight Wire, RCA.

With the Police; on A&M Records

Outlandos d' Amour, 1978.
Reggatta de Blanc, 1979.
Zenyatta Mondatta, 1980.
Ghost in the Machine, 1981.
Synchronicity, 1983.
Every Breath You Take: The Singles, 1986.
Message in a Box: The Complete Recordings, 1993.

With Animal Logic

Animal Logic, I.R.S., 1986.

Animal Logic II, I.R.S., 1991

Sources

Books

Sutcliffe, Phil, and Hugh Fielder, *The Police*, Proteus Books, 1981.

Periodicals

Christian Century, December 13, 1989.
Down Beat, May 1984.
Musical America, January/February 1992.
Opera News, October 1990.
Rolling Stone, February 19, 1981.

Additional information for this profile was obtained from the liner notes to *Message in a Box: The Complete Recordings*, A&M Records, 1993.

—*Debra Power*

The Cranberries

Rock band

Photograph by Kate Garner, courtesy of Island Records

Irish quartet the Cranberries burst onto the scene in 1992 with their ethereal hit "Dreams," the first single from a debut album that eventually went platinum. "What sets it apart—other, that is, from that continually astonishing voice and the effortlessly graceful arrangements—is a faintly tangible sense of ruptured innocence, of shattered hope," mused *Melody Maker* writer Andrew Mueller about the group's distinctive sound. Indeed, the youthful band survived a series of problematic encounters with bad management and a capricious press that nearly disbanded them; their astounding success in the United States was relatively unexpected but a welcome vote of confidence in their cohesive musicianship.

Fronted by lead singer Dolores O'Riordan, lead and bass guitars are the respective domains of brothers Noel and Mike Hogan; Feargal Lawler sits behind the drums. O'Riordan and Noel Hogan write most of the band's material. "Truth be told, what separates the Cranberries from much of the current flock is age and experience," wrote *Rolling Stone*'s Chris Mundy. "Or, in their case, the lack thereof."

O'Riordan, the Hogans, and Lawler all came into the world at Limerick's Maternity Hospital in the early 1970s. Like others in Ireland, the bandmates grew up in relatively reduced circumstances—O'Riordan was the youngest of seven children in a household supported by her mother; Noel Hogan collected unemployment for a time. The Hogans and Lawler were originally part of an ensemble called the Cranberry Saw Us, whose fourth member, another Limerick fellow, wrote all their material in addition to his singing duties. When the band's writer left the band in mid-1990, they began looking around for a new vocalist.

Entranced by a Country Girl's Voice

O'Riordan, then living just outside Limerick, heard about the band from a school friend and showed up at an audition. "They were all laughing at me and I was really embarrassed, [because] there was about nine fellas in the room and I was the girl from the country," the singer told Everett True in *Melody Maker.* "They thought I was a scream." The three young men, however, apparently liked the sound of O'Riordan's voice, with which she had been attracting attention since her preschool years; as a teenager she had won competitions for her solos with her church and school choirs.

Entranced, the Cranberry Saw Us members invited O'Riordan to join. After practicing and shortening the band's name to the Cranberries, they cut a three-song cassette titled *Nothing Left at All.* A second five-track release was sent out on a lark to a few record companies and to the band's surprise, Rough Trade Records—the former home of their idols, the Smiths—expressed interest. A bidding war ensued, and the Cranberries were signed to Island Records before a mention of their name had even appeared in the music press.

The band's obscurity was short-lived, however, as the energetic but snarky British music press instantly touted the Cranberries as the next big thing. "Wince-inducing interview after cringeworthy feature painted a picture of a band of four pristine, untainted, awestruck country souls, standing welly-deep in peat and creating the music of the Gods in between saying their rosaries and worrying the local sheep," wrote Mueller in *Melody Maker* of the articles that appeared in both his paper and the *New Musical Express* in 1991. In October of that year, after they had relocated to London, the band released their first single, "Uncertain." *Melody Maker's* True termed it "as fresh and stimulating as a breeze blowing in from the North Sea."

Debut Release Delayed

The Cranberries began playing various spots around Britain and wrote songs for a full-length album. In the studio, they teamed up with Stephen Street, who had produced a number of records for the Smiths and the

Psychedelic Furs. Problems with management, however, proved worrisome. They had recorded their demos and "Uncertain" with a Limerick producer and studio owner who was also their manager. Yet they eventually discovered that he had been lying to each of them to varying degrees. Contemplating a breakup, they sat down on a street corner and instead opted to fire Street. "We used to trust everybody," Noel Hogan told *Melody Maker's* Mueller. "We used to think everyone was here to help us. Then we realized that they were here to help themselves."

The resulting contractual delays and legal problems pushed back the release of the Cranberries' first full-length album, *Everybody Else Is Doing It, So Why Can't We?*, until March of 1993. *Melody Maker* was quick to call the LP "a superb coincidence of riches: six dozen immaculately-conceived melodies compressed into a mere 12 songs, and a voice that ravages your mood," according to critic Peter Paphides. Kara Manning of *Rolling Stone* described the album as "sublimely understated yet seductively, chillingly alive." *Melody Maker* reviewer Jennifer Nine noted, "Like many small things, Dolores' voice is neither as simple nor as frail as it seems, and there's a world of headstrong energy inside it."

Unexpected Success Abroad

O'Riordan's vocal style, in fact, has often been cited as the group's most undeniable hook and even sent Mueller into a reverie in his *Melody Maker* piece: "It comes down to the voice, doesn't it always? The Voice: A gentle, pure Irish whisper with a tinge of huskiness which sends melancholy-splattered shards of pain and hope and love straight to your heart. The Voice: a melodic mini-scream which oscillates and reverberates out into the darkening, overcast sky.... It can sound both young and ancient simultaneously. It can span the ages. It's so filled with emotion, it will break your heart with the merest slipped quaver."

The Cranberries' melodies, combined with O'Riordan's voice, struck a chord with the listening public, and by mid-1994 *Everybody's Doing It* had sold 2.8 million copies. Oddly, success in the United States from airplay on alternative and Top 40 radio helped spur sales in Britain. "I think the more the press stays away from us, the better we are," O'Riordan told *Rolling Stone's* Manning in mid-1993. "The American press is slightly more mature, but the British press is a very small group of people and they all jump on the same band at once, and they jump off the same band at once."

The Cranberries traveled to the United States to capitalize on the success of their debut album, doing a number of opening dates for rock band The The as well as headlining appearances on their own. They also used the between-gig time to write songs for a second album and headed back into the studio in the spring of 1994 with Stephen Street. The result was *No Need to Argue,* released in the fall of that year. Its first single, "Zombie," was a far cry from the band's other hits, featuring a hard-edged guitar sound and a more strident vocal style from O'Riordan that called to mind fellow Irish singer Sinead O'Connor. Additionally, the song's theme—a tirade against the sectarian violence that has rocked Northern Ireland, especially since 1968, was another step away from the dreamy love-struck songs of their first release.

People's Michael Small praised both *No Need to Argue* and "Zombie," noting that "O'Riordan's intense delivery brings out a slight tartness—which, of course, is the mark of a truly good cranberry." *Spin* reviewer Jonathan Bernstein termed "Zombie" the album's best song, "[lurching] between grindcore and whimsy, with O'Riordan mood-swinging from her normal soothing allure into growling and barnyard impersonations." Yet Bernstein conjectured that while the Cranberries offer more than the average dream-pop band, *No Need to Argue's* strong points might not be sufficient enough to sustain the group's lasting success.

The Cranberries, their legions of fans, and their label seemed to feel differently, however, and major concert tours—including ones in Asia and Australia—were set to coincide with the success of *No Need to Argue.* "By the time we came to do this album, we knew what we were capable of," Noel Hogan told *Billboard* writer Thom Duffy. "We're really happy with it. We did it the way we wanted to do it. It is what it's meant to be."

Selected discography

Singles

"Uncertain," Xeric, 1991.
"Dreams," Island, 1992.
"Linger," Island, 1993.

Albums

Everybody Else Is Doing It, So Why Can't We?, Island, 1993.
No Need to Argue, Island, 1994.

Sources

Billboard, August 14, 1993; August 20, 1994.
Entertainment Weekly, October 7, 1994; October 28, 1994.
Melody Maker, October 26, 1991; October 3, 1992; January 30, 1993; March 6, 1993; March 13, 1993; November 6, 1993.
Musician, November 1994.
People, October 17, 1994.
Pulse!, June 1994.
Rolling Stone, September 2, 1993; December 23, 1993; April 21, 1994; December 1, 1994; March 23, 1995.
Spin, November 1994.
Time, November 7, 1994.

—*Carol Brennan*

Crash Test Dummies

Rock band

Crash Test Dummies is an appropriate name for a band that got serious by accident and gained popularity faster than a speeding car. "Mmm Mmm Mmm Mmm," the band's first single off of their second album, swept across the United States driven by its quirky title and the unlikely bass baritone of its lead singer. If a bullfrog could sing appealingly, it would probably sound like Brad Roberts, the voice—and vaguely wacky songwriter—behind this "neo-folkie, pseudo-hippies, sort of Celtic, dryly humorous, exceptionally literate pop band." At least that's how *People* magazine contributor Craig Tomashoff described this quintet of Canadian natives.

Their beginnings are humorous too—and far from calculated. In the mid-1980s a loose group of friends from the University of Winnipeg in Manitoba started playing music together. Eventually they became the house band at a 50-seat after-hours club called the Blue Note. They played what Roberts described in *Rolling Stone* as "ridiculous cover tunes, everything from cheesy Irish traditionals to TV theme songs to acoustic versions of

Photograph by Timothy White, courtesy of Arista Records

Members include **Benjamin Darvill** (born January 4, 1967, in Winnipeg, Manitoba, Canada), mandolin, harmonica; **Michel (Mitch) Dorge** (born September 15, 1960, in Winnipeg), drums; **Ellen Lorraine Reid** (born July 14, 1966, in Selkirk, Manitoba, Canada), piano, keyboards, accordion, backup vocals; **Brad Roberts** (born January 10, 1964, in Winnipeg), lead vocals, guitar; and **Dan Roberts** (born May 22, 1967, in Winnipeg), bass.

Band formed in Winnipeg, Manitoba, Canada, mid-1980s; house band at a 50-seat after-hours club in Winnipeg called the Blue Note; signed with BMG Canada and Arista U.S., 1989; released first album, *The Ghosts That Haunt Me,* 1991; the single "Superman's Song" hit Number One on the Canadian charts, 1991; released *God Shuffled His Feet,* 1993; the single "Mmm Mmm Mmm Mmm" hit Number Two on the U.S. charts, 1994.

Awards: Grammy Award nominations for alternative performance for *God Shuffled His Feet,* for best pop vocal, group, for "Mmm Mmm Mmm Mmm," and for best new artist, all 1995.

Addresses: *Record company*—Arista Records, Inc., Arista Building, 6 West 57th St., New York, NY 10019.

Alice Cooper hits." The name the band picked was a joke: after considering Chemotherapists and Skin Graft, they agreed on Crash Test Dummies because they had written it down so many times.

Never Intended to Do This Professionally

After graduating with an honors degree in English literature from the University of Winnipeg, Roberts realized that the band had turned into something more than a way to pass the weekends. By then they had settled on their core members: Roberts singing lead and playing guitar; his younger brother Dan on bass; Benjamin Darvill on mandolin and harmonicas; Ellen Reid on a crop of instruments including piano, keyboards, and accordion, as well as singing backup; and Mitch Dorge on drums. They put together a five-song demo and shipped it around to Canadian music festivals, hoping to get some gigs outside of Winnipeg. The tape found its way into the hands of record company executives, who started calling with offers. Roberts nixed his plans for

completion of a master's degree and jumped into the music industry.

In 1989, when the band signed with BMG Canada and Arista in the United States, Roberts got to work trying to write enough songs for a first album. "I had only written five songs in my entire life by that time," he admitted to Fred Shuster in the *Los Angeles Daily News,* "I had to scramble to finish.... I had no intention of doing this professionally." As he told Larry LeBlanc in *Billboard,* "I often take three to four weeks to write a song, but when a song is finished, 99% of the time it's a keeper." They had only 13 songs to choose from for their first album; they picked 12 of them.

Released in the spring of 1991, *The Ghosts That Haunt Me* proved to be interesting, alternative music fare. A *People* reviewer likened it to "an improbable kiddie cereal made with bran," adding, "this Canadian group gives you sprightly Irish jigs and earthy-crunchy folk music, all rolled into one addictively sweet confection." Roberts described the sound to *Rolling Stone's* Elysa Gardner as "some country, and there's some folk, and there's some fairly aggressive rhythm section on a number of tunes that you wouldn't associate with country or folk." He called one song, "Here on Earth (I'll Have My Cake)," a "bagpipe-meets-fusion thing."

First Album Went Triple Platinum in Canada

That said, it should be noted that both Brad and Dan Roberts claim the heavy metal band Kiss as their greatest musical influence. Comparisons to David Byrne and the Talking Heads are more likely "inevitable," theorized Carter Alan in the *Boston Globe.* "The wit and intent [are] quite similar even if the Dummies are not as rhythmically relentless." It might also be noted that the Crash Test Dummies have covered country singer Johnny Cash and the alternative rock band Replacements, and that Brad Roberts dreams of touring with Andy Partridge of the alternative band XTC.

Within nine months of its release, and with the help of their Number One hit in Canada, "Superman's Song"—"a small masterpiece," according to *Newsweek's* David Gates—*Ghosts* reached sales of more than 300,000 copies in Canada, garnering three platinum albums. When the record first came out, the Dummies had been booked to play small clubs across Canada; after that first single, they had the power to sell out entire theaters.

After two years of touring—opening for rocker Sting on a few gigs—and spending quality time on their next recording, the band released their second album, *God Shuffled His Feet.* With more time and money on their side this time around, Roberts had the opportunity to demo all the material for the album on a 24-track studio in his home. That way the band had a better sense of Roberts's vision for a song before contributing their individual sounds to it. Ex-Talking Heads member Jerry Harrison coproduced the album. When asked about that choice, Roberts told *Billboard,* "We thought anybody who was in the Talking Heads must be at least halfway cool. He's also a keyboard player, and we wanted to stretch out into synthesized and sampling technology."

An even bigger stretch for the band, noted LeBlanc in *Billboard,* came with the jettisoning of "the sparse rock, country, and Celtic folk stance in favor of a new densely textured alternative-rock approach." "The shift in [that] direction has to do with me sitting down and wanting to write a body of work that was challenging, interesting, and new," Roberts explained in the same article. "The band welcomed that agenda. To me, it wouldn't be interesting to duplicate the sounds and genres we played around with on the first record."

"Mmm Mmm Mmm Mmm" Brought Acclaim

Arista was counting on this new approach to push the Dummies over the edge in the States. Although their first album had done respectably on the American college scene, it didn't come close to their Canadian acclaim. Since that time, however, two radio formats—commercial alternative and adult album alternative—had increased the band's profile, and that's what Arista was banking on. The company saturated U.S.-Canadian border stations with the first single, "Mmm Mmm Mmm Mmm," and in no time major stations, including the influential KROQ in Burbank, California, fell for the Dummies. Radio personnel weren't sure at first what their listeners would think of this odd song, but they didn't have to wait long for the calls to pour in. Outspoken radio personality Howard Stern was also fond of the single and plugged it incessantly on his syndicated radio show.

"Mmm Mmm Mmm Mmm," which takes its title from the hum-along chorus, tells the stories of three kids with somewhat unusual problems. Roberts's unearthly, deeply reverberating voice, along with lyrics "enveloped in shimmering atmospheric keyboards and a warm, finely wrought melody"—according to Shuster in the *Los Angeles Daily News*—add a serious and powerful feel to issues that would be a big deal from a kid's perspective.

The single reached Number Two on the American pop charts in the spring of 1994. The numbers of new fans buying the disc on the basis of that first song were rewarded with a weird and lovely album. *People's* Tomashoff found the dozen tunes sounded "like nothing you've ever heard before yet are completely hummable from the very first listening. The melodies are amiably pop, too laid-back to be rock and too upbeat to be ballads. And ... Roberts' throaty vocal style—sort of like a [manly-voiced television actress] Bea Arthur recording played back at slow speed—adds a quirky twist."

Critics and fans were charmed by this strange quintet. It's a rare Top 40-friendly tune that wonders, "If your eye got poked out in this life / Would it be waiting up in heaven with your wife?" (from "God Shuffled His Feet"). Assuming their sound keeps radio on its toes, as it has, and assuming Brad Roberts doesn't write a "normal" song too soon, or let loose that golden frog from his throat, these Manitobans look like they'll keep on singing their happy accidents.

Selected discography

On Arista Records

The Ghosts That Haunt Me (includes "Superman's Song" and "Here on Earth [I'll Have My Cake]"), 1991.
God Shuffled His Feet (includes title track, "Mmm Mmm Mmm Mmm," and "When I Go Out with Artists"), 1993.

Sources

Billboard, November 20, 1993.
Boston Globe, December 2, 1993.
Canadian Composer, summer 1991.
Entertainment Weekly, November 19, 1993; April 29, 1994.
Los Angeles Daily News, January 24, 1994.
Maclean's, January 27, 1992.
Newsweek, December 13, 1993.
People, October 11, 1991; January 10, 1994.
Pittsburgh Post-Gazette, November 5, 1993.
Rolling Stone, October 3, 1991; May 3, 1994.
Variety, February 3, 1992.

Additional information for this profile was obtained from Arista Records press materials, 1993.

—Joanna Rubiner

Das EFX

Rap duo

D as EFX appeared on the rap scene in 1992 with their platinum-selling album *Dead Serious,* which combined elements of hip-hop and hardcore rap with a novel, stammering vocal style and quickly established the East Coast group as versatile, freewheeling, and original. Their "diggity" style—in which they infused lyrics with the words "iggity," "diggity," or "wiggity"— was unique to the band and was relentlessly mimicked by other hip-hop musicians hoping to cash in on Das EFX's early success. The lyrics in Das EFX's first album have a whimsical, imaginative sound to them that is further underscored by heavy bass lines, unpredictable pauses, and a playful delivery.

Das EFX is comprised of Skoob and Krazy Drayz. The duo released their debut album in the spring of 1992 and expanded the delivery of words to stuttering triple-time syllables. *Dead Serious* went platinum in 1992, a fortuitous milestone for a debut. Their second album, *Straight Up Sewaside*, was released in November of 1993 and featured a more traditional hip-hop sound with unexpected breaks and stops.

Photograph by TAR, courtesy of EastWest Records America

For the Record . . .

Members include **Skoob** (also known as Books; born Willie Hines, November 27, 1972, in New York) and **Krazy Drayz** (born Andrew Preston, September 8, 1971, in New Jersey). *Education:* Skoob and Drayz attended Virginia State University.

Entered a rap contest judged by EPMD bandmembers and were offered a recording contract, 1991; released debut album, *Dead Serious*, EastWest, 1992; founded music management company Young & the Restless; toured 16 cities and appeared as guests on television shows, including *Late Night With Conan O'Brien, Arsenio Hall Show,* and Black Entertainment Television's *Video Soul* and *Video LP,* late 1993.

Addresses: *Record company*—EastWest Records, 75 Rockefeller Plaza, New York, NY 10019.

Skoob, or Books, was born Willie Hines and was raised in the middle-class section of Brooklyn known as Crown Heights. Drayz, born Andrew Weston, grew up in Tea Neck, New Jersey. The two met at Virginia State University while both were studying English literature. The duo later attributed their flippant, bouncy hip-hop sound to the fact that they were in Virginia, far from the musical influences of either New York City or Los Angeles.

Quiet Lives

While at Virginia State University, Skoob and Drayz entered a rap contest in 1991 in Richmond that was judged by members of the East Coast hip-hop group EPMD. Skoob and Drayz, who looked to EPMD as role models, felt confident they would win the contest's $100 first prize. Though they lost the contest, Skoob and Drayz were offered an EPMD-brokered record label deal with EastWest. They accepted on the spot and chose the name Das EFX, a shortened version of "Drayz and Skoob Effects." Drayz and Skoob both left Virginia State University and started working on their first album, *Dead Serious,* never suspecting the LP would blossom into one of 1992's best-selling rap and hip-hop records and go platinum.

In 1993, a year after Skoob and Drayz moved out of their Virginia State University dormitory and released their first album, they bought a house together in suburban Long Island with a pool, gym, music preproduction

studio, and basketball court. They felt they would rather live together than apart, which was a testament to their solid friendship. Although two young bachelors with an enormous house in Long Island would be expected to host massive parties, the two—as a rule—never threw parties in their home. They shunned crowds in favor of close friends, their production crew, current films, television, video games, and a peaceful, reflective solitude.

Das EFX's unique style was immediately imitated by other hip-hop bands who had heard the Das EFX demo tape long before *Dead Serious* was released. When the debut album turned out to be wildly successful, even more imitators cropped up, stuttering in the jerky manner invented by Das EFX. Discouraged—and as a result of this blatant pilfering—Das EFX dropped their signature "diggity" sound after their first album. *Straight Up Sewaside,* their second album, was less groundbreaking in terms of style and more heavily focused on clear narrative.

True to Tradition

After the release of Das EFX's second album, *Spin* magazine's Dream Hampton wrote, "Das definitely packs ... plenty of West Coast bass, [but] they're East Coast hip hop junkies first, keepers and lovers of the tradition." The duo's emphasis on narrative style on their second album is a choice usually associated with hardcore, L.A.-based rap musicians. This focus is generally less important to traditional East Coast hip-hop artists, who favor a novel, freestyle presentation and a unique lyrical signature. Although Das EFX experimented with the heavier bass notes and emphasized the narrative of the hardcore hip-hop sound, they remained close to their creative freestyle roots.

Jim Farber of the *New York Daily News* wrote of Das EFX's second album: "Confronting a hip-hop world crammed with too many fake gangstas, glitzy sellouts and flimsy gimmick acts, Das means to unearth old-school traditions." The *Boston Globe*'s Ken Capobianco noted of the duo on *Straight Up Sewaside:* "They don't break new ground here. Rather, rappers Krazy Drayz and Books firm up the foundation they laid down on their debut."

Das EFX is also true to longstanding, faithful friends: their production team, Silent Scheme, which consists of Derrick Lynch and Chris Charity, was with them when they started out in 1992. Their road manager, Anthony "Blitz" Butler, is a former Virginia State University student, and their original manager, Dennis Wade, has been with the duo since they first set out to record an album. Das EFX remain close to former EPMD members and other hip-hop musicians—such as KRS-One—who had been role models for the duo.

Eclectic Tastes

Skoob and Drayz are inspired by a wide range of music beyond the hip-hop and rap realm and cull their riffs from favorite rhythm and blues, jazz, reggae, dancehall, and classical music pieces. Some of the other recording acts sampled in Das EFX songs include Kool & the Gang, James Brown, and the Beastie Boys. Das EFX eventually founded their own music management company, the Young & the Restless, and handle an assortment of new talent, including a group of female rappers from New Jersey called Twice the Flava.

Das EFX often explores pop culture and television in a lighthearted, loose manner, alluding to television icons, memorable commercials, quirky consumer products, serial killer Jeffrey Dahmer, actor and filmmaker Woody Allen, and cartoon character Woody Woodpecker. Their single "Kaught in Da Ak" is a dark, vivid narrative about a gas pump attendant who becomes a robber. Another single on their second album that describes a tale of crime and deceit is "Undaground Rapper." *Creem* magazine's Marie Elsie St. Leger commented, "Das EFX has learned that the most important thing is musical integrity. And fat beats."

Das EFX has managed to recreate the English language in their music in a jubilant, tongue-twisting, seamless style, avoiding the bitterness or harshness associated with hardcore rap. Their reference to "sewaside" simply meant they did not stray far from the traditional underground hip-hop movement after the success of *Dead Serious*—"sewa" is a term for the underground. The duo also chose the single "Freakit" to introduce their second album because "freakin' styles" means to experiment in every direction; this is precisely what they intended to do on their second album to dispel the notion that they were a one-style ("diggity") wonder.

Das EFX toured 16 cities in late 1993 and traveled from east to west to remain visible. They also appeared on NBC's *Late Night With Conan O'Brien*, Black Entertainment Television's *Video Soul* and *Video LP*, and the *Arsenio Hall Show*.

Selected discography

Dead Serious, EastWest, 1992.
Straight Up Sewaside, EastWest, 1993.

Sources

Billboard, January 11, 1992; February 5, 1993; February 15, 1994.
Boston Globe, November 25, 1993.
Creem, March 1994.
Details, February 1994.
East Coast Rocker, March 18, 1992.
Entertainment Weekly, July 17, 1992.
New York Daily News, December 12, 1993.
New York Newsday, November 29, 1993.
Rap Masters, June 1992.
Request, May 1992; February 1994.
Rolling Stone, May 28, 1992.
Slap, March 1994.
Source, November 1992; January 1994.
Spin, May 1992, February 1994.

—B. Kimberly Taylor

Clive Davis

© Fotos International/Archive Photos

One of the most powerful figures in the recording industry, Clive Davis has presided over Arista Records for more than two decades. Davis has helped to shape the trends in the pop and rock music industries since the mid-1960s, and he has piloted Arista Records through the changing musical scene of the 1970s, 1980s, and 1990s—a period that gave birth to such innovative sounds as punk, grunge, and rap. Under Davis's management, the small but influential Arista label has averaged more than $300 million in sales yearly since 1990 with a catalog that includes Whitney Houston, Aretha Franklin, the Grateful Dead, the Kinks, Crash Test Dummies, Brooks & Dunn, and Alan Jackson. Entertainer Barry Manilow—an Arista mainstay—told *Newsday* that the energetic Davis "has the mind of an executive and the ears of a teenager." The singer added: "I don't know if the other artists at Arista appreciate him, but I do."

Davis is an unusual record company executive in that he takes an active role in guiding the musical development of his recording artists. He is recognized for his talent in matching artist, producer, and song so that a hit record is born. Singer Taylor Dayne described Davis's methods in *Newsday:* "What you see is his commitment and devotion to an artist. He's not alone out there, but because it is a more intimate label with a smaller roster, it allows him to get more involved with his artists. Sometimes, Clive gets down and dirty, really involved, and sometimes it's appreciated. Sometimes it's not. It's criticism, and you either take it correctly, or get insulted. He gets so involved, he really likes to listen and give his input. He cares enough to say, 'I want to like everything on [an album], I want to know everything on there.'"

Clive Davis was born on April 4, 1934, and raised in Brooklyn, New York, in a blue-collar, working-class family. He managed to attend New York University and Harvard Law School, both on full tuition scholarships. In both cases he graduated with top honors, and he was admitted to the New York Bar Association in 1957. Three years later, he took a position as a staff attorney with Columbia Records (a subsidiary of CBS) in New York City. As the 1960s progressed, so did his standing in the company. By 1967 he had been named president of the CBS Records Group.

New York Times Magazine contributor Geoffrey Stokes wrote: "As president of Columbia Records, Clive Davis was the most powerful man in the recording industry." With an ear for the vibrant rock music being played at the time—as well as a healthy respect for Tin Pan Alley-type popular tunes—Davis assembled one of the most impressive rosters of talent ever under the same record label. Columbia signed and produced such artists as

Born Clive Jay Davis, April 4, 1934, in Brooklyn, NY; son of Herman and Florence (Brooks) Davis; divorced; children: Fred, Lauren, Mitchell, Douglas. *Education:* New York University, B.A. (magna cum laude), 1953; Harvard University, LL.B. (magna cum laude), 1956.

Rosenman, Colin, Freund, Lewis & Cohen (law firm), New York City, attorney, 1958-60; Columbia Records, New York City, general attorney, 1960-65, president, 1966-73; Arista Records, New York City, president, 1974—. Director of Record Industry Association of America. Author, with James Willwerth, of *Clive: Inside the Record Business,* 1975.

Selected awards: Man of the Year citation from Martell Foundation for Cancer, Leukemia and AIDS Research, 1980; named Humanitarian of the Year by the American Cancer Society, 1985; Martin Luther King Humanitarian Award from Congress of Racial Equality (CORE), 1991; Man of the Year citation from the Friars, 1992.

Addresses: *Office*—Arista Records, Inc., 6 West 57th St., New York, NY 10019-3913.

Janis Joplin; Santana; Blood, Sweat and Tears; Pink Floyd; Billy Joel; and Bruce Springsteen. Davis also worked with the likes of Barbra Streisand, Paul Simon, and Laura Nyro, and he was a featured participant in the biggest and most highly publicized music industry parties of the time. Under his stewardship, Columbia's profits soared. The label became one of the most successful the music business had ever produced.

But in the summer of 1973, Davis was abruptly fired from his presidency of the CBS Records Group. Executives at CBS accused Davis of using $94,000 of the company's money for personal expenditures. To this day, Davis insists that the "official" reason for his firing was only a convenient excuse, and that, in reality, his quick ouster was a matter of personality conflict.

The United States' top record executive did not sit idle for long. In 1974 Davis took the helm of a small and struggling record company based in New York. He renamed the label Arista the following year and set about recruiting a stable of hit-producing stars. One of the first Arista success stories was Barry Manilow. Signed as a budding young pop singer in 1975, Manilow willingly accepted Davis's advice on what sorts of songs to record and which tunes would most likely hit the top of the charts. Within two years, Manilow was a pop superstar whose albums went platinum and whose concerts sold out in the largest venues. Other artists who joined the Arista label included Patti Smith, Lou Reed, the Kinks, and Hall & Oates.

Within its first three years of existence, Arista Records leaped into the Top Ten most profitable record companies in America. Davis, who was part-owner of the company, sold Arista to a German conglomerate, the Bertelsmann Music Group, in 1980. He retained his position as president of the company and continued to work closely with his artists and producers to create million-selling singles and albums.

Arista Records celebrated its fifteenth anniversary in 1990 with a huge, televised music special featuring many of the label's best-known artists. Chief among these was Whitney Houston. Her albums alone have generated more than $300 million in sales for Arista. Other performers who joined in the show that night were Manilow, Carly Simon, Taylor Dayne, the Eurythmics, Kenny G, and Dionne Warwick, to name a few. Also on hand was pop group Milli Vanilli—the duo of Rob Pilatus and Fab Morvan, who were subsequently discovered to be no more than effective lip-synchers. The Milli Vanilli scandal, however, did little to tarnish Arista's image as a top pop label. Davis and other Arista executives maintained they had no knowledge of the high-tech hoax, and with much fanfare they dropped Pilatus and Morvan from the label.

Forbes magazine termed Arista "the only bright spot in Bertelsmann's quest to become a major force in the U.S. entertainment business." Still dwarfed by labels like CBS and MCA, Arista nevertheless reports healthy profits on sales of recordings in categories as varied as country, rap, rock, and jazz. For his part, Davis has no plans to retire or even scale back his involvement with the company and its artists. "I find I love what I'm doing," he told *Newsday.* "When you find the Patti Smiths of the world, self-contained artists with something to say, it's wonderfully exciting."

Sources

Forbes, May 23, 1994.
Los Angeles Times, April 17, 1990; November 17, 1990; November 21, 1990; July 19, 1994.
Newsday (Long Island, NY), March 14, 1990.
Newsweek, June 11, 1973; July 7, 1975.
New York Times Magazine, April 24, 1977.
Rolling Stone, July 3, 1986.

—Anne Janette Johnson

El DeBarge

Singer, songwriter

Photograph by Mike Hashimoto, © 1994 Reprise Records

Eldra "El" DeBarge and his nine brothers and sisters all displayed musical talent at an early age. They sang in the gospel choir at the Bethel Pentecostal Church, where their uncle James Abney led the choir and another uncle, Reverend William Abney, served as pastor. Belting out gospel songs stimulated a love for music in the members of the DeBarge family, including Eldra. In time, however, the siblings outgrew the Bethel Pentecostal Church and looked to the recording industry to further their musical aspirations.

In 1978, when Eldra was just 18 years old, he moved from his home state of Michigan to Hollywood, California, with his three older brothers—Marty, James, and Randy—and his older sister, Bunny. They planned to impress the executives at Motown Records enough to land a record contract. Two other older brothers, Tommy and Bobby, already had a contract with the label as part of the funk group Switch, which was managed by Jermaine Jackson of the famous Jackson clan.

Under the name DeBarge, Eldra and his bandmates sent Jackson their demo tape; apparently, he didn't even listen to it. But the group didn't give up on their dream that easily. They found out when Jackson had his next scheduled meeting with Switch at the Motown offices and mounted an impromptu concert for him in the hallway. A few months later, DeBarge signed a contract with Motown. Label founder Berry Gordy, Jr., made DeBarge his own special project and personally worked with El DeBarge on his songwriting

Five years after DeBarge landed in Hollywood, they released their first album on Motown Records, *All This Love.* The title track became the band's first hit, and they received their first gold album. Comparisons between DeBarge and the Jacksons flew from everywhere, including the band's management and label. DeBarge's youngest member—producer and star performer El DeBarge—was tagged the next Michael Jackson.

DeBarge didn't perform live until they had cut their second album, *In a Special Way,* and once again sent sales soaring into gold status. In 1985, just two years after their first effort, DeBarge released *Rhythm of the Night,* their last album as a band. That same year, El DeBarge set out to prove to the world that he could make it on his own, without his brothers and sister: He decided to move on to a solo project with Motown Records. "I don't think people other than my most sincere fans are aware of just how much I had to do with those earlier DeBarge albums," the singer noted in *Billboard.*

El DeBarge released his self-titled solo debut in 1986, which produced the hits "Who's Johnny?" and "Love

For the Record . . .

Born Eldra DeBarge, c. 1960, in Grand Rapids, MI; formed band DeBarge with siblings Marty, James, Randy, and Bunny, 1978, and moved to Hollywood, CA; signed with Motown Records; released three albums, 1983-85; group disbanded, 1985; El DeBarge signed with Motown Records for his solo project; released two albums on Motown, 1986-89; signed with Warner Bros., 1991.

Addresses: *Record company*—Reprise, 3300 Warner Blvd., Burbank, CA 91505-4694.

DeBarge kept on working after the tour and started recording his next solo album in 1993. A year later, *Heart, Mind & Soul*—with its first single, "Can't Get Enough"—arrived in stores. DeBarge coproduced the album with luminaries Kenneth "Babyface" Edmonds, Jermaine Dupri, and Tony Dofat. Edmonds and De-Barge combined their talents with a duet on the track "Where Is My Love?"

"When I first began the album, I wanted to do some really hip music, music that was current, stylish," El DeBarge said in his Warner Bros. biography. "There's a whole new generation out there that I want to introduce to my music." DeBarge said of *Heart, Mind & Soul*, "Musically, it's where I am today. And everything on here is me speaking from my heart."

Selected discography

With DeBarge

All This Love, Motown, 1983.
In a Special Way, Motown, 1984.
Rhythm of the Night, Motown, 1985.

Solo albums

El DeBarge, Motown, 1986.
Gemini, Motown, 1989.
In the Storm, Warner Bros., 1992.
Heart, Mind & Soul, Reprise, 1994.

Sources

Billboard, April 21, 1984; July 19, 1986; June 17, 1989; April 11, 1992.
Keyboard, September 1985.
People, June 1, 1992.
Rolling Stone, April 26, 1984; May 28, 1992.
Spin, September 1994.
Variety, February 29, 1984.
Vibe, August 1994.

Always." Then he took his time before releasing his next effort, *Gemini,* three years later. After *Gemini* hit the stores, DeBarge's professional life took a sharp turn into turmoil. He went through a bankruptcy hearing that resulted in his release from his Motown contract and was forced to start on a new path. "It's like the beginning of a new era for me," he told David Nathan in *Billboard,* "and like one of the songs on the album [*Gemini*] says, it's all about turning the page. The storyline of that song 'Turn the Page' is actually more about a relationship. But you know what that song really means to me? It means that I am turning the page in my life. All that has passed is behind me."

DeBarge returned to Michigan and spent the early 1990s working on other artists' music. He performed on industry mogul Quincy Jones's *Secret Garden* with Barry White, James Ingram, and Al B. Sure! He also added guest performances to Fourplay's hit "After the Dance" and Tone Loc's *Cool Hand Loc.*

In 1991 DeBarge signed a recording contract with Warner Bros. Records. He admitted that Motown had stifled some of his creativity. "I was made to feel inse-cure," he said in *Billboard,* "because every time I would do something [musically], it would end up being changed.... It kinda made me shell up, made me to the point where I didn't want to create anymore." The following year he released *In the Storm* on Warner Bros., which he coproduced with Earth, Wind and Fire produc-er Maurice White. The first single, "My Heart Belongs to You," debuted on *Billboard*'s Hot R&B Singles Chart at Number 70. *In the Storm* also includes a song DeBarge cowrote with Prince called "Tip of My Tongue." After the album's release, DeBarge went on tour with singer Chaka Khan. Suddenly, the creative spark he felt he had lost at Motown came back with a vengeance.

Additional information for this profile was obtained from Warner Bros. Records publicity materials, 1994.

—*Sonya Shelton*

Manu Dibango

Saxophonist

Photograph by Vincent Soyez, © 1994 Giant Records

The most widely known musician from the French West African nation of Cameroon, Manu Dibango was one of the pioneers of world music in the early 1970s and remained one of the most internationally celebrated African musicians into the mid-1990s. The *Boston Globe* considered his 1994 hit *Wakafrika* to be his "best album in years." *Wakafrika* also brought together African and European stars, including King Sunny Ade, Ladysmith Black Mambazo, Peter Gabriel, and Sinead O'Connor.

Long recognized for combining African, American, European, and techno sounds, Dibango first achieved global fame in 1973 with *Soul Makossa,* through which he popularized makossa music, a Cameroonian form of early-century West African dance music. Living in Paris, in Douala, Cameroon, around Western and Central Africa, and later also in Jamaica and New York, Dibango has experimented with jazz, reggae, hip hop, and electric music throughout his prolific career.

Although Dibango has been criticized at times for having a foreign sound—foreign from African, European, and American perspectives—he has strived for a musical universality inflected by his own identity. "What contribution have I made?" he asked himself in an interview by the *UNESCO Courier* in 1991. "I have built a bridge between my starting point and my curiosity. I contribute a sound which is unmistakably African. I add my difference."

Cameroonian Makossa Roots

Born Emmanuel Dibango on February 10, 1934, in Douala, Cameroon, to a civil servant and a dressmaker, Dibango first discovered his interest in music as a boy at home and in church. His mother led the women's choir in their Protestant chapel and sang with her dressmaker's apprentices and Dibango, while working during the days. "We sang all day long," recalled Dibango in an interview with the *UNESCO Courier*. "I was the conductor. What I liked most of all was to marshall the voices into a human instrument that sounded right and true."

In addition to church music, which included many classical European scores, Dibango also listened without his parents' knowledge or approval to modern music on their gramophone. There and at performances in Douala, Dibango as an adolescent heard African musicians playing an assortment of modern Western music and Cameroonian styles, including initiation music, with drums and wooden instruments, and "assico," percussive dance music played by guitar bands.

For the Record . . .

Born Emmanuel Dibango, February 10, 1934, in Douala, Cameroon; son of a civil servant and a dressmaker. *Education:* Received baccalaureate in France, c. 1956; took lessons in classical piano, c. 1949-54, and in jazz saxophone, 1954-56.

Played saxophone and piano in Parisian cabarets, c. 1954-56; met Joseph Kabasele, star Congolese singer, while leading house band at club *Anges Noirs,* Brussels, Belgium, late 1950s; joined Kabasele's band African Jazz on tour in Europe, 1960, and then in Zaire (formerly the Congo), 1963; led own band in Cameroon, 1963-65; reunited with Kabasele, backed up visiting African and African-American musicians, then worked as bandleader, Paris, 1965-73; recorded first album, *Manu Dibango,* 1968; international breakthrough with fourth album, *Soul Makossa,* 1973; directed Radio Orchestra of Cote d'Ivoire, 1975-79; signed with U.K. label *Island,* 1980; recorded with members of the Wailers, Jamaica, 1979-83; toured U.S., Europe, and Africa, mid-1980s—; released *Wakafrica,* Giant, 1994. Author of autobiography *Trois Kilos de Cafe,* 1990.

Awards: Gold album and Grammy Award nomination for best rhythm and blues instrumental performance, 1973, both for *Soul Makossa.*

Addresses: *Record company*—Giant Records, 111 N. Hollywood Way, Burbank, CA 91505.

Hearing these bands, Dibango gained early exposure to "makossa," a modern Cameroonian version of West African highlife music. Highlife developed in the 1920s and 1930s from African musicians who incorporated original dance tunes into their performances for colonial audiences. The form drew on Western music, including jazz. As a West African response to merchant trade under colonial rule during the first half of the twentieth century, highlife represented an early accomplishment for modern Africa. "[Seen] in historical perspective the music ... assumes enhanced status as a cultural achievement," wrote West African music critics and historians John Collins and Paul Richards in their essay "Popular Music in West Africa." As a form, makossa did not gain international prominence until Dibango introduced the sounds in 1973 on his globally popular album *Soul Makossa.*

After moving to France with his family at 15 to study for a diploma, Dibango heard American jazz and began to consider himself a musician for his love of the art form. "How happy I was the first time I heard Louis Armstrong humming on the radio!" he told the *UNESCO Courier.* "Here was a black voice singing tunes that reminded me of those I had learned at the temple." For Dibango, jazz meant "a kind of freedom, fresh scope for the imagination."

In Paris during the 1940s, Dibango redirected his efforts from the piano toward the saxophone and absorbed, with a number of African musicians, the jazz, Latin American mambo and samba, Caribbean beguine, and Creole music permeating the city. At the end of the 1950s, Dibango moved to Brussels, Belgium, where during the 1960 negotiations for the independence of the Congo, he "experienced the tensions and clashes between whites and Africans," he stated in the *UNESCO Courier* interview.

Dibango also played with leading African musicians living in Europe, including Joseph Kabasele, a star singer from the Congo whose album, *Independence Cha-Cha,* became a hit in both Africa and Brussels when the Congo gained its independence in 1960 and became Zaire. Dibango performed in Zaire with Kabasele in 1961 and with the band African Jazz until 1963, when Dibango returned to his native Cameroon after a 12-year absence. Dibango began composing in Zaire, made his first recording there as a pianist for *African Jazz,* and appeared on over 100 singles.

Scored International Success

In 1965 soul music was flourishing in Paris, and Dibango returned there to begin an international ascent as a saxophonist. After three albums, including his 1968 debut, *Manu Dibango,* Dibango's fourth record caught on big in the U.S. and across Europe and Africa. Released on Atlantic Records in 1973, *Soul Makossa* rode the phenomenal success of its title track to win a gold record for sales in the U.S. and a Grammy Award nomination for Dibango for best rhythm and blues instrumental performance of the year.

Henri Kala-Lobe described the album's stylistic success and enduring achievement in *West Africa:* "When *Soul Makossa* happened, it was a new lease of life for the eternal stylistic quarrel between traditional and modern. Its new sound, more electric and ragging, the using of alto-sax as main instrument, the jerky and spare rhythm and the horn riffs, gave a modern African soul approach to makossa." Similarly, on the basis of *Soul Makossa* and Dibango's earlier work in Paris and Brussels, *Billboard's* Emmanuel Legrand deemed Dibango "one of the founders of the world music movement."

Since that success, Dibango has released numerous albums of African dance music combined with jazz and rhythm and blues. In 1979 he experimented also with reggae, recording with some of the Wailers in Jamaica. Then, in 1984, he celebrated 30 years in the music industry with an "electric-pop" album called *Abele Dance,* according to John Collins in *West African Pop Roots. Abele Dance* exhibited the new hip-hop style from New York and was produced by Martin Meissonnier, whom *Vogue* described as "France's most active proponent of world music." The title single quickly became one of the top African songs of the year.

Bridged Cultures with Music

Still, Dibango received some criticism of his shows following *Abele Dance.* Lynden Barber of *Melody Maker* noted that Dibango's music was "less pure in source than ... other big-name African artists." In response to such questions of his authenticity as an African musician, Dibango asserted the freedom of all musicians to absorb and mix influences. "The musician, even more than the composer, hears agreeable sounds around him and digests them," Dibango said in an interview with the *UNESCO Courier.* "The voices of [Luciano] Pavarotti and Barbara Hendricks have taught me to love opera. In my imaginary museum they join Louis Armstrong, Duke Ellington, and Charlie Parker. I haven't found anyone better. Mozart doesn't stop me from being African. I like mixtures."

With his 1991 album, *Live '91* on FNAC Music, Dibango proved his "continuing ability to build bridges between cultures and traditions," according to Legrand of *Billboard.* The *Guardian's* Robin Denselow agreed, lauding Dibango as "still one of the pioneers of the African music scene." The record featured Dibango's "cool jazz saxophone" along with an African chorus, drums, and south London rap.

The U.K.'s Sinead O'Connor and Peter Gabriel joined with African stars Youssou N'Dour, King Sunny Ade, and Ladysmith Black Mambazo to record with Dibango on his 1994 album, *Wakafrika,* released on the Giant label. This collaboration helped establish *Wakafrika* as "his best album in years," according to the *Boston Globe,* and "shows that Dibango can hold his own with the best of the younger generation."

Incorporating a remake of Gabriel's "Biko," which "simmers percussively, with rich soulful vocals that reach from Soweto to Memphis," according to the *Atlanta Journal and Constitution,* and new versions of Dibango originals, including "Soul Makossa" and "Ca Va Chouia," the album "dazzles in its vitality," wrote Paul Evans of

Rolling Stone. Wakafrika reached Number Seven on *Billboard's* Top World Music Albums chart in 1994.

Entering the mid-1990s, Dibango continued to grow as a musician. Hailed in 1991 in the *Boston Globe* as "perhaps the most consistent African pop artist working at cross-cultural experimentation," his high level of energy remained apparent. "Now 60, having generated more than 20 albums, Dibango hardly sounds like he's slowing down at all," Paul Evans wrote in *Rolling Stone.* Reviewing a performance at the Central Park Summerstage in July of 1994 in New York City, Jon Pareles of the *New York Times* agreed, noting, "He's still creating Afroglobal fusions that are both slick and enjoyable." Judging also by the host of younger stars who joined him on his 1994 album, Dibango has clearly begun to exert a lasting influence on the world music scene.

Selected discography

Albums

Manu Dibango, 1968.
O Boso, 1971.
Soma Loba, 1972.
Soul Makossa, Atlantic, 1973.
Super Kumba, 1974.
Africadelic, 1975.
(With Sly Dunbar and Robbie Shakespeare) *Gone Clear,* Island, 1979.
(With Dunbar and Shakespeare) *Ambassador,* Island, 1981.
Waka Juju, Sonodisc, 1982.
Soft and Sweet, 1983.
(As solo pianist) *Melodies Africaines, Volumes 1 & 2,* 1983.
Abele Dance, RCA, 1984.
(With Herbie Hancock and Wally Badarou) *Electric Africa,* Celluloid, 1985.
Afrijazzy, Soul Paris, 1986.
Polysonic, Bird Productions, 1990.
Live '91, FNAC Music, 1991.
(With others) *Wakafrika* (includes "Soul Makossa," "Ca Va Chouia," and "Biko"), Giant, 1994.

Film scores

L'herbe sauvage, Cote d'Ivoire, 1976.
Ceddo, Senegal, 1976.
Le prix de la liberte, Cameroon, 1976.

Sources

Books

Collins, John, *Musicmakers of West Africa,* Three Continents Press, 1985.

Collins, John, *West African Pop Roots,* Temple University Press, 1992.

Collins, John, and Paul Richards, "Popular Music in West Africa," *World Music, Politics, and Social Change,* edited by Simon Frith, Manchester University Press, 1989.

Periodicals

Atlanta Journal and Constitution, July 31, 1994.

Billboard, November 30, 1991; February 13, 1993; July 23, 1994.

Boston Globe, July 12, 1992.

Guardian, May 21, 1992; March 15, 1994.

Melody Maker, November 24, 1984.

New York Times, July 29, 1994.

Rolling Stone, August 11, 1994.

UNESCO Courier, March 1991.

Vogue, May 1989.

West Africa, November 8, 1982.

—Nicholas Patti

Doc Pomus

Songwriter

The writer of some of rock and roll's most enduring songs, Doc Pomus was first among those that kept the music alive between rock icon Elvis Presley's 1958 entrance into the U.S. Army and the 1964 arrival of British band the Beatles. Among the songs—many now standards—that Pomus wrote with his partner Mort Shuman are "Save the Last Dance for Me," "This Magic Moment," "A Teenager in Love," "His Latest Flame," "Viva Las Vegas," "Little Sister," "I Count the Tears," and "A Mess of Blues."

Despite being crippled by polio at age six, Pomus loomed larger than life to his many friends and admirers. Even as rock forged on without him in the late 1960s and 1970s, Pomus continued to embody the traits of the hip, all-knowing, and kind empiricist—the guy who has seen it all yet retains a heart of gold.

Born Jerome Solon Felder in Brooklyn on January 27, 1925, Pomus began his career singing, not writing. He grew up middle class, his father a precinct politician and lawyer. In a grim bit of irony, young Jerome was shipped off to summer camp to avoid a polio epidemic in his neighborhood; while at camp he contracted the disease. Difficult times were eased only by his infatuation with the blues, and specifically with Big Joe Turner's "Piney Brown Blues," a record that transformed Doc's life.

"It all changed for me when I was about 15 or 16 and I heard Joe Turner's 'Piney Brown Blues,'" Pomus told Peter Guralnick in 1988, as quoted in *Lost Highway*. "From that moment on I knew what I wanted to do. I was going to be a blues singer. That to me was everything music was supposed to be. It was the way the male voice was supposed to sound."

At the age of 18, Pomus began hanging out in New York City at Greenwich Village nightclubs, often sitting in and singing blues and rhythm and blues. It was after such a night that he chose the name Doc Pomus—a complete fabrication—because it sounded cool to him. It was in this milieu—the sweaty, bohemian, democratic, and sultry atmosphere at places like George's Tavern—that Pomus began singing, standing before the mike on braces and crutches. Attending Brooklyn College by day, at 19, Pomus made his first record, for famed critic Leonard Feather. He would later record for Chess and Savoy Records and sing jingles, all without great note.

But Doc had found his world; he quickly endeared himself to black musicians and their reality. He began writing songs, he said, "to support my singing habit," which he gave up in 1957 after a bad business deal. A year earlier, Pomus had begun writing with Mort Shu-

Photograph by Sharyn Felder, courtesy of Forward Media Relations

For the Record . . .

Born Jerome Solon Felder, January 27, 1925, in Brooklyn, NY; died of cancer, March 14, 1991.

Songwriter. Began singing at Greenwich Village nightclubs, c. 1943; began writing songs, c. 1953-54; met writing partner Mort Shuman, 1956; collaborated with Leiber and Stoller on "Young Blood," 1957; quit writing and gambled, 1965-75; wrote "There Must Be a Better World Somewhere" for B.B. King, 1982.

Awards: Grammy Award for "There Must Be a Better World Somewhere," 1982; inducted into Rock and Roll Hall of Fame, 1991.

Addresses: *Record company*—Rhino Records, 10635 Santa Monica Blvd., Los Angeles, CA 90025-4900.

man, a younger composer and musician. "Young Blood," a song started by Pomus and completed by stellar songwriters Leiber and Stoller, was a hit for the Coasters in 1957, giving Doc an early taste of things to come.

Songwriter Otis Blackwell—of "All Shook Up" and "Don't Be Cruel" fame—brought Pomus and Shuman to the attention of Hill & Range, a publishing house that had shrewdly established a lifelong relationship with Elvis Presley. Pomus and Shuman were moved into a penthouse suite in the famed Brill Building, the song factory that also housed Goffin & King, Sedaka & Greenfield and Phil Spector. The deal brought Pomus his first steady money—$200 a week—and the opportunity to write and place his songs.

Between 1958 and 1965, Pomus and Shuman wrote some of rock's most vivid and romantic songs. It was a new kind of music, not quite blues, not quite pop. The duo was helping to construct what rock and roll would be—what it communicated, what its tempo would be, and to what degree the music would penetrate every day life.

"Well, it's always easy to come up with explanations after the fact," Pomus later said, according to Forward Records publicity materials, "but I feel like we were writing songs that couldn't be pigeonholed, and we weren't writing songs in a single voice. Now you take a song like "Save the Last Dance for Me," or any of the Latin songs that Mort and I wrote together, and I was trying to get the lyrics to sound like a translation. My job was to bring the thing back to some elemental point,

something palatable to the recording industry, so you would have the image in your mind."

In 1965 Doc took a bad fall while in England; he was hospitalized for two months and would remain for the rest of his life in a wheelchair. Meanwhile, everything changed in the mid-1960s: Self-contained groups like the Beatles, the Beach Boys and the Rolling Stones were in vogue, and Pomus's marriage ended, as did his collaboration with Shuman.

For the next ten years Pomus quit writing and became a professional gambler under the tutelage of Johnny Mel, playing cards with a the toughest of characters. He gave it up in 1975, ultimately calling his gambling "too risky, too violent," as he noted in Forward Records press materials. "But the [songwriting] was the same kind of thing. I always felt that writing songs was like gambling, a profession where the odds were definitely loaded against you. But the idea of being able to bet on yourself... playing cards in a way was just as extension of the rest of my life."

With the help of friends like musicians Dr. John and B. B. King and songwriter Spector, Doc gradually began penning tunes, noticing that his contributions to the music world were again gaining notice. Before he died on March 14, 1991, Doc enjoyed a decade of activity. He wrote the Grammy Award-winning "There Must Be a Better World Somewhere" for B. B. King in 1982; recorded with Roomful of Blues; was reunited with his old friends and idols Ray Charles and Big Joe Turner; and in 1991 was inducted into the Rock and Roll Hall of Fame.

Pomus's songs have been covered by numerous and diverse artists from Bruce Springsteen to Dolly Parton, Neil Diamond to the Dead Kennedys, and LaVerne Baker to the Beach Boys. There also exists the Doc Pomus Financial Assistance Grant Program, established by the Rhythm & Blues Foundation in Pomus's name. Since its inception, the Foundation has provided more than $400,000 in general and financial assistance to legendary R&B figures.

In March of 1995 Rhino released the long overdue *Till the Night Is Gone: A Tribute to Doc Pomus*. The album features performances by Bob Dylan, Shawn Colvin, Rosanne Cash, Los Lobos, John Hiatt, and Lou Reed, who provided Doc with this homage: "Doc was a great songwriter, poet, philanthropist, gambler, raconteur supreme. He was like a blazing sun—anybody in his orbit benefitted from him. He was the way you should be. When you grow up, you should be like Doc."

Selected discography

As songwriter

Elvis Presley, *Pot Luck,* RCA, 1962.
Dion Sings His Greatest Hits, Laurie, 1973.
B. B. King, *There Must Be a Better World Somewhere,* MCA, 1983.
Presley, *Rocker,* RCA, 1984.
The Drifters: 1959-1965 All Time Greatest Hits and More, Atlantic, 1988.
50 Coastin' Classics: The Coasters Anthology, Rhino, 1992.
'Til the Night Is Gone: A Tribute to Doc Pomus, Forward/Rhino, 1995.

Sources

Books

Guralnick, Peter, *Lost Highway,* Vintage Books, 1982.
Heilbut, Anthony, *The Gospel Sound,* fourth edition, Limelight, 1992.

Rees, Dafydd, and Luke Crampton, *Rock Movers and Shakers,* Billboard Books, 1991.
Rolling Stone Album Guide, edited by Anthony DeCurtis, James Henke, and Holly George-Warren, Straight Arrow, 1992.
Rolling Stone Encyclopedia of Rock & Roll, edited by Jon Pareles and Patricia Romanowski, Rolling Stone Press, 1983.
Rolling Stone Record Guide, edited by Dave Marsh, Rolling Stone Press, 1979.
Scott, Frank, *The Down Home Guide to the Blues,* A Capella Books, 1991.
Whitburn, Joel, *Top R&B Singles, 1942-88,* Billboard Books, 1990.

Periodicals

Billboard, February 18, 1995.
Village Voice Rock and Roll Quarterly, summer, 1988.

Additional information for this profile was obtained from Forward Records publicity materials, 1995.

—Stewart Francke

Enigma

Contemporary dance entity

Photograph by Barbel Miebach, courtesy of Virgin Records

Michael Cretu, the man who is Enigma, declared his creative philosophy in a Virgin Records press release: "Old rules and habits have to be rejected and dismissed so that something new can be created." Even though Europeans were hip to Cretu's identity, early U.S. press information billed Enigma as the creation of a German producer who preferred to remain anonymous. "With Enigma," Cretu explained to Larry Flick in *Billboard,* I have created a complete piece of music that I wanted to let stand alone. There is a sense of mystery in the music that I wanted to leave untouched by the perceptions and preconceived ideas that come with the past history of a producer or a songwriter." He continued, "Contrary to the usual record company philosophy, people *are* open-minded and starved for something unique. This is music that is different from any other available at the moment. I think people have responded to that."

Born on May 18, 1957, in Bucharest, Romania, Cretu pursued an early goal of becoming a concert pianist by studying classical music. In 1965 he attended Lyzeum No. 2—a college for young and gifted musical talents—with piano as his main subject, and he also studied for five months in 1968 in Paris, France. From 1975 to 1978 he attended the Academy of Music in Frankfurt, Germany, where he earned a degree in music. Deserting his goal of classical music, he claimed, "I started writing hits the day I sold my piano."

MCMXC a.D. Conceived as One Song

In 1980 Cretu won his first gold record for his production work. The artists with whom he has been associated include Hubert Kah, Peter Cornelius, Moti Special, and Sylvie Vartan. Cretu has also won gold record awards for producing albums by his wife, Euro-dance chanteuse Sandra, and multi-instrumentalist-composer Michael Oldfield. Since 1985 Cretu has produced seven albums for Sandra, including her first international hit single, "Maria Magdalena," which went to Number One in more than 30 countries. Cretu released his first solo album on Virgin, *Legionäre* (which means legionnaires), in 1983, but his solo efforts before taking the name Enigma failed to earn U.S. distribution.

Inspired by such groups as the Art of Noise and Pink Floyd, Cretu assembled Enigma's debut album, *MCMXC a.D.* (the roman numeral representation of 1990), on an AudioFrame system at his home studio in Spain. *MCMXC a.D.* was released on December 3, 1990, in Europe through Virgin Germany and on February 12, 1991, in the U.S. through Virgin/Charisma. The LP eventually sold more than 12 million units worldwide,

Band consists of Michael Cretu, born May 18, 1957, in Bucharest, Romania; married Sandra Lauer (a singer), 1988. *Education:* Studied classical music at Lyzeum No. 2 in Bucharest, 1965; studied music in Paris, France, 1968; attended Academy of Music in Frankfurt, Germany, 1975-78, and earned a degree in music.

Producer, composer, and arranger. As Michael Cretu, released first album, *Legionäre,* Virgin, 1983; as Enigma, released debut album, *MCMXC a.D.,* Virgin/Charisma, 1990 (Europe), 1991 (U.S.).

Awards: Gold records for producing albums by Michael Oldfield and Sandra in Europe; platinum album for *MCMXC a.D.* in U.S., 1991; platinum record for single "Sadeness Part I," 1991; double-platinum album for *MCMXC a.D.,* 1993; platinum album for *The CROSS Of Changes,* 1994; gold record for single "Return to Innocence," Virgin/Charisma, 1994; gold and/or platinum awards for *MCMXC a.D.* in 25 countries; Echo Award for most successful German production abroad, 1995, for *The CROSS Of Changes.*

Addresses: *Record company*—Virgin Records, 338 North Foothill Rd., Beverly Hills, CA 90210; or 1790 Broadway, 20th Floor, New York, NY 10019. *Management*—Nizzari Artist Management, 410 West 25th St., New York, NY 10001.

and won gold and/or platinum awards in 25 countries. In the United States *MCMXC a.D.* went platinum by the first week in May of 1991 and earned double-platinum status by the fall of 1993.

Cretu told Alan di Perna of *Keyboard,* "I conceived of the whole album as a single song. The words and sounds are like flashlight beams. They don't show you everything. You have to look at what's between the lines." A mixture of sixth-century Gregorian chants, bewitching French whispers—provided by Cretu's wife, Sandra—and hypnotic, ethereal music set to intoxicating dance rhythms, *MCMXC a.D.* is definitely more a cathartic aural journey than a collection of individual songs. The video import of *MCMXC a.D.* is a gorgeous swirl of images seamlessly interpreting the entire album. Even so, "Sadeness Part I," a song marked by its inclusion of Gregorian chant, was destined to become the album's runaway single. "The great misconception of people who have only heard 'Sadeness' is that the whole album is filled with chanting. This is a complete piece of work

with many different levels and sounds. 'Sadeness' is only one piece of the puzzle," Cretu explained to *Billboard's* Flick.

Marquis de Sadeness

The French lyrics in "Sadeness Part I" are actually a dark homage to the Marquis de Sade, an eighteenth-century erotic novel writer from France from whose name the word sadism comes. In analyzing this element of the debut Enigma album, Vince Aletti of the *Village Voice* stated, "Cretu isn't celebrating the notorious Marquis ... but his mere presence in this context is a provocation, surely a deliberate and delicious one. Sade reserved his fiercest contempt and some of his most exquisite literary tortures for the pious and the prim, so even if he remains offstage here, the writer is a devilishly successful device. Cretu uses him to introduce questions of virtue and vice, faith and sacrilege, love and lust."

Cretu related to *Keyboard's* di Perna, "I wanted to use things that there are questions about, that are mysterious. You don't have to go too far to read all kinds of accusations about the Catholic Church—scandals, inquisitions, and wars—and you wonder how you can reconcile this with the idea that the Church is supposed to stand for universal love. But at the same time, I've been told that the Marquis de Sade was a very religious man, that he wrote what he wrote as a revenge against certain pious people who were hypocrites. So again, there are questions, mysteries."

Single Created Controversy

The Marquis was apparently not the only one out for revenge. As Cretu revealed to Michael Azerrad of *Rolling Stone,* "[*MCMXC a.D.*] was like revenge against everything I was hearing. I didn't want to write songs, I wanted to write *moods.*" When Azerrad drew a comparison to the way pop icons Madonna and Prince explored sexuality, Cretu replied, "What Madonna and Prince did is pure marketing—it's predicated on causing scandal. It's not a sexual music that I did. It's a *sensual* music. And there's a big difference."

Some radio stations in Europe with a large Catholic audience could not see that difference. They banned "Sadeness Part I," considering it "pure blasphemy." Dutch national radio network TROS actually received three bomb threats from listeners said to be shocked by what they heard when the record was proclaimed single of the week—prompting Cretu to issue a statement refuting rumors about satanic material in the Gregorian passages and insisting he had no desire to offend "any public religious beliefs." Himself an atheist, Cretu told Azerrad of *Rolling Stone,* "The institution of the Church doesn't really fit with our times. I believe in destiny, which is a much more powerful belief."

In terms of record sales, Cretu's beliefs were apparently embraced by many listeners. By January of 1991 "Sadeness Part I" had reached Number One in seven European countries: Germany (where it eventually became Germany's biggest-selling single ever), Belgium, the Netherlands, Switzerland, Austria, the United Kingdom, and Greece. The record would ultimately attain the Number One position in 15 countries. In the American market, "Sadeness Part I" broke into *Billboard's* Hot 100 in February of 1991, and by April the record was in the Top Five after 11 weeks at Number One on the combined European charts. Peaking at Number Two on the U.S. pop charts, "Sadeness Part I" became a certified platinum single.

Sued by a Gregorian Choir

Although Enigma was perhaps singularly responsible for boosting interest in Gregorian chant music worldwide, there was a price to pay—literally. In August of 1991 Munich-based choir Kapelle Antiqua demanded a written apology in addition to financial compensation when the choir, according to Ellie Weinert in *Billboard,* "recognized its recordings of Gregorian choral works on Enigma tracks. The group sued for damages, claiming Cretu had infringed upon its 'right of personality' by distorting the records sampled on the 'Sadeness Part I' and 'Mea Culpa' album tracks and singles." Cretu and Virgin Germany agreed to pay compensation for samples used on *MCMXC a.D.* and settled out of court with Polydor and BMG/Ariola, which represented the German choir, for an undisclosed sum. In the end Virgin acquired authorization for the retrospective use of the Polydor and BMG/Ariola masters.

In 1993 film producer Robert Evans asked Cretu to write the title song for the motion picture *Sliver.* The result was "Carly's Song" and "Carly's Loneliness," both of which appeared as "Age of Loneliness" on Enigma's next album, *The CROSS Of Changes.* Other Enigma soundtrack credits include songs from *MCMXC a.D.* used in the films *Single White Female* and *Boxing Helena.*

In May of 1991 Cretu told Larry Flick of *Billboard,* "It is my plan for Enigma to be an outlet for music that boldly strays away from the norm of pop music. I have several ideas for the next album that I think are fascinating. Part of the fun of projects such as these is watching how all of the various elements come together in the studio." Though it was released in Europe in December of 1993, it was not until February 8, 1994, that Enigma's second album, *The CROSS Of Changes,* was released in the United States. Cretu's belief that "music is part of my soul—and this ultimately decides everything" perhaps best explains the three years it took him to produce his second album.

Reviewing *The CROSS Of Changes* for *Pulse!,* Michael Freedberg stated, "Cretu's Wagnerian symphonics [in the manner of composer Richard Wagner], crisscrossed by sleazy beats and train-like machinations, feel enough like midnight to make you dance across the Seine [River in France] with your headset on." Evidently others were dancing with him. *The CROSS Of Changes* went platinum in the United States just seven weeks after its release, and "Return to Innocence" reached gold status one month later, in July of 1994. In *Keyboard* Cretu summed up perhaps a major reason for Enigma's success: "Enigma is a vehicle for doing things outside the rules that you normally have to follow when you make a dance record." He went on to say, "Basically, I will keep on doing Enigma records until I run out of new ideas. Then I'll move on to something else."

Selected discography

MCMXC a.D., Virgin/Charisma, 1990.
The CROSS Of Changes, Virgin/Charisma, 1993.

Also contributed songs to soundtrack *Sliver,* Virgin, 1993, and others.

Sources

Billboard, January 26, 1991; February 16, 1991; May 18, 1991; September 14, 1991; February 19, 1994.
Entertainment Weekly, October 14, 1994.
Keyboard, September 1991.
Melody Maker, January 12, 1991.
Pulse!, June 1994.
Rolling Stone, May 2, 1991; May 16, 1991.
Village Voice, April 16, 1991.

Additional information for this profile was obtained from Virgin Records America publicity materials, 1993, and Nizzari Artist Management, 1995.

—*Lazae Laspina*

Marianne Faithfull

Singer, songwriter

Photograph by Michael Comte, courtesy of Island Records

As an artist, Marianne Faithfull has resurrected herself many times over. Yet for many years the singer-songwriter's endeavors were consistently upstaged by dalliances with a number of vices. Her early years as a Euro-waif pop singer coincided with a well-chronicled relationship with Rolling Stone Mick Jagger, and her recordings during this time were often overshadowed by the couple's legendary exploits.

Faithfull began her musical career while still a teenager with timely, well-packaged singles that never quite achieved their assured potential; meanwhile, life among the Stones entourage led to bouts with heroin and alcohol. Faithfull was implicated in a notorious 1967 drug bust involving the band, and her relationship with Jagger came to an end in 1969. She spent much of the 1970s battling her addictions while intermittently acting in theater productions and recording a few overlooked albums.

The singer made a dramatic comeback in late 1979 with the release of *Broken English,* a critical success that prompted *Rolling Stone* writer Greil Marcus to remark, "Fifteen years after making her first single, Marianne Faithfull has made her first real album." She went on to record several other albums during the 1980s, which, like *Broken English,* were lauded by critics for their searing vocals and choice backing musicians. She also regained some ballast in her life in the mid-1980s after a serious confrontation with her addictions, an achievement that renewed her faith in her abilities.

In the summer of 1994, as the Rolling Stones, by now all in their 50s, began yet another mammoth stadium tour, Faithfull completed a saucy autobiography and put finishing touches on another innovative album. By the onset of the media blitz surrounding the Stones' multi-million-dollar extravaganza, Faithfull's 1973 comment to a television reporter about the vagaries of the music business, reported in *Rolling Stone,* had been long forgotten. "You can't go on doing that thing for years," the prescient Faithfull had snorted. "I mean just imagine having to sing 'Satisfaction' when you're forty-five."

Girl of the Moment

Faithfull was born on December 29, 1946, in Hampstead, London, to an Austrian baroness and a British intelligence officer who had met in Vienna during World War II. Her father, a devotee of Utopian social schemes, relocated his family to a communal farm in Oxfordshire in 1950, but after two years the Faithfulls' marriage disintegrated and Marianne and her mother moved to Reading, England. There they were forced to live in rather reduced circumstances, and Faithfull's girlhood was marred by bouts with tuberculosis and her charity-boarder status at the local convent school.

Despite these early hardships, Faithfull emerged as a vivacious teenager and soon began partaking in the exploding social scene in London. In early 1964 she attended a record-industry party with John Dunbar—an art student she later married—and there a chance meeting with Andrew Loog Oldham, the Rolling Stones' manager, led to a contract with Decca Records. Her first single, "As Tears Go By"—a reworking of an old English lyrical poem—was written by Oldham, Jagger, and Stones guitarist Keith Richards; it reached Number Nine on the U.K. charts by September of 1964. Faithfull was a few months short of her eighteenth birthday.

Faithfull became an overnight Top 40 sensation, known for her ethereal, whispery vocals and angelic face. Artistic differences led to a falling out with Oldham, but the teenager continued to record singles for Decca over the next few years, including covers of Bob Dylan's "Blowin' in the Wind" and the Beatles' "Yesterday." She had her biggest successes in 1965 with "Come and Stay With Me" and "This Little Bird." Her first full-length album, *Marianne Faithfull,* appeared in April of 1965, followed by *Go Away From My World* in November of the same year and *Faithfull Forever* in 1966.

Faithfull's dramatic personal life matched the fast-lane lifestyle her high-profile career demanded. She had a son with Dunbar in November of 1965, but the couple separated shortly thereafter. By then she and Jagger had become an item, and their drug-fueled, jet-set exploits together made a household name of Faithfull for all the wrong reasons. In 1967 a party at Richards's fourteenth-century manse was raided by English law enforcement authorities, and Jagger and Richards were brought up on drug-related charges. It was assumed that the unnamed vixen wearing nothing but a fur rug, a scandalous detail widely reported in news stories about the bust, had been Faithfull.

Drugs, Alcohol, and a Suicide Attempt

In an interview 27 years later with A. M. Homes for *Details,* Faithfull discussed her wilder days and admitted that the drug bust-fur rug incident had ravaged her personal life: "It destroyed me. To be a male drug addict and to act like that is always enhancing and glamorizing. A woman in that situation becomes a slut and a bad mother."

The young singer's recording career never fulfilled its early promise of pop stardom, but the industry's ready availability of drugs and alcohol offered some temporary solace. In 1969 she cut her last single for Decca, "Something Better," a record more notable for its B-side, "Sister Morphine." Faithfull had cowritten this song—a harrowing tale of heroin addiction—with Jagger and Richards but didn't receive official credit for it until 1984. Another version of the song appeared on the Stones' 1971 album *Sticky Fingers,* along with the cut "Wild Horses." The latter is considered to be Jagger's lyrical parting tribute to Faithfull, written around the time their relationship was disintegrating in 1969; the break-up was apparently precipitated by her suicide attempt in an Australian hotel room.

Faithfull also played a small part in the genesis of "Sympathy for the Devil," released on the 1968 Stones album *Beggar's Banquet* and considered by some critics to be one of their most noteworthy compositions. Jagger penned the lyrics to the song after Faithfull encouraged him one night to read an obscure novel written by early-twentieth-century Russian writer Mikhail Bulgakov entitled *The Master and Margarita.*

Despite her continuing drug problems, Faithfull harbored ambitions for greater things than cutting Top 40 records. In 1967 she appeared in two films, *I'll Never Forget Whatsisname* and the racy *Girl on a Motorcycle,* the latter with French actor Alain Delon. Two years later she made her stage debut at London's Royal Court Theatre in Anton Chekhov's *Three Sisters* and the following year played Ophelia in a film version of *Hamlet.* In the early 1970s Faithfull's heroin addiction led to intermittent hospitalization, and at one point she registered with Britain's National Health Service as an addict in order to receive a regular ration of the drug for free. Small royalties from "Sister Morphine" were sometimes her only source of income. She produced little in the way of recording, and the attempts made were disastrously ignored, such as 1975's country-and-western-inspired *Dreaming My Dreams* and *Faithless,* released in 1978.

> "Broken English *is a stunning account of the life that goes on after the end, an awful, liberating, harridan's laugh at the life that came before."*
> —Greil Marcus

By the late 1970s things were beginning to look better for Faithfull. She had put together a band and began touring British clubs, and the gigs led to a deal with Island Records. In June of 1979 she married punk bassist Ben Brierly, and a few months later her new label released *Broken English,* a fierce comeback that garnered critical acclaim. In a raspy, harsh voice light years away from her whispery teenage vocals, Faithfull sang of despair, jealousy, rage, and redemption. Her backing band included Brierly and guitarist-songwriter Barry Reynolds. Faithfull cowrote the title track as well as two other songs, but the album earned special praise for her covers of John Lennon's "Working Class Hero" and Shel Silverstein's "Ballad of Lucy Jordan."

In a *Rolling Stone* review, Greil Marcus looked back at the long road the singer had traveled since her 1964 debut, calling *Broken English* "a stunning account of the life that goes on after the end, an awful, liberating, harridan's laugh at the life that came before." The profanity-laden track "Why D'Ya Do It?," a terrifying rant against a faithless lover based on a poem by Heathcote Williams, contributed to a decision by EMI—Island's U.K. distributor—to boycott the record, although it did manage to reach Number 57 on the U.K. charts and Number 82 in the United States.

"I'm so, *so* strong," Faithfull told Debra Rae Cohen of *Rolling Stone* a few months after the release of the album. "People have no clue." Her pride in *Broken English* was apparent: "I've never worked very hard at anything before; it's the first time musical demands have been made on me." In his review Marcus termed the album "a perfectly intentional, controlled, unique

statement about fury, defeat and rancor.... It isn't anything we've heard before, from anyone."

Despite her newfound success, Faithfull continued to battle the demons of heroin and alcohol. A disastrous appearance on *Saturday Night Live* was blamed on too many rehearsals, but it was suspected that drugs had caused her vocal cords to seize up. A second album for Island, *Dangerous Acquaintances,* was released in 1981 and featured a more upbeat mood and a track written by Steve Winwood, formerly of the Spencer Davis Group, Traffic, and Blind Faith. The album just missed breaking the Top 100 in the United States but reached Number 45 in the U.K. "Faithfull fairly revels in her newfound strength," wrote Parke Puterbaugh in *Rolling Stone.* "*Dangerous Acquaintances* quakes with a darkly luminescent power, as the singer meditates on the transience and intransigence of affairs of the heart."

During the 1980s Faithfull moved between London and New York, her heroin addiction helping to obliterate the reality of her sometimes squalid living conditions and equally squalid acquaintances. Her third LP for Island, *A Child's Adventure,* was released in 1983 but achieved only scant commercial success. Though he praised the musicianship of the record, *Rolling Stone's* Puterbaugh mused that Faithfull had perhaps "overextended her poetic license, for the allusions are far too vague, the protagonist of these living nightmares too swollen with her own suffering."

Recovery

In the mid-1980s Faithfull's chemical addictions began to catch up with her—in a chemical-induced stupor she took a bad fall down a flight of stairs, and in another incident her heart actually stopped. Extensive rehabilitation, including a stint at the famed Hazelden facility, helped her overcome her demons by the time *Strange Weather* was released in 1987. The album of covers was produced by Hal Willner after the two had spent numerous weekends listening to hundreds of songs from the annals of twentieth-century music. They chose to record such diverse tracks as Bob Dylan's "I'll Keep It With Mine" and "Yesterdays," written by Broadway composers Jerome Kern and Otto Harbach. The work also includes tunes first made notable by blues luminaries like Billie Holiday and Bessie Smith; latter-day virtuoso Tom Waits penned the title track.

Coming full circle, the renewed Faithfull cut another recording of "As Tears Go By" for *Strange Weather,* this time in a tighter, more gravelly voice. The singer confessed to a lingering irritation with her first hit. "I always childishly thought that was where my problems started, with that damn song," she told Jay Cocks in *Time,* but she came to terms with it as well as with her past. In a 1987 interview with Rory O'Connor of *Vogue,* Faithfull declared, "forty is the age to sing it, not seventeen."

In 1990 Faithfull released *Blazing Away,* a live retrospective recorded at St. Anne's Cathedral in Brooklyn. The 13 selections include "Sister Morphine," a cover of Edith Piaf's "Les Prisons du Roy," and the controversial "Why D'Ya Do It?" from *Broken English.* Alanna Nash of *Stereo Review* commended the musicians whom Faithfull had chosen to back her—longtime guitarist Reynolds was joined by former Band member Garth Hudson and pianist Dr. John.

Nash was also impressed with the album's autobiographical tone, noting "Faithfull's gritty alto is a cracked and halting rasp, the voice of a woman who's been to hell and back on the excursion fare—which, of course, she has." The reviewer extolled Faithfull as "one of the most challenging and artful of women artists," and *Rolling Stone* writer Fred Goodman asserted: "*Blazing Away* is a fine retrospective—proof that we can still expect great things from this graying, jaded *contessa.*"

Released Candid Autobiography

Faithfull next took a hiatus from performing and lived in relative isolation in Ireland for a few years. She returned to the stage for a 1991 Dublin revival of *The Threepenny Opera* and played a ghost who comes back to torment her abusive husband in the film *When Pigs Fly.* She also spent time with writer David Dalton in compiling her 1994 autobiography, *Faithfull,* and released an album of the same name in August of that year. The book, as expected, is loaded with the singer's forthright reminiscences of being caught up in the orbit of the Rolling Stones and her difficult attempts to break free of those years, recounted "with witty, humorous detachment and in a voice as distinctive as her latter-day rasp," according to *Billboard* writer Chris Morris.

The 1994 album *Faithfull,* subtitled *A Collection of Her Best Recordings,* contains Faithfull's original version of "As Tears Go By," several cuts from *Broken English,* and a song written by Patti Smith scheduled for inclusion on an Irish AIDS benefit album. This track, "Ghost Dance"—suggested to Faithfull by a friend who later died of AIDS—was made with a trio of old acquaintances: Rolling Stones drummer Charlie Watts and guitarist Ron Wood backed Faithfull's vocals on the song while Richards coproduced it. The retrospective album also features one live track, "Times Square," as well as Faithfull's return to songwriting with "She," penned with acclaimed composer and arranger Angelo Badalamenti.

Best known for his work scoring projects for filmmaker and *Twin Peaks* creator David Lynch, Badalamenti teamed up with Faithfull for *A Secret Life,* her first full-length studio effort since 1987. *Vanity Fair* writer Cathy Horyn predicted in September of 1994 that this Island Records collaboration, released in March of 1995, "will almost certainly restore this fallen angel to her rightful place: as one of the great interpretive singers of our time."

Selected discography

Singles; on Decca

"As Tears Go By" / "Greensleeves," 1964.
"What Have I Done Wrong?" / "Come and Stay With Me," 1965.
"This Little Bird" / "Morning Sun," 1965.
"Summer Nights" / "The Sha La La Song," 1965.
"Go Away From My World" / "Oh Look Around You," 1965.
"Counting" / "Tomorrow's Calling," 1966.
"Is This What I Get for Loving You?" / "Tomorrow's Calling," 1967.
"Something Better" / "Sister Morphine," 1969.

Solo albums; on Decca

Marianne Faithfull, 1965.
Go Away From My World, 1965.
Faithfull Forever, 1966.
North Country Maid, 1966.
Love in a Mist, 1967.
Marianne Faithfull's Greatest Hits, 1969.

On Island

Broken English, 1979.
Dangerous Acquaintances, 1981.
A Child's Adventure, 1983.
Strange Weather, 1987.
Blazing Away, 1990.
Faithfull: A Collection of Her Best Recordings, 1994.
A Secret Life, 1995.

Other

Faithless, NEMS, 1978.
Marianne Faithfull's Greatest Hits, Abkco, 1988.

Sources

Books

Faithfull, Marianne, and David Dalton, *Faithfull: An Autobiography,* Little, Brown, 1994.
Lillian Roxon's Rock Encyclopedia, Grosset & Dunlap, 1969.
Nite, Norm N., with Ralph M. Newman, *Rock On: The Years of*

Change, 1964-1978, Harper & Row, 1984.

Penguin Encyclopedia of Popular Music, edited by Donald Clarke, Viking, 1989.

Rees, Dafydd, and Luke Crampton, Rock Movers & Shakers, ABC/CLIO, 1989.

The Rolling Stone Encyclopedia of Rock & Roll, edited by Jon Pareles and Patricia Romanowski, Rolling Stone Press/Summit Books, 1983.

Scaduto, Tony, Mick Jagger: Everybody's Lucifer, David McKay, 1974.

Periodicals

Billboard, July 30, 1994.

Details, September 1994.

Entertainment Weekly, August 26, 1994; March 24, 1995.

Melody Maker, July 31, 1965.

Newsweek, August 22, 1994.

Rolling Stone, April 12, 1973; January 24, 1980; April 17, 1980; December 10, 1981; January 21, 1982; April 14, 1983; May 17, 1990; October 20, 1994.

Spin, April 1995.

Stereo Review, October 1990.

Time, December 7, 1987.

Vanity Fair, September 1994.

Vogue, November 1987.

Additional information for this profile was obtained from an Island Records press biography.

—Carol Brennan

Mirella Freni

Opera singer

Photograph by Christian Steiner, courtesy of Columbia Artists Management, Inc.

Mirella Freni is not as instantly recognizable as opera stars Luciano Pavarotti or Maria Callas, but she is among the great sopranos of the twentieth century and holds a special appeal for opera lovers worldwide. Her gentle, fresh-sounding voice coupled with a simple and direct performing style made her ideally suited for romantic leads, vaulting her into the top ranks of the opera world in the early 1960s. In later years, in response to the urgings of her mentor, Herbert von Karajan, and her own desire to enlarge her horizons, she adapted her performing style to encompass more dramatic roles, easily making the kind of transition that has caused other singers' careers to founder. Since her debut in 1955, Freni has enjoyed a near-continual string of stage successes, something few other singers can claim. In the 1990s she remained one of the dominant figures on the opera scene.

Freni, the eldest daughter of Ennio, a civil servant, and Gianna Fregni, was born on February 27, 1935, in the northern Italian industrial town of Modena. She began her artistic development as a toddler, telling her mother at the age of two that she wanted to be an opera singer. Her grandmother, Valentina Bartolomasi, was a well-known soprano of the 1920s, and Mirella, growing up in a musical family, manifested a natural ability for singing. In fact, it was one of Freni's uncles who first recognized her talent when he heard her singing along with a recording of nineteenth-century Italian composer Gaetano Donizetti's *Lucia di Lammermoor.*

Musical Beginnings

When she was ten years old, Freni made her first public appearance at a music pupils' concert, singing "Sempre libera," a difficult aria from the first act of Giuseppe Verdi's 1853 opera *La Traviata.* At age 12, she won an international contest for young singers with the aria "Un bel di" from Giacomo Puccini's *Madama Butterfly.* One of the judges, renowned tenor Beniamino Gigli, warned her that she should not begin performing before her voice was fully developed, and Freni heeded his words, spending most of her teenage years training with maestro Ettore Campogalliani of Mantua, Italy, and watching operas from the upper galleries of Modena's local opera house, the Teatro Communale.

On January 3, 1955, Freni made her stage debut at the Teatro Communale in the role of Micaela in French composer Georges Bizet's *Carmen.* Though she was an immediate success and attracted notice from scouts for major opera companies, she chose to put her career on hold after marrying Leone Magiera—an instructor at the Bologna Conservatory who would serve as her

For the Record . . .

Born Mirella Fregni, February 27, 1935, in Modena, Italy; professionally known as Mirella Freni (surname pronounced "*Fray-nee*"); daughter of Ennio (a civil servant) and Gianna (a factory worker; maiden name, Arcelli) Fregni; married Leone Magiera (a choral instructor and conductor), 1955 (divorced 1982); married Nicolai Ghiaurov (an opera singer), 1982; children: (first marriage) Micaela (daughter). *Education:* Studied with maestros Ettore Campogalliani and Leone Magiera. *Religion:* Roman Catholic.

Opera singer. Made stage debut as Micaela in *Carmen* at Teatro Communale, Modena, Italy, 1955; Glyndebourne Opera Festival debut as Zerlina in *Don Giovanni,* 1960; debuted as Nannetta in *Falstaff* at the Royal Opera, London, England, 1961, and at La Scala, Milan, Italy, 1962; made Metropolitan Opera debut as Mimi in *La Bohème,* New York City, 1965. Has also made operatic appearances at New York City's Carnegie Hall; Houston Grand Opera; Lyric Opera of Chicago; San Francisco Opera; Paris Opera; Bolshoi Opera, Moscow; Amsterdam Opera; Vienna State Opera; and Salzburg Music Festival. Starred in film adaptations of *La Bohème* and *Madama Butterfly.*

Selected awards: First prize, Concorso Viotti, 1958; Cavalier of the Great Cross, 1989.

Addresses: *Home*—Modena, Italy. *Management*—Columbia Artists Management, Inc., Wilford Division, 165 West 57th St., New York, NY 10019.

teacher and mentor for the first two decades of her career—and giving birth to their daughter, Micaela, in 1956. Word of her talent was spreading, however, bringing numerous offers of roles with smaller Italian opera houses, and in 1957 Freni, at the urging of her husband, resumed performing.

The next year Freni won first prize in the prestigious Concorso Viotti in Vercelli, Italy. The award had a catalyzing effect on her career. After a round of appearances on mid-level Italian opera stages such as those in Palermo, Bologna, Naples, and Rome, Freni appeared with the Netherlands Opera for the 1959 season. In 1960 she made her debut at the Glyndebourne Opera Festival as Zerlina in Wolfgang Amadeus Mozart's 1787 opera *Don Giovanni* and the following year debuted at the Royal Opera in London as Nannetta in Verdi's

Falstaff, a role she took on less than ten days' notice to meet a casting emergency. In 1962 she appeared again at Glyndebourne as Susanna in Mozart's *The Marriage of Figaro,* a performance that Andrew Porter of *Opera* described as "bewitching," adding, "Everything she did, vocal and dramatic, was alive, credible, and unforced."

Discovered by von Karajan

On January 9, 1962, Freni bowed for the first time at La Scala in Milan, Italy, once again as Nannetta in *Falstaff.* Then she tackled the role of Liù in Puccini's last opera, *Turandot,* during the 1962-63 season. Appearing at the most prestigious of all Italian opera houses was a considerable personal benchmark for Freni; of greater consequence was that she came to the attention of Herbert von Karajan, the reigning conductor in Milan, Berlin, and Vienna and one of the foremost maestros in the world. Von Karajan, immediately taken by Freni's stage manner and the lyric quality of her singing, played a significant part in her rise into the opera elite, serving as her mentor over the course of the next decade and pushing her to accept new and challenging roles.

At von Karajan's insistence, Freni was cast as the female lead, Mimi, in a new production of Puccini's *La Bohème.* The opera had its debut on January 31, 1963, and Freni's performance was greeted rapturously by audiences and the opera press alike. Mimi became a signature role for Freni, and her interpretation of it set a standard against which other singers attempting the role are often judged. In November of 1963 she performed the part with the State Opera in Vienna, Austria; two years later she reprised the role with the Metropolitan Opera in New York for her American debut. Critic Alan Rich of the *New York Herald Tribune* wrote of that performance: "[Her voice] is pure and fresh, operating without seam ... marvelously colored at every point by what seems to be an instinctive response to the urging of the text." Freni recorded *La Bohème* for Angel in 1964, and in 1965 starred in a Franco Zeffirelli film of the opera. The role remained her favorite throughout her career, and she continued to perform it into the 1990s.

A Career Setback

Intending to capitalize on the enthusiasm for Freni, von Karajan pushed for her to sing Violetta, the female lead in Verdi's *La Traviata,* at La Scala. Freni was reluctant at such an early point in her career to take on a role that is considered one of the most difficult in the soprano repertory, but she eventually acceded to von Karajan's urging. Her decision turned out to be a serious misjudgment. Renata Scotto, a veteran singer and favorite performer at La Scala, had originally been cast as Violetta, and her replacement by a relatively inexperienced newcomer deeply angered many Milanese opera fans. Although Freni was probably up to the demands of the role, she never had a chance to prove herself.

The opera's debut in December of 1964 degenerated into a near-riot of shouting, whistling, and disturbances in the audience, and after a single performance, Freni was replaced by Anna Moffo, another well-known soprano. The experience must have been disheartening for such a young singer, but it taught her a valuable lesson. Thereafter, Freni refused roles for which she was ill-prepared, artistically unsuited, or that she thought might overtax her voice. This approach no doubt contributed to her longevity as a singer.

Freni recovered quickly from her setback with *La Traviata*. Throughout the winter of 1964, she toured with the La Scala company in the former Soviet Union. In 1965, in addition to her debut as Mimi, she appeared as Adina in Donizetti's *L'Elisir d'Amore* at New York's Metropolitan Opera. During the 1966 season, Freni performed the roles of Marguerite in nineteenth-century French composer Charles Gounod's *Faust* and Liù from *Turandot*, both at the Metropolitan, and the following year she sang the female lead in Gounod's *Romeo et Juliette*, solidifying her reputation as a reigning queen in the transatlantic world of opera. In spite of the adulation she received in the United States, however, Freni was increasingly reluctant to spend so much time away from her family, and her portrayal of Juliette at the Metropolitan in 1968 was her last American appearance until 1976.

The Dramatic Transition

Although Freni limited herself to European performances after 1968, she was hardly idle. She had debuted at the Salzburg Festival in Austria in 1966, and it was there in 1970—again at the urging of von Karajan—that Freni made the transition to dramatic roles, in this case that of Desdemona in Verdi's *Otello*. Her move surprised audiences and critics, who had previously thought her suited only to light or "soubrette" roles. Although taking the part could have been disastrous for her career, Freni's flexibility and intuitive grasp of the demands of a dramatic role allowed her to make an easy transition. English critic Noel Goodwin, writing in *Music and Musicians*, remarked, "Her radiant innocence and tragic despair ensured that our sympathies were with her throughout. In the last act, her expressive inflection of the vocal line was deeply moving in its warmth of character."

Freni followed this success with other dramatic roles, notably Elisabeth de Valois in Verdi's *Don Carlo* in 1975 and the title role of Verdi's *Aida* in 1979. Exhibiting her usual caution in career matters, she worked on each new role for at least a year before performing it, avoiding the problems singers often face when rushing into dramatic parts without sufficient preparation.

> *The opera's debut degenerated into a near-riot of shouting, whistling, and disturbances in the audience, and after a single performance, Freni was replaced. The experience must have been disheartening for such a young singer, but it taught her a valuable lesson.*

In the summer of 1976, with her daughter grown to adulthood, Freni returned to the United States, touring with La Scala and the Paris Opera. In October of the same year, a film version of Puccini's *Madama Butterfly*—starring Freni and Spanish tenor Placido Domingo and conducted by von Karajan—was telecast as part of the *Great Performances* series. Later that fall Freni appeared at Carnegie Hall in New York for a performance of Verdi's *Requiem Mass*. The enthusiasm she left behind in 1968 was quickly revived, and Freni subsequently became a fixture on the American opera scene, appearing in such locales as Houston, San Francisco, and Chicago, as well at the Metropolitan Opera in New York.

Freni's personal life underwent a transition in tandem with her career. Her marriage to Leone Magiera gradually dissolved, and in the early 1980s they amicably divorced. In the meantime, she had fallen in love with Bulgarian bass Nicolai Ghiaurov, a frequent stage partner, and they were married shortly after Freni's divorce from Magiera was finalized. Just as Magiera helped in the development of Freni's early career, Ghiaurov strongly encouraged her to branch out in later years. It was with his help, for example, that in 1985 she undertook the role of Tatyana in Tchaikovsky's *Eugene Onegin* for the Lyric Opera of Chicago, a project she had refused in the 1970s out of reluctance to sing in Russian.

In the 1980s and early 1990s, having reached the height of her career, Freni performed widely in the United

States and Europe. She appeared in numerous television opera broadcasts, including Mozart's *The Marriage of Figaro* with Kiri Te Kanawa, Verdi's *Don Carlo* and *Aida,* both with Placido Domingo, and *La Bohème* with Luciano Pavarotti. She also continued to expand her repertory, adding the title roles in *Adriana Lecouvreur* and *Manon Lescaut,* along with other parts in *Eugene Onegin* and *La Pique Dame.* When not performing, she spent a considerable amount of time in the studio. By the mid-1990s Freni had recorded over 50 complete operas with most of the major classical record companies, including Angel/EMI, RCA, London, Philips, and Deutsche Grammophon.

As she approached the fortieth anniversary of her Modena debut, Freni remained much in demand, with a solidly booked schedule. In the 1993-94 season alone, she performed in Barcelona, London, Paris, New York, Zurich, Milan, Athens, and Lisbon. Her operatic skills are largely undiminished, thanks to judicious choices in the roles she accepts, a constant attention to not straining her voice, and a simplicity and ease of manner that has allowed her to maintain a strong rapport with her audiences and fellow performers. Freni is an audience favorite on both sides of the Atlantic, and in the mid-1990s—at an age when most singers would be contemplating their retirement—she stood on the threshold of a fifth decade at the pinnacle of the opera world.

Selected discography

Alcina, London, 1963.
La Bohème, Angel, 1964, reissued, EMI Classics, 1988.
Don Giovanni, Angel, 1966.
L'Elisir d'Amore, Angel, 1967.
Donizetti & Bellini Arias and Duets, Angel, 1967.
French and Italian Opera Arias, Angel, 1968, reissued, 1985.
Mirella Freni Sings Favorite Arias, Vanguard, 1969.
Romeo et Juliette, Angel, 1969.
L'amico Fritz, Angel, 1969.
Carmen, RCA, 1971.
Messa da Requiem, Deutsche Grammophon, 1972.
La Bohème, London, 1973.
Don Giovanni, Philips, 1973.
Madama Butterfly, PolyGram, 1974.
Mirella Freni—Arias, Angel, 1977.
Simon Boccanegra, Deutsche Grammophon, 1977.

Turandot, Angel, 1978.
Cavalleria Rusticana/Pagliacci, London, 1978.
Faust, EMI Classics, 1979.
Aida, EMI Classics, 1980.
Guglielmo Tell, Decca, 1980.
The Great Voice of Mirella Freni, London Jubilee, 1982.
Ernani, EMI Classics, 1983.
Don Pasquale, EMI Classics, 1984.
Manon Lescaut, Deutsche Grammophon, 1984.
Mefistofele, London, 1985.
La Forza del Destino, EMI Classics, 1986.
Great Sopranos of Our Time, EMI Classics, 1986.
Madama Butterfly, Deutsche Grammophon, 1988.
Otello, EMI Classics, 1988.
Don Carlos, EMI Classics, 1988.
Opera Arias (recorded 1964-67), EMI Classics, 1988.
Eugene Onegin, Deutsche Grammophon, 1988.
Carmen, Philips, 1989.
Falstaff, London, 1989.
La Traviata, Rodolphe, 1991.
La Forza del Destino: Highlights, EMI Classics, 1991.
La Pique Dame ("The Queen of Spades")—Highlights, RCA Victor Red Seal, 1992.
Tosca, Deutsche Grammophon, 1992.
Manon Lescaut, London, 1993.

Sources

Hifi/Stereo Review, October 1964.
High Fidelity & Musical America, March 1965.
Music and Musicians, June 1967; October 1970.
New York Herald Tribune, September 13, 1965.
New York Times, November 13, 1965; March 23, 1980.
Opera, autumn 1962; June 1963; April 1967; July 1972.
Opera Monthly, January 1990.
Opera News, October 1977; October 1987; September 1990.
Ovation, March 1989.
Stereo Review, September 1965; November 1990.
Time, August 3, 1981.
Variety, December 30, 1965.

Additional information for this profile was provided by Columbia Artists Management, Wilford Division, New York City, and EMI Records publicity materials, 1994.

—Daniel Hodges

Grandmaster Flash

Rap DJ

AP/Wide World Photos

Grandmaster Flash was one of the founding fathers and a true innovator of hip-hop music. Dubbed "the [conductor Arturo] Toscanini of the turntables," he pioneered the art of deejaying in the 1970s by inventing many of the scratch-mixing techniques that later became the backbone of hip-hop and rap songs. His group Grandmaster Flash and the Furious Five was one of the first rap acts to break out of the local New York rap scene and become an international success. Their groundbreaking musical and lyrical styles laid down the building blocks of modern rap and influenced virtually every rap and hip-hop artist that came after them. Grandmaster Flash was truly one of rap's first superstars, but his climb to the top was tumultuous, and his stay there was brief.

Born Joseph Saddler on January 1, 1958, in New York City, Grandmaster Flash began his career in the early 1970s as a mobile DJ spinning records at outdoor parties in the streets and parks of New York's South Bronx. Fascinated by music and audio circuitry, he aspired to do more than just play other people's music. "Most deejays at parties would simply play a record all the way to the end, but I was too fidgety to wait," Flash explained in *Rap: Portraits and Lyrics of a Generation of Black Rockers,* "so I wanted to do something to enhance the music."

Pioneered Scratching

Experimenting with two turntables and a homemade cueing system, Flash began mixing together two copies of the same record—a technique that would become the basis for all scratch mixing. He practiced his new craft for nearly a year before taking it to the streets in late 1973. It was an instant hit but with one unexpected drawback. "Half an hour into my thing, in my experimental stage, people would just start watching me," Flash told Eric Berman in a *Rolling Stone* interview. "This got me very angry. I wanted to excite the crowd, to make people dance."

Searching for a way to take some of the attention off himself while still complementing his mixing, Flash invited his friend Keith Wiggins to join him on stage. While Flash mixed, Wiggins would shout improvised rhymes to the crowd in time with the music. The arrangement clicked and Wiggins, who would later adopt the name Cowboy, became one of the first rap MCs (mike controllers).

Over the next few months, four more MCs joined Grandmaster Flash—the Glover brothers, Melvin and Nathaniel, who took the names MC Melle Mel and Kid Creole;

Rahiem (Guy Todd Williams); and Scorpio (Eddie Morris). Now six in all, they dubbed themselves Grandmaster Flash and the Furious Five and quickly became one of the hottest groups in the New York metropolitan area. They were even offered a record deal with a small local label, but Flash turned the offer down, not believing that anyone would pay money for a rap record.

First Single Caught Sugarhill's Attention

The group played to packed houses at shows around the South Bronx for the next few years but failed to gain more than local success. Then, in 1979, the world of rap music changed forever. A small New Jersey record company called Sugarhill Records released the single "Rapper's Delight" by a group called Sugarhill Gang. One of the first rap singles ever recorded and distributed, "Rapper's Delight" shot to the top of the charts. Record companies scrambled to sign hip-hop and rap acts. Flash and the Five were approached by Enjoy Records owner Bobby Robinson and asked if they wanted to make a record. This time, Flash jumped at the chance. The group quickly recorded their first single, "Super Rappin'," which was released in late 1979.

Though not as successful as "Rapper's Delight," "Super Rappin'" brought Flash and the Five to the attention of

Sugarhill Records' owner Sylvia Robinson, who bought the group's contract from Enjoy. They released their first Sugarhill single, "Freedom," in 1980. The record went gold, selling over 500,000 copies nationwide and spurring Sugarhill to send the group on a 40-city U.S. tour. The following year, Flash and the Five released two more singles on Sugarhill, "Birthday Party" and "The Adventures of Grandmaster Flash on the Wheels of Steel," both of which went gold. The latter track featured the first serious use of sampled music and sounds on a rap record.

The group's biggest success came in 1982 when Sylvia Robinson asked them to record "The Message," a song she cowrote, featuring graphic lyrics about the horrors of growing up in the streets of a crime-infested ghetto. "The Message" became known as the first "conscience rap" song and opened up rap as a medium for serious social commentary. In the United States, the single went gold in 21 days and platinum in 41 days. It also introduced Flash and the Five to an English audience, reaching Number Eight on the British charts. By then a worldwide success, the group went on tour again, this time playing shows in both the States and Europe.

Royalty Dispute Led to Split

In June of 1983 discord broke out between Flash and Sugarhill over royalty payments for "The Message." Unable to settle the dispute, Flash left Sugarhill in November and sued the label for $5 million and the right to use the group's name at another label. The suit split the members down the middle. Rahiem and Kid Creole sided with Flash; Melle Mel, Cowboy, and Scorpio sided with Sugarhill. Flash later lost the court case. He was awarded no money and retained only the right to use the name Grandmaster Flash.

In 1985 Flash signed a ontract with Elektra Records and released his first solo album, *They Said It Couldn't Be Done,* which made a one-week appearance on the UK charts at Number 95. Over the next two years Flash released two more albums on Elektra, *The Source* in 1986 and *Ba Dop Boom Bang* in 1987. Both were commercial failures.

A lack of solo commercial success forced the original lineup of Flash, Melle Mel, Rahiem, Cowboy, Kid Creole, and Scorpio to reunite as Grandmaster Flash, Melle Mel and the Furious Five in 1987 for a charity concert at New York's Madison Square Garden. The reunion sparked renewed interest in the group. The six artists began working together on new songs, including a remake of the Steppenwolf classic "Magic Carpet Ride," and released *On the Strength* on Elektra in 1988.

But the album went nowhere and the reunion failed. The group split up a second time and the members faded into relative obscurity. Depressed and despondent, Flash turned to cocaine for escape. "It really messed me up," he said later in a *Rolling Stone* interview. "I walked away from my beats. Lost touch with what I loved. I no longer had the freedom, like back in the park." With the help of his sister, Flash eventually kicked his cocaine habit and set his sights on a new profession, that of producer. "I had always wanted to put music together for other people," he said in *Rolling Stone*. In 1993 he did just that, coproducing Public Enemy DJ Terminator X's album *Super Bad*.

The resurgence of interest in "old school" rap brought Flash back to his turntables in 1994. In the spring, he toured Germany, Japan, and the United States, deejaying for rappers Whodini and Kurtis Blow. He later hooked up with MC Melle Mel to help Duran Duran record a remake of his and Mel's 1983 hit "White Lines."

When asked in an *Entertainment Weekly* interview what he thought of younger music acts remaking his songs and building on the techniques he innovated, Flash replied, "It's great that the newer artists know where it came from, because it wasn't easy. In hip-hop, the formula was set so that it could be constantly re-innovated. So I would say to the hip-hop world, don't hold back anything, because that thing that you hold back might be the next big thing."

Selected discography

With the Furious Five

"Super Rappin'," Enjoy, 1979.
"Freedom," Sugarhill, 1980.

"Birthday Party," Sugarhill, 1981.
"The Adventures of Grandmaster Flash on the Wheels of Steel," Sugarhill, 1981.
"The Message," Sugarhill, 1982.
"White Lines (Don't Do It)," Sugarhill, 1983.
On the Strength, Elektra, 1988.

Solo albums

They Said It Couldn't Be Done, Elektra, 1985.
The Source, Elektra, 1986.
Ba Dop Boom Bang, Elektra, 1987.

Sources

Books

Adler, B., and Janette Beckman, *Rap: Portraits and Lyrics of a Generation of Black Rockers*, St. Martin's, 1991.
Rees, Dafydd, and Luke Crampton, *Rock Movers & Shakers*, Billboard Books, 1991.

Periodicals

Billboard, March 26, 1988.
Entertainment Weekly, June 6, 1994.
Keyboard, November 1988.
Melody Maker, December 11, 1982; December 18, 1982; May 24, 1986; July 19, 1986; February 28, 1987.
Musician, June 1988.
Rolling Stone, September 16, 1982; May 26, 1983; December 23, 1993.
Source, November 1993.
Spin, April 1991.
Variety, March 28, 1984.

—*Thaddeus Wawro*

Grant Green

Guitarist

Archive Photos/Frank Driggs Collection

Upon winning the new star category in *Down Beat's* critics' poll in 1962, jazz guitarist Grant Green attracted national attention as a major new force in the New York jazz scene. Green's guitar style—rooted in the swing approach of Charlie Christian, the blues, and African American religious music—is renowned for its warm, inviting tone and flowing single-note lines.

Critically acclaimed for his work with small combos and organ trios, Green recorded with the finest musicians on the famous Blue Note label in sessions that often paired him with saxophonists Hank Mobley and Ike Quebec as well as organists Jack McDuff and Larry Young. Though his name has fallen into obscurity in recent years, Green is no stranger to die-hard jazz fans and musicians who regard him as one of the premier guitar talents of the 1960s.

Grant Green was born on June 6, 1931, in St. Louis, Missouri. Green's father, a guitarist versed in Muddy Waters-style blues, bought him an inexpensive Harmony guitar and amplifier at an early age. After performing in a St. Louis gospel group, Green landed his first job with an accordion player, Joe Murphy, whose repertoire included gospel, boogie woogie, and rock and roll tunes. Drawn to the sounds of bebop modernism, he began to study the music of alto saxophonist Charlie Parker. Green recalled in *Guitar Payer* that "listening to Charlie [Parker] was like listening to a different man every night." After only one year of formal study, with St. Louis musician Forrest Alcorn, Green began playing with the St. Louis bands of organist Sam Lazar and tenor saxophonist Jimmy "Night Train" Forrest, with whom Green made his recording debut on the Delmark label.

After hearing Green play in a local nightclub, jazz saxophonist and singer Lou Donaldson contacted Francis Wolff of Blue Note Records. Upon the invitation of Donaldson, Green moved to New York in 1960, and within a few months signed a contract with Blue Note. After recording an unissued date with Miles Davis's quintet in 1961, he recorded his first album as a leader, *Grant's First Stand.* The LP includes Grant's composition "Miss Anne's Tempo," a driving blues that has emerged as a guitar/organ trio classic.

Following the release of the albums *Green Street* and *Grantstand* in 1961, Green recorded *Born to Be Blue* in 1962. His 1963 release *Idle Moments,* featuring tenor-saxophonist Joe Henderson and vibraphonist Bobby Hutcherson, has been considered by many critics as one of the finest jazz guitar records of the 1960s. Throughout the decade Green became a regular session man at Blue Note, recording on such dates as trumpeter Lee Morgan's LP *Search for the New Land.*

Born June 6, 1936, in St. Louis, MO; died of a heart attack, January 31, 1979, in New York, NY. *Education:* Studied guitar with St. Louis musician Forrest Alcorn.

Played guitar with a gospel group and accordion player Joe Murphy; performed with the bands of organist Sam Lazar and saxophonist Jimmy "Night Train" Forrest; moved to New York and began a career as sideman and solo artist on the Blue Note label, 1960; recorded numerous sides for Blue Note before leaving the label in 1966; became inactive after recording for several smaller labels, late 1960s; returned to Blue Note, 1969; moved to Detroit, 1970; continued to record and make appearances, 1970s.

Awards: Named best new star in *Down Beat* critics' poll, 1962.

Grant's recordings and live performances soon made him a formidable talent on the New York music scene. While working at a club on 142nd Street, Green participated in "The Battle of the Guitars"—an impromptu jam session that often included guitarists Wes Montgomery and Detroit veteran Kenny Burrell, whom Green considered one of his favorite guitarists.

Though his career became overshadowed by the popularity of Wes Montgomery, Green remained a unique talent who, along with Montgomery and Burrell, formed the great triumvirate of postwar jazz guitar—a style exhibiting a strong swing/blues feel and advanced harmonic ideas. Green's early recordings with organist Jack McDuff, trumpeter Harry "Sweets" Edison, and Donaldson were followed, in 1964, by several sessions featuring members of John Coltrane's legendary quartet, drummer Elvin Jones and pianist McCoy Tyner. Along with Jones and Tyner, Green recorded the outstanding albums *Solid* in 1964 and *Matador* in 1965.

In the years 1964 to 1965 and 1969 to 1972, Green recorded more than 30 sessions as a leader for the Blue Note label. His work as a sideman included dates with trumpeter Lee Morgan, pianist Herbie Hancock, saxophonists Stanley Turrentine, Ike Quebec, and Hank Mobley, and most of the label's organists. In 1966 Green periodically left Blue Note to record on several labels, including Muse, Verve, and Cobblestone. Due to personal problems and the effects of drug addiction, Green became intermittently inactive from 1967 to 1969.

In an effort to find new artistic avenues outside New York, Green moved to Detroit in 1970, where he lived for over five years. Although he returned to the studio a number of times during the decade, his commercially oriented recordings failed to live up to the quality of his earlier work. While in New York to play an engagement at George Benson's Breezin' Lounge, he collapsed in his car of a heart attack and died on January 31, 1979. Survived by six children, Green was buried in his hometown of St. Louis, Missouri.

Indebted to the horn-like phrasing of his early mentor Charlie Christian, Green's guitar style is reliant on single-note phrases, rather than the chordal inflections and octave figures of his contemporaries Wes Montgomery and Kenny Burrell. As music producer/writer Bob Porter stated, as quoted in the liner notes of *Born to Be Blue,* Green had the ability to "take any good melody and make it sing." It is this inherent skill that prompted Green to record both blues-inspired originals as well as ballads written by composers from Duke Ellington to Rogers and Hammerstein.

Like so many jazzmen, Green, after a brief, meteoric career, passed from life at an early age, leaving behind a musical legacy that became overshadowed by popular music trends and rock guitar heroes. In a review of one of Green's performances nine months before the guitarist's death, Gene Gray wrote in *Down Beat,* "Green, for those who may be unaware, does things on guitar better than anyone." To fans and serious students of jazz guitar, Green stands as an integral figure among the blues-based modernists of the postwar era. More than ten years after his passing, Green's guitar work remains a testament to genius—a music filled with soulful inspiration and broad artistic vision, which over time will no doubt earn its proper place in the history of modern American music.

Selected discography

Grant's First Stand, Blue Note, 1961.
Green Street, Blue Note, 1961.
(With others) *Quebec: Blue and Sentimental,* Blue Note, 1961.
Feelin' the Spirit, Blue Note, 1962.
Am I Blue, Blue Note, 1963.
Idle Moments, Blue Note, 1963.
Street of Dreams, Blue Note, 1963.
Matador, Blue Note, 1964.
Grant Green Alive!, 1970.
Iron City, Cobblestone, 1976.
Solid, Blue Note, 1976.
The Final Comedown (film soundtrack), 1976.

Nigeria, Blue Note, 1980.
Born to Be Blue, Blue Note, 1989.
Grant Green: The Best of Grant Green, Volume 1, Blue Note, 1993.

Sources

Books

Ramsey, Doug, *Jazz Matters: Reflections on the Music and Some of Its Makers,* University of Arkansas Press, 1989.

Periodicals

Down Beat, July 19, 1962; February 17, 1972; March 22, 1979; December 25, 1979; November 1980; April 1994.
Guitar Player, January 1975.

Additional information for this profile was obtained from the liner notes to *Matador,* by Michael Cuscuna; to *Grant Green: The Best of Grant Green, Volume 1,* by Tom Evered; and to *Born to Be Blue,* by Richard Seidel.

—*John Cohassey*

Joe Henderson

Saxophonist, educator

Photograph by Susan Ragan, courtesy of Verve Records

A lasting figure on the jazz scene, tenor saxophonist Joe Henderson has quietly pursued his craft with a learned passion. A central contributor to the classic Blue Note sessions of the 1960s and a composer, bandleader, and educator through the 1970s and 1980s, he stepped out of the shadows of the industry's saxophone giants in the early 1990s, recording tributes to jazz greats Billy Strayhorn and Miles Davis. Fame finally caught up with Henderson in 1992, when his career was properly reevaluated in light of the Strayhorn disc.

The broad-minded Henderson views his performing in terms of the other creative arts. "I think of music on the bandstand like an actor relates to a role," he told Michael Bourne in a 1992 interview for *Down Beat*. "I've always wanted to be the best interpreter the world has ever seen.... The creative faculties are the same whether you're a musician, a writer, a painter. I can appreciate a painter as if he were a musician playing a phrase with a stroke, the way he'll match two colors together the same as I'll match two tones together." Henderson's synthesis of script and improvisation, of tradition and originality, epitomizes the fresh and distinctive power of great jazz art.

Born April 24, 1937, in Lima, Ohio, Henderson was one of 15 children. The range of musical taste in his family was wide; he heard one sister's opera records, another sister's Bo Diddley, and country and western on the radio. "I happened to have grown up listening to [country music legend] Johnny Cash ... as much as I did [innovative jazz saxophonist] Charlie Parker," he told Lee Hildebrand of *Request*. One of Henderson's brothers was addicted to the noted ensemble Jazz at the Philharmonic, and Henderson was thus listening to horn players Lester Young and Ben Webster at the ripe age of six—though the sax wasn't his first love. "I wanted to play drums," he explained to Bourne. "I'd be making drums out of my mother's pie pans." When Henderson was nine, his schoolteachers tested his musical abilities. "They said I'd gotten a high enough score that I could play anything, and they gave me a saxophone." He bought his first horn with money from a paper route.

Henderson's musical appreciation and exploration continued in high school, where he listened to classical composers and pianists. "I started playing in high school bands, which didn't play bebop," he revealed to Mark Gilbert in *Jazz Journal International*. Instead he trained on marches and classical music. He was prepared for the atonal, free-jazz experiments of 1960s figures like Ornette Coleman and Eric Dolphy by listening to the works of Russian-American composer Igor Stravinsky and Austrian composer Arnold Schoenberg. Henderson also befriended pianists in Lima, who intro-

For the Record . . .

Born Joseph A. Henderson, April 24, 1937, in Lima, OH. *Education:* Attended Kentucky State University, 1955, and Wayne State University, 1956-60.

Studied saxophone as a teenager, 1951-55; played professionally while in college, 1956-60; led his first band in Detroit, 1960; served in military and performed in troupe, 1960-62; moved to New York City; leader and sideman for Blue Note Records, 1963-67; signed with Milestone Records, 1967; performed briefly with Blood, Sweat and Tears, 1969; moved to San Francisco and began career as an educator, 1972; experimented with electric jazz recordings, 1971-75; left Milestone and recorded for various labels, c. 1976-84; performed and toured with Freddie Hubbard, c. 1980-83; made live recordings in traditional lineups, 1980-92; re-signed with Blue Note, 1985; *Lush Life* and *So Near, So Far* released on Verve, 1992 and 1993, respectively. *Military service:* U.S. Army, 1960-62.

Awards: Grand Prix du Disque, 1981; Grammy Award for best instrumental jazz solo, 1992; Jazz Musician of the Year, Top Tenor Saxophonist, and Record of the Year honors from *Down Beat,* 1992, for *Lush Life,* and 1993, for *So Near, So Far;* Grammy Award for best jazz instrumentalist, 1993; Jazz Record of the Year honors from the *Village Voice* and *Billboard,* 1993, for *So Near, So Far;* named Number One Jazz Artist of the Year by *Billboard,* 1993.

Addresses: *Home*—San Francisco, CA. *Record company*—Verve, Worldwide Plaza, 825 Eighth Ave., New York, NY 10019.

duced him to a range of classical piano compositions and bebop. When he was 14, he subbed for an ailing saxophonist in the Lionel Hampton Band as the group passed through town. At the same age, he traveled to a dance in Detroit and there met the immortal Charlie Parker.

Henderson attended Kentucky State University in 1955 and transferred to Detroit's Wayne State University the following year. In the four years he studied there, Detroit was a fertile city for jazz. Henderson's classmates at Wayne State included Yusef Lateef and Curtis Fuller, and he spent evenings playing with Barry Harris, Pepper Adams, Donald Byrd, and Sonny Stitt. He also met John Coltrane during this time; in 1960 Coltrane recommended Henderson as a replacement for the Miles Davis Quintet. The U.S. government beckoned, however, and Henderson was drafted. He spent two years in the U.S. Army playing with a vaudeville group called the "Rolling Along Show"—performing everywhere from the Aleutian Islands to Japan to Paris.

Blue Note and Beyond

Discharged from the army in 1962, Henderson settled in New York City and began a stellar span of session work and public gigging—often with his peers from Michigan. During his early days in New York, he played with Brother Jack McDuff, an organist whose bluesy jazz recalled occasional work Henderson found in Detroit. He next met trumpeter Kenny Dorham and formed a band that put out Dorham's *Una Mas* on Blue Note in 1963. Henderson's first recording as a leader—*Page One*—soon followed, and he was well on his way to becoming a staple member of the Blue Note roster during its peak years.

Backing the experiments of pianist Andrew Hill, the juke and funk of pianist Horace Silver, or the cool trumpet of Lee Morgan, Henderson adapted to the diverse talents of the Blue Note crew. He joined Silver's band in 1964 and toured extensively with them for two years. In 1965 he recorded with Hill, and three years later—paired with Wayne Shorter on sax and an ever-shifting rhythm section—he finally got his chance to play with Miles Davis. But the arrangement lasted only a few months.

All the while, Henderson was leading his own band, which recorded five albums for Blue Note. In the middle to late 1960s, he was also composing charts for a big band he and Dorham had created; the band met weekly during certain stretches and featured such artists as Pepper Adams, Chick Corea, Ron Carter, Curtis Fuller, and Michael and Randy Brecker.

Jazz Educator

In 1967 Henderson left Blue Note for Milestone Records. Then, in an unexpected move, he joined the successful pop/rock group Blood, Sweat and Tears for a brief sojourn in 1969. BS&T sought credibility through Henderson; he told Ray Townley in a 1975 *Down Beat* piece: "I was sort of three-in-one oil for them: I was black, I had a rep as an improvising musician, and there were soul possibilities there." But what might have been a lucrative step for Henderson simply fizzled after four months, as the band fell into disarray.

Henderson's work from the late 1960s and early 1970s revealed his increasing sense of social consciousness.

"I got politically involved in a musical way," he commented to Bourne. "Especially in the '60s, when people were trying to affect a cure for the ills that have beset this country for such a long time." He cited song titles such as 1969's "Power to the People" and 1976's "Black Narcissus" as expressions of these sentiments. This period also produced "Invitation" on 1972's *In Pursuit of Blackness,* an oft-performed signature piece.

In 1972 Henderson moved to San Francisco, continued performing, and also began life as a private instructor. Teaching, he told Michael Ullman of *Schwann Spectrum,* "is another bandstand for me"—another form of interpretation. He encourages his students to study the greats and their performances, so that each aspirant might learn to vary and alter the original. "You get so far removed from the source," he explained to Ullman, "that the solo becomes your own."

A Genius Heralded

Henderson's recordings were typically varied during the 1970s but showed some signs of electrification. *Black Is the Color* seems rock-oriented, while *The Elements* features synthesizers in an avant-garde setting. He even turned to contemporary fusion for a 1975 recording date, but his crew of jazz expatriates and fusion renegades—such as George Duke and Ron Carter—were so pleased to be playing with a traditionalist that the set, according to Henderson, sounded more like bebop than electrified crossover.

Having left Milestone in the mid-1970s, Henderson freelanced through the early 1980s—he recorded with Enja, Contemporary, and Elektra/Musician—and concentrated on his teaching. His session work turned increasingly to collaborations with trumpeter Freddie Hubbard in ensembles known as Echoes of an Era, the Griffith Park Band, and the Griffith Park Collective. In 1985 Henderson returned to Blue Note, delivering a two-volume set entitled *The State of the Tenor* that confidently defined his own mastery.

The sessions were Henderson's first recordings in a trio format, and they highlighted his virtuosity. *An Evening with Joe Henderson,* released in 1987, showed him in similar form. For the rest of the decade, he recorded live sets and seemed content with life as a musician's musician, performing at Berlin's Jazzfest in 1987, playing sideman and leader on occasional Blue Note and Red Records releases, and even touring Europe with an all-female band in 1991.

Henderson's classic and versatile approach to music-making complemented the early 1990s interest in neo-

traditional jazz, and his Verve Records debut in 1992 changed his stature considerably. The Polygram-backed label encouraged Henderson to perform a set of covers, and he chose the work of Duke Ellington collaborator Billy Strayhorn. Henderson was fulfilling his goal of becoming "Professor Emeritus at interpretation," as he put it in *Jazz Journal International.* The resulting release, *Lush Life,* was phenomenally successful, earning Henderson a Grammy Award and *Down Beat's* triple crown—jazz musician of the year, top tenor saxophonist, and record of the year—among readers *and* critics. Previously, only Ellington had achieved this feat.

> "The creative faculties are the same whether you're a musician, a writer, a painter. I can appreciate a painter as if he were a musician playing a phrase with a stroke, the way he'll match two colors together the same as I'll match two tones together."

Lush Life was the best-selling jazz instrumental disc of the year. Henderson's 1993 effort, *So Near, So Far (Musings for Miles),* a tribute to Miles Davis, was similarly conceived. The disc covers a range of the trumpeter's songs from 1947 to 1968 and features Henderson in everything from solo to quintet settings. It was similarly successful, winning another Grammy and *Down Beat's* trio of awards, as well as Number One jazz record of the year honors from the *Village Voice* and *Billboard.* In 1993 Henderson was welcomed to Washington, D.C., twice—for the inaugural celebrations of President Bill Clinton and for a June White House performance. In 1995 *Billboard's* Jeff Levenson reported that Henderson was recording another homage album, this one for Brazilian composer Antonio Carlos Jobim, who died in December of 1994. *Double Rainbow: The Music of Antonio Carlos Jobim* was due to be released in March of 1995.

Amused and slightly overwhelmed by all of the attention, Henderson refused to view his early 1990s success as a "comeback." "I'm busy doing what I've been doing all the time, for over 20 years," he told Zan Stewart in *Down Beat.* The saxophonist did become much busier with tour dates, however, and reduced his teaching load from 20 students to five. But by recording with young musicians like Stephen Scott and Renee Rosnes, he maintained his commitment to passing on jazz tradition. That tradition has been invoked, as well, in Henderson's plans to record the big-band compositions he began with Dorham in the late 1960s. By the mid-1990s, Henderson's commitment to the jazz heritage had awarded him the wider notice he so justly deserved.

Selected discography

Page One, Blue Note, 1963.
Our Thing, Blue Note, 1963.
In 'n' Out, Blue Note, 1964.
Inner Urge, Blue Note, 1966.
Mode for Joe, Blue Note, 1966.
The Kicker, Milestone, 1967.
Tetragon, Milestone, 1967.
Power to the People, Milestone, 1969.
If You're Not Part of the Solution, You're Part of the Problem, Milestone, 1971.
In Pursuit of Blackness, Milestone, 1972.
Black Is the Color, Milestone, 1973.
Joe Henderson in Japan, Milestone, 1973.
Multiple, Milestone, 1974.
The Elements, Milestone, 1974.
Canyon Lady, Milestone, 1975.
Black Narcissus, Milestone, 1976.

Barcelona, Enja, 1977.
Relaxin' at Camarillo, Contemporary, 1979.
Mirror, Mirror, MPS/Pausa, 1980.
Griffith Park Collective: In Concert, Elektra/Musician, 1982.
The State of the Tenor, volumes 1 and 2, Blue Note, 1985.
An Evening with Joe Henderson, Red, 1987.
The Best of Joe Henderson, Blue Note, 1991.
Lush Life, Verve, 1992.
The Standard Joe, Red, 1992.
So Near, So Far (Musings for Miles), Verve, 1993.
Double Rainbow: The Music of Antonio Carlos Jobim, Verve, 1995.

Sources

Down Beat, January 16, 1975; March 1992; June 1992; May 1993; June 1994; July 1994.
Jazz Journal International, August 1985.
Los Angeles Times, March 12, 1993.
Musician, April 1992; February 1994.
New York Times, September 20, 1991.
Request, March 1993; April 1993.
San Francisco Chronicle, October 25, 1989; October 24, 1993.
Schwann Spectrum, summer 1994.

—*Matthew Brown*

Bernard Herrmann

Composer, conductor

MICHAEL OCHS ARCHIVES/Venice, CA

Bernard Herrmann is considered by some music critics to be the most important film composer in the history of the medium. For more than three and a half decades, he crafted scores that integrated music with the action of a movie, thereby making background tracks more than just an auditory diversion. Herrmann was also one of the few film composers to have worked steadily as a composer and conductor outside of cinema, serving—among other posts—as guest conductor at the New York Philharmonic, Hallé Orchestra, and BBC Symphony Orchestra.

Herrmann is probably best known for his long association with esteemed motion picture director Alfred Hitchcock, having composed the scores to seven of his thrillers. Many of his works served as models for other film composers. In fact, Herrmann's chilling music for the shower scene in Hitchcock's legendary 1960 film *Psycho* may be the most imitated piece in the history of movie music; it provides an especially good example of his ability to capture the psychological and emotional intensity of movie action.

Although his parents demonstrated no particular musical talent, Herrmann revealed his at a young age. He won a prize for musical composition at 13 and after high school began training in composition and conducting. Developing his skills first at New York University and then with a fellowship at Juilliard Graduate School of Music, Herrmann studied with noteworthy teachers such as Philip James, Percy Grainger, and Albert Stoessel. While attending Juilliard, Herrmann wrote scores for ballets that were presented in the 1932 Broadway musical *Americana*.

Music Translated Complex Emotions

Around the age of 20, Herrmann established the New Chamber Orchestra, which performed concerts in New York City and at the Library of Congress. In 1934 he began a 25-year affiliation with the Columbia Broadcasting System (CBS Radio), rising to the rank of chief conductor of the CBS Symphony Orchestra in 1942. On radio, Herrmann developed a reputation for airing programs of works by lesser known, progressive composers such as Charles Ives, Constant Lambert, Frederick Delius, and Arnold Bax.

As a composer, Herrmann began writing pieces that utilized just a few players and unusual mixes of instruments. This experience served him well when he first began writing music to be used in dramatic presentations. With his concert music, he displayed an aptitude for musically transmitting complex emotions and psy-

chological states. This skill is clearly evidenced in the
highly individual music he wrote for works such as *Moby
Dick* and *Wuthering Heights.*

A critical juncture in Herrmann's career came in the late
1930s when he began writing scores for radio broadcasts on Orson Welles's Mercury Theater. Welles then
asked the composer to score his 1941 cinematic masterpiece *Citizen Kane.* Realizing Herrmann's genius,
Welles broke Hollywood precedent by allowing him on
the set to gather ideas for his music. While watching the
action, the composer made musical sketches that he
later incorporated into the film score. Welles even cut his
movie in order to accommodate some of Herrmann's
musical sequences. The result was the first of a number
of Academy Award nominations. Herrmann loved working on *Citizen Kane;* he once said, as quoted in *Listening to the Movies,* that "the film was so unusual techni-
cally ... it afforded one many unique opportunities for
musical experiments."

Herrmann's experience in composing radio scores
served him well in the movies. One of his greatest assets
was an extraordinary sense of timing that made it almost
unnecessary for him to use cue marks for scoring

passages in a film. Following up on his success with
Citizen Kane, Herrmann proceeded to win the Academy
Award for best score on his very next film, 1941's *The
Devil and Daniel Webster* (also known as *All That Money
Can Buy*). Before long he had gained notice for creating
music that meshed ideally with film themes but was also
worth listening to on its own.

Turning out yet another acclaimed score for Welles's
1942 film *The Magnificent Ambersons,* Herrmann earned
himself a spot in the highest ranks of movie composers.
He was sometimes compared to other giants of movie
music such as Miklos Rosza, who also had the ability to
heighten the intensity of suspenseful scenes. Over the
years, Herrmann became noted for his orchestral variety and short impressionistic phrases, which marked a
contrast to the scores of more melodic film composers
of the 1940s and 1950s, including Max Steiner and
Victor Young. He often utilized shifts from major chords
to minor chords in two-note themes, thereby creating a
sense of foreboding.

Required Complete Control

Despite being in constant demand as a film composer,
Herrmann limited his output to about one film score per
year during his career. One of the few composers
working in film who insisted on doing his own orchestrations, he required complete control over his music.
Herrmann greatly resented any interference from both
producers and directors; according to *Listening to the
Movies,* he felt that producers "of a ... film will pander in
the score to the lowest common denominator," and
added, "If you were to follow the taste of most directors,
the music would be awful."

Herrmann was very selective in his choice of instrumentation, always trying to find the perfect match for the
emotion of a given scene. He continually experimented
with instruments in his scoring and made the most of
recording technology to heighten the sounds of certain
instruments. His use of electric violin and electric bass
in the 1951 sci-fi drama *The Day the Earth Stood Still* was
one of the first times electronic music was implemented
in a film score; soon other composers were following his
precedent. While Herrmann often returned to musical
themes he had used in previous films, he would frequently incorporate new orchestrations.

Herrmann's greatest fame as a film composer resulted
from his association with Alfred Hitchcock. Once brought
together, the pair maintained a relationship that spanned
eight films over nine years. Although both men were
uncompromising in their creative visions, they shared
sensibilities that solidified their alliance. Donald Spoto

wrote in *The Dark Side of Genius* that "Hitchcock and Herrmann shared a dark, tragic sense of life, a brooding view of human relationships, and a compulsion to explore aesthetically the private world of the romantic fantasy."

Their partnership resulted in some of the most intense music ever heard in films, with Herrmann often using atonal devices to support the unique eeriness of Hitchcock's movies. He succeeded in sustaining the dream mode that pervades 1958's *Vertigo* and two years later crafted one of the scariest string compositions ever for *Psycho.* Herrmann also served as sound consultant on Hitchcock's 1963 frightfest *The Birds* and wrote music for the television show *Alfred Hitchcock Presents.*

Refused to Embrace Pop

Creative differences over the score for *Marnie,* released in 1964, ended the collaborative relationship between Hitchcock and Herrmann. The director complained that Herrmann had not given him a pop song that he wanted for the film, and Herrmann shot back that he did not write pop music. While Herrmann had successes scoring fantasy films such as *Fahrenheit 451* in the 1960s, his inability or unwillingness to shift into the pop direction, which was gaining favor at the time, caused a decline in his appeal. He moved to London in the mid-1960s and remained a resident of England for the rest of his life, working on both recording and composing.

Herrmann's style of music made a comeback in the 1970s, when he was hired to write scores for top directors such as Brian De Palma and Martin Scorsese. Working relentlessly despite failing health and the warnings of doctors, Herrmann died on Christmas Eve of 1975, right after he had finished conducting the score for Scorsese's *Taxi Driver.*

While Herrmann was highly critical of film music in general throughout his life, he scoffed at critics who thought it unworthy of serious composers. "A film score will live longer than any other kind of music," he was quoted as saying in *Listening to the Movies.* Demonstrating a rare ability to capture and heighten shifts of emotion and mood in subtle yet effective ways, Bernard Herrmann may very well have been the most influential of all American film composers.

Selected compositions

Film scores

Citizen Kane, 1941.

The Devil and Daniel Webster (also known as *All That Money Can Buy*), 1941.
The Magnificent Ambersons, 1942.
Jane Eyre, 1944.
Anna and the King of Siam, 1946.
The Ghost and Mrs. Muir, 1947.
The Day the Earth Stood Still, 1951.
The Snows of Kilimanjaro, 1952.
The Man Who Knew Too Much, 1956.
The Man in the Gray Flannel Suit, 1956.
A Hatful of Rain, 1957.
Vertigo, 1958.
The Naked and the Dead, 1958.
North by Northwest, 1959.
Journey to the Center of the Earth, 1959.
Psycho, 1960.
Cape Fear, 1962.
Marnie, 1964.
Fahrenheit 451, 1967.
Sisters, 1973.
Taxi Driver, 1976.

Other

Currier and Ives (suite), 1935.
Nocturne and Scherzo, 1936.
Symphony No. 1, 1940.
Fiddle Concerto, 1940.
Moby Dick (cantata), 1940.
Johnny Appleseed (cantata), 1940.
Wuthering Heights (opera), 1941.
The Fantasticks (for vocal quartet and orchestra), 1944.
A Christmas Carol (opera for television), 1954.
Echoes (for string quartet), 1966.
Souvenirs de Voyage (clarinet quintet), 1967.

Selected discography

Bernard Herrmann, Decca, 1975.
The Mysterious Film World of Psycho, Unicorn, 1975.
Sisters, Entr'acte, 1975.
Taxi Driver, Arista, 1976.

Sources

Books

The Faber Companion to 20th Century Popular Music, edited by Phil Hardy and Dave Laing, Faber, 1990.
Karlin, Fred, *Listening to the Movies: The Film Lover's Guide to Film Music,* Schirmer Books, 1994.
The New Grove Dictionary of Music and Musicians, Volume 8, edited by Stanley Sadie, Macmillan, 1980.

Slonimsky, Nicholas, *Baker's Biographical Dictionary of Musicians,* eighth edition, Schirmer Books, 1992.

Spoto, Donald, *The Dark Side of Genius: The Life of Alfred Hitchcock,* Little, Brown, 1983.

Thomas, Tony, *Film Score: The Art & Craft of Movie Music,* Riverwood Press, 1991.

Periodicals

Films in Review, June 1970; March 1976.
New York Times Magazine, March 28, 1976.

—Ed Decker

Hole

Rock band

As the late Kurt Cobain was to Nirvana, his widow, Courtney Love, is to the rock group Hole, although many critics tend to focus more on her flamboyant personality than on her musicianship. Love, the band's lead singer, songwriter, and guitarist, is truly the image of the "bad girl of rock." Every interview with her seems to be pockmarked with profanity, though it is profanity eloquently stated. In spite of her outspoken nature, exhibitionist behavior, outrageous appearance, and alleged drug use, she comes off as articulate, intelligent, utterly entertained by the culture she is enmeshed in—and very angry at it, too. With Love as its driving force, Hole has emerged as a provocative mainstay on the rock scene. As Billy Corgan—Smashing Pumpkins singer and Love's former boyfriend—put it in *Entertainment Weekly,* "No girl rock band has come close to [Hole's] fury."

Hole reportedly takes its name from two sources: Love's mother's maxim "You can't walk around with a big hole inside yourself" and the line "There's a hole that pierces right through me," from Greek dramatist Euripides's

Photograph by Kevin Cummins, © 1994 Geffen Records, Inc.

For the Record . . .

Members include **Melissa Auf Der Maur** (born March 17, 1972, in Montreal, Canada; joined group 1994), bass; **Jill Emery** (bandmember 1989-93), bass; **Eric Erlandson** (founding member; born January 9, 1963, in Los Angeles, CA) guitar; **Courtney Love** (founding member; born July 9, 1964, in San Francisco, CA; raised in Eugene, OR; daughter of Linda Carroll [a therapist] and Hank Harrison [an author and publisher]; married James Moreland [a musician], 1989 [divorced 1990]; married Kurt Cobain [a musician], 1992 [died of self-inflicted gunshot wounds, April 5, 1994]; children: [with Cobain] Frances Bean), vocals, guitar; **Kristen Pfaff** (joined group 1993; born in 1967; died of a heroin overdose, June 1994), bass; **Caroline Rue** (bandmember 1989-92) drums; **Patty Schemel** (born April 24, 1967, in Seattle, WA; joined group mid-1992), drums.

Love formed band with Erlandson, Emery, and Rue in Los Angeles in 1989; relocated to Seattle, WA; released *Pretty on the Inside* on independent label, Caroline, 1991; band re-formed; released *Live Through This,* DGC, 1994.

Awards: Gold record for *Live Through This,* 1994.

Addresses: *Record company*—David Geffen Company, 9130 Sunset Blvd., Los Angeles, CA 90069.

tragedy *Medea.* The group was formed in Los Angeles in late 1989 after Love sought bandmembers through an ad in the *Recycler,* an L.A. weekly featuring free ads. She, guitarist Eric Erlandson, bass player Jill Emery, and drummer Caroline Rue went on to record Hole's debut album, *Pretty on the Inside,* which was released by independent label Caroline in 1991. While *Entertainment Weekly* contributor David Browne found *Pretty on the Inside* "mostly an excuse for Love to throw a musical temper tantrum," David Fricke, writing in *Rolling Stone,* deemed the album "a classic of sex-mad self-laceration, hypershred guitars and full-moon brawling."

After *Pretty on the Inside,* Hole re-formed, adding drummer Patty Schemel and bass player Kristen Pfaff to original members Love and Erlandson. (Pfaff would die of a heroine overdose in June of 1994.) The band's second full-length effort, *Live Through This,* came out in April of 1994, just days after a stunned rock world learned of Cobain's suicide. Only a few months after its release, the album had sold four times as many copies

as *Pretty on the Inside,* according to *Entertainment Weekly.*

A few critics missed the rawness of *Pretty on the Inside* when confronted with the more conventional accomplishments of *Live Through This. Melody Maker*'s Everett True mourned—even while he appreciated—the change. "Hole 1993 are (whisper it) a polished, accomplished rock band, brimming with carefully fashioned hooks and choruses," he wrote ruefully. Fricke, however, saw progress and noted that *Live Through This* is "prettier on the outside, with a greater emphasis on crushed-velvet guitar distortions and liquid poppish strumming.... Love and Hole [have] managed to harness the ugliness that drove *Pretty on the Inside* to a more controlled but still cutting extreme."

Love seems to spend considerable time honing her image and defending herself against that image. Her self-proclaimed "Kinder-whore look"—"white skin, red lips, blond hair with black roots," and "either ripped dresses from the thirties or one-size-too-small velvet dresses from the sixties," as described by *Vanity Fair*'s Lynn Hirschberg—has proven to be a big hit on the West Coast. In fact, the singer's unusual style and wild exploits have been sparking frenzied media coverage since the early 1990s. But Love's background as a stripper, rumors of her alleged heroin use while pregnant with her daughter, coverage of her sometimes stormy marriage to Cobain and their well-publicized trips to detoxification facilities, and finally Cobain's suicide have all detracted from Hole as a group.

Indeed, with the press so sharply focused on Love, Hole has had a hard time establishing its own identity as a musical unit. Appreciation for the band's dynamics notwithstanding, it is Love who continues to draw the most attention—for her unabashed sexuality, her distinctive sound, and her reputation as a creative powerhouse. *Entertainment Weekly*'s Browne characterized Love's voice as "a thick, reedy instrument that makes her sound like the younger, brattier sister of Johnny Rotten," and added, "She has charisma and attitude to burn." Fricke commented: "The sheer force of Love's corrosive, lunatic wail—not to mention the guitar-drum wrath unleashed in its wake—is impressive stuff."

Love's complex personality comes through in her lyrics. Her aspirations are far from casual: the singer-songwriter told Kim Neely of *Rolling Stone* that she aims "to have some sort of emotional impact that transcends time." Love has been praised by a number of critics for her honest, insightful, and intelligent lyrics—many autobiographical, and nearly all astute commentary. On "Asking for It" from *Live Through This,* for instance, she comments on the place of women in today's culture, stating: "Every time that I sell myself to you / I feel a little bit cheaper than I need to." Charles Aaron noted in *Spin* that Love "constantly plays patty-cake with the idea that she deserves everything she gets, good or bad."

For Fricke and many others, Courtney Love serves as the notorious queen of the perilous world of rock, representing both strength and anger alongside vulnerability. She claims that the influences of female rock pioneers Patti Smith and Chrissie Hynde "saved my life," according to an article by Lorraine Ali in *Entertainment Weekly*. Fricke stated that even before gaining fame via Cobain, "Love was the scarred beauty ... of underground-rock society, a fearless confessor and feedback addict, ... part ravaged baby doll, part avenging kamikaze angel." *Newsweek's* Karen Schoemer, however, wrote that Love is "no feminist," adding, "her rabid quest for attention in any form fulfills too many archaic female stereotypes."

Schoemer also noted, "There's only one band that can be credited with turning around the listless course of rock music in the '90s, and it's not Hole—it's Nirvana." Still, Hole is getting plenty of MTV airplay and *Live Through This* has gone gold. Furthermore, *Spin's* Craig Marks mentioned that the band is talking about performing at the 1995 version of the annual alternative rockfest Lollapalooza. To attest to the group's popularity, Marks also reported on the variety of celebrities that showed up at Hole's sold-out gig at the Hollywood Palladium, including actress Juliette Lewis and former Beatle Ringo Starr.

Courtney Love's still-young biography is disturbingly typical in the world of rock. Her story will forever be written with Kurt Cobain's. In response to suggestions that she thrives on music-world publicity, Love rhetorically asked Tom Sheehan of *Melody Maker,* "I saw something I wanted, and I got it.... What is so f——ing

bad about getting what you want?" One suspects that she—and Hole, if they can hold on—will continue to get what they want.

Selected discography

Rat Bastard (EP), Sympathy for the Record Industry, 1990.
"Dicknail" (single), Sub Pop, 1991.
Pretty on the Inside, Caroline, 1991.
"Beautiful Son" (single), City Slang, 1993.
Live Through This, DGC, 1994.

Sources

Boston Phoenix, April 8, 1994.
Entertainment Weekly, April 15, 1994; July 8, 1994; August 12, 1994.
Los Angeles Times, April 10, 1994.
Melody Maker, April 3, 1993; July 24, 1993; December 4, 1993; January 29, 1994; February 19, 1994.
Metro Times (Detroit), April 4, 1994.
Newsweek, April 11, 1994; February 6, 1995.
People, May 2, 1994; May 23, 1994; July 4, 1994.
Request, May 1994.
Rolling Stone, December 23, 1993-January 6, 1994; April 21, 1994; June 2, 1994; August 11, 1994; November 3, 1994; November 17, 1994; December 15, 1994.
Spin, May 1994; February 1995.
Vanity Fair, September 1992.

Additional information for this profile was obtained from David Geffen Company publicity materials, 1994.

—*Diane Moroff*

House of Pain

Rap trio

House of Pain's lead rapper, Everlast, told *Melody Maker*'s Andrew Smith, "There's been a lot of people that have come up to us and said that we're the first white rap group they can really believe in." Aside from achieving an unusual fame within the confines of rap, the three men in House of Pain have illustrated that the initially African-American form of expression called hip-hop has grown beyond its birth in black neighborhoods to cross racial boundaries.

But Everlast learned that hip-hop didn't cross over easily to white musicians. As with its African-American origin, it still needed the frame of a well-defined and easily characterized national identity. So House of Pain gave their hip-hop the character of the American Irish, the community that had taken root in American cities over a century ago and wove itself into the fabric of the country's culture—much as emancipated African slaves did.

Erik Schrody and Daniel O'Connor, known as Everlast and Danny Boy, each made earlier attempts at the music industry before they discovered a pot of gold in their ethnic heritage. Born in the early 1970s, both claimed their Irish heritage from their grandparents' immigration and both had some experience of cohesive Irish communities in Long Island and Brooklyn, New York. Everlast's father was a construction worker; Danny Boy identified his as "a drunk" to Smith. "I'm not kidding," he added. "He was a criminal, but I never really knew him, he was always locked up in one jail or another." Through separate family moves, both ended up in the San Fernando Valley outside of Los Angeles around the age of 11. The San Fernando Valley turned out to be a suburban sprawl with points of reference—like the freeway and the mall—that have little to do with history or identity.

Everlast and Danny Boy became one another's only significant white friend in high school; otherwise, they found themselves most at home with the black students at Taft High School. Everlast told Smith that rap "was just something you did where we grew up. You had to have a rap if you wanted to hang." Several of Everlast's friends knew Ice-T, one of the gurus of the genre known as gangsta rap, and one of those friends took Everlast's rap demo to Ice-T. "Ice-T said he'd like to meet me," Everlast told Julian Dibbell in an interview with *Details*. "Then they told him I was white, and he said he *really* wanted to meet me."

Soon, Everlast was recording an album under the auspices of the Rhyme Syndicate, Ice-T's subsidiary label on Warner Bros. Released in 1990, the album made little or no impression. Dubbing the effort "hip-hop lite," Dibbell noted that "the rapper was packaged as a boxer with a Sean Penn pout and greased back locks." Clearly, the generic white rapper image wouldn't be Everlast's ticket to fame.

Pals Paired Up for Hip-Hop

Subsequent to that tepid recording effort, Everlast migrated toward collaborating with Danny Boy, who decided to try hip-hop after some work with a local punk band. Danny Boy, described by *Details'* Dibbell as "a [rap group] Beastie Boys-worshipping skate punk," had become familiar with Los Angeles's Mexican gangs after a stay in juvenile detention at 16, and he knew the inner-city culture well through that route. "Most of what I've learned has been from people, not books," Danny Boy told *Musician's* Smith, adding, "I always admired the slick talkers and the criminals, you know, people who'd beaten the system. People who worked their asses off and got away with it. I mean I've never had an honest job in my life: there have been lots of jobs, but none that lasted. I don't mind hard work, but why work to make someone else rich when I'm getting nothing out of it."

One of Danny Boy's jobs included working in a record store warehouse; he simultaneously supplemented his income with stolen credit scams, which he shared with Everlast. Everlast expressed a similar feeling to Smith, though with a slightly more deliberate political edge: "How am I s'posed to appreciate the work ethic in a country that's telling me I'll make more money being a drug dealer or a mailman or a garbage collector than if I wanted to be a teacher?"

Everlast and Danny Boy teamed up with a deejay known as D.J. Lethal, or Leor DiMant, whose forebears came from nowhere near Ireland: his Jewish parents had emigrated from Latvia. Like Everlast and Danny Boy, his early years were characterized by rebelliousness. He didn't last in Hebrew school to the age of five, since he put classmates in the garbage can and, as he told Dibbell, threw "their yarmulkes up on the roof like Frisbees." Nonetheless, the trio began carving an image that drew on Everlast and Danny Boy's heritage, and they had their first official jam as House of Pain in 1990.

Catchy Single Jumped Onto Charts

House of Pain's first single, "Jump Around," succeeded at combining cutting-edge hip-hop fashion with abundant references to Irish-American tradition. The makeover worked. "House of Pain unabashedly borrow a pose from hard-ass rappers like Ices Cube and -T, yet claim their own gangster birthright as well—the shit-kicking, liquor-soaked, hoodlum stereotype of Irish-American urban folklore," *Details'* Dibbell wrote of the "Jump Around" video.

After an extended life on the college radio and underground rap circuit, "Jump Around" broke spectacularly into the mainstream. The reviewers raved, hip-hop fans took more than a million copies home from the stores by that fall, and a hardcore rap following in Ireland revealed itself. By the fall of 1992 the single was a common sight in the Top Five in *Billboard's* Hot 100 Singles. Noting that the "song wasn't ever intended for pop radio," Everlast told *Billboard's* Gil Griffin that "When I was watching MTV and saw our video as one of the top five, then saw our single in the Top Five on the pop charts, I bugged."

When the debut album, also called *House of Pain,* was released in 1992, Dibbell noted that "everything is dosed incongruously with nods to corned beef and cabbage, Mickeys and Guiness [beer], the luck of the Irish, and assorted other too-ra loo-ra loo-ralisms." "Jump Around" appeared in the midst of songs with titles like "Shamrocks and Shenanigans" and "Top O' the Morning to Ya." *Rockpool's* reviewer declared the album "one of the best debuts out in a long time, not to mention one of the five best albums of the year," characterizing it as "an extremely raw record that kicks you upside the head." One of the few dissenting voices came from England, where *Melody Maker's* Stephen Trousse panned the album at the end of the year. "Aesthetically paltry, morally repugnant," Trousse declared, "little more than an ugly, pathetic emerald bile. One for the little people." Nonetheless, the album went platinum.

A European tour in the fall took the outfit to Dublin, where they discovered the effect they had on Irish youth. "We played at a pub called the Dublin Castle Inn, in front of 200 people," Everlast told Griffin. "Kids came up to me and said, 'Welcome home,' and brought me gifts. One even handed me a small stuffed leprechaun. We got so many gifts I started to feel like a game show host."

> *"There's been a lot of people that come up to us and said that we're the first white rap group they can really believe in."*
> —Everlast

The trio pursued many other tours in the years that followed, one of which combined them with some of the other highly successful non-black rap bands: Cypress Hill, Funkdoobiest, and the Whooliganz. Danyel Smith, writing for *Rolling Stone* in 1993, noted Everlast's live power: "his cartoonish crazed-convict look and demeanor honed to a science ... fired up the crowd with his hoarse, desperate rhymes."

Between the first and second albums House of Pain managed about a half dozen tours, sharing the bill with groups like Public Enemy and L7. The bandmembers also have pursued non-musical avenues. Everlast appeared in a role in the film *Judgment Night* and is involved in an independent film called *Lowball,* and he started a business venture with Danny Boy and actor Mickey Rourke: House of Pizza. Danny Boy is also scheduled to costar in a gangster film, *Bullet,* with Rourke, while DJ Lethal has been producing numerous up-and-coming bands.

House of Pain all have other interests, but they have continued to record with the band. *Spin's* Chuck Eddy declared that their 1994 release, *Same As It Ever Was,* "feels more punk overall" than their self-titled debut, and Dimitri Ehrlich in *Entertainment Weekly* deemed the release "consistently more innovative—and funky" than the prior effort. And although the trio has been compared to another white rap act with a punk rock background, the wildly successful Beastie Boys, *Vibe's* Tom Sinclair noted that "while the Beastie Boys' music has evolved into a more ambiguous sound, House of Pain have kept the hardcore beats that put them on the charts." House of Pain's second LP has its share of requisite rap topics such as guns and gangs, but it reveals a lighter side—also witnessed on the first al-

bum—with mentions of pop culture personalities as diverse as Ruth Buzzi, Phil Collins, and Henry Rollins.

The Irish theme in House of Pain's lyrics and logo has been a source of debate. "They're playing the Irish card to the full—the group logo is a shamrock," *Melody Maker's* Smith noted, adding, "and I admit to entertaining the notion that this might be a gimmick." House of Pain's success has been, as Griffin noted, "an issue for fans and critics alike." The issue straddles two points of contention: the authenticity of the band's much-touted "Irishness" and the appropriateness of rap as a medium of expression for white youth. "The media has questioned how Irish we are," Everlast confessed to Griffin. "The Irishness is just something Danny Boy and I had in common and we just brought it out in our music. I guess we fit one major Irish stereotype in that we drink and get loud and rambunctious, but we don't perpetuate that stereotype in our music."

In an interview with *Spin's* Jonathan Bernstein, Everlast confessed that "People always say, 'You guys are bringing a bad name to the Irish, you're reinforcing stereotypes.'" Ultimately, House of Pain's claim to Irishness may express a loss of any meaningful connection with ethnic identity, which is also part of their ability to appropriate meaningful African-American forms of expression. *Details'* Dibbell attributed the phenomenon to Los Angeles, "the rootless sprawl, a postmodern exile from any sort of fixed identity, a place where kids like Everlast play with race like it was a box of Tinkertoys, reinventing themselves on the fly."

"Broke the Rules for White Boys"

Declaring that "House of Pain have broken the rules of engagement for white boys on hip-hop turf," Dibbell argued that "While other wannabes have tiptoed softly around their own lack of color ... House of Pain come on very hard *and* very white." Everlast echoed the comment himself, telling Dibbell, "Well, I do have some white pride. I don't believe in white supremacy or anything like that. But I have pride in what I am: I'm a white guy. A white, Irish guy." In retrospect, Everlast argued that he adopted rap as his vehicle for expressing that ethnic identity. "It's like when a regular kid from the Bronx is rhymin', he's talking about where his ancestors came from. That's all we're doing, letting people know what our background is," he explained to Bernstein.

Carol Cooper, writing for the *Village Voice,* found some constructive possibility in House of Pain's musical caricatures. "HOP know that if you want better transracial relations, you better straighten out intragroup psychoses first," she argued, adding that *House of Pain* is largely street-corner philosophy on the theme of needing to understand and love yourself before you can love others." More specifically, she sensed that "they resurrect all the derogative epithets for impoverished Caucasians in 'One for the Road' much the way Black rappers use 'nigger' among themselves. By deflating and defanging the entire concept of being 'white trash,' HOP invent their own form of remedial social work."

Selected discography

House of Pain (includes "Jump Around," "Shamrocks and Shenanigans," and "Top O' the Morning to Ya"), Tommy Boy, 1992.
Same As It Ever Was, Tommy Boy, 1994.

Sources

Billboard, October 31, 1992.
Details, November 1992.
Entertainment Weekly, July 8, 1994.
Melody Maker, October 10, 1992; December 12, 1992.
Rockpool, August 1, 1992; November 11, 1993.
Rolling Stone, October 29, 1992.
The Source, June 1992.
Spin, November 1992; January 1994.
Vibe, September 1994.
Village Voice, September 8, 1992.

Additional information for this profile was obtained from Tommy Boy Records publicity materials.

—*Ondine E. Le Blanc*

Mark Isham

Composer, instrumentalist

It is not surprising that versatile composer and recording artist Mark Isham, born into a family of musicians in New York City, chose to pursue a career in music. Both of his parents played violin professionally, and Isham began studying classical piano, violin, and trumpet as a child. By the age of 12, he performed his debut as a professional trumpet player with a small symphony orchestra.

When Isham started high school, he expanded his musical interests into jazz. While in his late teens, he and his family moved to the San Francisco Bay area, where Isham played trumpet with the Oakland Symphony Orchestra, San Francisco Symphony, San Francisco Opera, and a diverse range of contemporary jazz and rock bands. He performed with the Beach Boys, Esther Phillips, Charles Lloyd, Horace Silver, Pharoah Sanders, and Dave Liebman, then recorded and toured with the Sons of Champlin. Before long, Isham discovered yet another area of music—electronics. "It was about '74 or '75," the musician recalled in *Billboard*. "I had joined the Sons of Champlin, and it was there that I found

Courtesy of Vector Management

Born in New York, NY; son of professional violin players; married Margaret Johnstone.

Made debut as professional trumpet player at the age of 12; moved to San Francisco as a teenager and performed with the Oakland Symphony Orchestra, San Francisco Symphony, San Francisco Opera, and area bands; performed with artists Rubisa Patrol, 1976-78; Group 87, 1979-84; and Van Morrison, 1980-1983; signed with Windham Hill Records, recorded first solo LP, *Vapor Drawings,* and scored first film, *Never Cry Wolf,* 1983.

Awards: Grammy Award nomination for *Castalia* and Los Angeles Critics Award for best score for *The Moderns,* both 1988; Grammy Award nomination for *Tibet;* Grammy Award, 1991, for best New Age artist; Academy Award nomination for best film score, 1993, for *A River Runs Through It.*

Addresses: *Management*—Vector Management, P.O. Box 128037, Nashville, TN 37212.

the impetus to go out and buy one of the first ARP Odysseys [music equipment]."

In 1976 Isham joined pianist Art Lande to form an acoustic ensemble called Rubisa Patrol, and they released a self-titled album on ECM Records. Two years later, Rubisa Patrol recorded *Desert Marauders* on ECM. "That became the first really exciting learning experience for me," Isham remarked in *Down Beat* about working with Rubisa Patrol. "The whole way that band worked together was at a much higher level than anything else I had done before."

Isham performed with Van Morrison as a member of the musician's stage and studio bands on the 1979 album *Into the Music.* Along with guitarist Peter Maunu, synthesist Patrick O'Hearn, and drummer Terry Bozzio, Isham formed the fusion band Group 87 that same year. The band released their self-titled debut on Columbia Records in 1980, on which they explored strict composition and veered away from improvisation.

Van Morrison asked Isham to make return appearances on his subsequent releases *Common One* and *Beautiful Vision* in 1980 and 1982, respectively. But in 1983, Isham made the move from sideman to leader with debuts in two genres. He released his first solo LP on Windham Hill Records, *Vapor Drawings,* then received his first credit as a film composer for the music in Caroll Ballard's film *Never Cry Wolf.*

More Forays Into Film Scoring

Isham next joined Van Morrison on two more albums—*Inarticulate Speech of the Heart* and *Live at the Belfast Opera House.* This time, however, Isham collaborated with Morrison on some of the songwriting. Though Isham had garnered a fair amount of writing and performing credits, financial success had yet to hit. At the time, the musician lived in a leaky, two-bedroom basement apartment in Sausalito, California, working as hard as he could to make things happen.

Group 87 released their second album in 1984, *A Career in Dada Processing,* on Capitol Records. Isham also scored music for the films *Mrs. Soffel* and *The Life and Times of Harvey Milk,* which won an Academy Award for best documentary. He also created a new partnership with Japanese singer David Sylvian on the album *Brilliant Trees.*

By 1985 Isham had done enough film scoring that Windham Hill Records decided to release some of his compositions on the compilation *Film Music.* A year later, Island released his score for the movie *Trouble in Mind* on a soundtrack. Isham also provided music for *The Hitcher.*

After Isham had produced two solo albums for Art Lande, the two decided to renew their performing partnership on a duo recording called *We Begin* in 1987. Isham also composed the music for *Made in Heaven,* released as a soundtrack on Elektra Records. Then, adding more work to his already active year, he teamed up with David Sylvian once again for the album *Secrets of the Beehive* and collaborated with David Torn on *Cloud About Mercury.*

Formally Recognized at Last

Moving to a record company with bigger distribution, Isham came out with his next solo LP on Virgin Records, *Castalia,* which received a Grammy Award nomination in 1988. Success had finally arrived, but Isham didn't slow down. "I don't suffer from these new diseases they're dreaming up about yuppie workaholism," Isham told Chris Morris in *Billboard.* "I just enjoy it. For a long time, I didn't [make] any inroads into the mainstream or even [earn enough money] to pay the rent on time. In the last five or six years, that has changed. And I'm relishing the fact that it's changed."

Isham scored the music for the film *The Moderns,* which was released by Virgin Records and won the 1988 Los Angeles Critics Award for best score. Working continually as always, Isham also scored *The Beast,* a movie based on the former Soviet Union's incursion into Afghanistan. A review of the album in *Keyboard* noted, "*The Beast* aches with the sorrow of war, tempered by Asian vocal modalities and instrumentation. Yet, Isham blends these disparate elements into a linear flow, suggesting that the emotions underlying all the musics of the world are deeper than the stylistic differences his vision so easily absorbs."

Isham continued his collaborations, working with Patrick O'Hearn on *Ancient Dream, Rivers Gonna Rise,* and *Eldorado,* and with Was (Not Was) on their *What' Up Dog?* album. Also in 1989, Isham worked with XTC on *Oranges and Lemons.*

Isham released his next solo album on Windham Hill, *Tibet,* which earned the musician a Grammy Award nomination. In 1990 he returned with another album on Virgin Records, called simply *Mark Isham,* which included guest performances from Tanita Tikaram and Chick Corea. With the songs on his self-titled LP, Isham strove to close the gap between popular music and alternative progressive music.

A Tireless Worker and Genre Jumper

Isham continued his film scoring with the composition for *Reversal of Fortune,* and in 1990, the American Film Critics named him, along with Ennio Morricone and John Williams, one of their three choices for the best film music of the 1980s. "It's something that seemed very natural to me," Isham commented in *Billboard,* referring to his film work, "and the way I think about music—what I ask the musical experience to be, what I ask myself to put into music and ask music to then pass on to the audience. There's a relationship to size and space and scope and depth and color."

Isham returned to the group format when he launched the Mark Isham Jazz Band to provide him with an outlet to play acoustic jazz again. Then, in 1991—the same year he earned a Grammy Award for best new age artist—he released another solo album on Windham Hill Records, *Songs My Children Taught Me.* Isham had originally written the four suites that make up the LP for a series of children's audio and video recordings based on classic children's stories. He assembled different groups to invoke different periods and cultures from ancient China to Renaissance England.

Throughout the early to mid-1990s, Isham focused mainly on film scoring. He wrote the music for the motion pictures *Point Break, Crooked Hearts, Mortal Thoughts, Freejack, Billy Bathgate, Little Man Tate, Fire in the Sky,* and *Made in America* and received a 1993 Academy Award nomination for the music to *A River Runs Through It.* Traversing genres and mediums, Isham continued generating music at a startling rate. His love for music has seen him through tireless work in the industry and myriad experiments with sound and direction.

Selected discography

(With Rubisa Patrol) *Rubisa Patrol,* ECM, 1976.
(With Rubisa Patrol) *Desert Marauders,* ECM, 1978.
Vapor Drawings, Windham Hill, 1983.
(With Group 87) *A Career in Dada Processing,* Capitol, 1984.
Film Music, Windham Hill, 1985.
Trouble in Mind, Island, 1986.
(With others) *Made in Heaven,* Elektra, 1987.
(With Art Lande) *We Begin,* 1987.
The Beast, A&M, 1988.
Castalia, Virgin, 1988.
The Moderns, Virgin, 1988.
Tibet, Windham Hill, 1989.
Mark Isham, Virgin, 1990.
Reversal of Fortune, Milan America, 1991.
Songs My Children Taught Me, Windham Hill, 1991.

Composer of numerous film scores, including *Never Cry Wolf, Mrs. Soffel, The Life and Times of Harvey Milk, Trouble in Mind, The Hitcher, Made in Heaven, The Moderns, The Beast, Reversal of Fortune, Point Break, Crooked Hearts, Mortal Thoughts, Freejack, Billy Bathgate, Little Man Tate, Fire in the Sky, Made in America,* and *A River Runs Through It.*

Sources

ASCAP in Action, fall 1991.
Billboard, February 11, 1984; October 15, 1988; April 6, 1991.
Down Beat, March 1984; June 1984; August 1985; April 1988; January 1991.
Keyboard, November 1985; September 1987; October 1988; December 1988; October 1993.
Musician, June 1984; December 1988.
Pulse!, July 1992.
Stereo Review, January 1991.
Variety, August 20, 1986.

Additional information for this profile was obtained from Windham Hill Records publicity materials, 1991.

—*Sonya Shelton*

Millie Jackson

Singer, songwriter, producer

Photograph by Bud Smith, courtesy of Ichiban Records

Millie Jackson has built her singing career on her rich, smoky voice, her musical talent, her business acumen, and her sense of humor. Jackson has always made her own business and career decisions; for many years she has acted as her own manager. A coproducer of her own recordings, she also owns a production company, Keishval Enterprises. She writes many of her own songs and all of her own raps, the spoken sections in her concerts and on her records. In these raps, she has consciously chosen to continue the blues tradition of explicit honesty. She talks about every angle of sex, relationships, and everyday life. As Vertamae Grosvenor wrote in *Ms.* magazine, "Her buck-naked everyday truth-telling style is pure raunch.... When Millie sings and raps about love and relationships, the liberated lyrics of her spokesongs proclaim that there *are* choices. Alternatives."

Jackson grew up in the middle of the blues-oriented South, in Georgia. Her mother died when she was two years old; her father left her to go find work in the north when she was 11. For years, she lived with her strictly religious grandparents. When she was 15, she moved to New Jersey to live with her father again, but left shortly thereafter to live with an aunt in Brooklyn.

Jackson began singing professionally in her late teens on a dare. One evening she was with friends at the Palm Café in Harlem. A friend challenged her to get up and sing with the band. Not one to shy away from any such challenge, she got up and sang "Stand By Me," and the audience loved her. One member of the audience liked her so much he offered her a job singing at a nearby club, the Crystal Ballroom.

Secretary by Day, Chanteuse by Night

Jackson wanted a singing career, but also was quite aware of the pitfalls and insecurities of such a life. For ten years, she sang at night and on weekends while still holding down a full-time day job. "I didn't quit my secretarial job until I had two records on the charts," she told *Essence.* "I wasn't sure I was gonna continue because so many singers come out there and get hits then disappear. I told my agent that if he could book me three months in advance, I'd quit. I came in the next day and I was booked. That was it."

Beginning with little formal musical training, Jackson learned what she needed to know about music on the road. She described her musical education in *High Fidelity:* "[My road band] taught me a lot, and I familiarized myself enough with the piano to write.... I took a test at Juilliard in order to enroll. I told the professor 'You

For the Record . . .

Born July 15, 1944, in Thompson, GA; divorced; children: Keisha, Jerrol.

Singer, songwriter, and producer, early 1970s—. Performed in first singing job at Harlem's Crystal Ballroom, c. 1962; worked as a full-time secretary, singing evenings and weekends, c. 1962-72; recorded Top Ten singles "Ask Me What You Want" and "My Man a Sweet Man," early 1970s; recorded first album, *Millie,* 1973; recorded gold albums *Caught Up,* 1974, and *Still Caught Up,* 1975; cast member and regular performer on radio program *Young Man, Older Woman,* KKDA-FM, Dallas, TX, 1990s—. Works as own producer and manager; founder of production company Keishval Enterprises.

Awards: Named best female rhythm and blues vocalist, *Cash Box,* 1973.

Addresses: *Office*—Keishval Enterprises, Inc., 2095 High Point Tr. S.W., Atlanta, GA 30331. *Record company*—Ichiban Records, P.O. Box 724677, Atlanta, GA 31139-1677.

know I came here to better my career. Why do I have to name three Russian composers? I could give a damn!' He said, 'Well, you have to know theory—about major and minor, about diminished and augmented.'"

When Jackson told the Juilliard professor that she knew theory, she related, "He said, 'Go home. You're further ahead now than the majority of students graduating this year. You say you've got a record? How many of my students do you think would love to have one? If you go through these classes you're going to think about the right way of doing things and kill your artistic side. Go home.'" She went home, and has been writing many of the songs she sings ever since.

Jackson's early recordings fit squarely into traditional rhythm and blues categories, and included two singles that made the Top Ten: "Ask Me What You Want" and "My Man a Sweet Man." She developed her stage personality as she developed her raps in her live performances, in which she often talked about sex. "Sex is always a good subject," she told *Essence.* "People always been cheatin' and always will be.... [My songs] give people something to talk about and keeps their minds off their problems." She has also acted as something of a role model and spokesperson for women. "Women come to me all the time to comment on what I'm

doing," she explained to *Essence.* "Maybe it's because I'm saying something they want to say."

In 1974 Jackson scored a big hit with the release of *Caught Up.* This album, which contained country-western and rock tunes as well as soul, was the first successful concept album by a female singer, describing a love triangle from the perspectives of both the wife and the "other woman." It was her first album to contain raps developed from her concerts, and it was the first to contain explicitly sexual talk. It was also her first album to go gold.

Jackson's next album, *Still Caught Up,* continued with the same themes and also went gold. After her initial albums drew some complaints about her frank language and subject matter, she recorded a couple of tamer albums. She described the results in *High Fidelity:* "After I saw the sales I tapped on a few desks and said, 'I'm gonna do what the hell I want and if it doesn't sell it's my career.'... I went back into the studio and did *Feelin' Bitchy* and it was the biggest album I ever had." She did not change her style again.

Albums Went Gold Despite Little Airplay

Jackson's success has been something of an anomaly in the music industry. Usually a song's financial success depends almost completely on how much airplay it gets—recordings that are played frequently on the radio sell well. In the late 1970s and early 1980s, few radio stations played Jackson's songs because of their explicit lyrics, and few radio and television talk shows invited her to appear.

Even when Jackson did appear on shows, she rarely had a chance to really talk. "They always expect you to go completely off [the air] and say all those dirty words. You get to sing your song sometimes, but they never let you say anything," she explained to *Rolling Stone.* "Then when the show's over and you're backstage talking, they realize you have a brain in your head slightly larger than the size of a pea, but the show is over with, so you gotta wait until you get your next hit record maybe."

Even Jackson's clean albums did not receive radio play. "When I have a clean album, nobody'll play it. They say it's not Millie," she told *Rolling Stone.* In the long run, she does not waste too much time worrying about the radio. "I found out it doesn't make too much sense to gear yourself for radio anyway," she observed in *Rolling Stone.* "I'm one of those few artists whose albums people will buy without hearing. But I've had Number One R&B records that got no pop play at all."

In 1994, however, Jackson released *Rock N' Soul*, a collection of 11 tracks of varied styles, ranging from a cover of country singer Vince Gill's "Whenever You Come Around" to rockers Def Leppard's "Pour Some Sugar on Me." *Billboard*'s J. R. Reynolds noted that the album marked "a more conservative approach" in the singer's career, as it left out the racy lyrics and off-color poetry in favor straight-ahead rock and R&B. Reynolds reported that the move was due to Jackson's disapproval of much of what is on the airwaves. Jackson remarked in *Billboard*, "It all sounds the same, and I wanted to show you can make different kinds of good music."

Managed Own Career

Jackson has spent much time during her career deciding what does make sense (and cents), for she manages herself and runs her own production company, Keishval Enterprises. "It's a pain in the neck," she told *High Fidelity*, "and very time consuming, but no one has given me a better offer. I haven't given a manager 20, 25, or 30 percent of my money because I've found that I can speak for myself very well. He'd have the right to place me with a booking agency, but I've already got one that I like. I've never had any trouble collecting money or saying whether or not I want to work this week."

After almost 20 years of recording and performing in concert, Jackson felt it made sense for her to begin expanding her career. The woman who could not get radio airplay in the 1980s got her own radio show on KKDA-FM in Dallas in the 1990s. She took her concert raps to their logical conclusion, and created an entire program, "set up more as a play than a concert," as she told the *Atlanta Constitution*.

The show, *Young Man, Older Woman*, includes monologues, dancing, and comedy; the cast features not only Millie Jackson, but her daughter, singer Keisha Jackson. Like the rest of her work, *Young Man, Older Woman* talks about life and relationships, telling the story of a married woman who becomes complacent in her relationship, ceases to take pride in herself, and then regains control over her life.

Having command over one's own life has been a personal theme for Jackson, and her gift to her audience and younger female performers. While her many recordings constitute a rich legacy of their own, Jackson has given the music industry much more than songs. Through her individuality and independence, she has been a role model for many young women. She paved the way for aggressive female rappers in a genre famous for its misogyny. In her business dealings, she showed other female performers like Janet Jackson and Madonna that women can manage their own careers. Just as her songs feature raps about choices and alternatives for women, Millie Jackson's life course has been determined by her own choices.

Selected discography

Millie, Spring, 1973.
Caught Up, Spring, 1974.
Still Caught Up, Spring, 1975.
Free and In Love, Spring, 1976.
Lovingly Yours, Spring, 1976.
Get It Out'cha System, Spring, 1978.
A Moment's Pleasure, Spring, 1979.
Royal Rappin', Spring, 1979.
Live and Uncensored, Spring, 1979.
I Had to Say It, Spring, 1980.
For Men Only, Spring, 1980.
Just a Little Bit Country, Spring, 1981.
Live and Outrageous, Spring, 1982.
Hard Times, Spring, 1982.
ESP, Spring, 1984.
An Imitation of Love, Jive, 1987.
Back to the S—t, Jive, 1989.
Young Man, Older Woman, Jive, 1992.
The Very Best! of Millie Jackson, Jive, 1994.
Rock N' Soul, Ichiban, 1994.

Sources

Books

New Grove Dictionary of American Music, volume 2, Macmillan, 1986.

Periodicals

Atlanta Journal and Constitution, February 7, 1992.
Billboard, December 10, 1994.
Essence, July 1975.
High Fidelity, February 1981.
Jet, August 16, 1979; January 14, 1985; October 21, 1985; February 9, 1987; February 12, 1990; October 25, 1993.
Ms., October 1979.
New York Times, June 13, 1988; July 20, 1989.
Rolling Stone, April 3, 1980.
Vibe, September 1993; September 1994.

—Robin Armstrong

Kenny G

Saxophonist, composer

AP/Wide World Photos

Soft-spoken saxophonist Kenny G is a lot tougher than either his boyish grin or his mild, atmospheric records would tend to suggest. Ever since the release of the multimillion-selling *Duotones* in 1986, he has withstood a veritable onslaught of abuse from critics and fellow musicians alike. The heaps of invective flung in Kenny's direction intensified when his follow-up, 1988's *Silhouette,* went platinum. In fact, critical disparagement seems to run inversely to Kenny's popularity. Kenny himself tries to take it in stride. "I don't think anyone has been exceptionally mean to me," he explained in *Entertainment Weekly.* "It's the intellectuals who write the reviews. People read these things and think that these are the people who know the most. Maybe I'm a dreamer, but I think the ordinary guy has as much right to say, 'This is a good song' as somebody who is in the music business."

Kenny G is certainly one dreamer whose fantasies have come to life. In little more than a decade he went from being just another backup sax player to selling millions of records worldwide and, following an onstage jam with Bill Clinton, being billed as the U.S. president's favorite artist. In truth, his rapid and seemingly effortless rise to success may be part of the reason critics and musicians come down so hard on him. "I'm lucky," Kenny admitted in the *Detroit Free Press.* "I remember when *Duotones* came out, and I had a hit with 'Songbird.' The history of instrumentalists in pop is that you get a big hit and that's the end of it. They're not going to hear from you again. I've been lucky so far that it hasn't happened to me."

"A Serious Dork"

It was a combination of luck and musical prowess that landed Kenny his first gig. While still in high school, he was invited to play with R&B singer Barry White's Love Unlimited Orchestra. "They needed a sax player who could read and solo in a soulful style, and I really was the only person in Seattle [Washington] that could do both," Kenny recalled in *Down Beat.* "It was very funny, because I hadn't played professionally before. I didn't know anything about the business world of playing. They said suit and tie—and everybody knows that means dark suit, dark tie. And I came on with the whole bar mitzvah look—plaid jacket, maroon pants, and maroon tie to match, of course. I was a serious dork. When I showed up, the band could not believe it—here was this little tiny kid. But I did a great job—I even got a standing ovation because I had such a long solo. After that, I was a hero at school!"

Kenny continued to broaden his musical horizons over the next few years, playing with visiting performers such

For the Record . . .

Born Kenneth Gorelick, c. 1957, in Seattle, WA. *Education:* Graduated magna cum laude in accounting from the University of Washington.

Played backup for such musicians as Barry White and Liberace; played with Jeff Lorber Fusion, 1979-82; left to pursue solo career and released self-titled debut album on Arista, 1982; released *Duotones,* Arista, 1986; has made extensive world tours.

Awards: Grammy Award for best instrumental composition, 1993, for "Forever in Love"; *Billboard* magazine selected *Silhouette* as the Number One jazz album of 1988 and named Kenny G the Number One jazz artist of the 1980s.

Addresses: *Home*—Seattle, WA. *Record company*—Arista Records, 6 West 57th St., New York, NY 10019.

as White and famous pianist Liberace. His first big break came when he was asked to audition for jazz-fusion pioneer Jeff Lorber. Lorber was impressed, and Kenny joined the band—but only after graduating magna cum laude in accounting from the University of Washington, just in case he didn't make it in music. Lorber was Kenny's first and strongest influence. "I ended up playing with him for four years, from '79-82, and I learned so much," he reflected in *Down Beat*. "I think he was one of the pioneers of fusion—that blend of bebop, funk, and r&b—he had it down. I loved his style. And when you're in a band for four years, you live in that style—you really don't do anything else."

Early Producer Dilemmas

After a while, however, Kenny began to feel that it was time to strike out on his own. His first album, 1982's *Kenny G,* was produced by Lorber and released by Arista, Lorber's record company. The result was not exactly what Kenny had in mind. "I was a little frustrated, because the record was very much a Jeff Lorber album—it really had Jeff's sound," he revealed in *Down Beat*. "I'm not faulting him for that. He's a good producer who has strong ideas and he wanted to hear it his way. [But] I had Kashif produce my second album, *G Force,* and it sold almost 200,000 copies! I'm an r&b guy, and Kashif is an r&b producer, and I liked working with him."

Still, even that situation was less than ideal. "Kashif

turned out not to be the right producer for me either," Kenny continued in *Down Beat*. "He's more of a vocal producer, and he was hearing hit vocal songs and I was hearing instrumentals. The second album we did together didn't do as well." Kenny persevered, however, and with help from Arista released his breakthrough smash, *Duotones,* in 1986. "I wouldn't have blamed the record company if they had dropped me because it was shaky. But I wanted to do the next record in a certain way, and Arista agreed to try to work it out. So when we made *Duotones,* we still included some vocal tunes, but I wanted to make sure they fit in with the whole vibe of the record. My main concern was to make an album that people could listen to from top to bottom and like it, because that's what I like about a record."

Kenny was not the only one who liked *Duotones*. The album was an unequivocal smash hit, with the single "Songbird" shooting up to Number Four on the pop charts. The enormous success of *Duotones* surprised everyone, including Kenny, who told a *Down Beat* contributor, "When I wrote 'Songbird,' it wasn't as if I said to myself, 'Okay, it's 1987 and it's time for another instrumental hit.' I wrote the song, I played it, and I thought it was beautiful. I didn't think it was going to be a hit. I wasn't trying to do that."

When Kenny's follow-up albums—1988's *Silhouette* and 1992's *Breathless*—set new sales records the world over, the saxophonist realized that his success was not just a fluke. "It's my commitment to put a record out there that is really great and not to release it from a business standpoint," he explained. "It's the thing that makes people successful in life or not successful."

Connected With His Audience

Another aspect of Kenny's success is his ability to reach out to his audience. A highlight of his live performances is when he descends from the stage to walk and play among his many fans. Fellow saxophonist Eric Marienthal of Chick Corea's Elektric Band was quoted in *Down Beat* as saying: "One thing I thought Kenny G had going for him was that he had a great way of communicating with his audience. It's important to be proficient with your instrument. Also you want to try to communicate with people. Kenny's a master at that. He was able to get that real connection that a lot of musicians aren't as successful at doing." Kenny explained it this way in *Down Beat:* "Physically walking through the seats, to me that's the best. I like the sound better out there than the sound on the stage. Any time there's a performance, there is a wall separating me and the audience. You can leave it up there or take it down. I like to put myself in the audience's place."

Kenny's innate ability to relate to the nuts and bolts of record promotion has also helped him gain popularity. "The radio stations are not my enemy, and the record company is not my enemy," he explained in *Down Beat*. "If a record does well, then everybody's happy. Some artists look at the record company as the enemy. I look at it as part of a team." Indeed, his willingness to display his talents in remote locations has made him a dream artist to the business end of the music industry. "Kenny's his own best salesman," stated Heinz Henn, a senior vice-president at Arista's distributor, BMG, in *Billboard*. "He's just a genuine nice guy, who people warm to."

Kenny G is the embodiment of the musical success story. Dedication, hard work, and a bit of luck have taken him from relative obscurity to international super-stardom in little more than a decade. Still, he tries to keep a level head. "I take my music and playing very seriously," he was quoted as saying in *Down Beat*. "I think it's a great position to be in. I remember the time when I didn't have a gig. It's a dream. I'm waiting for the dream to end, and I hope it doesn't."

Selected discography

On Arista Records

Kenny G, 1982.
G Force, 1984.
Gravity, 1985.
Duotones (includes "Songbird"), 1986.
Silhouette, 1988.
Live, 1989.
Breathless, 1992.
Miracles: The Holiday Album, 1994.

Sources

Billboard, October 13, 1990; November 26, 1992; June 26, 1993; July 3, 1993; December 10, 1994.
Detroit Free Press, August 27, 1993.
Down Beat, January 1988; November 1992.
Entertainment Weekly, April 2, 1993; November 18, 1994.

—*Alan Glenn*

Hal Ketchum

Singer, songwriter

Singer-songwriter Hal Ketchum, the 71st member of the Grand Ole Opry, combines rock, folk, and country strains in songs that explore everything from the darker side of relationships to the frustrations of the working class. Ketchum, who was a carpenter for more than a decade before he started playing and singing professionally, began his country music career in his mid-30s. Since then the silver-haired musician has found stardom in Nashville and enthusiastic audiences elsewhere through his songs of heartache, desperation, and fragile love.

Country Music magazine contributor Bob Allen wrote: "In their best moments ... [Ketchum's] performances hook you and hold you and simply won't let you go. Palpable intimations of fear, helplessness, desire, compulsion and confusion all swirl just beneath the music's seemingly placid surface.... Ketchum's singing ... sounds ... hushed and effortlessly compelling." *Los Angeles Times* reviewer Mike Boehm praised the artist for his "simple, plain-spoken songwriting approach that tries to take a closer, more personal look at emotional situations than you'll find in most of the cliched, surface-oriented stuff churned out by Nashville song mills."

An Isolated Childhood

Ketchum was born and raised in Greenwich, New York, a small town nestled in the Adirondack Mountains near the Vermont border. His world was as insular as that of the frustrated teens he sings about in his hit song "Small Town Saturday Night." He told the *Chicago Tribune:* "Where I grew up, because the towns are separated by 8 or 10 miles of mountainous terrain, I never knew anybody in the next town until I was 18 or 19 years old. Except playing against them on a football team." Ketchum went on to describe himself as a "game" teen who was "always looking for some way to tear it up a little bit."

The Ketchum household was a musical one. The singer's father liked country and bluegrass music; his mother preferred popular singers such as Frank Sinatra. Ketchum told *Country Music* that he was particularly affected by his mother and her perceptions. "She had multiple sclerosis and went through some real hard periods," he recalled. "She had to perceive her own mortality. I spent a great deal of time with her when she was incapacitated, and she had a great deal to teach my brother and I before she went on her way. And all the things I perceive and write and sing about and the things I'm drawn to are relative to the philosophy I got from her in a very formative period of my life."

As a young man Ketchum dabbled in music, playing

Photograph by Randee St. Nicholas, courtesy of Curb Records

banjo in a bluegrass ensemble and drums in a rock band. Performing was strictly a hobby, however. Trained in carpentry, he made a living as a furniture craftsman and cabinetmaker. One favorite profit-making venture was restoring old houses. The artist told *Country Music* that he and his first wife used to "buy a house that I could get for next to nothing and live in the kitchen for a year or two while we fixed the rest of it up."

Received Music Education in a Dance Hall

In the early 1980s, Ketchum moved his wife and two young children south to Texas, where he continued to support the family by doing carpentry work. In 1982 they bought a house near Gruene, a historic town with a thriving music scene. On his very first night in his new home, Ketchum heard music wafting in through the bedroom window.

He left the house to investigate and discovered a dance hall nearby that played host to such notable artists as Asleep at the Wheel, Townes Van Zandt, Jimmie Dale Gilmore, and Lyle Lovett. Ketchum began to spend most of his spare time at the hall, absorbing performances that inspired him to try his own hand at singing and songwriting. "The whole experience ended up being like a four-year college course in music for me, with some of the best teachers in the world," he told *Country Music.*

By 1985 Ketchum was earning pocket money playing in small Texas clubs. One night Jerry Jeff Walker caught Ketchum's act and invited the erstwhile carpenter to open some show dates for him. The following year Ketchum released an album, *Threadbare Alibis,* on a small Texas label. He also worked more club dates and folk festivals, dodging audience requests for popular country fare in favor of his own quirky songs. "There were some down times, but I never quit," he noted in the *Chicago Tribune.* "I'm just a little hard-headed. There were occasions when I thought I might just stop by the side of the road and smash my guitar against a tree. Usually it would be about 3 o'clock in the morning after playing someplace where everybody had wanted to hear songs they'd heard before."

Recording artist Pat Alger introduced Ketchum to esteemed country-folk producer Jim Rooney in 1987. It was Rooney who convinced Ketchum to move to Nashville. For Ketchum, the decision to relocate brought personal pain: his wife and children stayed behind in Texas, and he was eventually divorced. "I was enthralled with being on stage and singing my own songs," he explained in the *Los Angeles Times.* "I didn't know anything about the music business, and it was difficult to reassure somebody else about something I didn't understand."

Inducted Into Grand Ole Opry

Ketchum signed with the independent label Curb, engaged Rooney and Allen Reynolds as his producers, and released his album *Past the Point of Rescue* in 1991. That album has since yielded four Top Ten country hits: "Past the Point of Rescue," "Five O'Clock World," "I Know Where Love Lives," and "Small Town Saturday Night." In "Small Town Saturday Night"—a typical Ketchum excursion into despair and frustration—restless teenagers seek release from the confining boundaries of their small-town lives.

Ketchum told the *Washington Post:* "As an up-and-coming musician, you spend a long time just looking for the door. You go through a naive, trial-and-error process before you realize this is not a magic show; this is a lot of work. You have to say to your family, 'I'll see you three days a week this summer, if I'm lucky.' You have to put a lot of personal habits and desires aside. You have to overcome a lot of self-doubt. Then one day the door opens, and you're suddenly in this big room with all these legendary personalities. It's like going to a dinner party in a better part of town than you've ever been before; it takes a while to get comfortable. But if you just relax and be yourself, all the rewards eventually come to you."

One reward that Ketchum has reaped is membership in the Grand Ole Opry, the ultimate benchmark of country stardom. Ketchum was inducted into the Opry in 1994, after his three Curb albums, *Past the Point of Rescue, Sure Love,* and *Every Little Word* had collectively sold in excess of a million copies.

The world according to Hal Ketchum is not necessarily a very happy place. In his songs, homeless families live in cars while searching fruitlessly for work; a longshoreman gets drunk and pines for his lost love; a broken-hearted lover feels that he is "wasting God's time" praying for reconciliation with his sweetheart. Ketchum delivers these songs in a "verge-of-a-teardrop" baritone, to quote *Los Angeles Times* contributor Boehm, with an occasional growl or yodel for punctuation.

Ketchum contributes a few of his own songs to each album and says that he works in bursts whenever he is inspired. "I just seem to have an open channel: occasionally something comes rushing through," the artist explained in the *San Francisco Chronicle.* "Sometimes I'll work on two or three songs at once; there's no pushing. I return to the well, check my traps; I just try to stay open. I write when and where I can, as long as I have something to write with and something to write on."

Ketchum typically spends between 250 and 300 nights on the road each year, performing with his band, the Alibis. Married again, to a Nashville businesswoman, the former carpenter is still somewhat bewildered by his success in country music. "I'm sitting on this flat rock and catching my breath," he told the *San Francisco Chronicle.* "It's a short life and a small planet, and I'm really enjoying it."

Selected discography

Threadbare Alibis, Watermelon, 1986.
Past the Point of Rescue, Curb, 1991.
Sure Love, Curb, 1992.
Every Little Word, Curb, 1994.

Sources

Chicago Tribune, August 30, 1991; January 10, 1994.
Country Music, January/February 1994.
Los Angeles Times, September 27, 1991; May 29, 1993.
San Francisco Chronicle, September 27, 1992.
USA Today, December 15, 1992.
Washington Post, August 5, 1994.

—*Anne Janette Johnson*

Charles Koppelman

Record company executive

Courtesy of EMI Records Group North America

Music industry mogul Charles Koppelman didn't always have a popular philosophy. Starting as a musician in the late 1950s, Koppelman always believed in the music side of the music business, when many of his contemporaries focused on the business. His direction and determination made him one of the most powerful men in music.

Koppelman joined the band Ivy Three while he attended Adelphi University in Long Island, New York. With his friend and future business partner, Don Rubin, the Ivy Three wrote and recorded the song "Yogi," about the cartoon bear. In 1960 the Ivy Three's "Yogi" reached the Top Ten on the *Billboard* charts, and Koppelman and Rubin entered the music business.

Koppelman landed a job previewing songs by aspiring songwriters for Aldon Music Chief Executive Officer (CEO) Don Kirshner. Koppelman and Rubin also joined the company's impressive songwriting staff, which included Carole King, Neil Sedaka, Barry Mann, and Cynthia Weil. When Kirshner noticed Koppelman had a track record for picking winners, he promoted Koppelman to director of his publishing company. Columbia Pictures bought Aldon Music, and as a result, Koppelman became the director of the new company—Screen Gems/Columbia Music.

In 1965 Koppelman and Rubin left Columbia Music to form their own entertainment company called Koppelman/Rubin Associates. The two college buddies ignited the careers of artists like the Lovin' Spoonful, the Turtles, Bobby Darin, and many others. Three years later, Commonwealth United purchased Koppelman/Rubin Associates, and the two executives stayed on to run the music division. During the early 1970s, Koppelman moved on to CBS Records and held numerous positions, including Vice President/National Director of A&R (artists and repertoire). While heading the A&R division, Koppelman signed many successful acts, including Billy Joel, Dave Mason, Janis Ian, Journey, and Phoebe Snow.

By the middle of the decade, Koppelman had stepped up to Vice President/General Manager of worldwide publishing for CBS Records. Then in 1975, he decided to once again break out on his own to form the Entertainment Company with attorney Martin Bandier and New York real estate developer and Bandier's father-in-law, Sam LeFrak. The multifaceted organization independently administered and promoted song catalogs and produced music artists. At the Entertainment Company, Koppelman cultivated top musicians like Barbra Streisand, Dolly Parton, Diana Ross, the Four Tops, and Cher. "His production company, based in New York, is

Born March 30, 1940, in Brooklyn, NY. Married; three children. *Education:* Attended Adelphi University, Long Island, NY.

Member of band Ivy Three until 1961; Aldon Music, songwriter and director, 1961-64; Screen Gems/Columbia Music, director, 1964-65; Koppelman/Rubin Associates, cofounder and partner, 1965-68; Commonwealth United, music division head, 1968-70; CBS Records Group, vice president/national director of A&R and vice president/general manager of worldwide publishing, c. 1970-75; Entertainment Company, cofounder and CEO, 1975-86; SBK Entertainment World, Inc., cofounder, 1986-89, Chairman/CEO, 1989-91; EMI Music Publishing, Chairman, 1989-91; three-label consolidation of EMI Records Group North America, Chairman/CEO, 1991-93; EMI Records Group North America, Chairman/CEO, 1993—.

Awards: Under Koppelman's leadership, EMI Music Publishing was named publisher of the year by American Society of Composers, Authors and Publishers and Broadcast Music, Incorporated, c. 1990; Abe Olman Publishers Award from Songwriters Hall of Fame, 1990; Humanitarian of the Year Award from T. J. Martell Foundation of Leukemia, Cancer, and AIDS Research, 1991; Distinguished Achievement Award from Yeshiva University, 1992.

Addresses: *Record company*—EMI Records Group North America, 1290 Avenue of the Americas, 42nd Floor, New York, NY 10104.

the darling of the recording business," *Billboard* reported of Koppelman's Entertainment Company, "custom tailoring songs and records to produce hits for its clients."

Created World's Largest Publishing Company

By 1981 the Entertainment Company had grown into a production company with its own staff of producers and 20 in-house songwriters. Koppelman and Bandier partnered with record companies in putting together packages, or they signed artists directly to their company to place them with a record company. Then, in 1984, they purchased the Combine Music catalog of 25,000 country songs.

Koppelman and Bandier continued to pursue new artists during this time of expansion. They published Gregory Abbot's Number One hit song "Shake You Down," and signed then-unknown Tracy Chapman. Koppelman and Bandier took on a new partner in 1986—financier and carpet and furniture magnate, Stephen C. Swid. They formed the partnership as part of a plan to purchase the interests of CBS Songs, Inc.

On October 24, 1986, the new partnership, named SBK Entertainment World, Inc., bought the 250,000 titles owned by CBS Songs for $125 million, the highest price ever paid for a music publishing setup. SBK also developed into the largest independent music publisher in the world. Koppelman and SBK published and played a major role in the success of artists like Michael Bolton, Robbie Robertson, New Kids on the Block, Ice House, Al B. Sure!, and Eric B. & Rakim.

An Influential Force in Music

Three years later, SBK sold the company, including all of its music publishing interests, to EMI Music for about $300 million. As part of the deal, Koppelman and Bandier formed a partnership with EMI Music Worldwide to create their own record label, SBK Records. EMI put up $15 million in seed money, while Koppelman and Bandier invested $10 million. In addition, Koppelman took the positions of Chairman and CEO of the new label and Chairman of EMI Music Publishing. Bandier received the posts of President and Chief Operating Officer of SBK Records and Vice Chairman of EMI Music Publishing. SBK Entertainment also purchased a film company called Cinecom, which Stephen Swid managed. SBK Records opened their doors in June of 1989.

While Koppelman led EMI Music Publishing, the company won many industry awards, including publisher of the year honors, bestowed by both the American Society of Composers, Authors and Publishers (ASCAP) and Broadcast Music, Incorporated (BMI). Koppelman received the 1990 Abe Olman Publishers Award through the Songwriters Hall of Fame. And only one year after they started the company, SBK Records received their first platinum album with Technotronic's *Pump Up the Jam.* SBK Records went on to sign successful new artists like Jesus Jones, Wilson Phillips, and Vanilla Ice. On April 27, 1991, Koppelman earned an award for his achievements outside of music—the Humanitarian of the Year Award from the T. J. Martell Foundation for Leukemia, Cancer, and AIDS Research.

Later in 1991, Koppelman and Bandier sold their 50 percent share of SBK Records to EMI Music, making EMI the sole owner of the label. EMI Music then decided to consolidate its operations and formed EMI Records Group North America. Koppelman was subsequently appointed Chairman and CEO.

Promoted to EMI's Chairman/CEO

When Capitol-EMI's CEO Joe Smith decided to leave his position in March of 1993, Koppelman became responsible for the North American operations of Angel/EMI Classics/Virgin Classics, Blue Note Records, Capitol Records, EMI Latin, EMI Music Canada, EMI Records (EMI/Chrysalis/SBK), I.R.S., and Liberty Records. He also oversees the group's recording studios, manufacturing, and distribution in North America. Koppelman publicly stated his mission for the company in the *Los Angeles Times:* "to make EMI the No. 1 record corporation in the world by 1998." During the first two years of his post, EMI experienced the success of such artists as Duran Duran, Bonnie Raitt, Blind Melon, and Eternal, also the Barrio Boyzz and Jon Secada. Koppelman played an integral role in the reunion of singer Frank Sinatra with Capitol Records, which spawned the five-million-selling album *Duets.*

Koppelman told Chuck Phillips in the *Los Angeles Times,* "No matter what anybody says, all that matters to me is the music. What people forget is our business starts with the music. If you have the belief in your gut about a song and artist, you have to have the nerve to stand behind the thing, to stay the course." Koppelman summed up his career in an interview with Thom Duffy in *Musician.* "When I listen to the radio, I hear more songs that I've been involved with than anyone," he explained. "I've just rattled off number ones. Classics. Appeal to everybody, little kids, adults. Everybody. You know what my image is? Hits."

Sources

Billboard, January 7, 1978; January 17, 1981; February 28, 1981; June 20, 1981; July 4, 1981; November 8, 1986; January 21, 1989; June 30, 1990; May 11, 1991; November 30, 1991; January 16, 1993; January 23, 1993.
Entertainment Weekly, October 30, 1992.
Forbes, September 30, 1991.
Los Angeles Times, June 13, 1993.
Musician, December 1991.
Variety, January 12, 1983; October 22, 1986; October 29, 1986; January 11, 1993.

Additional information for this profile was obtained from an EMI Records Group North America press biography, 1994.

—Sonya Shelton

Bill Laswell

Bassist, producer

Photograph by Thi-Linh Le, courtesy of Axiom/Island/PLG

Bill Laswell once said in *Down Beat* that "good music is just a product of searching for new things. The priority is really to grow and not kill the idea of self-expression, spontaneity, or experimenting with sound and music." As a bassist and producer, Laswell has pursued "good music" with a pragmatic eye and visionary heart. In ensembles such as Material and Last Exit, his musical philosophy has led him to the extremes of jazz, dance music, and rock experimentation. In production work that has ranged from Marrakeshian Gnawa music to heavy metal band Motörhead, Laswell has sought a unique sound to match what he considers the independence of the particular artists with whom he chooses to work.

A successful combination of noise, electronic experimentation, and dance rhythms in the production of Herbie Hancock's 1983 hit "Rockit" attracted artists like Mick Jagger and Yoko Ono to Laswell, who produced their mid-1980s solo records. But popular success has been of less interest to Laswell than the years of "street" credibility he has attained through work with New York City jazz and rap musicians since the late 1970s. The bassist/producer's commitment to unconventional, fiercely collaborative music found industry approval when he landed a 1990 deal with Island Records to manage a label devoted to world music, experimental jazz, and anarchic fusion. A tireless worker with a "jaded hipster" image, Laswell made Island's Axiom and Rykodisc's Black Arc uncompromising places to search for new things—as well as places to rediscover the work of older visionaries like Cream's Ginger Baker and P-Funk's Bootsy Collins.

Born on February 14, 1950, Laswell spent his early years in Salem, Illinois. His father was an oil businessman who died when Laswell was young. In 1958 the family moved to a predominantly black section of Detroit. Music did not play a large role in Laswell's family life. At school, instructors led him to the drums and the baritone sax, but Laswell had other ideas. True to his collaborative philosophy, he chose the bass. He explained to *Down Beat's* John Diliberto: "I was interested in forming groups at that time, and everyone had guitars and drums. So if you had a bass you were in a group." By age 13, Laswell was performing at local gigs.

During his fifteenth year, Laswell's work in rhythm and blues bands put him on the road, playing black clubs in the South and Midwest. At the same time, Detroit's late 1960s melting pot—as it mixed together the MC5, Motown, Iggy Pop, and Funkadelic—proved influential, if only retrospectively. "I remember concerts of Funkadelic and the MC5 on the same bill," he told *Musician's* Jerome Reese in 1986. "Which was really interesting to me; because you're there you think that's what's hap-

For the Record . . .

B orn William Laswell, February 14, 1950, in Salem, IL; son of an oil businessman.

Learned bass and played in local Detroit bands, 1963-64; toured rhythm and blues clubs in the South and Midwest, 1965; performed periodically in Detroit, c. 1966-76; moved to New York City, 1977; formed band Material and recorded three discs with group, 1979-82; earned acclaim with production of Herbie Hancock hit "Rockit," 1983; producer with major labels and Celluloid Records, 1983-89; continued performing with Material, 1983—; founded Axiom Records, 1989; founded Greenpoint Studio, Brooklyn, NY, with first Axiom productions released, 1990; manager and producer for Axiom, 1990—; created Black Arc label, 1994.

Addresses: *Home*—New York, NY. *Record company*—Axiom/Island Records, 400 Lafayette St., 5th floor, New York, NY 10003.

pening. You don't realize that it's not like that anywhere else."

The rare combination of noisy punk and deep funk seemed natural to the young Laswell. He kept his listening horizons broad; he was also interested in the 1960s experimentations of John Coltrane, James Brown, Wayne Shorter, and Jimi Hendrix. By the 1970s, he was attracted to the European progressive sounds of Henry Cow, Gong, and Magma.

Material Boy

In 1977 Laswell relocated to New York City. He reported to Vikki Tobak of *Paper* in 1994 that his theory of ensemble work had evolved at this point: "When I moved to New York, I had no interest in forming a band or playing with one. I was more interested in interacting with different musicians and playing all different styles rather than being tied down."

Laswell initially took part in the "no wave" scene then forming in downtown New York, performing with such artists as DNA and James Chance. He then met Michael Beinhorn, an electronic musician whose atonal synthesizer work was influenced by avant-garde composer Karlheinz Stockhausen. The Zu Band was formed in 1978, featuring Laswell, Beinhorn, Cliff Culteri, and Fred Maher; the band would complement the esoteric designs of Gong and Soft Machine contributors David

Allen and Giorgio Gomelsky in a 14-hour performance. In 1979 the Zu Band toured the U.S. with Allen's latest version of Gong.

Material—the group that would establish Laswell's reputation—materialized out of this quartet of Zu musicians. Principally the collaboration of Laswell and Beinhorn from 1979 to 1982, the ensemble recorded *Temporary Music, One Down,* and *Memory Serves* during this period. The discs showcased, according to *Down Beat's* Diliberto, "musique concrete, free improvisation, electronics, and rock ... wrapped around relentless rhythms." Culteri and Maher orbited around these projects, but the collaborative ethic precluded fixing the group permanently. Laswell told *Down Beat* in 1982, "It's really just an experience of meeting people and influencing them or trying to be influenced by them."

Material cohorts during this period included Fred Frith, Archie Shepp, Henry Threadgill, Nile Rogers, Billy Bang, George Lewis, Sonny Sharrock—and, on 1982's *One Down,* an unknown named Whitney Houston. Beinhorn's philosophy—"By doing a lot of different things," he told Diliberto, "people can associate the name Material and various projects that happen alongside that name with a language or way of approaching music"— contrasted with Laswell's straightforwardness. Laswell told *Musician* in 1986, "There has never been an idea behind Material, it's just been a means to work and create with other people, to have a situation where a lot of people can have interplay."

Laswell's innovations during this period were not only conceptual. As a jazz bassist, Laswell struck *Down Beat's* Diliberto as "[reconciling] the virtuosic development of the electric bass in the mid 70s with its original role as an anchoring instrument." *Musician's* Jerome Reese wrote that Laswell's bass playing "sounded ominous, brooding, and yet elastic, right in the pocket." As an instrumentalist, Laswell played on Brian Eno and David Byrne's *My Life in the Bush of Ghosts,* and he joined other groups, such as Massacre (a trio composed of Laswell, Maher, and Frith, whose first show was in Paris in 1980) and Anton Fier's Golden Palominos. As a producer, he contributed to Nona Hendryx's dance hit "Bustin' Out," forged ties with rap artists Afrika Bambaataa and Fab 5 Freddy, and helped develop Celluloid Records.

"Rockit" Put Career on a Roll

By 1983 these various projects had caught Herbie Hancock's ear. A premier keyboardist in the 1960s and 1970s jazz scenes, Hancock had Laswell concoct "Rockit," the single that sold one and a half million copies. A staple of early MTV, the single's mix of synthesizer, DJ scratching, and drum machine dance beats helped introduce the hip-hop sound to a wider public. Cowritten and produced by Laswell, the album *Future Shock* garnered Herbie Hancock a Grammy Award for best rhythm and blues instrumental performance.

The success of "Rockit" led to a streak of high-profile work. Laswell produced portions of Mick Jagger's *She's the Boss,* Yoko Ono's *Starpeace,* Laurie Anderson's *Mr. Heartbreak,* and Public Image Ltd.'s *Album.* As this varied list attests, the Hancock record did not create a formula—indeed, Laswell told *Down Beat's* Bill Milkowski in 1986 that its success was "totally based on the fact that we used a Bronx DJ to scratch a record particularly at the correct time."

Laswell's mid-1980s production work was sometimes controversial. Occasional Nigerian political prisoner and international pop star Fela Kuti was incensed by Laswell's treatment of his record *Army Arrangement.* Laswell chose to drop Fela's principal saxophone solos from the disc, substituting instead Bernie Worrell's organ playing. With typical bluntness, Laswell explained to Milkowski: "The fact is, Fela can't play the sax. His solos were awful.... Prison or not, politics or not, he can't play saxophone. So we just erased everything."

Remained Tied to Experimental Music

In addition, Laswell refused to reveal the names of the musicians on the Public Image Ltd. record (which fit with the aesthetic of the "generic" packaging that adorns *Album*). Tagged a drum machine specialist, Laswell wanted critics to judge his music, not the names (or machines) attached to the music. Ginger Baker and Tony Williams are the rumored drummers on the album.

Laswell also maintained his ties to experimental music and independent labels. The mid-1980s found him in a number of improvisatory bands—not only Material, Massacre, and the Golden Palominos, but also two more outfits: Curlew, with Tom Cora, Nicky Skopelitis, and George Cartwright, and, in 1986, Last Exit, with Sonny Sharrock, Peter Brötzmann, and Ronald Shannon Jackson.

Originally named the Sex Beatles, Last Exit was an incendiary quartet that returned Sharrock's guitar work to public notice. Loved in jazz circles overseas, the band recorded three discs through 1989. In 1984 Laswell paired Bambaataa and John Lydon on an apocalyptic rap called "World Destruction," and in 1987 he worked with James Blood Ulmer for Blue Note Records.

Laswell's most creatively significant production efforts during the period were perhaps his "world music" forays on Celluloid Records. Synthesizing African and Middle Eastern music with digital technology and city sounds, Laswell produced music by Manu Dibango, Toure Kunda, and Mandingo. "Back then it was the beginning of rap and hip hop," he told *Billboard's* Ed Christman in 1993. "I incorporated that and other musical elements such as drum machines with [non-Western music], and at that time I received a lot of criticism. It turned out that many others have since blended different music in the same manner."

> "*Good music is just a product of searching for new things. The priority is really to grow and not kill the idea of self-expression, spontaneity, or experimenting with sound and music.*"

As Laswell's relationship with Celluloid concluded in 1989, he looked for other opportunities to pursue his vision. Having met Island Records president Chris Blackwell after working with reggae rhythm section Sly and Robbie in the early 1980s, Laswell approached the industry executive. Blackwell agreed to back a project whereby Laswell would manage a subsidiary label, produce records, and maintain complete creative control. Thus Axiom Records was born. With an average of five Axiom releases per year from 1990 to 1994, Laswell was able to explore spontaneous collaboration on a much grander scale than had been the case in the early days of Material.

Nicky Skopelitis, longtime Laswell partner and mainstay of the label, reported to *Billboard* in 1993 that Axiom was "the only existing catalog of recordings that defies genre, formula, and obsolescence." Laswell detested explaining Axiom's product; he told Vikki Tobak of *Paper* that writers "demand too many descriptions for things that should be felt rather than described." The label's exploratory function was both figurative and literal for the bassist/producer. Releases ranged from world music (Arabic music by Simon Shaheen and Gambian music by the Mandinka and Fulani), to cutting-edge jazz (Henry Threadgill and Ronald Shannon Jackson), to ruthlessly eclectic mutations (Ginger Baker, Mandingo, and Skopelitis). Tracking down these artists was a global affair. Laswell ventured to Italy's olive farms to coax Baker out of retirement; he toured Gambia and Morrocco with a 12-track recorder to capture the sounds of the Mandinka and Fulani and the Master Musicians of Jajouka, respectively. As he proclaimed in *Musician,* "People that know about music are people who are well-traveled."

But in the early 1990s Laswell was also rooted to his first New York conceptual ensemble, to the city itself, and to the black popular music he grew up on. He continued Material (though not with Beinhorn) and released two albums on Axiom: 1991's *Third Power,* with contributions from Shabba Ranks, the Jungle Brothers, Sly and Robbie, and Fred Wesley, and 1994's *Hallucination Engine,* featuring Indian instrumentalist Ravi Shankar, Beat writer William Burroughs, organist Worrell, and Chinese singer Liu Sola.

Gathered Funk Pioneers

In 1993 Laswell started working out of a Brooklyn studio called Greenpoint, a relaxed if rudimentary facility he owned and ran. Here Laswell recorded and mixed not only a variety of Axiom projects, but also, in 1994, a new series of "black rock, cyberfunk, and future blues" on the Rykodisc-sponsored, Laswell-managed label Black Arc. In seeking out and working with Hendrix drummer Buddy Miles, bassist Bootsy Collins, P-Funk guitarist Michael Hampton, and classic rapper Melle Mel, among others, Laswell helped mitigate the underrecognition of funk pioneers.

Laswell elaborated to *Vibe's* Tom Moon: "You've got all these rappers out there building off of what guys like [these] did, while the originators can't get any attention. It's not right. I just wanted to create an outlet so that these guys could work more." And here, too, he mixed and matched performers, intuitively seeking a singular combination of sounds.

Summarizing his rigorously eclectic career, Laswell told Tobak that he has been "fortunate to work with such a variety of musicians from different backgrounds and cultures. But to me there's nothing strange about bringing them together. It's no stranger than putting a guitar with a bass; it all boils down to how far you want to go with the music."

Selected discography

Solo recordings

Baselines, Elektra/Musician, 1983.
Praxis, Celluloid, 1984.
Hear No Evil, Virgin, 1988.
Deconstruction: The Celluloid Recordings, Metrotone, 1993.

With Material

Temporary Music, Celluloid, 1981.
Memory Serves, Elektra/Musician, 1982.
One Down, Elektra, 1982.
Seven Souls, Virgin, 1989.
Third Power, Axiom, 1991.
Hallucination Engine, Axiom, 1994.

With Massacre

Killing Time, Celluloid, 1982.

With the Golden Palominos

The Golden Palominos, Celluloid, 1983.
Visions of Excess, Celluloid, 1985.
A Dead Horse, Celluloid, 1989.

With Last Exit

Last Exit, Celluloid, 1986.
The Noise of Trouble, Celluloid, 1987.
Cassette Recordings '87, Celluloid, 1988.

As Producer

Herbie Hancock, *Future Shock,* Columbia, 1983.
Nona Hendryx, *Nona,* RCA, 1983.
Laurie Anderson, *Mr. Heartbreak,* Warner Bros., 1984.
Herbie Hancock, *Sound-System,* Columbia, 1984.
Nona Hendryx, *The Art of Defense,* RCA, 1984.
Time Zone (John Lydon and Afrika Bambaataa), "World Destruction," Celluloid, 1984.
Fela Kuti, *Army Arrangement,* Celluloid, 1985.
Mick Jagger, *She's the Boss,* Columbia, 1985.
Yoko Ono, *Starpeace,* Polydor, 1985.
Toure Kunda, *Natalia,* Celluloid, 1985.
Afrika Bambaataa, *Beware (The Funk Is Everywhere),* Tommy Boy, 1986.
Motorhead, *Orgasmatron,* Profile, 1986.
Public Image Ltd., *Album,* Elektra, 1986.
James Blood Ulmer, *America—Do You Remember the Love?,* Blue Note, 1987.
Iggy Pop, *Instinct,* A&M, 1988.
Ronald Shannon Jackson, *Red Warrior,* Axiom, 1990.
Ginger Baker, *Middle Passage,* Axiom, 1991.
Jonas Hellborg, *The Word,* Axiom, 1991.
Mandingo, *New World Power,* Axiom, 1991.
Sonny Sharrock, *Ask the Ages,* Axiom, 1991.
Master Musicians of Jajouka, *Apocalypse Across the Sky,* Axiom, 1992.
Henry Threadgill, *Too Much Sugar for a Dime,* Axiom, 1993.
Buddy Miles Express, *Hell and Back,* Black Arc Records, c. 1994.
Hardware, *Third Eye Open,* Black Arc Records, c. 1994.

The Slavemasters, *Under the Six,* Black Arc Records, c. 1994.
Zillatron, *Lords of the Harvest,* Black Arc Records, c. 1994.
O. G. Funk, *Out of the Dark,* Black Arc Records, c. 1994.

Sources

Billboard, June 12, 1993; May 21, 1994; August 20, 1994.
Down Beat, July 1982; August 1986; November 1994.
Musician, February 1986.
New Art Examiner, June 1994.
New York Times, July 6, 1994.
Paper, 1994.
Vibe, August 1994.

—Matthew Brown

Leiber
and
Stoller

Songwriters, producers

MICHAEL OCHS ARCHIVES/Venice, CA

If Elvis Presley was the king of rock and roll, then Jerry Leiber and Mike Stoller were the power behind the throne. The songwriting duo of Leiber and Stoller, two white kids from the East Coast transplanted to Los Angeles, wrote African-American style blues songs and helped to popularize them. What was rhythm and blues to a black audience became rock and roll to a white audience, and a new kind of music was born. After several years of writing songs for the recording industry, the pair began to produce music—first the songs they wrote themselves, and then songs others wrote for them; they were the first independent recording producers, a common job in the industry today. In these ways, the two men significantly changed the American music industry.

Jerry Leiber met Mike Stoller in 1950, when they were both 17 years old. Leiber told *Audio* magazine that he "was writing songs with a drummer ... in Los Angeles. The drummer lost interest and suggested I call Mike Stoller.... I called Mike. He said he was not interested in writing songs. I said I thought it would be a good idea if we met anyway." Leiber went over to his house that afternoon, but Mike wasn't sure about the collaboration until he had seen some of Leiber's lyrics. Stoller told *Audio,* "The thing that cemented our relationship was when Jerry showed me his lyrics and I saw that they were blues in structure." Stoller, while not interested in writing sappy pop songs, was excited by the blues. That afternoon, they started writing, and they have been working together ever since.

Caught Success With "Hound Dog"

Leiber and Stoller's early years were filled with long days of writing at the piano. Leiber told *Rolling Stone,* "We used to go to Mike's house, where the upright piano was. We went there every day and wrote. We worked ten, 11, 12 hours a day." Stoller continued, "When we started working, we'd write five songs at a session. Then we'd go home, and we'd call each other up. 'I've written six more songs!' 'I've written four more.'"

After a year or so of writing songs, Leiber and Stoller's first real professional opportunity came when they met Lester Still, who worked for a local independent label, Modern Records. Still took the boys around to different studios to meet artists and executives and to play some of their songs. Leiber described for Robert Palmer in his book *Baby That Was Rock & Roll: The Legendary Leiber & Stoller,* just how they got their first song recorded by the Robbins: "The group was there, sitting around the room, and they said 'Come on, play us some stuff.' Mike played the piano and I sang our song, 'That's What the

For the Record . . .

Jerome Leiber born April 25, 1933, in Baltimore, MD; **Michael Stoller** born March 13, 1933, in New York, NY (one source says Belle Harbor, NY).

Songwriters. Met in Los Angeles and began collaboration, 1950; wrote first song, "That's What the Good Book Says," recorded by Bobby Nunn and the Robbins, 1951; first rhythm-and-blues hit composition recorded by Charles Brown, 1952; produced first major hit recording, "Hound Dog," for Willie Mae "Big Mama" Thornton, 1953; formed Spark Records, 1953; became independent producers for Atlantic records, 1956; "Hound Dog" recorded by Elvis Presley, 1956; other big hits include "Yakety Yak," recorded by the Coasters, 1958, "There Goes My Baby," recorded by the Drifters, 1959, "Spanish Harlem," recorded by Ben E. King, 1960, and "Is That All There Is," recorded by Peggy Lee, 1969; wrote songs for Presley's first movie, *Love Me Tender*, Twentieth Century Fox, 1956; other Presley films include *Jailhouse Rock*, MGM, 1957; *Loving You*, Paramount, 1957; and *King Creole*, Paramount, 1958.

Awards: Inducted into Songwriter's Hall of Fame, 1985; inducted into Rock and Roll Hall of Fame, 1987; Founder's Award, American Society of Composers, Authors and Publishers, 1991.

Addresses: *Office*—9000 Sunset Blvd., Los Angeles, CA 90069.

Good Book Says.' And they said, 'Groovy, yeah, we'll do that.' It was as easy as that. We couldn't believe it."

Songs came fast and easy for them in those days. Leiber and Stoller wrote their first big hit, "Hound Dog," in less than a quarter of an hour. In 1952 Johnny Otis, a leader of a popular blues band, asked the pair to come to a rehearsal, meet the singers, and write some songs for them. One of the singers, Big Mama Thornton, was one of "the saltiest chick[s]" they had ever seen, as Leiber told Palmer. They wanted to capture her personality in the song by writing a mean one, and the first printable line that came out was "You ain't nothin' but a hound dog." Big Mama's recording was a huge local hit in 1953.

When Elvis Presley recorded Leiber and Stoller's "Hound Dog" in 1957, their national success was assured. Presley was so pleased with the success of "Hound Dog" that he asked the two to write songs for his movies,

including *Jailhouse Rock* and *King Creole*. Because Presley was the most popular singer of his day, these two became the most popular song writers.

Became Independent Producers

"Hound Dog" was not only Leiber and Stoller's first big hit, it was the first song they also produced. Normally at this time, record companies kept people on staff to arrange the songs and oversee the recording process. When Leiber and Stoller wrote a song, they conceived the final sound as they wrote it. But when others produced their songs, the pair were not satisfied with the results. When Thornton and Otis went to record "Hound Dog," Stoller and Leiber explained and demonstrated how they thought it should sound to the band, and sat in control in the sound booth.

The following year, in 1953, Leiber and Stoller established their own label, Spark Records, so that they could always produce their own songs. A few years later, they got tired of the business end of the process, sold Spark Records, and contracted to Atlantic Records as the first independent producers ever: they became musical arrangers who were not on staff, but were instead brought in for specific recordings.

In the following few years, Leiber and Stoller produced some of the biggest hits of the day, including "Yakety Yak," recorded by the Coasters, and "There Goes My Baby" and "This Magic Moment," both recorded by the Drifters. As independent producers, Leiber and Stoller also oversaw recordings for other major labels, including RCA Victor, Verve, Atco, Big Top, Kapp, Capitol, United Artists, MGM, and A&M. Today, most producers work independently.

Moved on to Other Things

Leiber and Stoller's phenomenal success in the late 1950s and early 1960s as both songwriters and producers gave the pair the freedom to do whatever they wanted; when they got bored with one activity, they went on to the next. After writing songs for a few Elvis Presley movies, they looked for something more challenging, and started producing more and more songs for Atlantic and other labels, including their own Red Bird Records between 1964 and 1966. When they needed to move on to something else, they returned to songwriting, but changed their style as the popular style of the day changed. In the mid-1960s, they worked with singer Peggy Lee. After Lee sang their song "I'm a Woman," they wrote their cabaret-style hit "Is That All There Is," which she recorded in 1969.

Because of their monetary and professional success, the challenges Leiber and Stoller faced were few, and they were becoming bored. The song "Is That All There Is" presents a jaded, cynical, and at least in part, autobiographical view for the pair. Leiber explained the song to *Audio* in 1986: "We were thinking of moving on. We were getting older, and we weren't writing for kids anymore; we weren't kids anymore. We were looking for another, more mature audience. We thought perhaps the theater would be the place for us. So I started experimenting with some ideas, and Mike and I got together on that. 'Is That All There Is' was one of the first ideas of that genre that we completed." The two did move on into work for the theater, writing songs for both Broadway and films.

While Leiber and Stoller's work as producers helped to change the way records were made, their songs have left a more tangible legacy; many of them are still known and popular nearly 40 years after their first recording. Not only were many of them reissued on CD format in the late 1980s and early 1990s, but some of the best have found new venues. Their 1961 hit "Stand by Me," first recorded by Ben E. King, became a hit again 15 years later, when it became the title track of the 1986 movie of the same name. Twice, their songs have been reused in theatrical revues: *Smokey Joe's Cafe,* put on in Seattle in 1990, and *Baby, That's Rock 'n' Roll: The Songs of Leiber and Stoller,* which opened in Chicago in 1994. Their songs "Hound Dog" and "Jailhouse Rock" defined the new sound of rock and roll in the mid-1950s, and will forever evoke that era.

Selected discography

Charles Brown, "Hard Times," 1952.
Willie Mae "Big Mama" Thornton, "Hound Dog," Peacock, 1953.
The Cheers, "Black Denim Trousers and Motorcycle Boots," Capitol, 1955.
The Coasters, "Down in Mexico," Atco, 1956.
Elvis Presley, "Hound Dog," RCA Victor, 1956.
The Coasters, "Searchin'," Atco, 1957.
(With Doc Pomus) The Coasters, "Young Blood," Atco, 1957.
Elvis Presley, "Don't," RCA Victor, 1957.
The Coasters, "Yakety Yak," Atco, 1958.
The Coasters, "Along Came Jones," Atco, 1959.
The Coasters, "Charlie Brown," Atco, 1959.

The Coasters, "Poison Ivy," Atco, 1959.
The Clovers, "Love Potion Number Nine," United Artists, 1959.
Wilbert Harrison, "Kansas City," Fury, 1959.
(Leiber only, with Phil Spector) Ben E. King, "Spanish Harlem," 1960.
(With Ben E. King) Ben E. King, "Stand by Me," Atco, 1961.
(With Barry Mann and Cynthia Weil) The Drifters, "On Broadway," Atlantic, 1963.
Peggy Lee, "Is That All There Is," Capitol, 1969.
Dino & Sembello, *Dino & Sembello,* A&M, 1974.
Peggy Lee, *Mirrors,* A&M, 1975.
Elkie Brooks, *Elkie Brooks,* A&M, 1976.
Bolcolm and Morris, *Other Songs by Leiber & Stoller,* Nonesuch, 1978.
Elvis Presley, *Elvis Presley Sings Leiber and Stoller,* RCA, 1991.
There's a Riot Going On, Rhino Records, 1991.

Also contributed songs to soundtracks for Elvis Presley films *Love Me Tender,* 1957; *Jailhouse Rock,* 1957; *Loving You,* 1957; *King Creole,* 1959; and *Fun in Acapulco,* 1963.

Sources

Books

Hardy, Phil, and Dave Laing, *The Faber Companion to 20th Century Popular Music,* Faber & Faber, 1990.
Helander, Brock, *The Rock Who's Who,* Schirmer Books, 1982.
Palmer, Robert, *Baby, That Was Rock & Roll: The Legendary Leiber & Stoller,* Harcourt Brace Jovanovich, 1978.
Popular Music, 1920-1979, edited by Nat Shapiro and Bruce Pollock, Gale, 1985.
White, Mark, *"You Must Remember This": Popular Songwriters 1900-1980,* Scribner, 1983.

Periodicals

Audio, November 1986; December 1986.
Billboard, January 5, 1985; December 24, 1988; June 22, 1991; January 9, 1993.
Chicago Sun-Times, June 5, 1994; June 17, 1994.
Life, December 1, 1992.
Rolling Stone, February 12, 1987; April 19, 1990.
Variety, January 7, 1987; January 25, 1989; July 4, 1990.

—*Robin Armstrong*

Ute Lemper

Singer, actress, dancer, performance artist

Performer Ute Lemper has refused to pigeonhole herself into one realm of entertainment. Whether dancing, singing, or acting, Lemper has learned to command the stage and her audience. Consistently compared to actress and cabaret singer Marlene Dietrich, Lemper doesn't just sing; she grabs the audience's attention and leads them into the emotion of the music with her body language and vocal fluctuations.

Lemper was born to an opera singer mother and banker father in Muenster, Germany. Influenced by music at a young age, she studied piano, voice, and ballet. She grew up listening to American jazz and pop music. Her mother hoped that Lemper would decide on a career as a ballerina. "I was too crazy for that," Lemper told the London *Sunday Times.* "I have too much crazy passion to be disciplined as you have to be as a classical dancer. I was more interested in performing, entertainment, acting. If a song was acted, it was fine; if a song was just sung, I wasn't very good, because my voice wasn't extraordinary."

As she grew up, Lemper started getting up onstage, dancing, singing, and acting children's parts in operettas and plays at the theater where her mother worked. At age 15, Lemper kicked off her career performing in jazz and piano bars. From there, she continued her studies in acting at the Staatstheater Stuttgart. She went on to study classical theater at the prestigious Max Reinhardt Seminar in Vienna. Her first significant stage production came in two roles in Andrew Lloyd Weber's *Cats* when she was 21. She alternated between the parts of Grizabella and Bombalurina. She also performed in other stage productions like *Peter Pan,* in which she played the title role, and in *Cabaret* as Sally Bowles.

European Stardom

While she performed in *Peter Pan,* Lemper also appeared in a Berlin revue of Kurt Weill's music. Once the revue ended, the State Theatre in Stuttgart offered her an engagement to perform classical and contemporary drama. Starting with the music she learned and listened to in Berlin, Lemper wrote the script for a musical biography of Weill, from his early collaborations with playwright Bertolt Brecht and his flight from Nazi Germany in 1915, to his American citizenship and his American musicals. The news of her production spread throughout Europe.

"I am very curious about the period between the two world wars," Lemper told the *Sunday Times.* "Everyone who was important in the 1930s had to emigrate be-

For the Record . . .

Born in Muenster, Germany, in 1963. Daughter of a banker and an opera singer. *Education:* Studied theater at the Staatstheater Stuttgart and Max Reinhart Seminar.

Began performing as a child at a municipal theater in Germany; sang in jazz and piano bars when she was 15 years old; received roles in *Cats* at age 21; signed with London Records and released debut album, *Ute Lemper Sings Kurt Weill,* 1989; performed in several theater productions, films, and a ballet.

Addresses: *Record company*—London Records, 825 Eighth Ave., New York, NY 10019.

cause their art was revolutionary and anti-convention. The artists who stayed worked later for the Nazis." Lemper's curiosity and background led her to infuse her work with political passion. She wanted to revive interest in this era's music and theater, which the Nazis had eliminated. In 1989 Lemper released her first album on London Records, called *Ute Lemper Sings Kurt Weill.* She made a strong impression in America, and the LP reached Number One on *Billboard's* classical crossover chart. The following year, she earned a nomination for the Laurence Olivier award for her Weill recital in London. Her second Weill performance, *Three Penny Opera,* was released the same year.

Danced into Ballet and Film

Lemper made her mother's dreams come true when she performed as a principal dancer in a ballet Maurice Bejart created specifically for her. The ballet, *La Morte Subite,* premiered in Paris in 1991 and continued on to Germany. By this time, Lemper's popularity in Germany had grown to such an intensity that she decided to move to London. "In Germany, I cannot live a free life anymore," she told the *Sunday Times.* "I'm watched in the streets. Everything about my private life—whenever I go out with someone—is reported in the newspapers. I can't go to the supermarket because everybody knows my face. I did too many television shows.... And I want to live in a city which is culturally interesting. London is the Mecca at the moment, more interesting than New York."

Lemper's third album for London Records, *Seven Deadly Sins,* made a splash on the music scene, and she also released *Crimes of the Heart* on CBS Records that year. She made her film debut as the haughty Queen Marie-Antoinette in the French production of *L'Austrichienne.* Later, Lemper worked on two other French films—*Pierre Qui Biule,* a contemporary political film, and *Jean Galmot,* a nineteenth-century adventure.

In 1992 Lemper collaborated with Michael Nyman to record *Songbook.* The two artists created music to accompany lyrics based on classic verse by such famous poets as Paul Celan, Arthur Rimbaud, and William Shakespeare. Lemper also performed the role of Lola in Berlin's five-month run of *The Blue Angel* in 1992. After her performance, she moved back to Berlin and recorded *Kurt Weill Songs, Volume II,* on London Records. Later in the year, she released another LP, *Illusions*—her personal interpretation of Edith Piaf and Marlene Dietrich songs.

Illusions spent more than 15 weeks in the Number One slot of *Billboard's* crossover charts, and became the best-selling crossover album of the year. *Billboard* named Ute Lemper the Number One classical crossover artist of 1993. "Lemper ... can best be described as a very tasteful cabaret artist," wrote Susan Elliot in *Billboard,* "one with a good deal more emotional authenticity than, say, Barbra Streisand or Liza Minnelli, both of whom she has been compared to."

Complete Artistic Expression

Though critics have praised her glamorous image, Lemper has attributed that characteristic to her portrayal of emotion. "The glamorous part of the image is not really me," she said in the *Los Angeles Times.* "I am not at all glamorous, and it's really contrary to what I want to do on stage. I prefer to think I am very straightforward ... although maybe still with a secret. Glamour is not what I'm looking for in my performance. I'm looking for emotional expression, not in a sentimental or stylized way, but with complete honesty and directness." Lemper sings mostly in German and French, and uses visual enhancement as much as her vocals to enliven her performances.

Constantly expanding her credits, Lemper performed at La Scala in Milan in an homage to opera singer Cathy Berberian. She also made her debut with the London Symphony Orchestra with conductor Kent Nagano. She took her talents into yet another area with an exhibition in Paris of her oil paintings, which received a warm reception from the press.

In 1994 Lemper began working with acclaimed director Robert Altman on his film *Ready to Wear,* which depicts the inner workings of the fashion industry. Lemper played the role of an eight-months-pregnant model named Albertine. Continuing her trend of nonstop work, Lemper released *City of Strangers* on London Records in 1995, which included songs by American composer-lyricist Stephen Sondheim.

Selected discography

Ute Lemper Sings Kurt Weill, London, 1989.
Three Penny Opera, London, 1990.
Seven Deadly Sins, London, 1991.
Crimes of the Heart, CBS, 1991.
Songbook, London, 1992.
Kurt Weill Songs, Volume II, London, 1993.
Illusions, London, 1993.

City of Strangers, London, 1995.

Sources

Billboard, April 29, 1989; July 3, 1993.
High Fidelity, May 1989.
Los Angeles Times, January 16, 1993; January 29, 1993.
New York Times, February 4, 1993.
Stereo Review, July 1990; September 1991; November 1993.
Sunday Times (London), March 17, 1991.
Variety, March 22, 1989.

Additional information for this profile was obtained from London Records press material, 1994.

—Sonya Shelton

Ramsey Lewis

Pianist, composer

Courtesy of GRP Records, Inc.

Ramsey Lewis's recording history—more than 60 albums in his four-decade career—attests to his enduring popularity. Although considered a jazz artist, Lewis is known for mixing a variety of genres, including blues, soul, pop, and classical into his repertoire. But the album that propelled him from a popular nightclub performer to a phenomenal success, *The In Crowd,* also marked the end of his critical acclaim. Since its release in 1965, Lewis has frequently been accused of commercializing his music and not playing to his potential as a jazz artist. Lewis, however, points out that his albums have always included non-jazz pieces, and his fans have ignored the criticism for decades.

Lewis began playing the piano at the age of four and was receiving lessons by age six. In his early teens, he served as pianist at the church where his father was the choir director. His introduction to jazz came at 16, when he was invited to join the Clefs, a seven-piece band that played at college proms and social functions. Lewis described it to Mike Bourne in *Down Beat* as "a very hip R&B jazz type thing." He performed with the band for a couple of years, until it broke up because of America's military involvement in the Korean War. Daddy-O Daylie, a popular Chicago DJ, advised the players who had escaped the draft—bassist and cellist Eldee Young, drummer Red Holt, and Lewis—to stay together as the Ramsey Lewis Trio.

Daddy-O Daylie gave another boost to the group's career when he introduced them to Leonard Chess of the Chess recording company. And although Chess recorded the trio's first album, it was shelved until Daylie intervened, promising to air it on his show. That radio exposure in 1956 contributed to the group's growing popularity.

Increased Exposure and a Hit Record

Meanwhile, Lewis had been studying music, first at the Chicago Music College and later at De Paul University. In 1959 the trio was playing at the Cloister Inn in Chicago when an invitation came to perform at the legendary club Birdland in New York City. Lewis decided to leave school to take advantage of the opportunity. Although Birdland had only invited the trio for three weeks, the exposure led to performances at Randall's Island Jazz Festival, the Newport Jazz Festival, and the Village Vanguard. One gig led to another, and Lewis never returned to school.

The trio performed steadily in nightclubs, achieving moderate recognition in Chicago and elsewhere. In 1965 their album *The In Crowd* catapulted the Ramsey

Born May 27, 1935, in Chicago, IL; married twice; children: four, including sons Robert and Frayne. *Education:* Attended Chicago Music College and De Paul University.

Formed trio with bassist-cellist Eldee Young and drummer Red Holt, 1956; group recorded first album, 1956; also recorded with Max Roach, Clark Terry, and Sonny Stitt, late 1950s; trio played at Birdland and Island Jazz Festival, New York, 1959; released *The In Crowd,* 1965; trio dissolved and Lewis formed another with bassist Cleveland Eaton and drummer Maurice White; also formed quintet, including Henry Johnson (guitar), Chuck Webb (bass), Michael Logan (keyboards), and Steve Cobb (drums), 1990s; hosted nationally syndicated weekly radio show and weekly cable show; served as artistic director for Ravinia's Jazz in June series, beginning in 1993.

Selected awards: Gold album for *The In Crowd,* 1965; Grammy Award for best small-group jazz recording, 1965, for "The In Crowd"; gold album for *Sun Goddess,* 1975; Grammy awards for "Hold It Right There" and "Hang on Sloopy."

Addresses: *Home*—Chicago, IL. *Record company*—GRP Records, Inc., 555 West 57th Street, New York, NY 10019.

Lewis Trio to national prominence. The title track, one of the first "fusion" hits, won a Grammy that year for best small-group jazz recording. Soon after, the trio recorded hit versions of the popular rock songs "Hang on Sloopy," "A Hard Day's Night," and "Wade in the Water." One of the few instances of a jazz instrumental being played on Top 40 radio stations, Lewis's version of "Hang on Sloopy" eclipsed the original by the McCoys.

Trio Disbanded

But fame did not sit well with the 15-year-old group. According to Lewis, things had grown stale. "We weren't relating to each other musically," he told Bourne in a *Down Beat* interview. He admitted that the other bandmembers resented the attention he received as the group's namesake. The group broke up in the mid-1960s, and Lewis formed a new trio with bassist Cleveland Eaton and drummer Maurice White, who later joined the rhythm and blues group Earth, Wind and Fire.

By 1970 Lewis had more than 30 albums to his name. His popularity had remained strong, despite substantial criticism from the jazz press since his success with *The In Crowd.* Accused of "selling out" and diluting his jazz with pop formulas, Lewis maintained that he had always played a mix of jazz, R&B, rock, and classics. "I've always had a broad outlook," he explained to Bourne in 1973. "If it was good music, I could dig it." With the new trio, Lewis made several albums with orchestral backing, and drummer White added *kalimba,* an African thumb piano, to some pieces. Lewis told *Down Beat* that the group didn't "want to be fenced in by old jazz patterns, or any patterns, for that matter." Fans ignored the critical disrespect and continued listening; several Lewis albums from this period went gold, including *Sun Goddess* in 1975.

Lewis abandoned the trio format in the 1970s in favor of a seven-piece group. The septet, following the success of *Sun Goddess,* toured twice with Earth, Wind and Fire. However, Lewis reported feeling more like a bandleader than a pianist, and in the early 1980s he returned to playing with a trio. He varied his surroundings several times in the late 1980s and early 1990s, playing in quartets, quintets, piano duets, and as a soloist.

Critical Scorn and Audience Approval

Although the fervor Lewis had inspired in the late 1960s and the early 1970s waned in the 1980s, he continued to draw a substantial following. But critics, for the most part, remained unimpressed. In 1982 Brian Harrigan, reviewing *Live at the Savoy* for *Melody Maker,* admitted Lewis still had "brilliant technique," but protested that his playing was "totally submerged by the presence of horn sections, additional keyboards, backing singers and—although I didn't actually hear it—probably someone tapping on the side of a kitchen sink.... [This work has] all the backbone of a musical jellyfish." Richard Palmer reviewed the 1984 album *Ramsey Lewis and Nancy Wilson* for *Jazz Journal International* in a similar vein: "I must say that the vulgar commercial intent and packaging of this album is not something I warm to greatly. If I'm wrong, and this was an honest and sincere project—well, I feel a bit sorry for them both." Listeners disagreed, however, expressing their approval by continuing to attend performances and buy albums.

Lewis moved into new arenas in the 1980s and early 1990s. He started hosting a jazz radio show on WNUA Chicago, which had been syndicated in 15 markets by 1994. He also began hosting a weekly Black Entertainment Television (BET) cable program called *Sound & Style,* which was nominated for an ACE award. In addition, BET chose Lewis as the official spokesperson for the new cable channel BET on Jazz, which was set to launch in the autumn of 1994. And in 1993, Lewis became the artistic director for Ravinia's Jazz in June concert series in Chicago.

Signed With GRP

Lewis also continued to tour and record. He ended his 20-year relationship with Columbia Records in the early 1990s and signed on with GRP, a label he feels is more enthusiastic in its promotion of jazz musicians. *Sky Island,* released by GRP in 1993, received the usual complaints from critics, including Larry Birnbaum, who wrote in *Down Beat:* "[Lewis's] acoustic piano breezes blandly through a set of diluted pop tunes and insipid originals, lightly scattering bluesy signature riffs upon the tepid waters."

However, *Sky Island* was popular with jazz listeners; it hit the Top Five on the contemporary jazz albums chart and sold 37,000 units within three months of its release. Sons Frayne and Robert had helped Lewis produce the album, along with Carl Griffin and Maurice White. With plans to collaborate with fusion saxophonist Grover Washington on a mid-1990s release, Lewis held true to his claim in *Down Beat* in 1991 that he would be "concertizing and recording until they are throwing dirt in my face six feet under."

Selected discography

Something You Got, Chess, 1964.
Live at the Bohemian Caverns, Chess, 1964.
The In Crowd, Chess, 1965.
Sound of Christmas, Chess, 1966.
Another Voyage, Cadet, 1969.
Sun Goddess, Columbia, 1975.
Live at the Savoy, Columbia, 1982.
Ramsey Lewis and Nancy Wilson, Columbia, 1984.
Ivory Pyramid, GRP, 1992.
Sky Island, GRP, 1993.
Tequila Mockingbird, Columbia.
Keys to the City, Columbia.
A Classic Encounter, Columbia.

Sources

Billboard, February 12, 1994.
Down Beat, May 14, 1970; October 25, 1973; March 1991; July 1993; November 1993.
Jazz Journal International, December 1984.
Melody Maker, March 13, 1982.

Additional information for this profile was provided by GRP Records.

—*Susan Windisch Brown*

Little Texas

Country band

The success of country-rock band Little Texas reflects the changing demographics of country music. The group's contemporary, rock-and-pop-influenced sound is meant to appeal to the fans of "young country" and the disc jockeys at big-market, urban radio stations. Young and handsome, the members of Little Texas have capitalized on music videos and frequent live appearances to bolster their popularity. The formula has worked: six of the group's first seven singles reached the country Top Ten, and two of those—"God Blessed Texas" and "What Might Have Been"—crested at Number One. "We're appealing to a young, new generation that probably didn't listen to country music before," vocalist Tim Rushlow told *Country Music* magazine. "And that's something we're real proud of."

Despite their relatively tender ages, the artists in Little Texas are seasoned professionals who spent years together developing their signature harmonies, writing songs, and practicing their stage presence. At the urging of Warner Bros. executives, the group travelled the country in a beat-up van, playing small clubs six or

AP/Wide World Photos

143

Members include **Del Gray** (born May 5, 1968, in Ohio), drums; **Porter Howell** (born June 21, 1964, in Longview, TX), guitar; **Dwayne O'Brien** (born July 30, 1963, in Ada, OK), guitar; **Duane Propes** (born December 17, 1966, in Longview, TX), bass; **Tim Rushlow** (born October 6, 1966, in Arlington, TX), lead vocals; **Brady Seals** (born March 29, 1969, in Ohio), keyboards.

Band formed in Nashville, TN, when members were signed to a development deal by Warner Bros. Records, 1988; released first single with Warner Bros., "Some Guys Have All the Love," 1991; released debut album *First Time for Everything,* 1992.

Addresses: *Management*—Square West Entertainment, P.O. Box 120053, Nashville, TN 37212.

seven days a week. This forced camaraderie has served the members well now that they have established themselves in Nashville. "You put six guys in an unair-conditioned van in the middle of July, and you find out real quick if they're really a band," Rushlow said in the *Chicago Tribune.* "We became six brothers instead of just six people who wanted to make money together."

The earliest hints of Little Texas began in 1984. That year, in Arlington, Texas, Rushlow and acoustic guitarist Dwayne O'Brien started playing together. In the meantime, lead guitarist Porter Howell and bassist Duane Propes—both natives of Longview, Texas—were attending college together in Nashville. The four musicians got together in Nashville in 1986 and began earning pocket money by playing "golden oldies" in a hotel lounge. In those days they called themselves the Varsitys.

In 1988 the four-man group took a tour of the Northern states, playing at fairs and clubs. On one stop they met Del Gray and Brady Seals, who were at the time touring with Sandy Powell. "We hit it off and they asked us to be in the band, but we were committed to the rest of Sandy's tour," Gray told *Country Music.* "We kept in touch, and about two months later, they called and said that a guy from Warner Bros. had seen them and liked everyone except the drummer and the keyboard player. So we went down and met with them, and two weeks later we were in the band." Gray was 20 at the time; Seals 19.

Warner Bros. did indeed express interest in the group in 1988, but what the company offered was hardly ideal. The group was basically given the opportunity to record some demonstration tapes. When the tapes were completed, the executives were not particularly impressed. "They demanded that we be a country act and hit the road rather than hang around Nashville playing motel lounges," Rushlow told the Fort Wayne, Indiana, *News Sentinel.*

The band scraped up enough money to buy a well-used van, hooked on a homemade trailer, and hit the road. "We'd do a week at a time in each city, five sets a night, six to seven nights a week," Rushlow recalled. "We'd write a song, put it in our show, and see how people liked it. It gave us a chance to experiment and see just what our little niche was."

That "niche" was the same one occupied by soft-rock bands like the Eagles and Restless Heart—a country-flavored pop sound with emphasis on vocal harmonies and rock rhythms. Finally, after three years of almost nonstop road work, the group's sound suited both Warner Bros. and the artists themselves. Little Texas's first album, *First Time for Everything,* was released in 1992, and the debut single, "Some Guys Have All the Love," hit the country Top Ten.

The name Little Texas derived from the name of the street on which Warner Bros. producer Doug Grau lived in Nashville. The band members discovered that the street was named after a community south of Nashville that was famous for moonshine activity. Grau agreed that "Little Texas" would be a far better name than another the group was considering—Possum Flat.

With their long, flowing hairstyles and rock stylings, Little Texas had to fight stereotyping as a "hair act." O'Brien told *Billboard* that the longhair image "almost killed us.... Nobody took us seriously. They thought we were all thrown together and that we didn't play our instruments or write our own songs." With the budding popularity of pop-oriented "young country," the group soon found an audience, proving particularly popular with country radio stations in larger markets. Within two years Little Texas had produced two gold albums and a string of hit singles, including "What Might Have Been."

"We *want* to bring something new to country music—it's not the same chord structure, the same lyrics, the same situations," Seals told *Country Music.* "Nowadays, country is opening up so much, and you can see so many different influences in it. And a lot of people out there won't even admit that they listened to [pop icons] Prince or Michael Jackson or [rock group] Kiss when they were growing up, but you know they did."

The long years of struggle have brought maturity and drive to the members of Little Texas. Members collaborate on songs, and each album contains numbers written by the band. Their touring schedule still keeps them on the road almost 300 days a year. Rushlow summed up the group's strengths in *Country Music:* "We're a real band. We're self-contained: We play our own stuff, write our own stuff and sing our own stuff. People will come up to us after a show and say, 'Man, you sound just like the record!' And we just kind of smile, 'cause it is—it's us in the studio and it's us live. So that's the best compliment in the world."

Selected discography

On Warner Bros.

First Time for Everything, 1992.
Big Time, 1993.
Kick a Little, 1994.

Sources

Akron Beacon Journal, October 14, 1993.
Billboard, February 19, 1994.
Chicago Tribune, March 19, 1992; November 19, 1993.
Country Music, March/April, 1994.
News Sentinel (Fort Wayne, IN), October 7, 1993.

—Anne Janette Johnson

Little Walter

Courtesy of the Institute of Jazz Studies

The most commercially successful Chicago blues performer of the postwar era, harmonica stylist Little Walter Jacobs continues to attract a devoted legion of followers. His recordings as a solo artist and side musician with the bands of Muddy Waters and Jimmy Rogers are among the finest performances of Chicago blues—sessions that continue to be studied and idolized by musical artists around the world. Fusing the style of his mentor John Lee Williamson with the jump blues of saxophonist Louis Jordan, Walter varied the harmonica, to quote Paul Oliver in his work *The Blackwell Guide to Blues Records,* as a "capable but crude horn substitute." A country-bred musician with a modern sensibility for swing music, Walter created an amplified sound filled with dark, haunting tones and flowing melodic lines that became an integral element in the emergence of Chicago blues.

Born to Adams Jacobs and Beatrice Leveige on May 1, 1930, in Marksville, Louisiana, Marion Walter Jacobs was raised on a farm in Alexandria. Taking up the harmonica at age eight, he learned to play blues by listening to the recordings of John Lee "Sonny Boy" Williamson. After leaving home at age 13, the young musician played small night spots in Louisiana, Arkansas, and Missouri.

In 1947 Little Walter arrived in Chicago and supported himself by playing on street corners and in the Jewish market district of Maxwell Street. Performing for tips and handouts, Walter's repertoire included waltzes, polkas, and blues numbers. On Maxwell Street he performed with guitarists Johnny Young, Othum Brown, and Big Bill Broonzy, who became his informally adopted guardian. At this time he also took up playing guitar. Arkansas-born guitarist Moody Jones recalled in *Chicago Blues* how Walter displayed a deep interest in studying the instrument: "[Walter] played harmonica y'know but he used to follow me to try to play the guitar. Me and him be playing together, we'd go out to make some money and he wouldn't want to play the harmonica. He'd want to play what I was doing. So he finally learned."

Little Walter's burgeoning talent led to his recording debut for Ora Nelle—a small, obscure label located in Bernard and Red Abrams's Maxwell Street record shop —in 1947. Backed by Othum Brown on guitar, Walter cut the number "I Just Keep Loving Her," a blues boogie emulative of Williamson. The reverse side featured Walter playing behind Brown on his original composition "Ora Nelle Blues."

During this time, Little Walter's performances on Maxwell Street began to attract the attention of many musicians. A resident of the Maxwell district, guitarist Jimmy

Born Walter Marion Jacobs, May 1, 1930, in Marksville, LA; died from a blood clot sustained in a street fight, February 15, 1968; son of Adams Jacobs and Beatrice Leveige.

Began playing harmonica at age eight; left home at age 13 to play nightspots in Louisiana, Arkansas, and Missouri; arrived in Chicago, 1947, and performed as a street musician until joining the Muddy Waters band, 1948; left Waters after scoring first hit record, 1952; joined the Four Aces and recorded a string of hits under own name, including "My Babe," 1955; continued to record and perform, late 1950s; toured Europe, early 1960s.

Awards: Won *Blues Unlimited* Reader's Poll as best blues harmonica player, 1973.

Rogers recalled his early association with the young harmonica great in *Blues Guitar:* "I met Little Walter ... down on Maxwell Street. He was about seventeen. So I took him down and introduced him to Muddy [Waters], and I told him he was a good harmonica player. In fact, Little Walter was about the best harmonica that was in Chicago—for the blues, at that time."

Joined Muddy Waters Band

In 1948 Waters added Little Walter to his road band, which included Rogers on guitar, Big Crawford on bass, and Baby Face Leroy on drums. Departing from his guitar/bass Chess Records studio line-up, Waters recorded with Walter in a trio that produced the nationwide hit "Louisiana Blues" in 1951. Waters also joined Walter on the Parkway studio recordings of the Little Walter Trio and the Baby Face Trio. Guitarist Baby Face Leroy's cut of "Rolling and Tumbling," featuring Walter's harmonica and Waters's stinging slide work, has been considered by many critics and historians as one of the most powerful Chicago blues songs ever recorded. On subsequent sessions for Chess, wrote Jas Obrecht in *Blues Guitar,* "Waters and Walter further forged their instruments into a seamless voice or created stunning call-and-response dialogues."

This powerful musical exchange is featured on a number of Chess sides, including Little Walter's 1951 Top Ten rhythm-and-blues hit "Long Distance Call." Featured on second guitar on the recording of "Honey Bee," Walter played single-line figures with subtle, yet driving intensity. On "Just a Fool," he was paired on guitar with Jimmy Rogers to create a strong Mississippi Delta setting behind Waters's vocals.

Little Walter's contribution to Waters's band, observed blues researcher Alan Lomax in *The Land Where the Blues Began,* resulted in the transformation of "the blues combo from a country string band into a wind-plus-string orchestra." With the addition of drums and the piano of Otis Spann, Little Walter remained the primary soloist of the Waters band, his amplified harmonica producing haunting tones and long, drawn-out, horn-like bends. The powerful Waters-Rogers-Walter combination gained a formidable reputation. As Waters recalled in *Blues Guitar,* "Little Walter, Jimmy Rogers, and myself, we would go looking for bands that were playing. We called ourselves 'the headhunters,' 'cause we'd go in and if we get the chance we were gonna burn 'em."

Little Walter and His Jukes

After landing a hit with the Waters band's stage theme song for Chess in 1952, Little Walter left the group. Originally an untitled boogie instrumental, the number was released as "Juke." The reverse side featured "Crazy About You Baby," an original song based on Sonny Boy Williamson's "Crazy About You Gal." During a tour of Louisiana the band discovered that "Juke" had hit the charts. In an interview in *Blues Review,* Rogers remembered that he was sitting in a club when "here comes this song, so we gets up and runs to the jukebox 'fore the record is out. So we're looking to find what's the number, and we found it and it said 'Juke.' And we kept looking at it; it said 'Little Walter and his Jukes.' We said, 'Who's them Jukes, man?' Wasn't no Jukes."

Little Walter became so excited upon hearing "Juke" that he left the group and rushed back to Chicago. Returning to the city, he discovered that the Four Aces' harmonica player, Junior Wells, had left that outfit to fill his spot with the Muddy Waters band; thus, he immediately welcomed the opportunity to join the Aces, a group that included Louis and Dave Myers on guitars and Freddie Below on drums.

Dave Myers explained in *Blues Access,* "We gave him the framework. The work he needed was our type of work to be able to express himself at his level of playing. We was all fast and flexible, and we was all in the process of learning much different types of music and different expressions of music." At the helm of the band, Walter brought to it a vibrant sense of energy and creativity. "Walter was simply a person you could always learn something from," recalled drummer Below in the liner notes to *Little Walter.* "He was always calling rehearsals for us to go over tunes or tighten up our old ones. It was like Walter was running a school where you could really learn something you interested in."

At Chess studios, the band—now billed as Little Walter and His Jukes and Little Walter and His Nightcats—recorded a string of hits, many of which outsold those of the Muddy Waters band, including the 1952 recording "Mean Old World," and the 1953 releases "Blues with a Feeling" and the instrumental classic "Off the Wall." When Louis Myers left the band in 1954, he was replaced by guitarist Robert Junior Lockwood, whose brilliant jazz-style fills were featured on numbers like "Thunderbird," "Shake Dancer," and the haunting slow blues "Blue Lights."

Although Little Walter remained on the rhythm and blues charts throughout 1954, it wasn't until 1955 that he had his biggest hit, with Willie Dixon's "My Babe"—a song adapted from the gospel number "This Train." Despite Walter's initial dislike for the tune, Dixon, as he wrote in his autobiography, was determined to persuade him to record it: "I felt Little Walter had the feeling for this 'My Babe' song. He was the type of fellow who wanted to brag about some chick, somebody he loved, something he was doing or getting [away] with. He fought it for two long years and I wasn't going to give the song to nobody but him. [But] the minute he did it, Boom! she went right to the top of the charts."

Hard Years: The End of an Era

But as Little Walter hit the charts with "My Babe," his career faced several setbacks. Soon afterward, Dave Myers left the band, followed by drummer Below. Excessive drinking and an erratic lifestyle greatly affected Walter's ability as a bandleader. "He was behaving like a cowboy much of the time," wrote Mike Rowe in *Chicago Blues,* "and would roar up to a clubdate in his black Cadillac with a squeal of the brakes that sent everyone rushing to the door to stare."

Though Little Walter's studio performances of the late 1950s continued to produce first-rate material, his rough lifestyle began to take its toll. By the 1960s he bore facial scars from drunken altercations. As Muddy Waters told Paul Oliver during the 1960s in *Conversation With the Blues,* "He's real tough, Little Walter, and he's had it hard. Got a slug in his leg right now!" Walter's street-hardened behavior resulted in his death, at his home, on February 15, 1968, from a blood clot sustained during a street fight. He was 37.

Upon his death, Little Walter left a recording career unparalleled in the history of postwar Chicago Blues. His musicianship has influenced nearly every modern blues harmonica player. In the liner notes to *Confessin' the Blues,* Pete Welding wrote: "Honor Little Walter, who gave us so much and, who like most bluesmen, received so little." But as a man who lived through his instrument, Walter knew no other source of reward than the mastery of his art and the freedom to create music of original expression.

Selected discography

Little Walter: Confessin' the Blues, Chess.
Little Walter: I Hate to See You Go, Chess.
The Best of Little Walter, Chess.
The Best of Little Walter, Volume II, Chess.
Boss of the Blues Harmonica, Chess.
The Blues World of Little Walter, Delmark.
Little Walter, Chess, 1976.
The Essential Little Walter, Chess, 1993.

With others

More Real Folk Blues: Muddy Waters, Chess, 1967.
Muddy Waters: Trouble No More, Singles 1955-1959, Chess, 1989.
Jimmy Rogers: Chicago Bound, Chess.

Anthologies

The Best of Chess, Volume I, Chess.
The Best of Chess, Volume II, Chess.
Chicago Boogie! 1947, St. George Records, 1983.

Sources

Books

Blues Guitar: The Men Who Made the Music, From the Pages of Guitar Player Magazine, edited by Jas Obrecht, Miller Freeman Books, 1993.
Dixon, Willie, and Don Snowden, *I Am the Blues: The Willie Dixon Story,* Da Capo, 1989.
Lomax, Alan, *The Land Where the Blues Began,* Pantheon Books, 1993.
Oliver, Paul, *Conversation With the Blues,* Horizon Press, 1965.
Oliver, Paul, *The Blackwell Record Guide to Blues Records,* Basil Blackwell, 1989.
Palmer, Robert, *Deep Blues,* Viking Press, 1989.
Rowe, Mike, *Chicago Blues: The City and the Music,* Da Capo, 1975.

Periodicals

Blues Access, summer 1994.
Blues Revue, fall 1994.

Additional information for this profile was obtained from the liner notes to *Confessin' the Blues*, by Pete Welding.

—John Cohassey

Live

Rock band

Two words are consistently used to describe Live's music: honest and serious. This seems to be a reflection of what the bandmembers are all about. Not many people keep in touch with the friends they had when they were 13 years old, much less work with them into adulthood. This small-town band, with their strong values, were propelled into popularity thanks to their deep, personal lyrics and their intense live performances. Elysa Gardner in *Spin* remarked that despite lead singer Ed Kowalczyk's usually mild-mannered demeanor, "A physical metamorphosis seems to occur when he performs, transforming boyish singer into whirling dervish."

Live started out in their hometown, York, Pennsylvania, as four 13-year-olds called Public Affection. In 1984, singer Kowalczyk, guitarist Chad Taylor, drummer Chad Gracey, and bassist Patrick Dahlheimer decided to form a band for their eighth-grade talent show, and they kept playing together. The members of Public Affection faced a crossroads when they all graduated from William Penn Senior High School in 1989. They each had to

Photograph by Michael Wilson, courtesy of Radioactive Records

For the Record . . .

Members include **Patrick Dahlheimer,** bass guitar; **Chad Gracey,** drums; **Ed Kowalczyk,** vocals; **Chad Taylor,** guitar.

Band formed in York, PA, as Public Affection, 1984; released independent album *Death of a Dictionary,* 1989; signed with Radioactive Records and changed band name to Live, 1991; released EP *Four Songs*; released debut album, *Mental Jewelry,* 1992; appeared on *MTV Unplugged,* 1995.

Addresses: *Record company*—Radioactive Records, 70 Universal City Plaza, 3rd Floor, Universal City, CA 91608.

make the choice between college and pursuing the band. "We were bound for college and decided not to do it," recalled Kowalczyk in *Musician.* "That was the serious turning point, deciding not to go to college," echoed Taylor.

Determined to take the band to the next level, Public Affection independently released their first album, called *Death of a Dictionary,* in 1989. Two years later, Talking Heads keyboardist Jerry Harrison named Public Affection his choice for up-and-coming rock and roll rookies in *Rolling Stone.* "Public Affection has rock appeal, but they still have acknowledgment of other types of music," said Harrison. "That's what excites me about them."

Soon, word had spread about Public Affection from York, Pennsylvania. Radioactive Records heard their demo tape and signed the band to a contract. "You listen to so many bad tapes and see so many bad showcases that it gets discouraging after a while," Phil Schuster, a representative of Radioactive Records, said in *Musician.* "I listened to the first two songs on the tape, and I knew they had something unique. With a band like that, you just know. I saw them play several times, and they always performed with the same intensity, whether it was to a full club or 15 people. They just love to play."

Once the group joined the Radioactive roster, they decided to change their name to Live. Next, they started working on their first project. Harrison produced the band's *Four Songs* EP debut. "Unlike most demo tapes, theirs had real melodies," Harrison told *Musician.* "Ed can sing in the classical sense, but it doesn't cut down

on the fervor. He has honesty and intense beliefs. I think that living in York, out of the mainstream, has made them less derivative, more indigenous. When I made suggestions, they weren't looking over their shoulders at what some other band was doing."

In 1992, Jerry Harrison took over production once again, and Live released their first full-length album, *Mental Jewelry.* The band kicked off the beginning of their success with the hit "Operation Spirit." *Mental Jewelry* focused on four young individuals struggling with the outside world. As part of the tour supporting the album, Live joined Big Audio Dynamite, Public Image Ltd., and Blind Melon on the "MTV 120 Minutes" tour.

The music industry took note of Live's potential, as did the press. "I'm really excited about this band Live," radio consultant Jeff Pollack told *Rolling Stone.* "The lyrics are really impressive, and this from a bunch of unjaded kids from York, Pennsylvania. It's the sort of record that reminds me of the old days. It just refuses to be ignored. There's just something irrepressible about their talent." Don McLeese wrote in *Rolling Stone,* "It's hard to imagine a more serious band than Pennsylvania's Live, whose moral earnestness makes early U2 sound frat-band frivolous."

Live went back into the studio and released their next effort, *Throwing Copper,* in 1994. Elysa Gardner in *Spin* remarked that the release, like their previous album, was "rife with spiritual imagery and social commentary." The first single from the album, "Selling the Drama," delves into the relationship between musicians and their audience. "Being on stage and talking at people is a strange thing," Kowalczyk explained in the band's label publicity bio. "You can rape your audience with ambiguity and distance, and they can rape you with prejudice and preconception." "Selling the Drama" and "I Alone" went into heavy rotation on MTV, furthering the band's popularity.

Another song on *Throwing Copper,* "White Discussion," describes a conversation between two people just before the world ends. "We've tried to make *Throwing Copper* more than your average trip down angst lane," continued Kowalczyk in the bio. In all, Kowalczyk felt *Throwing Copper* marked significant growth for Live. "We like to say that the soundscape of Live has totally transformed," he said. "A lot of good things happen to guitar amplifiers when you turn them up all the way, and a lot of good things happen to lyrics when you don't think about them as much." The *New York Times'* Neil Strauss wrote, "The difference between Live and many of its slacker contemporaries is that Live treats songs reverentially, as if they are truly inspired by a higher force."

Live recorded *Throwing Copper* live in the studio, as opposed to the technique of each musician recording his part separately, to be mixed with the other instruments later. They played together, as a band, the way they've worked since junior high school. "We're always out playing," Chad Taylor told Jon Sutherland in *RIP* magazine. "Even if we are writing songs for a new album, we'll go out and play. That's how we remain a good band." That's also how they earned the right to their name. Live will continue to stay on those stages performing their serious rock and roll, just like they did when they were 13 years old, competing in the school talent show.

Selected discography

Death of a Dictionary (independent release), 1989.
Four Songs (EP), Radioactive, 1991.
Mental Jewelry, Radioactive, 1992.

Throwing Copper (includes "Selling the Drama," "I Alone," and "Lightning Crashes"), Radioactive, 1994.

Sources

Entertainment Weekly, March 17, 1995.
Guitar Player, February 1995.
Musician, April 1992.
New York Times, April 23, 1992; June 9, 1994.
RIP, August 1994.
Rolling Stone, April 18, 1991; April 16, 1992; May 14, 1992; August 11, 1994.
Spin, February 1995.
Variety, May 11, 1992.

Additional information for this profile was obtained from Radioactive Records publicity materials, 1994.

—*Sonya Shelton*

Israel "Cachao" Lopez

Bassist

© 1994 Sony Music

Film actor Andy Garcia told Lynette Rice in a *Chicago Times* article about Cuban bassist Israel "Cachao" Lopez, "In the music world, [Cachao is] a legend. In the ... commercial world, he's unknown." While fame and fortune have not always been his, Lopez, who has been performing Cuban jazz for decades, has had an enormous influence on the direction this music has taken. He and the musicians he played with in the late 1930s and early 1940s in Havana developed the *mambo* from the more staid and traditional ballroom dance the *danzón.* In the mid-1950s, they applied the jazz jam session to Cuban music and created the improvised *descarga.*

Many members of the Lopez family were famous professional musicians. Young Israel began learning various instruments at an early age, and began playing professionally when he was only eight. While he could play guitar, trumpet, and bongos, he chose the bass as his main instrument because, as he explained to Gigi Anders of the *Washington Post,* "It's the most important instrument, the foundation. There has to be a beat. An orchestra without a bass cannot speak. Just like a building, without an underlying structure, falls. It's a rhythmic, accompanying instrument that carries the beat for all kinds of music. The ear always searches for it, and once it's perceived, you relax."

Lopez's first job was in the movies, playing in an orchestra that accompanied silent films. When talkies put these musicians out of business, he moved on; by the age of 12, Israel Lopez was a full-time member of the Havana Philharmonic, as well as a number of dance bands. In 1937, he joined flautist Antonio Arcaño's Las Maravillas. While his musical background included many types of music, Lopez preferred a distinctly Cuban music. "I was always attracted to [Cuban music] because it belonged to my country, my origins," he told the *Washington Post.* "As a Latino, playing our music for Hispanic and Anglo ears is a chance to unite the Hispanic and Anglo cultures. Music is the closest way to reach all people."

Lopez and his brother Orestes, also in the Orquesta Arcaño y las Maravillas, composed and arranged most of the group's performing repertoire of *danzón,* frequently more than 20 pieces in one week. The *danzón,* the most popular ballroom dance in Cuba in the late nineteenth and early twentieth centuries, was itself a mixture of the European contradance and the Afro-Cuban syncopated rhythms of the *habañera.* The Lopez brothers added riffs and swing and other jazz characteristics, and changed the *danzón* into the *mambo.* "Orestes and I wanted to give a spin to our music, turn it around a little, 180 degrees from what it was," Lopez told the *Washington Post.* "So we made some

For the Record . . .

Born Israel Lopez, September 14, 1918, in Havana, Cuba; married, 1946; children: one daughter.

Joined the Havana Philharmonic, 1930; joined *Orquesta Arcaño y las Maravillas*, 1937; made 16 albums in Cuba, 1945-60; left Cuba, 1962; joined the Miami Symphony, 1978; played at Alice Tully Hall in the Jazz at Lincoln Center program, 1991, and at Radio City Music Hall, 1993. Television appearances include *Showbiz Today*, 1994; subject of film documentary *Cachao: Como Su Ritmo No Hay Dos*, 1994.

Awards: Latin Music Award, *Billboard*, 1994; inducted into *Billboard's* Latin Music Hall of Fame, 1994; Grammy Award for best tropical Latin performance, 1995, for *Master Sessions, Volume 1*.

Addresses: *Record company*—Crescent Moon/Epic, 550 Madison Ave., New York, NY 10022.

modifications, while always respecting the tradition. The idea was to give a bit more velocity to the old style."

Lopez and his group made this new music mostly for themselves, not knowing who, if anyone, would appreciate it. Lopez said in the *Washington Post:* "You can never tell what will please people. When I made the *mambo* with Orestes, I thought 'Nobody will like this.' It was a very explosive, spontaneous treatment. We were trying to advance our music and expected nothing to come of it. We thought people would think we were loco [crazy]." Instead, his audiences thought the new sound was marvelous, and it soon spread, quickly becoming the hottest dance worldwide. Interest in jazz by Cuban musicians kept growing in the 1940s and 1950s, and soon Lopez and his colleagues started playing and recording jam sessions—sessions of improvisation—called *descarga,* meaning 'discharge.' Lopez continued to play *mambas, danzón,* and *descarga* for the next 40 years, inside and outside of Cuba.

Lopez remained with the Havana Philharmonic for 30 years, until Communist dictator Fidel Castro came to power in Cuba. The following years were difficult for Lopez, for he was unable to achieve the same level of success outside of Cuba that he had found inside. He played in New York and Las Vegas for a number of years, finally settling down and joining the symphony orchestra in Miami, Florida. Aside from the orchestra, he played with bands in clubs, remaining in quiet obscurity

until the early 1990s, when Latin jazz and *descarga* began to enjoy something of a renaissance.

Due in great part to the efforts of Cuban-born American film star Andy Garcia, Lopez received attention when Latin jazz began to become popular again. In the early 1990s, Garcia began to promote Lopez's performances. In 1992, he hosted a Lopez concert as part of the Cuban Music Festival in Miami. For the next two years, Garcia produced the film documentary *Cachao: Como Su Ritmo No Hay Dos* (*Cachao: Like His Rhythm, There Is No Other*). The film takes the festival concert as its point of departure. A lot of footage is of the show, interspersed with other biographical and musical material and shots of rehearsals as well as a few interviews. The film chronicles Lopez's career from his early days in Havana up to the 1992 concert.

In 1994 Andy Garcia also produced a new recording for Lopez, *Master Sessions, Volume 1*. Despite his advanced years (he made the recording when he was 75), Lopez had energy to spare. As Garcia, who played percussion on the album, told the *Chicago Tribune,* "It's one thing to hear them play, but to see how they play. Cachao is like no other.... We had no overdubbing. We did it in one or two takes. Everyone was playing at the same time.... It was masterminded by Cachao. It was a historical event. The music was like a live organism of sound ... and he's the driving force of the rhythm."

Lopez started the recording session with four arrangements, and six days later had recorded 30. He arranged one piece on a cocktail napkin during a coffee break. "He then passed the pieces of paper out, saying, 'This is your piece for the trombone,' and so on," Garcia related in the *Chicago Tribune.* "When performing, he is like a child. He has the exuberance of a teenager."

What has given Israel Lopez the 'exuberance of a teenager' and what has kept him going through the lean years has been a deep, abiding love for what he does. He told Anders that "with music, I'm generating happiness and good humor twenty-four hours a day." Lopez considers himself lucky, and explained to *Washington Post* contributor Anders that "somewhere in Heaven there must be a star called 'Contrabass' that guided me to my instrument." He also told Anders that he believes that "a world without music would not be possible. It's our spiritual artery. It lifts us, makes us feel better."

Selected discography

Cuban Jam Session in Miniature 'Descargas,' Panart, 1957.
Jam Sessions with Feeling, Maype, 1958.
Cuban Music in Jam Session, Bonita, 1961.

Cachao y su Descarga '77, Volume 1, Salsoul Records, 1977.
Cachao y su Descarga Dos, Volume 2, Salsoul Records, 1977.
Cuban Jazz, Gema, 1981, reissued, Palladium, 1988.
Walpataca, Tania Records, 1981.
Maestro de Maestros/Israel Lopez 'Cachao' y su Descarga '86, Tania Records, 1986.
Master Sessions, Volume 1, Crescent Moon/Epic, 1994.

Sources

Billboard, May 7, 1994; May 21, 1994; August 6, 1994.
Buffalo News (NY), January 16, 1993.
Chicago Tribune, August 12, 1994; September 18, 1994.
Down Beat, January 1991; February 1991.
Entertainment Weekly, August 12, 1994.
Los Angeles Times, September 15, 1993.
Montreal Gazette, September 3, 1994.
New York Times, December 20, 1991; December 23, 1991; January 21, 1993; August 19, 1994.
Wall Street Journal, August 26, 1992.
Washington Post, September 14, 1994.

Additional information for this profile was provided by the film documentary *Cachao: Como Su Ritmo No Hay Dos,* Epic Home Video, 1994, and Crescent Moon Records publicity materials, 1994.

—*Robin Armstrong*

Martina McBride

Singer

Photograph by Ron Keith, courtesy of RCA Records

When she moved to Nashville in 1989, budding country singer Martina McBride had but one goal: to make the perfect traditional country album. Raised on the sounds of classic country music, McBride strove for the authenticity of time-honored country style and substance. She achieved her goal with the 1992 release of *The Time Has Come.* Since then, McBride has expanded on the traditional roots of that first album with business savvy and intuition, and has joined the top strata of talented "New Country" performers lighting country music's path into the next century.

McBride was born Martina Schiff in Medicine Lodge, Kansas, and grew up in nearby Sharon, a small town boasting a population that peaked at 200. Her father, a farmer who also owned a local cabinetry shop, was a musician at heart, and young Martina was exposed to the classics of country music at an early age. Her love of country tunes grew, along with her love of singing. She would spend hours after school singing along with the records of female vocalists like Linda Ronstadt and Bonnie Raitt.

At the age of eight, McBride began performing onstage with the Shiffters, a country band her father had formed; she would perform with them almost every weekend until she graduated from high school. Always a good student, McBride was offered a scholarship at a nearby college after graduation, but she attended for only one semester. A career in music was where her future lay, McBride decided, and she began working with local bands and performing throughout the Wichita area.

Armed with a new last name—courtesy of a new husband, sound technician John McBride—and a demo tape, McBride made the move to Music City in 1989. When she wasn't busy waiting tables in restaurants around Nashville, she knocked on doors up and down Music Row, hoping to attract the notice of a major record label. Her husband was fortunate enough to join the sound crew for country megasuperstar Garth Brooks, a career move that proved to be fortunate for both him and his wife. John went on to become Brooks's concert production manager, and, taking time off from waitressing, McBride accompanied her husband on the road with the stage crew during national tours and helped with concert souvenir T-shirt sales.

McBride's enthusiastic, upbeat spirit caught Brooks's eye; he offered the aspiring singer an opening-act slot during his 1992 concert tour if she could obtain a recording contract. Brooks kept his word: McBride soon signed on with RCA, and during her first year under contract she opened for Brooks as well as several other top country acts. In keeping with his support of

For the Record . . .

Born July 29, 1966, in Medicine Lodge, KS; daughter of Darryl Schiff (a farmer and cabinetmaker); married John McBride (concert production manager for country singer Garth Brooks), 1988.

Sang with the Schiffters, c. 1975-86; vocalist with local bands, Wichita, KS; moved to Nashville, TN, 1989; signed with RCA Records, 1991; released debut LP, *The Time Has Come,* 1992; toured with Brooks, 1992-93; made acting debut in episode of television series *Baywatch;* appeared on *General Hospital,* 1994; toured Europe, 1994.

Awards: Grammy Award nomination for country vocal, female, 1995, for "Independence Day."

Addresses: *Record company*—RCA Nashville, One Music Circle N., Nashville, TN 37203-4310.

new country talent, Brooks provided vocal harmony on "Cheap Whiskey," a single from McBride's first album.

McBride's album, *The Time Has Come,* released by RCA in 1992, was praised by reviewers as the debut of a strong country vocalist, but the LP didn't get a lot of airplay, perhaps because its songs focused on thoughtful subjects. "The first time out, I was really concerned with being taken seriously as an artist," McBride commented in an RCA Records press release on her first effort. "I looked for songs that had a lot to say. I'm not sure that I didn't go over the line with the first album. Maybe it was too serious." Her 1993 follow-up, *The Way That I Am,* broke this trend for the young singer; it showed a lighter side. As she told Edward Morris of *Billboard,* "Somewhere along the line I realized that music has to be entertaining."

From the upbeat "Heart Trouble" to the strong uptempo rhythms that propelled "My Baby Loves Me" to Number Two on the *Billboard* charts, *The Way That I Am* reflects a more balanced choice of material. The album has a serious side, however: noted Nashville songsmith Gretchen Peters's "Independence Day," a proclamation of justice for the victims of domestic violence, is given soaring voice by McBride. Released by RCA as the album's third single, "Independence Day" received some resistance from radio stations that considered its storyline—a woman driven to arson by a violent and abusive spouse—too sobering for an entertainment-seeking radio audience.

McBride is careful about the music she chooses to perform and record, and about the way her songs portray women. There are no unfortunate victims in her vocals, only strong, self-assertive women looking ahead to a future that is better than present circumstances. On *The Time Has Come* the single "A Woman Knows" portrays the strength of feminine intuition. Songs like "Independence Day," "That Wasn't Me," and Pam Tillis's "Goin' to Work," all from *The Way That I Am,* depict women dealing with emotional issues in ways that are personally strengthening. In fact, "My Baby Loves Me" was adopted as an anthem by female country music fans because of its upbeat portrayal of a healthy relationship in which respect for the individual holds sway over surface appearance. And McBride, herself a woman of the 1990s, has demonstrated her ability to grow, to learn, and to constantly expand as an artist.

McBride's vocal talent pairs well with her drive to be successful and her definite sense of where her career is going. "There's a perception that you just show up, put on your makeup, don't worry your pretty little head about the business, and sing," McBride told Neil Pond in *Country America.* "But that's changing, I think. People like Reba [McEntire], Barbra Streisand, and Madonna, who are in control of their own careers and their destinies, have been big influences on me."

Since her first touring experience with Garth Brooks, McBride has gone on the road with many other acts, including Sammy Kershaw, Kenny Rogers, Ricky Van Shelton, and Marty Stuart. In the fall of 1994, plans were underway for her first trip to Europe to promote her brand of American country music. For McBride, the most important aspect of a performance is connecting with the audience. "I always make sure the spotlights aren't right in my eyes [so] that I can see people's faces," she told an interviewer in *Country Song Roundup.* "I love it when people interact with me during a show, when they yell out stuff or when they sing along."

Selected discography

The Time Has Come, RCA, 1992.
The Way That I Am (includes "My Baby Loves Me" and "Independence Day"), RCA, 1993.

Sources

Books

The Comprehensive Country Music Encyclopedia, Times Books, 1994.

Periodicals

Billboard, January 29, 1994; September 3, 1994.
Country America, June 1994.
Country Music, March/April 1994.
Country Song Roundup, March 1994.

Additional information for this profile was obtained from RCA
Records publicity materials, 1994.

—*Pamela L. Shelton*

Delbert McClinton

Singer, songwriter, harmonica player, guitarist

Courtesy of Curb Records

American honky-tonk music has gained a cult figure in roadhouse-rock and blues artist Delbert McClinton. With his unique fusion of earthy roots-based rock, rhythm and blues, and country-flavored honky-tonk, McClinton's gravelly vocals and sensitive lyrical ballads have gained him the name "King of the White Texas Bluesmen" since he appeared on the scene in the 1950s. From whatever source he draws his rhythms, the vocal intensity of McClinton's live performances has hit a universal chord with audiences of many musical tastes.

Born in Lubbock, Texas, McClinton moved to Fort Worth when he was 11. There, musical influences were all around him. "I was in my early teens at the beginning of rock and roll, and I grew up in West Texas listening to country music and Nat King Cole," he told Elizabeth Hilts in the *Westchester County Weekly.* "So I just sort of incorporated it all. I've never felt limited to any one style."

McClinton made his first public appearance in 1957, at the Big "V" Jamboree in Liberation Village. His first group, the Straitjackets, became the house band for Jack's Place, a Fort Worth blues club that brought the young singer into the company of blues greats Sonny Boy Williamson, Sonny Reed, and Big Joe Turner. In 1960, under the name Mac Clinton, he released his first single on the Le Cam label. "Wake Up Baby" was one of several sides McClinton would record with the Straitjackets before the group disbanded in the early 1960s.

Harp Licks for the Beatles

In 1962 McClinton toured with Bruce Channel, playing harmonica on the artist's hit "Hey! Baby" in venues throughout Europe. In England, he jammed with a then-unknown group called the Beatles, inspiring the harp licks on the group's smash hit "Love Me Do." By the early 1960s he was fronting for the Ron-Dels, a group who scored on the national charts in 1965 with McClinton's "If You Really Want Me to I'll Go," a single that was later covered by Waylon Jennings. But after 15 years with that band, McClinton returned to the bar circuit in Texas, and released his first solo LP, *Victim of Life's Circumstances,* in 1975.

McClinton's soulful roadhouse-style rock caught fire with fans, and his debut LP spawned *Genuine Cowhide* in 1976, followed by 1977's *Love Rustler.* Unfortunately, his association with ABC Records would not be long-lived, symptomatic of the bad luck McClinton would have with record companies throughout his early career. After issuing three McClinton discs, ABC went out of business in 1977. A deal with Capricorn, which

relative safety of the stage. "During the mid-'80s there, I was pretty much wondering whether or not it would ever happen," he told Jim Morrison of the *Virginian Pilot.*

Fellow musicians, who held his songwriting skills in high esteem, supported McClinton by covering his songs. Performers who recorded his tunes include country/folk singer Emmylou Harris—whose cover of his "Two More Bottles of Wine" made Number One on the country charts—country crooner Vince Gill, and John Belushi and Dan Akroyd's Blues Brothers team. Of his songwriting, McClinton told Hilts: "I never really set out to particularly write about anything. But there are things that command to be written about. You can write about two things.... You either love to hate somebody or you hate to love somebody. That's just about it."

In 1988, with the help of manager and close friend Wendy Goldstein, McClinton felt it was time to turn his career around. After a televised performance on the Public Broadcasting Service's *Austin City Limits,* he remixed a live album from the television tapes. His instincts proved right; as critic Robert Baird noted in *New Country,* "This album brims with the kind of sweaty, electric energy that makes McClinton and his crack group one of the best bar bands in the world." The long-awaited release of *Live from Austin* in 1989 earned him a Grammy nomination for best contemporary blues album.

picked him up in 1977, proved to be little better. After the release of two successful albums, *Second Wind* and *Keeper of the Flame,* and with one song poised to climb the charts, that label, too, succumbed to the recording industry's intense competition, and declared bankruptcy in 1979.

McClinton switched to the Muscle Schoals Sound (MSS) label in 1980, and recorded the first of two albums, *The Jealous Kind,* that year. The album's single "Giving It Up for Your Love" was a Top Ten hit for McClinton, and brought him a whole new circle of admirers.

In the Studio and Grammy-Bound

On the heels of this success, McClinton negotiated a recording contract with Curb Records that put him back in the studio. Clearly, McClinton's long absence from the charts hadn't fazed his fans, who eagerly awaited release of 1991's "I'm With You." The enthusiasm of fans in Scandinavia was such that "I'm With You" soared to the Top Ten position in that region.

Turns It Around on the Road

When his second album for MSS, *Plain from the Heart,* was on its way to record shops in 1981, the distributor, Capitol Records, dropped the label. McClinton's efforts on that LP languished due to lack of airplay and proper promotion. In frustration—and motivated also by a tax problem that resulted in a complete takeover of his assets by the Internal Revenue Service—the singer took a seven-year break from the studio to hit the road on a relentless touring schedule that numbered 250 live performance dates a year. Sharing the spotlight with performers as diverse as Jimmy Buffet, the Allman Brothers, and Elvis Costello, McClinton spent most of the decade of the 1980s observing the world from the

A few years later, a duet with blues slide-guitarist Bonnie Raitt gave McClinton the exposure that had so eluded him in the past. Together, the two recorded "Good Man, Good Woman"; the single appeared first on Raitt's *Luck of the Draw* LP and garnered the couple a Grammy Award for best rock duo. "To win a Grammy validates you to a lot of people," McClinton was quoted as saying in the *Charlotte Observer.* "Suddenly you get a lot more attention and a lot more calls." Whether touring with veteran rockers Lynyrd Skynyrd or appearing with country vocalist Tanya Tucker on her 1993 hit "Tell Me About It," doors began to open with no sign of closing.

The Grammy Award put impetus behind McClinton's own recording project. Don Was, who has produced such artists as Raitt, Bob Dylan, and Iggy Pop, shared credit with McClinton and saxophonist Jim Horn on his 1992 LP, *Never Been Rocked Enough.* The release proved to be more than just a successful album; as Rich Kienzle remarked of McClinton in *Country Music,* "[*Never Been Rocked Enough*] works as a reaffirmation both of his strengths and of the justifiable admiration his peers have for him."

McClinton's 1975 release, *Victim of Life's Circumstances,* has become a classic of eclectic country. And the performer, likewise, has become something of a classic himself. Praised as one of the world's best harmonica players, McClinton has uncannily sustained an undo amount of what can only be described as plain old bad luck. He has weathered the storm because of his love of his music. "It's the kind of music that makes you want to forget all your problems and have a good time," noted McClinton in a press release. "If it wasn't for a few people, the flame of this particular kind of music might have died. I like to think I'm helping to keep it alive."

Selected discography

Victim of Life's Circumstances (includes "Two More Bottles of Wine"), ABC, 1975.
Genuine Cowhide, ABC, 1976, reissued, MCA, 1994.
Love Rustler, ABC, 1977.
Second Wind, Capricorn, 1978, reissued, Mercury.
Keeper of the Flame, Capricorn, 1979, reissued, Mercury.
The Jealous Kind (includes "Givin' It Up for Your Love"), MCC/Capitol, 1980, reissued, Curb, 1994.
Plain from the Heart, MCA/Capitol, 1981, reissued, Curb, 1994.
The Best of Delbert McClinton, MCA, 1981.
Delbert McClinton Live from Austin, Alligator, 1989.
Best of Delbert McClinton, Curb, 1991.
Never Been Rocked Enough (includes "Good Man, Good Woman" and "Everytime I Roll the Dice"), Curb, 1992.
Delbert McClinton, Curb, 1993.
Honky Tonk 'N Blues (re-releases; includes "Two More Bottles of Wine"), MCA, 1994.

Sources

Country Music, September 1992; November/December 1994.
Fort Worth Star-Telegram (TX), July 5, 1992.
Los Angeles Times, September 24, 1992.
New Country, May 1994.
USA Today, February 26, 1992.
Virginia Pilot, October 2, 1992.
Westchester County Weekly (NY), March 17, 1994.

—*Pamela L. Shelton*

The Meters

Funk/R&B band

Archive Photos

Although the Meters polished their skills as a backing band, their original work as a recording act—particularly a few dozen instrumental sides recorded in the late 1960s—has served as a vital influence on the development of funk. Infusing the soul combo format with the wild syncopations of their native New Orleans, they introduced new rhythmic possibilities; their seemingly telepathic communication produced a groove that appeared both locked-in and loose. After courting mainstream audiences with mixed results in the 1970s and partially metamorphosing into the Neville Brothers, the group fragmented and has performed with rotating personnel ever since. Indeed, the rights to the Meters name and many of their recordings remained in dispute into the 1990s.

Keyboardist Art Neville, the eldest of a prodigiously musical group of brothers, began his musical career in New Orleans in the mid-1950s. With his band the Hawketts, he recorded "Mardi Gras Mambo"—an instant smash in the Crescent City that has since become a standard part of the town's yearly Mardi Gras festivities. He was soon offered a solo deal by Specialty Records and was able to earn a living recording and performing with the Hawketts.

After a stint in the navy, Art joined his brother Aaron to form an ensemble called the Neville Sounds, which soon included younger brother Cyril as well as the three musicians who would form the nucleus of the Meters. Bassist George Porter, Jr., and drummer Joseph "Zigaboo" Modeliste—the latter having briefly been a Hawkett—were cousins, while guitarist Leo Nocentelli had been a hot session player for Motown Records in Detroit, recording with major acts like the Supremes in his teenage years. Aaron Neville had scored a solo hit with 1966's "Tell It Like It Is," and the group backed him on tour. Then, in 1967, the Neville Sounds split up; Aaron and Cyril became part of The Soul Machine, while Art Neville, Porter, Modeliste, and Nocentelli branched off on their own.

Honed Sound in Tough French Quarter Gigs

That quartet—lacking a permanent moniker—honed a mixture of R&B dance tunes and a bit of jazz in the crucible of the nightclub scene in New Orleans's French Quarter, working long nights for little pay at places like the Nitecap and the Ivanhoe. "It was a six day a week thing, ten o'clock at night till four in the morning," Art told *Melody Maker* in a 1976 interview, adding, "We'd always improvise a lot to keep it from being monotonous, doing it every night. We'd always try something else."

For the Record . . .

Members include **David Russell Baptiste** (joined reunited group c. 1989), drums; **Joseph "Ziga-boo" Modeliste** (born December 28, 1948), drums; **Art Neville** (born December 17, 1937, in New Orleans, LA), keyboards, vocals; **Cyril Neville** (joined group 1975), percussion, vocals; **Leo Nocentelli** (born 1946), guitar; and **George Porter, Jr.** (born 1947), bass.

Group formed in New Orleans, 1967; worked as session players for Sansu Records; released instrumental single "Sophisticated Cissy," 1967; signed with Josie Records and released debut album, *Cissy Strut*, 1969; signed with Reprise Records and released *Cabbage Alley*, 1972; backed such artists as Lee Dorsey, the Pointer Sisters, the Neville Brothers, Dr. John, and Robert Palmer, 1960s-1970s; toured with the Rolling Stones, 1975; disbanded, 1977; Art and Cyril Neville joined the Neville Brothers, 1977; reunited periodically with various personnel under several names, 1980s and 1990s.

Awards: Named best rhythm and blues instrumental group by *Billboard* and *Record World* magazines, 1970.

Such improvisation refined the tight grooves for which the group would become known and injected the spice of New Orleans rhythm—particularly the syncopated "second-line" beat—into the hit songs they trotted out for the dance crowd. Art played organ exclusively (having demanded one from the tony Ivanhoe), supported by the complex interaction of the Porter-Modeliste rhythm section and what *Rolling Stone* called Nocentelli's "inspired rock & roll guitar, which is almost ghostly in its thin-sounding tone and eerie dissonances."

New Orleans impresario Allen Toussaint, an old friend of Art's, saw the group play and was sufficiently impressed to sign them to his record company, Sansu. The label—co-founded by Toussaint and local producer Marshall Sehorn—aspired to become for New Orleans what the Stax label had been for Memphis and Motown for Detroit, namely a soul music hit factory.

Thus, like Stax, which used the organ-guitar-bass-drums firepower of Booker T. & The MGs as its house band, Sansu deployed Art Neville's groove-heavy foursome as the backing group for a variety of performers, including Lee Dorsey, Ernie K-Doe, and many others. "We never knew who the artist was going to be," Porter

recalled to *Musical Gumbo* authors Grace Lichtenstein and Laura Dankner. "Allen would spell the music out, and then he'd find the artists and make the artists fit the track."

The quartet recorded a few singles under Art Neville's name and then, in 1967, cut a track that would establish them as serious contenders in the R&B world. Called "Sophisticated Cissy," the insinuating funk tune became a smash; Sehorn immediately inked a deal for the group with Josie Records. The label insisted that the band adopt a pithy name, however, and after several suggestions were picked out of a hat, "the Meters"—one of Toussaint's entries—won out. More hits followed, notably "Cissy Strut," which, like "Sophisticated," based its groove on the stride of local drag queens.

Unknowingly Made the Charts

In 1969 the band released its debut album on Josie, also called *Cissy Strut*. The title cut reached the Number Four position on the Billboard R&B chart—unbeknownst to the group. "We played six nights a week from six o'clock to five o'clock in the morning for almost two years and we didn't know we had a hit record," Art Neville told Lichtenstein and Dankner. Such omissions of information on the part of Toussaint and Sehorn, both of whom profited knowingly from the record's success, sowed the seeds of bitter discord down the line. The two of them, as *Rolling Stone* observed, "produced the records, managed the band and owned both the studio where the records were made and the songs' publishing rights." Meanwhile, as Neville reminded *Melody Maker,* the band endured "the bottom of the barrel type touring, the chitlin' circuit. Out of the way clubs where the promoters would run out with the money."

Despite their travails, the Meters earned a degree of recognition; *Billboard* and *Record World* dubbed them the best rhythm and blues instrumental group of 1970, the year they released *Look-ka Py Py*. Ben Sandmel, in his liner notes for the album's 1990 Rounder reissue, quoted Porter's recollection about the disc's percolating title track: the key riff came "from a burnt piston in the engine of our van," the bassist revealed. "It kept going 'ooka-she-uh, ooka-she-ah,' over and over. Leo and Zig started singing along to it, and beating on the seats. Zig would beat on the roof, too, 'cause it had such a great bass drum sound. Then Art started singing 'bom she bom bom,' and we worked the whole thing out right there in the van."

This anecdote speaks volumes about the intuitive group process that listeners found so compelling in the Meters, who, in 1972 signed on with Reprise Records. Though their debut on the label, *Cabbage Alley,* fared poorly, their 1974 album, *Rejuvenation*—a Toussaint-produced effort, which, like its predecessor, featured Art's singing—became something of an instant classic. "Although the Meters draw freely from a variety of sources, they make a music uniquely their own," enthused Jim Miller of *Rolling Stone,* adding that the recording "shows off the full extent of the Meters' skills, by including ballads as well as extended improvisation." Sampled frequently by hip-hop DJs, *Rejuvenation* includes such classic tracks as "Jungle Man" and "Africa."

Reached Tenuous Heights

In between these Reprise albums, the Meters had backed up New Orleans pianist Dr. John on an album that included the hit "Right Place, Wrong Time" and Robert Palmer on his *Sneakin' Sally Through the Alley.* 1975 saw the Meters expand to a quintet with the addition of Cyril Neville, the youngest of the Neville boys, on percussion and vocals. Around that time, the band also performed at a lavish Los Angeles bash hosted by ex-Beatle Paul McCartney and landed a high-profile opening spot on that year's tour by British rock superstars the Rolling Stones. All this success, Art Neville regretfully explained to Lichtenstein and Dankner, affected the easy chemistry of the Josie days. "Some of the attitudes changed," the organist recollected. "You know, heads went to swelling up." Various band members had begun using drugs as well.

Toussaint and Sehorn continued to profit from their management of the Meters, collecting publishing rights and royalties from Reprise and paying the group only after recording and other expenses had been recouped. The Meters' 1975 album, *Fire on the Bayou,* sold insufficiently to put them in the black, and they fared no better with the following year's *Trick Bag.* In 1977 the Meters recorded what would be their final album, *New Directions,* produced without Toussaint; that same year they were bumped from the television program *Saturday Night Live*'s Mardi Gras installment.

The Meters soon broke up and descended into a protracted legal battle over ownership of the band's name and rights to their recordings. Periodic reunions occurred, and the litigation was ultimately concluded with all parties but Modeliste satisfied; the drummer was replaced by David Russell Baptiste. Modeliste and Nocentelli also performed together periodically in the ensuing years (sometimes as "Zig and Leo"), while Porter, like his bandmates, became a respected session player. Art and Cyril joined Aaron and the rest of the Neville Brothers, who became a much more financially successful act than the Meters had ever been.

Yet the Meters left a profound legacy. Rounder's early 1990s reissues *Look-ka Py Py, The Meters Jam,* and *Good Old Funky Music* provide ample evidence of what latter-day funkateers like the Red Hot Chili Peppers had been saying all along: that the New Orleans foursome had been an integral and largely overlooked part of funk history. "Acts as diverse as the Jackson Five, George Clinton and his Funkadelic colleagues, and Prince clearly listened well to the sinuous syncopations of the Meters," attested *Musical Gumbo* authors Lichtenstein and Dankner. And as Sandmel declared in his liner notes, "Few other bands have ever balanced such subtle understatement and suspenseful use of silence with such powerful, creative funk." The writer went on to offer a tempting challenge to listeners: "Just try to keep still once the music starts."

Selected discography

Cissy Strut (includes "Sophisticated Cissy" and "Cissy Strut"), Josie, 1969.
Look-ka Py Py, Josie, 1970, reissued, Rounder, 1990.
Struttin', Josie, 1970.
Cabbage Alley, Reprise, 1972.
Rejuvenation (includes "Jungle Man" and "Africa"), Reprise, 1974.
Fire on the Bayou, Reprise, 1975.
Trick Bag, Reprise, 1976.
New Directions, Reprise, 1977.
Good Old Funky Music, Rounder, 1990.
The Meters Jam, Rounder, 1990.
Uptown Rulers: The Meters Live on the Queen Mary, Rounder, 1990.
Funkify Your Life: The Meters Anthology, Rhino, 1995.

Also appeared on recordings by Lee Dorsey, Ernie K-Doe, the Pointer Sisters, Dr. John, the Neville Brothers, Robert Palmer, and others.

Sources

Books

Lichtenstein, Grace, and Laura Dankner, *Musical Gumbo: The Music of New Orleans,* Norton, 1993.
Rees, Dafydd, and Luke Crampton, *Rock Movers & Shakers,* Billboard, 1991.

Periodicals

Cash Box, June 9, 1990.
Down Beat, December 1990.
Guitar Player, April 1991.
Melody Maker, May 29, 1976.

Rolling Stone, May 11, 1972; September 12, 1974; September 8, 1977; August 8, 1991.

Additional information for this profile was obtained from liner notes by Ben Sandmel to *Look-ka Py Py,* Rounder Records, 1990.

—*Simon Glickman*

The Mills Brothers

Pop vocal group

MICHAEL OCHS ARCHIVES/Venice, CA

Upon hearing the name "The Mills Brothers," parents of the baby-boom generation are apt to smile fondly. A puzzled look and the question "Is that group anything like the Ink Spots?" is a more common reaction from young people. Even young people familiar with a few Mills Brothers tunes from easy-listening stations are often surprised to learn that the Mills Brothers are black. According to *The Billboard Book of American Singing Groups,* the Mills Brothers are the most popular male vocal group ever, having charted 71 times over 40 years. This is all the more impressive considering that the Mills Brothers achieved their success when most black performers were excluded from entertainment media.

The four Mills Brothers—Herbert, Donald, Harry, and John, Jr.—began singing in their father's barbershop in Piqua, Ohio, in the late 1920s. Their father had been successful with a barbershop quartet called the Four Kings of Harmony. The boys' good-natured four-part harmony retained a barbershop quartet flavor until the end of their careers. That the Mills Brothers took up a mainstream musical form no doubt partly accounted for their tremendous appeal to white audiences during the first half of the 1900s.

Another musical influence on the Mills Brothers that did not have a traditionally black cultural heritage was opera. Their father, John Sr., sang in the light opera style. It was at the local opera house that the Mills Brothers began performing publicly, though they were not adverse to a little street corner harmonizing.

Sang Even the Instruments' Parts

The Mills Brothers claimed that their trademark vocal imitation of musical instruments began during a 1920s concert when they "forgot" their kazoos. This trick proved popular and they soon added impressive imitations of other instruments, mostly wind, including saxophones, trumpets, trombones, and bass. They kept the practice up through the 1950s. During these early years the brothers changed their group name to please various sponsors, singing as "The Steamboat Four" for Soho Motor Oil and, for Tasty Yeast, as the "Tasty Yeast Jesters." In addition, the group secured their own radio show on WLW in Cincinnati, Ohio. John, Jr., sang bass and accompanied the singing on guitar, the group's only real instrumentation at the time. By 1930 the lure of Big Apple clubs and theaters moved the quartet to New York. There they recorded with big-name orchestras, including the Duke Ellington Orchestra in 1932 and later with Benny Carter.

For the Record . . .

Members include **Norman Brown**, guitar; **Donald Mills** (born April 29, 1915, in Piqua, OH), vocals; **Harry Mills** (born August 19, 1913, in Piqua, OH; died June 28, 1982), vocals; **Herbert Mills** (born in April 1912, in Piqua, OH), vocals; **John Mills, Jr.** (born in Piqua, OH; died in 1935), vocals and guitar; **John Mills, Sr.** (born in Bellefonte, PA, in 1882; died in 1967), vocals.

Began singing in their father's barbershop, late 1920s; moved to New York City to sing with well-known orchestras, c. 1930; signed with Brunswick label; recorded hit songs "Tiger Rag" and "Nobody's Sweetheart," 1931; recorded over 70 hit songs, including "You Always Hurt the One You Love," "Paper Doll," and "The Glow Worm," 1931-late 1960s; signed with Decca label, c. 1934; signed with Dot Records, late 1950s.

The Mills Brothers did not limit themselves to harmonizing, and some authorities consider them to have played a role in jazz history. Mark Tucker wrote in *The New Grove Dictionary of Jazz* of "their spectacular forays into scat singing, as on their quartet recording of 'Tiger Rag/Nobody's Sweetheart.'" This record was one of the Mills Brothers' many singles to reach the Top Ten with both sides charting separately; "Tiger" went to Number One and "Nobody's Sweetheart" reached Number Four.

Loss of a Brother

During the Depression the Mills Brothers switched from the Brunswick label to the Decca label. Decca remained the brothers' label into the late 1950s, after which time they recorded on Dot Records. During the 1930s the Mills Brothers cut some songs with Ella Fitzgerald and Louis Armstrong. In 1935 the band suffered the death of their eldest brother, John. After auditioning replacement candidates without success, the surviving sons settled on their father, John, Sr., who sang bass until retiring in 1956. Norman Brown was hired to play guitar.

In 1943 the Mills Brothers had their biggest hit, "Paper Doll," which sold six million copies, an astonishing number back then. The song sat at Number One for three months. About a year later the group hit the top slot again with "You Always Hurt the One You Love," and these two songs became Mills Brothers staples.

The 1952 tune "Be My Life's Companion" became the Mills Brothers's first successful song using a band for accompaniment instead of simply a guitar. Also orchestrated that same year was the Mills Brothers' top-charting Johnny Mercer rewrite of an old German operetta song, "The Glow-Worm." And in 1952 the group cut a single on Harmony Records with Bing Crosby, Shine" backed with "My Honey's Lovin' Arms." A *Variety* concert review from October 14, 1959, suggests the flavor of Mills Brothers shows in this era. The group had played the Riverside in Reno, Nevada, performing for 25 minutes. According to the writer, the group sang in "the same polished manner, and the voices still hold that perfect blend."

The Last Decades

Most of the 1960s were a quiet time for the Mills Brothers. The group's popularity was revived somewhat, oddly enough, during the turbulent, rock-saturated late years of the decade. It is doubtful that the young people of that era, however, put tunes with names like "My Shy Violet" and "The Ol' Race Track" on the charts. "Race Track" was the last such success for the Mills Brothers. The following year, 1969, the vocalists, now in their late fifties, performed for the first time in their 43-year career at the legendary Coconut Grove, on Christmas and New Year's Eve. Singing along was encouraged at the shows.

During the 1980s German filmmakers made an English-language documentary about the Mills Brothers entitled *The Mills Brothers Story*. Available on video, the documentary is an excellent portrait of the group through its many decades of performing. In the film Harry Mills emerges as a warm, even somewhat jolly man, who traditionally took the role of spokesperson, introducing songs and maintaining an amusing though dignified patter. Other members of the quartet were more shy— Herb avoided the limelight even to the extent of shunning solos.

A touching moment in the film occurs during a 1971 concert when Harry quietly tells the audience how the band, then a trio, had lost first their brother 36 years before, then their father four years before, and only two years later, their longtime guitarist, Norman Brown. The trio then sang a feeling rendition of "Yellow Bird," with the heavyset Harry making surprisingly gentle yet comic bird-like gestures. Shortly thereafter, Harry would suffer blindness due to a longtime battle with diabetes. He continued to perform in his traditionally pleasant and mobile fashion so that audiences often failed to realize his condition. Harry Mills died in 1982. By the late 1980s, only Donald Mills was left singing. Donald carried on with a cane, successfully touring with his son John as a duo, still singing Mills Brothers tunes of another era.

Selected discography

Singles

"Tiger Rag"/"Nobody's Sweetheart," Brunswick, 1931.
"Dinah"/"Can't We Talk It Over," Brunswick, 1932.
"Smoke Rings"/"My Honey's Loving Arms," Brunswick, 1933.
"Miss Otis Regrets"/"Old Fashioned Love," Decca, 1934.
"Good Bye Blues"/"Sweet Sue, Just You," Decca, 1937.
"Georgia On My Mind"/"S-H-I-N-E," Decca, 1941.
"Paper Doll"/"I'll Be Around," Decca, 1942.
"Till Then"/"You Always Hurt the One You Love," Decca, 1944.
(With Ella Fitzgerald) "Dedicated to You"/"Big Boy Blue," Decca, 1948.
"Love Lies"/"Be My Life's Companion," Decca, c. 1951.
"The Glow-Worm"/"After All," Decca, 1952.
(With Bing Crosby) "Shine"/"My Honey's Lovin' Arms," Harmony, 1952.
"How Blue"/"Why Do I Keep Loving You?," Decca, 1954.
"Baby Clementine"/"Yellow Bird," Dot, 1961.
"Bye Bye Blackbird"/"Chum Chum Chittilum Chum," Dot, 1965.
"My Shy Violet"/"The Flower Road," Dot, 1968.
"But for Love"/"The Ol' Race Track," Dot, c. 1969.
"Coney Island Washboard"/"Nevertheless," Ranwood, 1976.

Albums

Greatest Hits, MCA, 1987.

Sources

Books

Kernfeld, Barry, *New Grove Dictionary of Jazz,* Macmillan, 1988.
Guiness Encyclopedia of Popular Music, Guiness, 1992.
Warner, Jay, *The Billboard Book of American Singing Groups,* Billboard, 1992.

Periodicals

Variety, October 14, 1959; January 1, 1969.

Additional information for this profile was obtained from the video *The Mills Brothers Story,* Storyville Films, 1986.

—Joseph M. Reiner

John Michael Montgomery

Singer

Reuters/Bettmann

John Michael Montgomery has not allowed stardom to change his Kentuckian country identity. Instead, he revels in it. After his second album, *Kickin' It Up,* hit Number One on both the pop and country charts in early 1994, Montgomery maintained residence in his new house in his home county, Jessamine, just outside of Lexington, Kentucky. He also shared his success with his family, continued to play occasionally in the Lexington club where he found his first break, and made time at last for his friends. Although some critics have charged his music with being more formulaic and commercial than creative, Montgomery asserts that he is simply playing the same kind of popular romantic ballads he had been for years before his success.

Before that success, Montgomery struggled for over ten years through often severe financial uncertainty as a "three-sets-a-night honky tonk singer in Lexington" and then for another year ceaselessly on the road promoting his debut album, 1992's *Life's a Dance,* according to Michael McCall of *Country Music.* Finally his hard work paid off: both albums received platinum awards for over one million sold, and Montgomery himself was named the Academy of Country Music's best new male artist of the year in 1994. He also became one of only three country musicians to have topped the *Billboard* 200.

Hard Times for Country Music

John Michael Montgomery was born on January 20, 1965, in Danville, Kentucky, into a family devoted to country music. By day, Montgomery's father, Harold, and mother, Carol, worked as meatcutters. By night, however, Montgomery's parents played together in their own country band, Harold Montgomery and the Kentucky River Express. The Montgomery children, including Eddie, John Michael, and Rebecca, eventually joined their parents in the family band. "Our family, it was a totally different lifestyle," Montgomery told Richard Cromelin of the *Los Angeles Times.* "We all lived around this big cravin', and that was music. We had musicians come over to our living room every night to play and practice. As a kid, at 2 and 3 o'clock in the mornin', I was allowed to sit there and watch 'em play, and get up the next mornin' and go to school."

The family traded their financial security for their passion, however, and eventually buckled under the subsequent strain. His parents divorced when Montgomery was 17; with their parents out of the band, Montgomery and his brother, Eddie, formed a new band called at first Early Tymz and later, John Michael Montgomery and Young Country. These bands played rural Kentucky honky-tonks for a few hundred dollars per week, which

Born January 20, 1965, in Danville, KY; son of Harold and Carol Montgomery (both meatcutters and country musicians).

Played guitar in family band, Harold Montgomery and the Kentucky River Express, 1980; sang and played lead guitar for and cofounded Early Tymz, later called John Michael Montgomery and Young Country, c. 1983; sang under his own name in rural Kentucky honky-tonks, then Lexington, KY, nightclubs, with regular gigs at Austin City Saloon; discovered by Estill Sowards, Congress Inn, Lexington, 1990; signed with Atlantic Records, 1991; released debut album, *Life's a Dance,* Atlantic, 1992; toured U.S., 1993; toured with Reba McEntire, 1994.

Awards: American Music Award for favorite new country artist, 1994; named best new male artist, Academy of Country Music, 1994; Country Radio Music Award, single of the year, 1994; platinum records for *Life's a Dance* and *Kickin' It Up*; Grammy Award nomination for country vocal, male, 1995, for "I Swear."

Addresses: *Record company*—Atlantic Records, 75 Rockefeller Plaza, New York, NY 10019.

1991, Montgomery signed with Atlantic Nashville for a one-song deal that grew into the release of his debut album, *Life's a Dance,* in October of 1992.

The album's title song, "Life's a Dance," reached Number Four on the country charts, and the second single, the ballad entitled "I Love the Way You Love Me," hit Number One. In 1993 Montgomery was on the road, performing a total of 204 shows to build a national audience. His target audience was primarily young females, 18 to 24 years old, who loved his power ballads.

In 1993 Montgomery also filmed a few music videos and cut a second album, *Kickin' It Up,* released in January of 1994. With the aid of Atlantic's clever marketing, in which the company withheld distribution of the album until the ballad "I Swear" had already reached Number Seven on the country charts, Montgomery's second album became an overnight success.

Unchanged by Fame

Montgomery also broadened his style somewhat on the latter recording. "I think this second album shows people a little bigger piece of me," he explained to Michael McCall of *Country Music* in 1994. "The first album didn't cover all of my influences. The second album doesn't cover them all either, as far as the versatility that I feel like I have to give to the people. But *Kickin' It Up* certainly comes a lot closer to showing my sides. I've always liked to rock it up a little bit." Also highlighting his proclivity for romantic ballads, Montgomery cited Lionel Richie as a primary influence, as well as Merle Haggard, George Strait, Bob Seger, Lynyrd Skynyrd, Charlie Daniels, and Kenny Rogers.

With *Kickin' It Up*, Montgomery became one of only three country musicians to have topped the *Billboard* 200. The other two are Garth Brooks, with three albums from 1991 to 1993, and Billy Ray Cyrus, with one in 1992. Co-headlining a tour with Reba McEntire in 1994, Montgomery also won favorite new country artist at the American Music Awards in February of that year. With that status, Montgomery led a trend of successful new country acts, including Faith Hill, Little Texas, Billy Dean, and the Gibson Miller Band.

Montgomery's recognition has not been universal, however. The *Los Angeles Times* reported that some reviewers regarded his music with disdain, charging him with a formulaic approach and limited vision as a vocalist. The *Times* also quoted his response: "The critics—a lot of 'em say I played it safe or whatever. Well, I grew up singin' hits off the radio, and that's the kind of

they split among the several band members, who shared apartments and expenses.

By 1988, however, Montgomery had hit bottom. His run of shows had slowed down, he was working in a liquor store to survive, and he had backed out of a three-year romance with Kelly Welch just a few weeks before their wedding. In addition, his driver's license had been suspended for nonpayment of a ticket, and when he was pulled aside for speeding in December of 1988, police found prescription muscle relaxers in his pocket and fined him for a misdemeanor count of possession of controlled substances.

Danced on to Stardom

When Montgomery left Welch, however, he devoted himself entirely to his music. He sang in Lexington clubs with the band, and in the Austin City Saloon with the house band. Then, in October of 1990, at the Congress Inn, Montgomery was discovered. Estill Sowards, a Pikeville, Kentucky, manager, was impressed and invited Atlantic Records executives to see him. In January of

songs I want to sing—hits that other people are gonna play in bars that might influence another guy out there one day."

Toward the summer of 1994, Montgomery slowed his pace finally to enjoy some of his success, which he shared with family and friends. His brother supervised his security, his mother presided over his 10,000-letter-per-month fan club, and his father appeared a few times onstage with him. "We went through the hard times," Montgomery's father told Paul Prather of the *Lexington Herald-Leader*. "If one of us had an apple, the other had an apple. When the good times came along, we still shared."

Montgomery's friends concurred. "I consider him one of my best buddies," his close friend Richie Farmer, 1992 University of Kentucky basketball star, was quoted as saying in *Country Music*. "I've always loved his music. But the thing I want you to understand is, well, you see so many people, once they make it big, they change.... The good ones, according to me, are the ones who stay the same. If John had 10 zillion or if he had a dollar, he'd be the same John. I think that's what's special about him."

Selected discography

Life's a Dance (includes "Life's a Dance" and "I Love the Way You Love Me"), Atlantic, 1992.
Kickin' It Up (includes "I Swear" and "Rope the Moon"), Atlantic, 1994.

Sources

Billboard, February 19, 1994; January 22, 1994.
Country Music, May/June 1994.
Entertainment Weekly, October 1, 1993.
Lexington Herald-Leader (KY), March 6, 1994.
Los Angeles Times, June 26, 1994.
Tennessean (Nashville, TN), April 2, 1994.

—*Nicholas Patti*

Nashville Bluegrass Band

Bluegrass band

The five-member Nashville Bluegrass band (NBB) has widened the appeal of a little-known musical genre through perseverance, creativity, and instrumental mastery. "Bluegrass is music built on virtuosity, with most groups boasting either a star vocalist or instrumentalist upon which the band's reputation is built," commented David Duckman in the *Chicago Tribune*. "The Nashville Bluegrass Band is the rare exception that combines all-star playing with flawless singing, choosing [instead] to emphasize ensemble unity." Guitarist Pat Enright, Alan O'Bryant on banjo, Stuart Duncan on fiddle and mandolin, Gene Libbea on bass, and legendary bluegrasser Roland White on mandolin—award winners all—unite their musical talents under the Nashville Bluegrass Band banner to produce some of the most popular bluegrass music being recorded today.

The seeds of the NBB took root early in the 1970s when Enright, then living in San Francisco, discovered bluegrass music's intricate acoustic and vocal harmonies. With the zeal of many latecomers to the music, he

Photograph by McGuire, courtesy of Keith Case & Associates

Members include **Stuart Duncan**, fiddle and mandolin; **Pat Enright**, guitar and vocals; **Gene Libbea**, acoustic bass; **Alan O'Bryant**, banjo; and **Roland White**, mandolin.

Group formed in Nashville, TN, 1984; signed with Rounder Records, c. 1984; signed with Sugar Hill Records, 1988; appeared at Carnegie Hall, New York City, 1991; toured with country singer Lyle Lovett, 1994; have toured Brazil, Iraq, Israel, Italy, and Japan, and were first bluegrass band to appear in People's Republic of China.

Awards: Named vocal group of the year, 1990, 1991, 1992, and 1993, and entertainer of the year, 1992 and 1993, by International Bluegrass Music Association (IBMA); Grammy Award for best bluegrass recording, 1993, for *Waitin' for the Hard Times to Go.*

Addresses: *Record company*—Sugar Hill Records, P.O. Box 4040, Duke Station, Durham, NC 27706.

formed the Phantoms of the Opry, a bluegrass band that became popular along the West Coast; by 1974 he was making tracks for Tennessee to get close to the wellspring of country music. Once in Nashville he linked up with O'Bryant, a talented songwriter who had been picking bluegrass banjo since his teen years in North Carolina.

Together, Enright and O'Bryant performed at local Music City clubs that included the Station Inn, a famous bluegrass mecca. Enright moved up to Boston four years later to play with then-teenage banjo artist Bela Fleck while O'Bryant continued performing and recording bluegrass with artists like Bill and James Monroe, Peter Rowan, and Doc Watson. Enright returned to Music City a year later and resumed the association that would lead to the formation of the Nashville Bluegrass Band in 1984.

A current list of the NBB's membership reads like a roster for an Ivy League bluegrass master class; in fact, multi-instrumentalist Duncan joins fellow NBB-ers in serving as master teachers at festivals around the United States, giving both time and expertise to less-seasoned players. A sought-after session man in Nashville recording studios, Duncan augments his time with the band by backing artists like Nanci Griffith, Del McCoury, Dolly Parton, and Ricky Skaggs. His aston-

ishing fiddle runs soar amid the NBB's crisp, unclouded instrumentals.

Also on the roster is mandolinist White, who got his start with brothers Clarence—a renowned bluegrass flat-picking guitarist who joined the Byrds during the late 1960s—and Eric, Jr., as part of the Kentucky Colonels in 1954. The Colonels made several highly acclaimed albums before disbanding in 1965. He further distinguished himself in the bands of Bill Monroe and Lester Flatt and in the Country Gazette. White's soulful signature is now instantly recognizable in the NBB's understated mandolin breaks.

A veteran performer who has played with a broad range of artists spanning both bluegrass and country music—and another former Californian—Libbea gives the music of the Nashville Bluegrass Band a strong grounding with his renderings on acoustic bass. And, in the years since they began performing together, the tight, blues-based vocal harmonies developed by O'Bryant and Enright have been joined by the vocal skills of their fellow bandmembers to good effect. The five men reach back into the mingled roots of bluegrass and black gospel for one *a cappella* number, producing soulful quintet counterpoints that are widely admired.

While each member of the Nashville Bluegrass Band is an award-winning performer in his own right, the NBB as a whole has received countless accolades from bluegrass judges across the country. And the band's recognition has transcended the bluegrass community, an amazing feat in itself for performers in a musical genre that has traditionally been sidestepped by Top 40 radio, talk shows, and hip tabloid fan magazines. Nominated for Grammy awards three times—in 1988 for *New Moon Rising,* in 1990 for *The Boys Are Back in Town,* and in 1992 for *Home of the Blues*—the achievements of the NBB were finally crowned outside the bluegrass music community with a 1993 Grammy Award for *Waitin' for the Hard Times to Go,* an album that still charted on *Bluegrass Now's* Top Ten more than a year after its release. Both *Home of the Blues* and *Waitin' for the Hard Times to Go* have been widely lauded by critics as exemplary recordings of contemporary bluegrass music.

While the NBB holds to the traditional bluegrass sound— bluesy, "high-lonesome" vocals painted against a hard-hitting, hard-driving acoustic canvas—it has introduced many new fans to the music. The fact that it was touted by the Nashville *Tennessean* as "the hippest, hottest new act in [bluegrass]" attests not only to the sound, but also to the band's ability to transcend the "backwoods bumpkin" image that erroneously attached itself to the genre for so many years. And in their selection of music, the NBB chooses not only from among the riches of the established bluegrass and gospel repertoire, but also from the works of modern songwriting talents like Michael Dowling, Mark Sanders, and the late Dave Allen as well.

The Nashville Bluegrass Band's collective talent is so prodigious that one listen can inspire conversion. Actress and vocalist Bernadette Peters heard the band open for eclectic country singer Lyle Lovett one night and promptly booked them to play on two tracks on her 1994 Angel Records release. And concerning that tour with Lovett, "His audience is the audience we're trying to reach," Enright told Jay Orr in the *Nashville Banner*. "We've played for 45,000 people, most of whom had never heard us before." With that country-wide tour, the NBB reached many more ears than they would have by only receiving airplay on the small but thriving network of bluegrass radio shows.

The NBB's appearance during the bluegrass series at Nashville's newly renovated Ryman Auditorium, the "high church of country music," broadened its audience even more. With a Grammy Award, appearances onstage at the Grand Ole Opry, and a 1994 guest spot on the Nashville Network's popular *Music City Tonight* to their credit, the Nashville Bluegrass Band has taken bluegrass music one step further into the spotlight. "We're starting to feel like more people are paying attention," Enright told Orr in the *Nashville Banner* about the band's increasing momentum. "It feels like we've got something going."

Selected discography

(With Peter Rowan) *New Moon Rising,* Sugar Hill, 1988.

The Boys Are Back in Town, Sugar Hill, 1990.
Home of the Blues (includes "Roll Jordan Roll"), Sugar Hill, 1992.
Waitin' for the Hard Times to Go (includes "Backtrackin'" and "On Again Off Again"), Sugar Hill, 1993.
My Native Home, Rounder.
Idle Time, Rounder.
To Be His Child, Rounder.

Sources

Books

Rosenberg, Neil V., *Bluegrass: A History,* University of Illinois Press, 1985.

Periodicals

Bluegrass Now, October 1994.
Bluegrass Unlimited, April 1994.
Chicago Tribune, December 7, 1992.
Dirty Linen, October/November 1993.
Kinesis, Vol. 2, No. 7, 1993.
Nashville Banner, April 22, 1993; August 3, 1994.
Tennessean (Nashville), September 27, 1992.

Additional information for this profile was obtained from Sugar Hill Records publicity materials, 1994.

—*Pamela L. Shelton*

Pavement

Rock band

Pavement has become one of independent (indie) rock's biggest success stories—almost against the bandmembers' will. The California-based group charmed critics and fans alike with their early collections of noisy, intermittently melodic postpunk laced with cryptic, self-conscious lyrics; after achieving fame in the world of independent recording, they were launched into the mainstream with 1994's *Crooked Rain, Crooked Rain.* Their ambiguity about large-scale popularity intact, the group—fronted by singer-guitarist Stephen Malkmus—faced reality by exploring the phenomenon of rock fandom in their songs. "Supported by tense, entrancing music that touches on everything from giddy pop and fake jazz to woozy country rock and sinister sonic tightropes," observed Jason Cohen in *Rolling Stone,* "Malkmus stares down rock mythology with a look that's part skeptical squint and part unforced smile. He's constantly careening between cynicism and sincerity, sarcasm and earnestness."

"Pavement was originally a pathetic effort by us to do something to escape the terminal boredom we were

Photograph by Gail Butensky, courtesy of Matador Records

experiencing in Stockton," Malkmus told *Melody Maker,* referring to the rough recordings he and his friend Scott Kannberg put together in their northern California hometown. The two had played together in a band in the early 1980s. Eventually Malkmus went off to college in Virginia; when he came home for a break, he and Kannberg decided to record a single. The studio they chose, Louder Than You Think, was run by engineer-drummer Gary Young, a hard-living 40ish progressive-rock fan who urged them to let him play drums on the songs.

Made Mark in Indie Universe

The result was a 7-inch disc called "Slay Tracks (1933-1969)," an opaque and, according to David Sprague of *New York Newsday,* "unabashedly sloppy" mini-collection that Kannberg released on a label he called Treble Kicker in 1989. Malkmus returned to school before "Slay Tracks" was issued, but the positive response it generated in the indie universe—and the fact that British cult heroes the Wedding Present recorded a version of one song from it—forced him to think of Pavement as something other than a lark.

Next came "Demolition Plot J-7" and *Perfect Sound Forever,* which appeared in 1990 and 1991, respectively, on the Drag City label. These releases increased the "buzz" in the music underground about this mysterious band; Malkmus and Kannberg had only heightened the mystique by referring to themselves as "S. M." and "Spiral Stairs" in the seemingly coded liner notes that accompanied their records. Along with Young, bassist Mark Ibold, and second drummer Bob Nastanovich, Pavement embarked on what Sprague called "startlingly unrehearsed live shows" characterized by what might charitably be called extremely loose renditions of their songs and—more notoriously—Young's drunken theatrics.

Signed With Matador Records

Young not only grabbed the spotlight during gigs, he also grabbed fans before them, greeting them outside and welcoming them to the show. While his energy was infectious, his prodigious consumption of alcohol was ultimately disruptive. "With Young behind the kit (or often on top of it), Pavement could potentially be really bad," wrote *Spin's* Jim Greer, "and you got a sense watching the band interact onstage that the rest of them found that idea kind of cool." Yet Malkmus swore to *Rolling Stone* that the band did not have this attitude. "We've gotten these labels, that we're a slacker rock band and that we don't give a shit about our live show," he said. "I can't remember a time that that's ever been the case. Usually, we're really trying hard as we can to be entertaining."

Among other pursuits, Pavement's early creations inspired myriad games of "spot-the-influence" among critics and fans; many heard the imprint of British experimentalists like the Fall in Malkmus's obscurantist lingo and detected more than a hint of New York postpunk giants Sonic Youth in the group's dissonant guitars and "lo-fi" sound. But Pavement also clearly adored melodic pop, as indicated by the fragments of melody that periodically floated up from the murk. "I've always liked [power-pop hitmakers] Cheap Trick and [rock-funk innovator] Prince and [symphonic Top 40 popsters] ELO as much as the Fall," Malkmus insisted to *New York Newsday's* Sprague. Lauren Spencer of *Spin* proclaimed that *Perfect Sound* "bubbles over with more ideas than on the last three Sonic Youth albums combined," and concluded, "Listening to Pavement is like trying to listen to three radio stations at once: One is playing [folk-pop duo] Simon and Garfunkel, one is playing [1960s rockers] the Bobby Fuller Four, and the third one's just static."

Pavement had yet to record a full-length album, despite having become one of the hottest independent acts in America. They signed to Matador Records and in 1992, at a cost of only around $10,000, released *Slanted and Enchanted*. Even prior to its release, the LP was acclaimed as one of the year's best, thanks to advance cassettes that had the effect of religious icons on the nation's reviewers.

> *"On the one hand, music is just songs, but there is this whole other side to the music world which is really dirty and not very noble, and which is reflected in consumer society."*
> —Stephen Malkmus

The authoritative *College Music Journal* declared *Slanted and Enchanted* "quite likely the first and last word in American indie rock for 1992," while *Entertainment Weekly's* Gina Arnold found the collection "brimming with beautiful pop songs, soured a bit by the rhythmic clamor of harder guitar rock"; she awarded it an "A-." *Spin* named the album the year's best, contending with characteristic abandon that *Slanted* "renders any and all competition meaningless." And the *Village Voice* ranked *Slanted and Enchanted* as the second best of 1992. Pavement's *Watery, Domestic* EP topped the *Voice's* list of the year's best EPs.

Despite the accolades, the band tended to evince a certain casualness with respect to its musical career; as Malkmus told *Option,* "We've actually spent less than 100 hours on Pavement—playing, recording, and practicing. We've had six practices. We don't even play together as a band when we record. Basically I send the guys into the studio and I sit there with a microphone and sing along and I have an idea of where I want them to stop. That's where I put the guitar."

Yet the obvious necessity of treating this enterprise more professionally gradually overtook Pavement's cavalier "indie" pose; original drummer Young left the band in 1993, exhausted from touring and unsatisfied with his pay. "It made me sad that it couldn't creatively work out with Gary," Malkmus reflected to Sprague. "He really wanted to be a rock star in capital letters, but it was clear that he wasn't emotionally centered enough to handle it." Steve West, a friend of second drummer Nastanovich's, replaced Young. Along with Ibold and

Malkmus, he took up residence in New York, while Kannberg continued to live in Stockton, and Nastanovich made his home in Louisville, Kentucky, so he could attend his beloved horse races. *Rolling Stone* explained, "Geography has made it difficult for Pavement to be well rehearsed."

1993 saw the release of *Westing (By Musket and Sextant),* a Drag City CD compilation containing all of Pavement's pre-*Slanted* releases. "You *could* argue that this noise-for-noise's sake approach is going nowhere," wrote *Spin* reviewer Simon Reynolds, "but it's going there in terrific style, and that's more than enough for me." The group also contributed selections to the high-profile alternative rock collections *Born to Choose* and *No Alternative;* their song for the latter pays skewed tribute to rock giants R.E.M., enumerating the cuts—including Malkmus's "least favorite"—on that group's sophomore album, *Reckoning.*

Expectations were so high after *Slanted* that Pavement's next full-length release appeared amid a flurry of hype and a full-scale promotional effort by Matador. The band filmed a video, submitted to a press junket, and, in a virtually unprecedented move for a group still occupying the fringe of American culture, appeared on television's *Tonight Show With Jay Leno.* The new album, *Crooked Rain, Crooked Rain,* bowled over critics; *Rolling Stone's* Matt Diehl called it "stunning," and Joe Levy of the *Village Voice* heartily admired Pavement's "invigorating noise and, crucially, melodies—and their ability to transform both into warmth at will."

"American Originals"

Malkmus told *New York Newsday's* Sprague, "I guess there was more of a decision to just make songs instead of a noisy, indie-signifying record" and expressed to *Melody Maker* his hope that people wouldn't "think this record is too bratty in a wrong way, or too know-it-all, when it was the only thing we could do." In any event, *Crooked Rain* devoted much of its content to the phenomenon of rock music as "career"—Malkmus sings the word into a mantra-like mush, which more than one listener has misconstrued as "Korea," on the single "Cut Your Hair"—exploring the ambivalence and the magic of relating to music not as a professional but as a fan.

Pavement's rise in popularity led to international tours. Drummer West commented in *Musician,* "Everywhere we went, from Prague, Vienna, to New Zealand, Australia, and Japan, we always had at least four or five hundred people out to see us, even in the smallest places.... That wouldn't have happened five years ago. For the Replacements, or even R.E.M. in '83 or '84, when they were at our level, to go to Prague, or even to fly to Australia would have been impossible."

Even after fame hit, though, Pavement remained remarkably independent. Kannberg continues to manage the group from a spare bedroom in his San Francisco apartment, and the members do their own roadie work. In early 1995 the band was working on an LP scheduled for release in April of that year. *Musician*'s Nathan Brackett noted, "Lack of pretense and the do-it-yourself aesthetic are the order of business in any Pavement enterprise."

"Pavement are American originals," remarked Levy in an attempt to sum up the band's appeal. "There are debts, to be sure, though Pavement acknowledge them with more mystery, style, and humor than R.E.M. or Sonic Youth ever did." *Spin*'s Greer, meanwhile, insisted that with *Crooked Rain,* "Pavement has once again proven that the enduring lesson of punk rock was that *not* everyone could do it." The band had begun to transcend cult status to make a stand in the mainstream rock world; what success in this new realm would mean to its members remained to be seen. Malkmus, however, indicated to *Melody Maker* part of the reason for his explorations of rock culture: "On the one hand, music is just songs and there are good melodies and bad melodies, but there is this whole other side to the music world which is really dirty and not very noble, and which is reflected in consumer society." He added, "The references [in the songs] to being in a band are just me trying to tell the truth."

Selected discography

"Slay Tracks (1933-1969)," Treble Kicker, 1989.
"Demolition Plot J-7," Drag City, 1990.
Perfect Sound Forever (EP), Drag City, 1991.
"Summer Babe," Drag City, 1991.

Slanted and Enchanted, Matador, 1992.
"Trigger Cut," Matador, 1992.
Watery, Domestic (EP), Matador, 1992.
Westing (By Musket & Sextant), Drag City, 1993.
"Greenlander," *Born to Choose,* Rykodisc, 1993.
"Unseen Power of the Picket Fence," *No Alternative,* Arista, 1993.
Crooked Rain, Crooked Rain (includes "Cut Your Hair"), Matador, 1994.

Sources

Billboard, January 15, 1994.
College Music Journal (CMJ), March 27, 1992.
Entertainment Weekly, July 31, 1993.
Interview, June 1993; February 1994.
Los Angeles Times, February 13, 1994.
Melody Maker, March 7, 1992; November 28, 1992; March 20, 1993; February 12, 1994.
Musician, January/February 1995.
New Musical Express (NME), July 4, 1992; August 1, 1992; January 9, 1993; April 3, 1993.
New York Newsday, February 15, 1994.
New York Times, December 30, 1992.
Option, July 1992.
Request, May 1994.
Rolling Stone, February 24, 1994; July 14, 1994; November 17, 1994.
Spin, September 1991; December 1992; June 1993; March 1994; April 1994; July 1994; March 1995.
Village Voice, March 2, 1993; August 3, 1993; February 22, 1994.

Additional information for this profile was obtained from Matador Records publicity materials, 1994.

—*Simon Glickman*

Liz
Phair

Singer, songwriter, guitarist

Photograph by Stephen Apicell-Hitchcock, courtesy of Atlantic Records

Liz Phair's recording debut, 1993's *Exile in Guyville,* landed her a spot in the annals of alternative-music history—the album became her label's best-selling release at 200,000 copies and was extolled by critics for the novice songwriter's refreshing, female-oriented spin on life and love among the Generation X set. The venerable *Village Voice* named it album of the year, making Phair the first woman artist to capture that honor since singer-songwriter Joni Mitchell in 1974.

Seeming to appear out of nowhere on the independent (indie) label scene, Phair received enormous amounts of press, which often quoted the more sexually explicit lyrics of her songs and pointed out her rather idyllic suburban upbringing. Later, in 1994, she released her sophomore effort, *Whip-Smart,* which, like her debut, is a complex paean to a subject dear to Phair's songwriting heart—men and the trouble they cause. Surprising many with its solid musicianship, *Whip-Smart* was a successful response to those waiting to dismiss Phair as a just another flash in the alternative music pan.

Phair, born April 17, 1967, is the adopted daughter of John and Nancy Phair; she spent her early childhood in Ohio. In 1976 the family, which includes an older brother, relocated from Cincinnati to the Chicago area. Phair's father is a physician and AIDS researcher, while her mother is an instructor at Chicago's premier art school. The family settled in Winnetka, a posh Chicago suburb, and Phair grew into a creative adolescent who wrote songs at the family piano but displayed a rebellious streak. She left Winnetka to attend Oberlin College, a small, quirky liberal arts school in Ohio.

Broke Out of Guyville

Oberlin, like other isolated outposts of middle-class intellectual rebellion, bred bands like other schools breed keg parties; Phair's art studies were supplemented by her informal education in the local music scene. "Oberlin is a really indie rock type of college," Phair told Annette Petruso of Detroit's *Metro Times.* "It was very much left of center, intellectual and scrawny. Those are the three really good markers of guyville. All of my boyfriends were guyville. They still sort of are." Her first album was full of songs inspired by this phase of her life. "I was really just trying to impress a bunch of guys," Phair noted of her early musical ambitions. "I am not the band wife. I am the band."

After college Phair relocated to San Francisco, where she stayed at a friend's loft for a time. It was there that she re-encountered Chris Brokaw, a guitarist with the band Come; they had briefly known one another at

For the Record . . .

Born Elizabeth Clark Phair, April 17, 1967, in Cincinnati, OH; daughter of John (a physician and AIDS researcher) and Nancy (a museology instructor) Phair. *Education:* Received degree from Oberlin College, 1990.

Worked as a free-lance artist, early 1990s; singer and songwriter, 1992—.

Awards: *Exile in Guyville* named album of year by the *Village Voice*; voted best new female vocalist in a *Rolling Stone* Critics' Poll; Grammy Award nomination for rock performance, female, 1995, for "Supernova."

Addresses: *Home*—Chicago, IL. *Record company*—Matador Records, 676 Broadway, 4th Floor, New York, NY 10012.

Oberlin. The two would play guitar together for amusement, but Phair decided to return to Chicago in late 1990. Brokaw convinced her to record some of the songs he had heard her play, so for a few months in 1991, Phair sat back in her room at her parents' home in Winnetka with a guitar and a simple four-track recorder. The result was two tapes, each with 14 songs. Phair called them *Girly Sound* and sent them to Brokaw.

The rough *Girly Sound* tapes stealthily began making the rounds of the alternative scene, passing from one college radio disc jockey to another, and eventually found their way to a Matador Records representative. The company signed Phair in the summer of 1992, and she began putting together a band. By then she had moved from Winnetka to the artsy Chicago enclave of Wicker Park, a mecca for the post-collegiate loft-dwelling crowd, and was selling sketches to make ends meet. Local musician Brad Wood, owner of Chicago's Idful Music recording studio, became her drummer and producer; LeRoy Bach was hired on as bassist; and Casey Rice shared guitar duties with Phair. The three musicians went into the studio and began putting together *Exile in Guyville*.

Phair mined her collection of *Girly Sound* recordings as well as her own personal history for the 18 tracks on *Exile in Guyville*. Although cagey on the subject, she occasionally admitted in later interviews that it was a response to an episode in her life with "a specific person that I had an undefined relationship with," as she put it to *Vogue*'s Moira McCormick. Listening to the Rolling Stones' acclaimed 1972 double album *Exile on Main Street* reminded her of certain facets of that relationship, and she conceived *Exile* as a female response to the sentiments expressed by both Stones vocalist Mick Jagger and her mercurial romantic interest. "Making my album helped me define my relationship with this person—and that was all I needed. It didn't get me what I thought I wanted, but it gave me peace of mind."

Exile was released in May of 1993, and over the next few months word-of-mouth, airplay, and sales resulted in astounding success for Phair. Reviews were filled with accolades. *Spin* writer Christina Kelly deemed the disc "a glorious pop album that concerns itself with the minutiae of male-female relations and girly empowerment" and described Phair as the "most hyperintellectual of indie-rock geeks." Katherine Dieckmann of *Musician* noted that Phair's persona, as reflected in the songs, "calls up the image of a cool, brainy chick with a major 'don't mess with me' [attitude]," and pointed out that "you don't really think of the Rolling Stones while listening to Liz Phair, save the stray riff or inversion. Instead, you're seduced by the rawness and pith of her lyrics, the stripped-back production and Phair's urgent yet deadpan vocals."

"Modern Girldom"

Another *Spin* writer, Craig Marks, noted that "while the music is basic and [traditional], and Phair's gift for melodies and rock 'n' roll linguistics ... recall the glory days of AM radio, it's her unflinching embodiment of modern girldom—giddy with the pleasures of sex, wary of loneliness, confused by the cowardice of men—that stamps Phair as a songwriter of prodigious talent." *Vogue*'s McCormick described *Exile* as "a startling blast of stripped-down, unpolished, thoroughly addictive guitar pop, a state-of-the-heart report on love, sex, and life from an above average, disarmingly honest American girl."

Exile in Guyville's first single, "Never Said," made its way from college radio stations to modern rock outlets across the country. While Phair and the album were attracting national media attention, the two were almost willfully ignored by the music scene in Chicago. Her coverage there was limited to periodic snarky comments about her Winnetka roots, and the city's two mainstream alternative rock stations jumped on the bandwagon in 1994 with "Never Said" only long after other major markets had given it generous airplay.

Soon Phair had to face something she'd dreaded—the necessity of touring. Never thinking of herself as a performer, but rather as a songwriter, her early appearances were tense and panned by critics. Phair's description of herself onstage to Jancee Dunn of *Rolling Stone* echoed those in the reviews: "My voice warbles, my projection diminishes. I have more of a sneer, I'll get threatened by the crowd, I'll look like I'm really angry. Inability to remember songs, that's a good sign of stage fright."

Settled Down With Success

Phair's sophomore effort, *Whip-Smart,* was released in September of 1994, and with Matador teaming with Atlantic Records for a distribution deal, the LP had the heavy weight of a major record label behind it. *Whip-Smart's* first single, "Supernova," began climbing the modern-rock charts and the song's video, directed by Phair, was given regular rotation on MTV. The album was compared endlessly with her first in reviews: Deborah Frost of *Musician* found that "where *Exile* seemed liberating and came off like personal confessions, *Whip-Smart* comes off largely like professional shtick," but conceded that the effort may just be "merely the transition between Phair's art hobbyist beginnings and a full-fledged major-label career."

David Browne of *Entertainment Weekly* also judged Phair's second LP against her first and described it as "basically the same story: easy to respect for its intelligence and low-fi rock (it's not, thank God, corporate grunge-by-numbers), yet at times so ... passive and self-conscious that it's easier to admire than fall in love with." Browne granted, however, that much of the record "is more musically fleshed out than the garage-level tracks of *Exile.*"

Other critics were more charitable in their reviews of *Whip-Smart*. In *Rolling Stone,* Dunn termed the LP "a stunner—and dare we say, better than the first—a perfect progression from *Guyville,* carrying over all of the [do-it-yourself] feel of her first offering but with greater accessibility and tighter arrangements." Dunn's colleague Barbara O'Dair reviewed *Whip-Smart* and declared, "Phair has once again written and 'directed' a bunch of entertaining, affected songs." While O'Dair felt that the release might have been too hastily completed, she allowed, "This brainiac bad girl deserves a lot of credit for not being cowed by her classic debut." *Newsweek's* Christopher John Farley liked the quirkiness of Phair's follow-up and remarked that "not many singer-songwriters manage to be so honest and so much fun at the same time." The reviewer further noted that Phair's "guitar playing has a likeable, warbling strangeness; she is developing into a stronger, more varied songwriter."

As the sure success of *Whip-Smart* became apparent in the weeks after its release, Phair's reticence to perform led her to cancel scheduled concert dates. She discussed this decision on *Modern Rock Live,* a syndicated radio show: "I really hated touring, and I don't think I'm a good performer.... I've had vicious stage fright.... It's a big old anvil hanging over my head." What Phair did feel confident about, on the other hand, was her creative abilities as both a songwriter and inspiration to others; she has become a path-clearing force in alternative music. "My whole thing was, 'I was a college kid who wrote songs, and *you can too,'* she told McCormick in *Vogue.* "Some day another girl will say, 'I can do that,' and it won't be because she saw a boy up there—but because she saw me."

Selected discography

Singles

"Never Said," Matador, 1993.
"Supernova," Matador/Atlantic, 1994.

Albums

Exile in Guyville, Matador, 1993.
Whip-Smart, Matador/Atlantic, 1994.

Sources

Billboard, November 27, 1993; August 6, 1994; October 15, 1994.
Details, July 1994; October 1994.
Entertainment Weekly, September 23, 1994.
Metro Times (Detroit, MI), June 30, 1993; September 1, 1993.
Musician, November 1993; October 1994.
Rolling Stone, January 27, 1994; September 22, 1994; October 6, 1994; November 17, 1994.
Spin, August 1993; November 1993; July 1994.
Time, October 17, 1994.
Vogue, August 1994.

Additional information for this profile was obtained from an interview with Phair heard on the syndicated radio program *Modern Rock Live.*

—Carol Brennan

Primal Scream

Rock band

Primal Scream, a band that combines a funky 1960s groove with 1990s technology, rose to the top of the U.K. music charts in 1991. Their album release that year, *Screamadelica,* was tinged with hippie hysteria, and the dispossessed youth of post-industrial, post-Cold War Britain bought it. Brantley Bardin in *Interview* magazine called the album "a visionary hybrid that pits Beach Boys harmonies against lost-in-space dub reggae, country riffs against gospel shouts, and Coltrane-ish cries of saxophone against acid house wiggles." Primal Scream's next LP, *Give Out but Don't Give Up,* released in 1994, also drew on various sources—England's acid jazz, rockabilly, funk, and heavy metal—and was an attempt to widen the band's audience.

Primal Scream came together in Glasgow, Scotland, in 1984, initially featuring Andrew Innes on keyboards and guitar, Robert "Throbert" Young on second guitar, and on vocals and bass, Bobby Gillespie—who also played drums for the Jesus and Mary Chain, which was becoming famous as well. At first, Primal Scream imitated bands like the Byrds, the influential 1960s group that

Photograph by Neil Cooper, © 1994 Sire Records Company

melded country, folk, and rock. An early admirer, disc jockey Andrew Weatherall, tried to transform one of Primal Scream's songs, "I'm Losing More Than I'll Ever Have," into a more danceable tune. The result was "Loaded," which became a hit among the denizens of the "acid house" nightclubs. The music of that scene was known as rave, which spawned feverish dancing and raw emotion in an atmosphere of slide shows and other psychedelia. Clubgoers demanded a rhythmic dance mix, which was the same impetus that had spawned disco in the 1970s.

Primal Scream soon signed with an independent label, Creation Records, and in 1986, released two singles, "All Fall Down" and "Crystal Crescent." Their success with young, party-going Britons also attracted the attention of Warner Bros. In the 1980s major record companies such as Warner adopted the role of distributor for smaller companies to keep tabs on the burgeoning alternative rock scene. Warner's subsidiary, Elevation, released *Sonic Flower Groove* in 1987. Primal Scream then recorded the single "Ivy Ivy Ivy" for Creation. When the song "Loaded" became a hit, the band was switched to another Warner subsidiary, Sire Records in New York City, for American distribution.

A period of arduous touring began, an obligatory career move for the nascent Primal Scream. The band traveled throughout the United Kingdom to growing acclaim. Producer Jimmy Miller, who had worked with the Rolling

Stones, then took Primal Scream into the studio. The group collected the songs written and performed on the U.K. tour onto an album, *Screamadelica,* which was released in 1991. The LP opened with the song "Movin' on Up," featuring acoustic guitars and congas, and concluded with the gospel hymn "Come Together," a song lasting more than eight minutes.

Bardin, in *Interview,* remarked that despite Primal Scream's "early love of Public Image Ltd.-like noise—and their heavy-metalish moniker—*Screamadelica* is no mere screechfest," and added, "In fact, songs such as the album's magnum opus, 'Higher than the Sun,' with its Walt Whitman-on-Ecstasy declarations of independence and bliss, are virtually soothing." Primal Scream also covered "Slip Inside This House," by Roky Erickson of the 13th Floor Elevators, to emphasize their alternative rock credentials. *Screamadelica's* success propelled the band into the international arena. In 1992 Primal Scream crossed the Atlantic to the United States, where they toured for five weeks. By that time they had hit the airwaves and earned heavy rotation on the nation's dance club turntables.

Primal Scream's next album, 1994's *Give Out but Don't Give Up,* drew some negative press. The band had purchased some gloss by hiring such noted studio hands as funkmeister George Clinton and Atlantic Records' veteran producer Tom Dowd. Dowd's resume includes work with Aretha Franklin, Rod Stewart, Lynyrd Skynyrd, and the Allman Brothers. The sixtyish sound man, a wizard on the volume controls, had been present at the birth of rock and roll. Clinton provided an additional link to the gospel and soul sound.

Imported to replace Primal Scream's bassist and drummer were expert studio musicians from Memphis, Tennessee, and Muscle Shoals, Alabama. George Drakoulias, who had given a commercial spin to the Black Crowes, performed the mix. Primal Scream's attempt to resurrect an earlier rhythm and blues sound, however, came across to many as derivative and exploitative. Some critics felt that Primal Scream had abandoned its happy blend of high-tech dance music and soul. *Rolling Stone's* Steven Daly called attention to this backlash, noting that in reaction to *Give Out but Don't Give Up,* critics "have lately been lampooning the Scream as repro-rock turncoats peddling reheated boogie à la the '73 Rolling Stones and flying in the face of progress."

Lead singer Bobby Gillespie defended the collaboration in *Request* magazine, remarking, "I enjoyed working with these people. I guess there's kind of a conversational quality and directness now. It's more instinctive." Alan McGee, who had signed Primal Scream to Creation Records, told *Billboard* magazine, "All great bands reflect their audience, and Primal Scream *is* their audience.... It's the perfect time for a funk record, because the kids in the clubs are going back to funk." In 1994, Primal Scream filmed an MTV video for the track "Rocks" from *Give Out but Don't Give Up* at a YMCA in London's West End.

According to Sire Records publicity materials, Bobby Gillespie sees Primal Scream's mission as therapeutic: "The healing power of music is vastly underestimated. It's a way to relieve tensions, to get the poisons out of the body, music is a way to love people, an example of how good we all can be. It's a form of liberation and where there's freedom, there's hope. Our hope is to make strange and beautiful records that take the process one step further."

Selected discography

Sonic Flower Groove, Elevation, 1987.

Come Together (EP), 1990.
Screamadelica, Sire/Reprise, 1991.
Dixie Narco (EP), 1992.
Give Out but Don't Give Up, Sire/Reprise, 1994.

Sources

Billboard, August 7, 1993; February 12, 1994.
Interview, January 1992.
Los Angeles Times, March 7, 1992; March 9, 1992.
Request, May 1994.
Rolling Stone, June 16, 1994.
San Jose Mercury News (CA), March 6, 1992.
Seattle Times, February 28, 1992.
Spin, May 1994.

Additional information for this profile was obtained from Sire Records publicity material.

—Paul E. Anderson

Prince

Singer, songwriter, guitarist, arranger, producer

Photograph by Terry Gydesen, courtesy of Warner Bros. Records, Inc.

Pop stars frequently alter their names, but rarely has a change of moniker caused a stir like the one motivated by the artist formerly known as Prince. After signing a lucrative record deal in 1993, the enigmatic multi-instrumentalist bandleader and singer-songwriter announced his retirement and changed his name to an unpronounceable symbol. It later became clear that this "retirement" applied only to the now-defunct Prince and not to the artist reborn as the symbol.

While he was Prince, of course, he was one of the most consistent hitmakers in contemporary music, fusing soul, funk, rock, and power pop into a distinctive, exuberant brew; his unflinchingly erotic (and often simply raunchy) lyrics managed a kind of sacredness, thanks to his apparent sincerity. He displayed an astounding versatility, both in the studio—playing some two dozen instruments, multitracking vocals, and arranging music for his bands—and onstage, where he would participate in elaborate choreography even while peeling off pyrotechnic guitar solos.

As *Guitar Player*'s Chris Gill commented, "Few artists of his stature are as talented in one area as Prince is in many." In his post-Prince existence the symbol-artist quickly embarked on a series of ventures—including a new independent record label (replacing Prince's defunct old one), a musical based on an ancient Greek text, a retail clothing outlet, and an interactive CD-ROM program—and promised that his new music would make the old pale by comparison.

Multi-Instrumental Prodigy

The artist was born Prince Rogers Nelson in Minneapolis, Minnesota, and was named for the Prince Rogers Trio, a jazz group fronted by his father, John Nelson. His mother, Mattie, occasionally sang with the combo, but the Nelsons ultimately found less harmony in their marriage than in the music and went their separate ways. Young Prince's relationship with Mattie's second husband, Hayward Baker, was difficult, but Baker unwittingly helped set his stepson's musical career in motion by taking him to a concert by singer-bandleader and "Godfather of Soul" James Brown. Prince was only ten years old, but Brown's electrifying stew of funk, soul, and energetic showmanship seared itself onto his imagination, as would the fiery guitar of Jimi Hendrix, the communal dance-uplift of Sly & the Family Stone, and the otherworldly funk of George Clinton's Parliament-Funkadelic in the coming years.

By age 12, Prince had begun teaching himself to play the guitar Nelson had given him, but the rockiness of his

Born Prince Rogers Nelson, June 7, 1958, in Minneapolis, MN; son of John Nelson (a jazz pianist) and Mattie Shaw (a singer).

Recording and performing artist, 1976—. Released debut album, *For You,* Warner Bros., 1978; formed, and headed own subsidiary label, Paisley Park, 1987-93; produced and/or wrote for other artists, including the Time, Mavis Staples, Vanity, and others, 1980—; starred in films *Purple Rain,* 1984, *Under the Cherry Moon,* 1986, *Sign O' the Times,* 1987, and *Grafitti Bridge,* 1990; provided songs for films *Batman,* 1989, and *I'd Do Anything,* 1993; wrote songs for stage musical *Glam Slam Ulysses,* 1993; published book of photographs, *The Sacrifice of Victor,* 1993; opened Glam Slam nightclubs, 1993; changed name to an unpronounceable symbol and announced retirement of "Prince" from recording, 1993; released EP *The Beautiful Experience,* NPG/Bellmark, 1993; debuted interactive CD-ROM software and New Power Generation retail establishments, 1994.

Selected awards: Academy Award for best original song score, 1984, for film *Purple Rain;* three Grammy Awards, 1984; People's Choice music awards, 1985, for best new song, for "Purple Rain," and best male musical performer; Grammy Award for best rhythm and blues performance, 1986, for "Kiss"; honored with "Prince Day" in Minneapolis, 1990; named top urban contemporary artist of the past 20 years, *Radio & Records* 20th anniversary celebration; World Music Award for outstanding contribution to the pop industry, 1994; numerous American Music awards and *Rolling Stone* readers' polls and critics' picks awards; 14 platinum albums, 12 gold singles.

Addresses: *Home*—Minneapolis, MN. *Record company*—(Prince) Warner Bros., 3300 Warner Blvd., Burbank, CA 91505, or 75 Rockefeller Plaza, 20th Floor, New York, NY 10019; (symbol) NPG/Bellmark, 7060 Hollywood Blvd., Suite 1000, Hollywood, CA 90028.

home life meant that he rarely had a firm address; he stayed with Nelson and with the family of his friend Andre Anderson. The Anderson clan eventually adopted him. Prince would soon master the drums, bass, piano, and saxophone. At age 14 he was the guitarist for Grand Central, a junior-high cover band begun by his cousin, drummer Charles Smith, and featuring Andre (who would later change his last name to Cymone) and Andre's sister Linda on bass and keyboards, respectively.

The following year, the group changed its name to Champagne and underwent various personnel changes; the new lineup included future stars Morris Day and Jimmy Jam—later of the funk band the Time—and Prince took over leadership duties. After various other musical endeavors, he recorded a demo—on which the 16-year-old played all the instruments and sang—that led to a recording contract with Warner Bros.

By 1978 Prince had released his debut, *For You,* which featured the single "Soft and Wet." Working with his band the Revolution, Prince developed his trademark mix of funk workouts, soul balladry, and metallic guitar wailing—overlaid with his silky falsetto vocals—on the subsequent efforts *Prince, Dirty Mind,* and *Controversy.* But he made his first huge splash with *1999,* an ambitious double-length recording that exploded thanks to the apocalyptic dance music of the title track and the crossover sensation "Little Red Corvette." The album remained on the charts for two years, by which time the film and album *Purple Rain* had established Prince as one of pop's megastars.

Though the movie *Purple Rain*—conceived by and starring Prince—was poorly reviewed, it earned nearly ten times what it cost to make. The soundtrack, meanwhile, was a sensation, and featured both his most daring and his most commercially successful work to date. Featuring the enigmatic single "When Doves Cry"—"His shining hour, in terms of a commercially viable artistic statement," according to *Down Beat*—as well as the barnburning "Let's Go Crazy" and the shimmering balladry of the title song, the collection earned Prince an Academy Award for best original song score. It eventually reached the 9 million mark in U.S. sales.

More Milestones

Rhythm and blues siren Chaka Khan scored a huge hit covering Prince's early song "I Feel for You," and several years later Sinead O'Connor sang a smash rendition of his "Nothing Compares 2 U." Yet Prince's artistic restlessness meant that he rarely attempted to emulate past successes, even multiplatinum ones. Thus, the artist recorded the baroque pop and winsome psychedelia of *Around the World in a Day*—with its playful hit "Raspberry Beret"—and the funkified *Parade,* which served as the soundtrack to the cooly received film *Under the Cherry Moon.*

But it was 1987's *Sign O' the Times* that suggested another milestone in Prince's varied career. Once again cramming a panoply of song styles into a double disc, Prince performed a duet with Scottish diva Sheena Easton on the hit "U Got the Look" and scored again with the single "I Could Never Take the Place of Your Man." Though he pulled his now-legendary *Black Album* from circulation because of its allegedly evil qualities—thus making it a sensationally lucrative item for bootleggers who got hold of advance copies—he charted again with *Lovesexy* in 1988.

While much of the entertainment press covered his unorthodox career moves with a combination of cynical gossip and dread, the artist formerly known as Prince simply—and, it seems, fearlessly—went his own way.

Prince's various proteges—including Apollonia and Vanity—fared poorly on his new record label/production complex, Paisley Park, which opened its doors in 1987. He himself hit what many regard as a fallow period in the next few years. His suite of songs for Tim Burton's film *Batman* sold well but suggested something of a creative letdown to critics, while 1990's *Graffiti Bridge* was a sprawling omnibus record featuring the Time, funk heavyweight George Clinton, Mavis Staples, newcomer Tevin Campbell, and others that lacked the focus of his mid-1980s work. But he assembled a stellar backup group that he called the New Power Generation and showed them off to fine effect on the 1991 collection *Diamonds and Pearls*. Prince was named best songwriter that year by *Rolling Stone's* readers and opened a nightclub franchise called Glam Slam a bit later, appearing at its various locales periodically and using them as showcases for Paisley Park acts.

The following year saw the release of an album bearing only a symbol as its title. The glyph appeared to be a combination of the symbols for male and female, with a hornlike flourish running through the middle. Though the album featured the song "My Name Is Prince," it wasn't long before the unpronounceable symbol became the artist's new moniker. Warner Bros. announced the dissolution of Paisley Park, while the former Prince announced his retirement from music, a proclamation met with some skepticism at his record label and elsewhere; Prince had promised to retire from performing in 1985 for a period of years, only to begin a tour a few months afterward. "Prince did retire," noted the artist to *Vibe's* Alan Light. "He stopped making records because he didn't need to anymore." Having allegedly stockpiled some 500 songs, enough Prince material existed to cover any remaining contractual obligation.

TAFKAP

In 1993 Prince released his long-awaited greatest hits package, a three-CD set that included favorites from all his albums and a number of B-sides and rarities. Despite some qualms, an *Entertainment Weekly* review was enthusiastic: "Mostly *The Hits* remind us that Prince started out his career breaking both musical ground *and* a few sociocultural taboos. Now that he's calling himself [symbol] and writing musicals based on Homer's *Odyssey,* we need all the reminders we can get." Next came what the *Los Angeles Times* called a "musically satisfying but lyrically uneven collection," *Come*—apparently the first of many Warner Bros. releases from the Prince vault. "This isn't near being a great Prince album," reviewer Ernest Hardy noted, adding, "stricter editing at least could have made it a very good one."

Meanwhile, "The Artist Formerly Known as Prince," or TAFKAP, as he came to be known among bewildered music writers, declared that his new music would surpass all of Prince's output. As if to prove the point, "The Most Beautiful Girl in the World," his first single as the symbol—released on NPG/Bellmark—hit the Number Three position on the U.S. charts. According to Light, on much of the new material Prince previewed in 1994 at shows and on mixes from his upcoming *Gold Album,* he appeared "freer than he has in years." *Spin's* Jason Cohen felt otherwise, calling the rendition of past hits during a 1993 performance "both sad and thrilling in its superiority to the newer material." Also during this period, NPG Records released a collection of work by artists formerly on Paisley Park, *1-800-NEW-FUNK.*

Prince's other ventures included a record store and a clothing outlet (both going by the name "New Power Generation"); the publication of a book of photographs; the production of other artists; his interactive CD-ROM software, which allows participants to remix some of his music in a simulated studio, among other things; *Glam Slam Ulysses,* the aforementioned musical based on the *Odyssey;* and, of course, performing and recording with his band.

New Power Generation guitarist Levi Seacer, Jr., told *Guitar Player's* Gill in 1993 that "Every night we try to out-funk each other. We know where the breaks are going to be, but after the break hits we play whatever we want. Each of us is thinking, 'What can I do to get Prince to make the funk face?' You know, when you play something funky and you make that face where it looks like something's stinkin'. Every night we try to come up with something new. When he makes that face we go, 'Okay. Got it.'" As *Vibe*'s Light put it a bit later, "Watching Prince cue them, stop on a dime, introduce a new groove, veer off by triggering another sample, you can only think of James Brown burnishing his bands to razor-precision, fining them for missing a single note." Indeed, several writers suggested that Prince had earned Brown's mantle of "The Hardest Working Man in Show Business."

Stayed Ahead of Pop Music Trends

As Alan Leeds noted in the liner notes to the Prince *Hits* collection, "Prince raced with the times and usually won." Leeds suggested that music historians might someday regard the artist's tenure under his former name as they have the early work of jazz greats Duke Ellington and Miles Davis—as a prelude to greater innovation. "He's 15 years into his career, a time when most stars are kicking back, going through the motions," noted Light. "But he is still rethinking the rules of performance, the idea of how music is released, the basic concepts about how we consume and listen to music, still challenging himself and his audience like an avant-garde artist, not a platinum-selling pop star."

Time's David Thigpen also noted Prince's tendency to be ahead of trends and innovations in pop music. The artist finally released *The Black Album,* recorded around 1987, in 1994, but made it available only for a limited time—two months—amid speculation that it was released against his wishes. Thigpen remarked after hearing the long-shrouded album's contents that Prince had "anticipated the decidedly unlovesexy anger and violence in the gangster rap of the 1990s," and added, "In [1987], listeners probably wouldn't have known what to make of its bitter outlook; today it is almost conventional." *Entertainment Weekly*'s David Browne, however, scoffed at *The Black Album*'s "dark" aura and commented, "For all its mysterioso qualities, it's essentially party music."

While much of the entertainment press covered his unorthodox career moves with a combination of cynical gossip and dread, the artist formerly known as Prince simply—and, it seems, fearlessly—went his own way. "[Athlete] Bo Jackson can play baseball and football," he noted to Light. "Can you imagine what I would do if I could do all I can?"

Selected discography

On Warner Bros.

For You (includes "Soft and Wet"), 1978.
Prince, 1979.
Dirty Mind, 1980.
Controversy, 1981.
1999 (includes "1999" and "Little Red Corvette"), 1982.
(With the Revolution) *Purple Rain* (soundtrack; includes "When Doves Cry," "Let's Go Crazy," and "Purple Rain"), 1984.
(With the Revolution) *Around the World in a Day* (includes "Raspberry Beret"), 1985.
The Black Album (recorded c. 1987), 1994.
Batman (film soundtrack), 1989.
Come, 1994.

On Paisley Park

(With the Revolution) *Parade* (soundtrack from *Under the Cherry Moon*), 1986.
Sign O' the Times (includes "U Got the Look" and "I Could Never Take the Place of Your Man"), 1987.
Lovesexy, 1988.
Graffiti Bridge (film soundtrack), 1990.
(With New Power Generation) *Diamonds & Pearls*, 1991.
(With New Power Generation) *[symbol]*, 1992.
The Hits/The B-Sides, 1993.
The Hits 1, 1993.
The Hits 2, 1993.

On NPG/Bellmark

The Beautiful Experience (EP; includes "The Most Beautiful Girl in the World"), 1993.

Sources

Books

Rees, Dafydd, and Luke Crampton, *Rock Movers & Shakers*, Billboard, 1991.

Periodicals

Billboard, May 8, 1993; June 19, 1993; July 24, 1993; August 28, 1993; February 12, 1994; May 21, 1994; November 5, 1994.
Down Beat, January 1994.
Entertainment Weekly, April 9, 1993; May 14, 1993; June 25, 1993; September 17, 1993; July 22, 1994; August 19, 1994.
Guitar Player, August 1993.

Jet, May 24, 1993.

Los Angeles Times, August 14, 1994.

Oakland Press (Oakland County, MI), May 2, 1993.

Q, July 1994.

Request, August 1994.

Rolling Stone, April 1, 1993; April 29, 1993; June 10, 1993;
   August 5, 1993; October 14, 1993.

Spin, September 1991; June 1993.

Vanity Fair, November 1993.

Vibe, August 1994.

Additional information for this profile was provided by Warner Bros. press materials, 1991-94, and liner notes to *The Hits/ The B-Sides,* Paisley Park, 1993.

—Simon Glickman

Tito Puente

Bandleader, percussionist, pianist, composer

Tito Puente is widely considered to be the godfather of Latin jazz and salsa, devoting more than six decades of his life to performing Latin music and earning a reputation as a masterful percussionist. Noted for merging Latin American rhythms with contemporary jazz and big band music, Puente's prolific output encompasses over 100 albums recorded between 1949 and 1994.

Puente was born in New York City's Spanish Harlem in 1923, where the hybrid of Afro-Cuban and Afro-Puerto Rican music helped create salsa music (the Spanish word for "spice" and "sauce" is salsa). By the time Puente was ten years old, he played with local Latin bands at neighborhood gatherings, society parties, and New York City hotels. Puente first performed as a young boy with a local band called Los Happy Boys, at New York City's Park Place Hotel, and by the age of 13, he was considered a child prodigy by his family, neighbors, and fellow bandmembers. As a teenager, he joined Noro Morales and the Machito Orchestra. Puente was drafted into the Navy in 1942—at the age of 19—to

Photograph by Ricardo Betancourt, courtesy of Tropijazz Talent Agency

Born Ernesto Antonio Puente, April 23, 1920, in New York, NY; married; three children. *Education:* Studied conducting, orchestration, and musical theory at the Juilliard School of Music, 1945-47.

As a child, performed as percussionist/pianist in Los Happy Boys band, New York City; as a teenager, performed with Noro Morales and the Machito Orchestra; performed with Fernando Alvarez and his Copacabana Group, Jose Curbelo, and Pupi Campo; formed Piccadilly Boys, 1948, then Tito Puente Orchestra; recorded first hit single, "Abaniquito," Tico, 1949; signed with RCA, 1949; released fusion of mambo/big band/jazz LPs, 1950s-1960s; performed compositions at Metropolitan Opera, New York City, 1967; hosted television show *The World of Tito Puente,* 1968; performed for U.S. President Jimmy Carter, 1979; founded Tito Puente Scholarship Foundation; appeared in films *Radio Days, Armed and Dangerous,* and *The Mambo Kings,* 1991; released 100th recording, *El Numero Cien,* 1991; with Golden Latin-Jazz Allstars, released *Master Timbalero,* 1994; with Latin-Jazz Allstars, released *In Session,* 1994. *Military service:* U.S. Navy, 1942-45.

Awards: Grammy awards for *A Tribute to Benny More,* 1979; *On Broadway,* 1983; *Mambo Diablo,* 1985; and *Goza Mi Timbal,* 1989; honorary doctorate from College at Old Westbury, mid-1980s; Founders Award, American Society of Composers, Authors and Publishers, 1994; eight Grammy Award nominations.

Addresses: *Record company*—RMM Records, 568 Broadway, Suite 806, New York, NY 10012.

orchestration, and musical theory under the G.I. bill. He completed his studies in 1947, at the age of 24.

While at Juilliard, and for a year after he completed his studies, Puente played with Fernando Alvarez and his Copacabana Group, as well as Jose Curbelo and Pupi Campo. When Puente was 25 in 1948, he formed his own group—or conjunto—called the Piccadilly Boys, which soon became known as the Tito Puente Orchestra. He recorded his first hit, "Abaniquito," on the Tico Records label a year later. Later in 1949, he signed with RCA Victor records and recorded the single "Ran Kan Kan."

King of the 1950s Mambo Craze

Puente began churning out hits in the 1950s while riding the crest of mambo's popularity, and recorded dance favorites such as "Barbarabatiri," "El Rey del Timbai," "Mambo la Roca," and "Mambo Gallego." RCA released *Cuban Carnival, Puente Goes Jazz, Dance Mania,* and *Top Percussion,* four of Puente's most popular albums in the 1950s, between 1956 and 1960. Puente established himself as the foremost mambo musician of the 1950s, and in the late 1950s, fused Cuban "cha-cha-cha" beats with big band compositions.

In the 1960s Puente began to collaborate more widely with other New York City-based musicians; he played with trombonist Buddy Morrow, Woody Herman, and Cuban musicians Celia Cruz and La Lupe. He remained flexible and open to experimentation by collaborating with others and fusing various musical styles such as mambo, jazz, salsa, and the big band sound of the 1940s. Puente epitomized the Latin-jazz crossover movement in music at the time. In 1963 on Tico Records, Puente released "Oye Como Va," which was a resounding success and is now considered a classic. Four years later in 1967 Puente performed a program of his compositions at the Metropolitan Opera at Lincoln Center.

Gained Global Recognition

Puente hosted his own television show called "The World of Tito Puente," broadcast on Hispanic television in 1968, and he was asked to be the Grand Marshall of New York City's Puerto Rican Day Parade. In 1969 Mayor John Lindsay gave Puente the key to New York City as a ceremonious gesture of widespread appreciation.

Puente's music was not categorized as salsa until the 1970s, as it contained elements of big band composi-

fight in World War II, which entailed a three-year reprieve from music.

In the late 1930s Puente had originally intended to become a professional dancer, but chose to continue performing and composing music after injuring his ankle in a bicycle accident. Puente befriended bandleader Charlie Spivak while in the Navy, and through Spivak, Puente became interested in big band composition. When Puente returned from the Navy after serving in nine battles, he received a Presidential Commendation and completed his formal musical education at the Juilliard School of Music, studying conducting,

tion and jazz as well. When Puente's classic hit "Oye Como Va" was covered by Carlos Santana in the early 1970s, a new generation was introduced to Puente's music. Santana also covered Puente's "Para Los Rumberos," which Puente recorded in 1956. Puente and Santana eventually met in 1977 in New York City's Roseland Ballroom.

In 1979 Puente toured Japan with his ensemble and discovered an enthusiastic new audience as well as the fact that he had achieved worldwide popularity. After returning from Japan, the musician and his orchestra played for U.S. President Jimmy Carter as part of the president's Hispanic Heritage Month celebration. Puente was awarded the first of four Grammy Awards in 1979 for *A Tribute To Benny More.* He also received Grammy awards for *On Broadway* in 1983, *Mambo Diablo* in 1985, and *Goza Mi Timbal* in 1989. In the course of his long career, Puente received eight Grammy Award nominations, more than any other musician in the Latin music field before 1994.

Released 100th Album

Puente recorded his last big band albums in 1980 and 1981. He toured European cities with the Latin Percussion Jazz Ensemble, and recorded albums with them as well in the 1980s. Puente continued to devote himself to composing, recording, and performing music throughout the 1980s, but his interests broadened at this time.

Puente founded the Tito Puente Scholarship Foundation to benefit musically talented children; the foundation later signed a contract with Allnet Communications to provide scholarships to music students nationwide. He appeared on *The Cosby Show,* and performed in a commercial for Coca-Cola with Bill Cosby. Puente also made a guest appearances in the films *Radio Days* and *Armed and Dangerous.* Puente received an honorary doctorate degree from the College at Old Westbury in the 1980s as well, and appeared at the Monterey Jazz Festival in 1984.

On August 14, 1990, Puente received a Hollywood Star in Los Angles for posterity. Puente's talent was elevated to an international audience in the mid-1980s, and he spent time in the early 1990s performing for audiences overseas. In 1991 Puente appeared—most appropriately—in the film *The Mambo Kings Play Songs of Love,* which prompted another new generation's interest in his music.

In 1991, at the age of 68, Puente released his 100th album, titled *El Numero Cien,* distributed by Sony for RMM Records. Puente released *Master Timbalero* with

his Golden Latin-Jazz Allstars—comprised mainly of other band leaders —in 1994, covering classics such as "The Peanut Vendor" and "Nostalgia in Times Square," as well as the album *In Session* with a separate ensemble of musicians called the Latin-Jazz Allstars, is his regular touring group. Puente was awarded ASCAP's most prestigious honor—the Founders Award—in July of 1994. *Billboard's* John Lannert wrote, "As Puente stepped up to the microphone, a segment of the audience broke into an impromptu rendition of the Puente anthem 'Oye Como Va.'"

Selected discography

Mambos with Puente, Tumbao Cuban Classics, 1949.
Tito Puente & Friends, Tropical, 1949.
Mambo On Broadway, RCA, 1951.
Cuban Carnival, RCA, 1956.
Puente Goes Jazz, RCA, 1957.
Let's Cha Cha with Puente, RCA, 1958.
Dance Mania, RCA, 1958.
Top Percussion, RCA, 1960.
Bossa Nova by Puente, Roulette, 1965.
My Fair Lady Goes Latin, Roulette, 1968.
Palante, Tico, 1972.
Pa Los Rumberos, Tico, 1974.
A Tribute to Benny More, Tico, 1979.
On Broadway, Concord, 1983.
El Ray, Concord, 1984.
Mambo Diablo, Concord, 1985.
Sensacion, Concord, 1987.
Un Poco Loco, Concord, 1987.
Salsa Meets Jazz, Concord, 1988.
Goza Mi Timbal, Concord, 1989.
El Numero Cien, Sony, 1991.
Mambo Macoco, Tumbao Cuban Classics, 1992.
Puente Goes Jazz, Bluebird, 1993.
Master Timbalero, Concord Picante, 1994.
In Session, TropiJazz, 1994.
Navidad en las Americas, 1994.
(Contributor) *I Like It Like That* (soundtrack), Sony, 1994.

Sources

Books

Gerard, Charley, *Salsa: The Rhythm of Latin Music,* White Cliffs Media Company, 1989.

Periodicals

Americas, January/February 1993.
Billboard, July 9, 1994.
Down Beat, June 1992; November 1993; August 1994.
Harper's Bazaar, June 1993.

Hispanic, May 1992; December 1992.
Musician, July 1994.
Newsweek, November 11, 1991; April 20, 1992.
New Yorker, March 2, 1992.
Rolling Stone, December 12, 1991.
Time, June 8, 1992.

—B. Kimberly Taylor

The Residents

Rock band

The members of the Residents have managed to keep their identities secret for over 20 years. It is rumored that the band name was chosen after Warner Bros. Records rejected the band's unlabeled demo tape and sent it back to "Residents" at the band's return address. Further biographical information about the Residents is limited to the members' claim of having come from Louisiana and of having formed the band in the San Francisco area.

In 1972 the Residents turned out a two-record set of 45 rpm disks called *Santa Dog*. This issue is sometimes confused with their 1978 45 rpm remake called *Santa Dog '78*, which was sent out to the mailing list of the experimentally-oriented label Ralph Records as a Christmas greeting and appreciation of support.

The band apparently did not have musical training, but since 1970 the members had been fooling around with tape recorders and had begun building a private studio, subsequently buying the first consumer four- and eight-track machines as they became available. Prior to *Santa Dog,* the band had limited themselves to demo tapes, one hatched in 1971 entitled "Baby Sex," for which cover art was designed—a woman performing fellatio on a male baby.

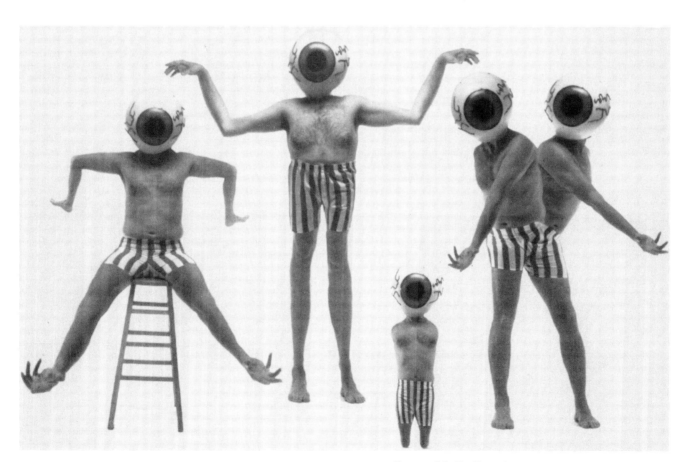

Photograph by Rex Ray and Jay Neel, © 1991, The Cryptic Corporation

For the Record . . .

Members' identities unknown.

Recording and performing artists, early 1970s—. Band formed c. 1971; released first album, *Meet the Residents,* 1974; released first video, *The Mole Show,* 1985; released CD-ROM *The Residents: Freak Show,* 1994.

Addresses: *Record company*—Cryptic Corporation, 566 Folsom Street, San Francisco, CA 94105. *Fan club*—U.W.E.B. The Official Residents Fan Club, P.O. Box 1599, Hoboken, NJ 07030.

The Residents' first album, *Meet the Residents,* appeared in 1974 and marked the birth of the mail-order only label Ralph Records. The Residents, who would become the most anonymous of musical groups, began by attacking the most well known, the Beatles. For the cover art on *Meet the Residents,* the group used a copy of the *Meet the Beatles* album cover, albeit embroidered with some sarcastic doodling. Drawing legal fire, the Residents backed down and changed the design to show people dressed like the Beatles labeled with names like Paul McCrawfish and Ringo Starrfish.

Similarity with the Beatles ended inside the cover. As Cole Gagne wrote of the album in *Sonic Transports,* "most often, one crazy patch of music abuts another, or else the songs dovetail in slippery segues, where a phrase abruptly collapses into a seizure of repetitions which draws in weird new life forms that crowd out the old piece all together." The songs were not discrete—where one composition ended and another began was often unclear. Similarly unclear was into what genre this music fell; certainly it was not easy listening.

The Residents again mocked early pop rock culture in the 1975 album *The Third Reich 'n' Roll.* The song "It's My Party" was performed not with the traditional whining of a teenage girl but by the raging thunder of "the 50-foot woman" as Gagne put it. Similarly, a deservedly ghastly rendition was in store for "Yummy Yummy Yummy I've Got Love in My Tummy." The album was punctuated by shrieks, sound effects, and electronic noise, trying to break down a sugary, sentimental culture, a mission the Residents have never really abandoned.

The Residents could not get enough Beatles music and again returned to the Fab Four in their 1977 45 rpm on Ralph entitled *The Beatles Play the Residents and the Residents Play the Beatles.* Side "A" was a remix of various original Beatles recordings; this dip into sampling was only one of numerous times the Residents used a technique years before mainstream pop.

The Residents' LPs of the 1970s included *Not Available* (1974), *Fingerprince* (1977), *Duckstab/Buster & Glen* (1978), and *Eskimo* (a 1979 effort based on Eskimo stories that included an appearance by longtime collaborator Philip "Snakefinger" Lithman and others). The band's prolific pace of an LP or two a year, along with 45s and other projects, continued through the 1980s. A partial list of these albums includes: *The Commercial Album* (1980); *Mark of the Mole* (the 1981 introduction to the saga of the oppressed Mole people of which two more volumes would appear); *George and James* (a 1984 exploration of George Gershwin and James Brown music, part of the band's American Composer series); *Hell* (1986); and *God in Three Persons* (1988).

The Residents have observed strict anonymity, always playing their infrequent concerts in disguise—they often appear dressed in black with giant bloodshot eyeballs covering each musician's head like a deep sea diver's helmet. Yet the Residents have not gone without a voice. Two people, Homer Flynn and Hardy Fox, are authorized to speak for the Residents—or at least, the band has not publicly objected to their doing so.

The Residents themselves do not make public statements. In 1993 a *Mondo 2000* interviewer queried Homer and Hardy (both of whom have Louisiana accents) on the band's musical influences and was told that these certainly existed, but due to the Residents' lack of traditional musical skills, the band was incapable of making them recognizable.

"Musically, Captain Beefheart was an early influence," Flynn added. "It was obvious to them [the Residents] that he was taking John Coltrane and Howling Wolf and twisting them around in a wonderfully unique and interesting way." The process of freely twisting influences is what interested the Residents, not so much imitation of Beefheart's style—except, perhaps, his strong and often cryptic lyrics.

In a 1989 album, *The King & Eye*—the "eye" perhaps a reference to the band members' favorite stage disguise—the Residents introduced some interpretations of Elvis Presley's music. While Elvis had performed "Teddy Bear" as a light pop number, the Residents spokesmen saw the ditty's dark "undercurrent of [sadomasochism]." Regarding the King's "Jailhouse Rock," the Residents emphasized what they saw as its concern with homosexuality.

In a June 1992 *Post* magazine article, Debra Kaufman painted an interesting picture of the Residents' complex meshing of performance art, music, and storytelling. Working from the theme developed in their album trilogy on the fantasy Mole people, the Residents had made a financially draining world tour, The Mole Show, in 1982-83. Penn, of the comic duo Penn and Teller, narrated the show. Kaufman wrote that the Mole people's emotional struggles after they were forced to live above ground was mirrored in Penn's performance and his expression of anger and confusion about his role in the show. The narration also allegedly reflected the Residents' ambivalent feelings "about their self-imposed underground status."

The band's interest in freakishness and new technology married nicely in their 1994 CD-ROM release, *The Residents: Freak Show,* which features such circus wonders as Herman the Human Mole and Wanda the Worm Woman. The characters' lamentable histories are revealed via photos, animation, and audio. In May of 1994 one *Billboard* reviewer admitted in viewing the CD that he had really felt as though he had entered "forbidden territory, enjoying an illicit thrill." Of course, that has always been the Residents' territory.

Selected discography

Santa Dog, Ralph, 1972.
Meet the Residents, Ralph, c. 1973.
The Third Reich 'n' Roll, Ralph, 1976.
Fingerprince, Ralph, 1977.
The Beatles Play the Residents and the Residents Play the Beatles, Ralph, 1977.
Duck Stab/Buster & Glen, Ralph, 1978.
(With Snakefinger) *Eskimo,* Ralph, 1979.
The Commercial Album, Ralph, 1980.
Mark of the Mole, Ralph, 1981.
The Tunes of Two Cities, Ralph, 1982.

George and James, Ralph, 1984.
Whatever Happened to Vileness Fats?, Ralph, 1984.
The Census Taker, Episode, 1985.
The Big Bubble, Ralph, 1985.
Hell, Rykodisc, 1986.
Pee Wee's Playhouse (television score), CBS, 1987.
God in Three Persons, Rykodisc/Torso, 1988.
The King and Eye, Enigma/Torso, 1989.
Not Available (recorded 1974), Ralph.

Other

The Mole Show/Whatever Happened to Vileness Fats? (video), Doublevision, 1985.
Video Voodoo—The Residents, Volume 1 (retrospective of album videos), Palacevideo, 1987.
The Residents: Freak Show (CD-ROM), Voyager, 1994.
"Midway" segment on *Inscape* (CD-ROM), Voyager, 1995.

Sources

Books

Bigazzi, Giampiero, and Annette Jarvie, *The Residents—An Almost Complete Collection of Lyrics, 1972-1988,* Stampa Alternativa/Nuovi Equilibri, 1989.
Culp, Philip, and others, *The Official W.E.I.R.D. Book of the Residents,* The Residents Official Fan Club, 1979.
Gagne, Cole, *Sonic Transports, New Frontiers in Our Music,* de Falco Books, 1990.

Periodicals

Billboard, May 14, 1994; July 23, 1994; August 20, 1994.
Mondo 2000, 1993.
New York Times, June 20, 1988; January 8, 1990.
Post, June 22, 1992.

—*Joseph M. Reiner*

Cliff Richard

Singer

Reuters/Bettmann

Considered the most successful artist in the history of British pop music, Cliff Richard has showed remarkable staying power in an industry known for short careers. From the late 1950s through the late 1980s, he placed nearly 100 songs on the British pop charts as he managed to survive through revolutionary changes in musical tastes. During this span he progressed from an Elvis Presley-like rocker, to a well-scrubbed teen idol, to a purveyor of mellow rock, to a singer of songs with a Christian theme.

After moving from India to England as a boy, Richard began learning how to play the guitar after he was given a used one as a present. Like many teens in Britain at the time, he became interested in the outgrowth of blues music known as "skiffle." He formed the Quintones vocal group in 1957, then sang with the Dave Teague Skiffle Group. Richard sang gigs around his Hertfordshire home on nights and weekends, while working as a credit control clerk at his father's factory during the day. Eventually he teamed up with drummer Terry Smart and guitarist Ken Payne to form the Drifters, who worked their way up on the club circuit until they were playing at London's famous 21's coffee bar. While performing they were seen by guitarist Ian Samwell, who then joined the group. With his musicians providing a Ventures-like background, Richard continued to develop his rocking style and grow in popularity.

Became U.K.'s Top Rock and Roller

In 1958 Cliff and the Drifters attracted the attention of theatrical agent George Ganyou while performing at a Saturday morning talent show at Gaumont cinema in Shepherd's Bush, London. Ganyou approached them about making a demo, then paid for their recording of "Breathless" and "Lawdy Miss Clawdy." Norrie Paramour, a producer at EMI, gave the group an audition after hearing the demo. He immediately saw Richard's obvious "Elvis-like" appeal and wanted to sign him up as a solo act who would be backed up by an orchestra. Richard insisted on retaining his band members, and the producer agreed to bring the Drifters on board as well.

For his first single with EMI, Richard recorded a cover of Bobby Helms's American teen ballad "Schoolboy Crush." However, when British television producer Jack Good heard the record, he preferred the B-side's "Move It." According to the *Guinness Encyclopedia of Popular Music,* "Good reacted with characteristically manic enthusiasm when he heard the disc, rightly recognizing that it sounded like nothing else in the history of UK pop." Richard and the Drifters had brought a much-desired American sound to British rock, and Good launched a massive publicity campaign to herald the arrival of the group's first single. His instincts turned out to be right, and "Move It" soared to Number Two on the U.K. charts. In no time Cliff Richard was hailed as Britain's top rock and roller, ousting Marty Wilde from the slot.

Samwell decided to quit the group and become a songwriter when Richard started receiving most of the attention, and by the end of 1958, the group included new members Hank B. Marvin and Bruce Welch. To avoid confusion with the American rhythm-and-blues group of the same name, the group then became Cliff and the Shadows. While the group enjoyed massive popularity, Richard also generated controversy with his highly physical gyrations on stage that were labeled offensive by some groups. The *New Musical Express* chastised him for his "hip-swinging" and "crude exhibitionism."

Expanded Career Into Acting

Richard really came into his own in 1959, reaching Number One with Lionel Bart's "Living Doll." By then he had already appeared on British television's *Oh Boy!,* and had also landed roles in two feature films. In *Expresso Bongo,* he played an average singer who is repackaged into a major pop star. The *Guinness Encyclopedia* said that it was "one of the most revealing and humorous films ever made on the music business and proved an interesting vehicle for Richard's varied talents."

After his sensational arrival on the entertainment scene at the end of the 1950s, Richard generated songs in the 1960s that were relatively tame but dependably popular. From 1960 to 1965 he enjoyed a streak of seven consecutive Top Ten singles, and appeared in two more popular movie musicals. He demonstrated his versatility by having success with both rocking numbers such as "Nine Times Out of Ten" and pensive tunes such as "Theme for a Dream." One of his best showings in the early 1960s was "The Young Ones" released in 1962. *Guinness* called it "A glorious pop anthem to youth, with some striking guitar work from Hank Marvin." During the first half of the 1960s, Richard toured actively in Europe, Japan, Australia, South Africa, and the U.S.

Converted to Christianity

Although Richard never got on the track of the British invasion or beat groups of the mid-1960s, he managed to keep churning out fresh material that kept him in the Top Ten in Britain. He became a fundamentalist Christian in 1966, and at first was going to quit the pop music scene. Instead, he used his voice to promote faith in God. He became active with the English Christian youth group the Crusaders and often spoke to groups on the merits of Christian living.

Popular culture was changing too fast for Richard to adapt in the late 1960s, and he was left somewhat behind as other British groups ushered in a new era in music. A new Richard song in the 1970s was no longer assured of Top Ten status, although he continued to break the Top 20 with songs such as "Sunny Honey Girl" in 1971 and "Sing a Song of Freedom" in 1972.

After being absent from the charts for nearly two years, Richard sprang back to pop life in 1976 when Bruce Welch of the Shadows took over as his producer. The collaboration led to the best-selling 1976 album *I'm Nearly Famous*, which contained the hits "Miss You Nights" and "Devil Woman," Richard's first song to chart in the U.S. since 1959. Following another creative trough after "My Kinda Life" was released in 1977, Richard resurfaced again with "We Don't Talk Anymore" in 1979. That song became his first Number One hit in the U.K. since 1968, and it heralded a new, well-arranged sound for Richard that sustained him on the hit parade through the 1980s. The success of the song overseas triggered a tour in the U.S., his first there since 1963.

Richard added another dimension to his career in the 1980s by demonstrating a keen ability to harmonize, as shown in duets with Olivia Newton-John, Phil Everly, Sarah Brightman, Sheila Walsh, Elton John, and Van Morrison. He also starred in Dave Clark's (of the Dave Clark Five) musical *Time,* which was first staged in the West End of London in 1985. Retaining his youthful good looks over the years, Richard retained a loyal army of fans well into his forties. By 1988 there were 29 Cliff Richard fan clubs in Britain, consisting mostly of middle-aged women. At age 50, he showed his continuing ability to adapt when he recorded his first anti-war song, "From a Distance," which proved to be a hit.

Cliff Richard managed to remain viable as a pop act for an incredible three decades, in an era when most singers fade from the scene in just a few years. As acknowledged in *New Statesman and Society,* he is "undoubtedly the most important pop symbol modern British culture has produced."

Selected discography

Singles; with others

(With the Drifters) "Move It," 1958.
(With the Drifters) "Living Doll," 1959.
(With the Shadows) "Fall in Love with You," 1960.
(With the Shadows) "On the Beach," 1964.
(With the Shadows) "The Minute You're Gone," 1965.
(With Hank Marvin) "Throw Down a Line," 1969.
(With Olivia Newton-John) "Suddenly," 1980.
(With Phil Everly) "She Means Nothing to Me," 1983.
(With Sarah Brightman) "All I Ask of You," 1986.

Solo singles

"The Twelfth of Never," 1964.
"Visions," 1966.
"Congratulations," 1968.
"Devil Woman," 1976.
"We Don't Talk Anymore," 1979.

Solo albums

The Young Ones, Columbia, 1961.
Summer Holiday, Epic/Columbia, 1963.
I'm Nearly Famous, Rocket/EMI, 1976.
40 Golden Greats, EMI, 1977.
Wired for Sound, EMI America/EMI, 1981.
Always Guaranteed, EMI, 1987.

Sources

Books

Ferrier, Bob, *The Wonderful World of Cliff Richard,* Davies, 1964.
Larkin, Colin, editor, *The Guinness Encyclopedia of Popular Music, Volume 3,* Guinness Publishing, 1992.
Doncaster, Patrick, and Tony Jasper, *Cliff,* Sidgwick & Jackson, 1981.
Tremblett, George, *The Cliff Richard Story,* Futura, 1975.
Winter, David Brian, *New Singer, New Song, The Cliff Richard Story,* Word Books, 1960.

Periodicals

Billboard, February 12, 1994.
Entertainment Weekly, November 19, 1993.
New Statesman and Society, September 23, 1988.
People, February 18, 1980.

—*Ed Decker*

Teddy Riley

While still in his early twenties, Teddy Riley rose up from the streets of Harlem, New York, to found a new kind of music—new jack swing. Riley described this new sound in *Rolling Stone* as "rap music with pop, rap with jazz, rap with R&B." Since his career began in 1984, Riley has directed his own bands—namely Wreckx-N-Effect, Guy, and Blackstreet—and produced and written hit songs for a host of stars, including Michael Jackson, Bobby Brown, Stevie Wonder, Kool Moe Dee, and Jane Child. With numerous Number One hits and platinum albums, Riley has impressed even industry executives, one of whom was moved to proclaim the value of top songwriters and producers in general. "You cannot have a hit record without good songwriters and producers. They are the very heart of the industry," LeBaron Taylor, CBS Records vice-president and general manager, was quoted as saying in *Ebony*.

Riley's success did not come without trials, however. He lost a bandmember and half-brother to gunfire on the streets and broke with his longtime manager and childhood father figure, Gene Griffen, in a lawsuit over money. Relocating then from New York City to Virginia Beach, Virginia, for relative serenity, the 1992 recipient of the American Society of Composers, Authors, and Publishers (ASCAP) prestigious rhythm and blues songwriter of the year award aspired to legendary heights of productivity and achievement: "I wanna be the hardest working man in the music industry, like James Brown," he commented in *Vibe*. Based on Riley's track record, *Vibe's* music writer Bönz Malone considered that dream plausible.

Learned Music in Church and on the Street

Born on October 8, 1967, in Harlem, Teddy Riley became something of a musical prodigy and star as an early teen in school. His mother provided the impetus to bring him out of the bad ways he developed and into aspirations in music at an early age—16. He had been "hustlin'" to make money when his mother was laid off, but she soon called him on his behavior. "I had to do something to help my family, but then I got busted by my Moms and she started losing faith in me, telling me I ain't gonna be nothin'," Riley told Malone for *Vibe*. "I said, 'Ma, I'm gonna make it in the music industry.' Then we sat and we hugged and I cried and she cried. That's when I cashed in my money and bought me about three or four keyboards."

At age ten Riley had already mastered several instruments—guitar, bass, several horns, and especially the keyboard. He gained his edge listening and playing

Born October 8, 1967, in New York, NY; son of Mildred and Edward (stepfather); two children. *Education:* Studied electronic music at Manhattan School of Music and composition at Columbia University.

First produced his own group, Kids At Work, 1981; recorded hit "New Jack City" with first band, Wreckx-N-Effect, 1984; produced *Kool Moe Dee,* 1984; produced first single, "The Show," for Doug E. Fresh; wrote and produced songs for Michael Jackson, Bobby Brown, Stevie Wonder, Jane Child, and many others, mid-1980s—; formed band Guy, 1987; released hit albums and toured U.S., c. 1987-90; formed band Blackstreet, early 1990s; founded independent label, LOR Records & Management, and formed own company, Future Entertainment Group Ltd., Virginia Beach, VA, 1990.

Awards: Named rhythm and blues songwriter of the year, American Society of Composers, Authors and Publishers (ASCAP), 1992; platinum album for *The Future,* MCA, 1990.

Addresses: *Home*—Virginia Beach, VA. *Record company*—Interscope Records, 75 Rockefeller Plaza, New York, NY 10019. *Management*—Harvey Gallagher Communications, Inc., 1501 Broadway, Suite 2001, New York, NY 10036.

with friends at impromptu pick-up concerts on Harlem streets and in church, according to the *Village Voice.* "I come from a rap family," he told Mark Coleman of the *Los Angeles Times.* "I was there when it was happening, back in the days rap wasn't even out yet when I first heard about deejays' scratching and beatboxes. That stayed in my head, and at the same time, my mother was sayin' 'Let's go to church.' So that stayed in my head too. All those different keyboard players—uh, preachers. There was one in particular, a Rev. Caulfield, who was a genius on the organ. That's really where I learned everything about playing keyboards."

Invented New Jack Swing

After forming his first band, Wreckx-N-Effect, with his brothers, Markell, and Brandon Mitchell, a few years later in 1987 he formed a second band, Guy, with Aaron Hall and Timmy Gatling. Wreckx-N-Effect released the hit single "New Jack Swing," while Guy debuted in 1987 with a self-titled album on the Uptown/MCA label. That

album hit Number One on Billboard's top rhythm-and-blues albums chart in 1988 while the group traveled on sold-out tours.

Guy's second album, 1990's *The Future,* went platinum and won rave reviews. Peter Watrous of the *New York Times* called the album "an example of unadulterated pop brilliance." The successful tunes included "Long Gone," a song of dedication to the late Sarah Vaughan and Riley's half-brother Brandon Mitchell, "D-O-G Me Out," and "Do Me Right." Watrous credited Guy on their first album with "inventing the genre called New Jack Swing," while on *The Future,* the band brought in more dance music and singing, particularly by Aaron Hall, described by Watrous as possibly "the most gifted pop music singer to emerge in the late 80's."

All of that success brought its troubles, however. First, Riley lost his younger brother, Brandon Mitchell of Wreckx-N-Effect, to gunfire in 1989. Soon after, Riley wrote "Long Gone" from *The Future* and decided to move to Virginia Beach. "The day my little brother got killed, I said, 'We got to go. We got to move.' We got a lot of angry people up here, a lot of jealousy. The new jacks don't mean to hurt you, they don't mean to harm you, but they want to be where you are. We want to help them, but at the same time, they're going too fast. Everybody's living in the fast lane up in New York." Next, he and his longtime manager and father figure, Gene Griffen, broke up in a dispute over money. Finally, internal problems separated Guy itself.

Began Own Label and Band Blackstreet

Riley has applied himself vigorously to a number of projects throughout his career, however, and continued to do so after his move in 1990. Over his career, he has written or produced such songs as Michael Jackson's "Remember the Time," Keith Sweat's "Why Me Baby," Wreckx-N-Effect's "Rump Shaker," Bobby Brown's "My Prerogative," and Kool Moe Dee's "How Ya' Like Me Now?" On film soundtracks, his work can be heard on the Number One rhythm and blues single "My Fantasy" for the Spike Lee film, *Do the Right Thing,* and in the title track of the film *New Jack City.* After moving to Virginia Beach, Riley set up a $3 million, 72-track recording facility, Future Records Recording Studio, and his own label and management company, LOR Records & Management, as part of his company, Future Entertainment Group Ltd.

Meanwhile, after the breakup of Guy, Riley set up another band called Blackstreet. One of the band's lead vocalists, Chauncey "Black" Hannibal, started as a backup singer for Guy, with roots in the church choirs of

Paterson, New Jersey; another, Dave Hollister, began in the church in Chicago and subsequently sang for Al B. Sure! and Mary J. Blige; and the third, Levi Little, had "phantom" origins, according to *Vibe*'s Bönz Malone, but "[they] just know he's down and he *rocks*." Malone described the sound as a combination of "Chauncey's sweet voice ... and Teddy's airtight drum drops." The band hoped to stay together and move funk music into the future. "This is the group forever," Riley maintained in *Vibe*. "We already have in our minds that none of us is gonna make it solo. It's like a marriage. We're gonna stick this out together."

Dubbed "the single most influential producer in the music business today," in *Ebony Man,* and "a genius," according to *Village Voice* music writer Barry Michael Cooper, by his late twenties Riley had already achieved prominence. With a new band and his own recording facilities in Virginia, Teddy Riley showed no signs of slowing down.

Selected discography

Singles

(As songwriter) Doug E. Fresh, "The Show," Reality, 1985.
(With Wreckx-N-Effect) "New Jack Swing," c. 1987.
(As coproducer and coarranger) Johnny Kemp, "Just Got Paid," CBS, 1988.
(As producer) Classic Two, "Rap's New Generation," Jive/RCA, 1988.
(As arranger) Al B. Sure!, "If I'm Not Your Lover," Warner Bros., 1988.
(As coarranger and songwriter) Billy Ocean, "Tear Down These Walls," Jive/Arista, 1988.
(As remix producer) Stevie Wonder, "My Eyes Don't Cry," Motown, 1988.

(As songwriter and producer) Wee Papa Girl Rappers, "Faith," Jive/RCA, 1988.

Albums

(As producer) Heavy D. and the Boyz, *Living Large,* MCA, 1987.
(As coproducer) Kool Moe Dee, *Kool Moe Dee,* Jive/RCA, 1987.
(As songwriter and coproducer) Kool Moe Dee, *How Ya Like Me Now?* Jive/RCA, 1987.
(As songwriter and coproducer) Keith Sweat, *Make It Last Forever,* Elektra, 1987.
(With Guy) *Guy,* MCA, 1988.
(With Guy) *The Future* (includes "Long Gone," "D-O-G Me Out," and "Do Me Right"), MCA, 1990.
(As producer of several tracks) Michael Jackson, *Dangerous,* 1992.
(As producer of several tracks) Bobby Brown, *'Till the End of Time,* MCA, 1992.
(With Blackstreet) *Blackstreet,* Interscope, 1994.

Sources

Billboard, December 11, 1993.
Ebony, June 1990.
Ebony Man, July 1992.
Entertainment Weekly, February 7, 1992.
Los Angeles Times, February 3, 1991.
New York Times, December 23, 1990.
Rolling Stone, May 18, 1989; January 10, 1991; February 7, 1991.
Spin, March 1992.
Vibe, June/July 1994.
Village Voice, Rock & Roll Quarterly, fall 1988.

—*Nicholas Patti*

Red Rodney

Trumpeter

MICHAEL OCHS ARCHIVES/Venice, CA

Red Rodney was the last of the original bebop trumpeters. After cutting his musical teeth playing swing with big bands, Rodney converted to jazz under the guidance of Dizzy Gillespie and Charlie Parker. Joining Parker's quintet at the age of 21, for more than a half a century he carried on the legacy begun by Gillespie and Miles Davis. Although a true bebop innovator in the 1940s and 1950s, Rodney's early contributions to jazz were overshadowed by his chaotic personal life. It was not until his later years that he gained respect as a driving creative force of bebop's developmental era.

Red Rodney was born Robert Rodney Chudnick on September 27, 1927, in a Jewish ghetto of Philadelphia, Pennsylvania. He began playing bugle in a Jewish veterans' drum and bugle corps at the age of ten. Originally, he wanted to play the drums, but because he was too small to carry them he was forced to switch instruments. He received his first trumpet at the age of 13 as a bar mitzvah present. He studied music at Philadelphia's Mastbaum High School, where he was a classmate of future jazz greats Buddy DeFranco and John Coltrane. His main influence at that time was swing trumpeter Harry James, whose solos he learned to play when he was 14 years old.

In 1942 Rodney ran away to Atlantic City, New Jersey, where he got a job playing in a house band that warmed up the crowd before the big bands performed. Flamboyant, talented, and too young to be drafted, he caught the attention of big-band leaders looking to replace trumpeters who had been drafted to fight in World War II. Over the next few years Rodney played with various big-band greats including Jerry Wald, Jimmy Dorsey, Tony Pastor, Les Brown, and Georgie Auld.

By the mid-1940s, Rodney had returned to Philadelphia, where he played in a studio band for CBS radio. He became interested in jazz after hearing Dizzy Gillespie perform and began sitting in with bands in clubs around the Philadelphia area. It was in one such venue, the Downbeat Club in South Philadelphia, that he met and befriended Gillespie. Impressed by the young man's musical ability, Gillespie took Rodney to New York to hear his quintet play. There, Gillespie introduced Rodney to Charlie Parker.

Hearing Parker's brand of bebop was an epiphany for Rodney. He told Craig Steinburg in an interview in *Diabetes Forecast:* "Even though my instrument was trumpet, and Dizzy was my hero, when I heard Charlie Parker, I knew right then, at 18 years old, what I wanted to do the rest of my life. It all came together then—that one night was like a religious experience." Rodney formed his own bebop band in 1946 and recorded his first album as a leader. Over the next two years he played as a featured soloist with Gene Krupa and Claude Thornhill, before joining Woody Herman's Four Brothers Band in 1948.

A Call From Bird

In 1949 Rodney got the call of a lifetime. It was Charlie "Bird" Parker asking him to join his quintet and replace trumpeter Miles Davis, who was leaving to form his own band. Parker didn't have to ask twice. Rodney moved to New York City and took his place beside a legend. His experiences with Parker would have a profound and lasting effect on both his music and life. "I got to stand next to this colossal giant each night and hear outpourings of raw genius," Rodney said in an interview in the *Philadelphia Inquirer.* "I really didn't feel that I deserved to be there, but he saw some potential, of course. I think it was more that he liked me. And I took advantage of the experience and reached a plateau that I never would have accomplished in so short a time. It was my college and graduate school at the same time."

Between 1949 and 1951, Rodney recorded albums for Keynote, EmArcy and Mercury both with Parker and under his own name. In the 18 months he spent with Parker he mastered the intricate harmonics of bebop and gained a reputation as one of the most talented

young bebop artists in the world. Unfortunately, he also learned about drugs. By the time he left Parker's band in 1951, he was addicted to heroin. Rodney faded in and out of the jazz spotlight for most of the 1950s. He played brief stints with Charlie Ventura's Big Band and recorded six albums (1952-57), including the now-classic *Modern Music From Chicago* with Ira Sullivan. After serving two prison terms for possession of heroin, Rodney returned to Philadelphia in 1957.

Walked Away From Jazz

Rodney kicked his heroin habit in prison, but because of his drug convictions, under Pennsylvania law he was not allowed to work in cabaret clubs. Unable to play the music he loved in the clubs he practically grew up in, Rodney turned his back on jazz and took a job as the leader of the house band at a banquet hall. Playing for weddings and bar mitzvahs was light years away from Rodney's experiences with Parker, but he was tremendously successful. By 1958, he was leading and managing five different dance bands and making more money than he had ever earned in his life. But the money wasn't enough to keep him happy. Frustrated by not playing jazz, he began using heroin again. Two years later, he found himself strung out and broke in San Francisco. Out of desperation, he impersonated an Army officer and stole $10,000 from the Atomic Energy Commission.

Finally apprehended in 1964, Rodney received a 27-month sentence for theft. While in prison he gave up heroin for good, got his bachelor's degree, and took a correspondence course in law. After his release, Rodney met celebrity lawyer Melvin Belli, who gave him a job as an investigator and enrolled him in law school. Rodney finished his law studies in just three years, but he was unable to become a practicing lawyer because of a California law that prevented convicted felons from taking the bar exam. He moved to Las Vegas and spent the remainder of 1960s in Las Vegas casino orchestras backing Strip headliners including Elvis Presley, Barbra Streisand, and Sammy Davis, Jr.

Comeback Led to Recognition as Jazz Great

Rodney led the good life in Vegas, but he longed to play bebop again. So he moved to Los Angeles in 1972 and began making frequent appearances at Donte's jazz club. Rodney made his return to jazz official in late 1973 with the release *Bird Lives!,* his first album in nearly 14 years. His comeback was briefly delayed by a stroke that left him temporarily paralyzed, but by the fall of 1974 he had recovered sufficiently to tour Europe with W.G.

Wien's *Musical Life of Charlie Parker.* He remained in Europe until April of 1975, making numerous television appearances and playing clubs and concerts in Denmark, Sweden, Portugal, Belgium, Holland, and England.

Upon returning to the United States, Rodney recorded three albums between 1976 and 1979, before forming a quartet with Ira Sullivan in 1980. The group played, recorded, and toured together until 1985, releasing five albums and garnering a 1982 Grammy nomination for the album *Sprint.* After parting ways with Sullivan, Rodney formed several new bands featuring up-and-coming jazz musicians whom he had taken under his wing. He recorded an incredible five albums between 1986 and 1988, including *Code Red,* which marked his first venture into jazz fusion and rap. During that time he also acted as a consultant on actor and director Clint Eastwood's biographical film of Charlie Parker's life, *Bird.* In addition to adding his fiery licks to the soundtrack, he coached actor Michael Zelnicker, who portrayed him in the film.

Rodney officially joined the ranks of the jazz greats in 1990. The Mellon Jazz Festival was dedicated to his honor and he was elected to the *Down Beat* Hall of Fame. In the *Down Beat* article announcing his induction he said: "Some people begin to slip after 50.... It's strange, but I seem to be playing better than ever." Rodney returned once more to his bebop roots in 1993 with *Then and Now,* a collection of updated bebop standards and new originals. He was planning a follow up album for Chesky records when he was diagnosed with lung cancer. He made his last public appearance in the summer of 1993 at the Charlie Parker Jazz Festival in New York City.

Red Rodney died of lung cancer on May 27, 1994, at his home in Boynton Beach, Florida. He was one of the last living links to Charlie Parker and bebop, and his death marked the end of an era. Although Rodney experienced his share of hardships and problems during his rollercoaster 52-year career, he overcame all odds to record more than 40 albums and to inspire and encourage four decades of jazz trumpeters.

Selected discography

Advance Guard of the '40s, EmArcy, 1945.

Early Bebop on Keynote, Mercury, 1947.
The New Sounds—Red Rodney, Prestige, 1952.
Modern Music From Chicago, Fantasy, 1955.
Fiery Red Rodney, Savoy, 1957.
The Red Arrow, Onyx, 1957.
Red Rodney, Signal, 1957.
Red Rodney Returns, Argo, 1957.
Bird Lives!, Muse, 1973.
Superbop, Muse, 1974.
Red Tornado, Muse, 1975.
Red, White & Blues, Muse, 1976.
Home Free, Muse, 1977.
The Three R's, Muse, 1979.
Hi Jinx (At the Vanguard), Muse, 1980.
Live at the Village Vanguard, Muse, 1980.
Night and Day, Muse, 1981.
Sprint, Elektra, 1982.
The 3 R's, Muse, 1983.
Alive in New York, Muse 1986.
No Turn on Red, Denon, 1986.
One for Bird, Steeple Chase, 1988.
Red Giant, Steeple Chase, 1988.
Red Snapper, Steeple Chase, 1988.
Red Alert!, Continuum, 1990.
Then and Now, Chesky, 1992.

Sources

Books

Carr, Ian, Digby Fairweather, and Brian Priestley, *Jazz: The Essential Companion,* Prentice Hall, 1988.
Feather, Leonard G., *Encyclopedia of Jazz in the Seventies,* Horizon Press, 1976.

Periodicals

Billboard, June 6, 1994.
Diabetes Forecast, July 1989.
Down Beat, December 1990; August 1994.
JazzTimes, December 1993.
Philadelphia Inquirer, June 17, 1990; March 13, 1992.
Stereo Review, February 1989.

Additional information for this profile was obtained from the *All-Music Guide,* Matrix Software, 1994.

—Thaddeus Wawro

Jimmy Scott

Singer

James Victor Scott, nicknamed Little Jimmy Scott by jazz artist Lionel Hampton in the late 1940s, often appears ambivalent about the difficulties in his life. He related in a *Vibe* article that Kallmann's syndrome, a rare hormonal disorder affecting both Scott and his brother, has been a blessing and a curse. His diagnosis late in life with the disease, whose sufferers do not undergo puberty, has finally explained the most mysterious and memorable aspect of this jazz singer's voice.

First-time listeners often assume Scott's voice is that of a woman. But it is not just his range that mesmerizes: he sings slowly, drawing out notes across measures, playing havoc with time. Sometimes leaving supporting musicians behind, Scott continues a cappella, evocatively delivering painful ballads in his own time. A difficult childhood, failed marriages, and questions about his sexuality and drug use—as well as ill treatment by the music industry—have left a mark of sadness on the singer's life. In *Pulse!* he observed: "A lot of people, like me, carry sadness with them for the rest of their life. I don't think I'll ever lose the expression of that. But, in a strange way, that sadness has finally brought about some happiness in my life."

Indeed, in the late 1980s, after spending some 20 years outside the music business, Scott reemerged as a powerful song stylist. His career was bolstered by both Jimmy McDonough's 1988 article on the singer in the *Village Voice* and Scott's rendition of the George and Ira Gershwin tune "Someone to Watch Over Me" at the 1991 funeral of rhythm and blues songwriter Doc Pomus, after which, according to *Bazaar,* he was signed to a five-album deal by the president of Sire Records, Seymour Stein. Since then Scott has sung for celebrity-filled audiences on both coasts, with Lou Reed on *Magic and Loss,* and with Bruce Springsteen on the film soundtrack *Philadelphia.* He even appeared as a ghost on the final episode of director David Lynch's TV series *Twin Peaks,* singing an original tune, "Under the Sycamore Tree." The man for whom *Jet* magazine "had printed an erroneous obituary in 1965," according to *LA Weekly,* was back.

Sang Away the Blues

One of ten children, Jimmy Scott was born in 1925 in Cleveland, Ohio, with his umbilical chord wrapped around his neck—a sign, remarked one of his father's friends, that he would become a singer. Scott's father, Arthur "Scottie" Scott, was a skilled asphalt layer; his mother, Justine Scott, played piano at Hagar's Universal Spiritual Church and would gather the children to sing gospel songs, noted Jimmy McDonough in the

For the Record . . .

Born July 17, 1925, in Cleveland, OH; married four times; fourth wife's name, Earlene.

Singer and recording artist. Prior to World War II, toured with Vaudeville acts; toured with shake dancer Estelle "Caledonia" Young, 1945-49; member of Lionel Hampton's band, until 1953; started recording for small record labels, 1950; recorded with Savoy Records, until 1975; cut record with Ray Charles on Charles's Tangerine label; entered semiretirement and started work as a hotel shipping and receiving clerk, 1965; renewed music career with a radio appearance, Newark, NJ, 1984; sang at musician Doc Pomus's funeral and signed to first major record deal, 1991.

Awards: Grant from Rhythm and Blues Foundation, 1989; Grammy Award nomination for best jazz vocal, 1992, for *All the Way.*

Addresses: *Management*—Harriet Sternberg Management, 15250 Ventura Blvd., Ste. 1215, Sherman Oaks, CA 91403. *Record company*—Sire Records, 75 Rockefeller Plaza, New York, NY, 10019.

Village Voice. In the same article, Scott reported that his mother was a stern music teacher: "She'd make you feel guilty for voicing wrong notes. She was a very spiritual woman, a cornerstone of strength. My father just didn't give a damn." Her death in 1938 after being hit by a car caused the family to be split up into foster homes and created a lifelong desire for family unity that Scott has never reconciled.

Although he has told many tales about his youth, it appears that Scott first embraced big band music while serving as an usher at the Metropolitan Theater. He then went on the road with two tap dancers, working as their valet and pestering them to let him sing. In Meadville, Pennsylvania, in the mid-1940s, Scott got his chance. He was a hit in front of a band that included Lester Young, Ben Webster, and Jo Jones. "Even that first night, the people screamed and hollered," Scott recounted in the *Village Voice.*

From 1945 to 1949 Scott went on tour with shake dancer Estelle "Caledonia" Young, during which he met comedian Redd Foxx and R&B crooner Big Maybelle. According to McDonough in the *Village Voice,* Foxx would later team up with boxer Joe Louis and actor Ralph Cooper to arrange Scott's first New York City gig at the

Baby Grand in 1948. Scott joined Lionel Hampton's band a year later and recorded his first hit, "Everybody's Somebody's Fool," along with "I've Been a Fool" and "I Wish I Knew." Record producer Quincy Jones, who was a trumpeter in the band, commented in the *Village Voice:* "It was dramatic when [Scott] came out in the solo spot. He'd just stand there with his shoulders hunched and his eyes closed and his head tilted to one side. He sang like a horn—he sang with the melodic concept of an instrument. It's a very emotional, soul-penetrating style. He'd put me on my knees, give me goose bumps. Jimmy used to tear my heart out every night."

Making Records, But Not Making It

Scott eventually left the Hampton band, settling into the thriving Newark, New Jersey, music scene and recording some sessions with Roost Records between 1950 and 1952 before signing with Savoy Records. At Savoy he was to cut memorable sides with producer Fred Mendelsohn—some of which are available on the first Savoy reissue, *Little Jimmy Scott*—but poor management crippled the singer with inferior material and cheap production while at the same time failing to effectively distribute the recordings or compensate Scott adequately for his work. McDonough noted in the *Village Voice* that though Scott had some modest hits, he never really fit the R&B market. Changing musical tastes even occasioned a 1958 rock and roll session, on which Scott perhaps fittingly sang, "I'll be what I'm not, if that's what you want."

Scott's difficulties in the industry where compounded by the abuse he suffered for the effeminate way he looked and sang, according to Robert Baird in *Pulse!* Homophobes called him names and others thought he was a woman posing as a man. His association with such jazz greats as Charlie Parker—his vocal on Parker's "One Night in Birdland" is credited to a woman— aroused rumors that he was a junkie. This made him a target for police in Philadelphia, who insisted that he was a woman transporting heroin and publicly stripped and humiliated him.

By the early 1960s Scott's career was floundering. He stayed on in California after a performance and wound up recording an album on Ray Charles's own label, Tangerine. The singer was accompanied by Charles— whom he had known from his days with Lionel Hampton—on piano and a live string section. Scott declared in the *Village Voice,* "I finally got a chance to sing with the instrumentation I wanted" and called his collaboration with Charles "a meeting of the souls." Returning to Cleveland to await the record's release, Scott learned that an injunction was being filed by the owner of Savoy claiming that Scott was still under contract. Tangerine subsequently halted distribution.

Scott took a job as a shipping and receiving clerk at a Sheraton Hotel in 1965 and restricted his music to occasional gigs. In 1969, with Joel Dorn as producer, he recorded *The Source,* an album that was ill promoted and misunderstood. Scott cut one last record with Savoy in 1975, entitled *Can't We Begin Again,* but it too was a failure. In 1970 the singer suffered a severe back injury in a fall at work. This, along with the end of his third marriage, occasioned his move to a senior citizens home, where he became president of the building's council.

Scott spent the 1970s in the rest home, helping others and caring for his ailing father. After his father's death he reestablished communication with a woman he had met in Newark 40 years earlier. Earlene moved to Cleveland, where she eventually married Scott and encouraged him to renew his career. A successful radio appearance in 1984 was followed by a packed engagement at Newark's Mirage Club. Scott was back in business.

Business Slowly Improved

Despite the warm reception by old and new fans, it took several years of tough club dates before Scott began to get the attention he deserved. The time Jimmy McDonough spent with him during this period became the basis for McDonough's seminal 1988 article in the *Village Voice,* the proceeds from which he used to produce a demo for Scott. In 1989 the singer received a Rhythm and Blues Foundation Grant, and three years later, his first release on Sire, *All the Way,* earned good reviews and a nomination for a Grammy Award. Produced by Tommy LiPuma, it featured Scott in front of an orchestra performing such classics as "Embraceable You," "At Last," and "Every Time We Say Goodby." People were impressed by his unique style as well as his influence on other musicians. As Doc Pomus noted in *LA Weekly* in 1990, Nancy Wilson, Marvin Gaye, Stevie Wonder, and Johnnie Ray "all began with 'watered down versions' of [Scott's] sound."

The year 1994 marked the release of *Dream,* an album produced by Mitchell Froom and featuring Junior Mance on piano, Ron Carter on bass, Peyton Crossley on drums, and Milt Jackson on vibes. Saxophone players

Red Holloway and Patience Higgins also contributed, along with guitarist Rick Zuniger and Froom himself on keyboards. Scott seemed pleased with the sessions, recalling in his Sire Records biography: "Everyone who was there had really wanted to make it, and that made all the difference. A lot of the tracks we got in the first take. We wanted something friendly and intimate on the album and that came right out of those sessions and the feelings we were sharing at the moment."

For Scott singing has always been about feeling, whether to help bear the pain of his mother's death or the many pains that followed. As he confided in *Bazaar:* "I've learned that music is such a healer. As long as I could sing my songs, I wasn't as angry about what had happened, about being shoved back for this or shoved back for the other. I'm a singer, and I never lost sight of that."

Selected discography

The Source, 1969.
Can't We Begin Again, Savoy, 1975.
All the Way, Sire, 1992.
Regal Records Live in New Orleans: Little Jimmy Scott and the Paul Gayten Band, Specialty, 1992.
Lost and Found, Rhino, 1993.
Dream, Sire, 1994.
Little Jimmy Scott, Savoy.

Sources

Bazaar, April 1994.
Billboard, July 23, 1994.
Cadence, November 1991; March 1992.
Cash Box, July 30, 1994.
CD Review, October 1994.
Entertainment Weekly, August 5, 1994.
Jazztimes, October 1994.
LA Weekly, December 21, 1990; July 15, 1994.
Mirabella, September 1994.
Out, October 1994.
Pulse!, September 1994.
Village Voice: Rock and Roll Quarterly, winter 1988.

Additional information for this profile was obtained from Sire Records publicity materials, 1994.

—*John Morrow*

Seal

Singer, songwriter

Photograph by Tim France, © 1994 Sire Records Company

Eclectic British pop artist Seal told *Rolling Stone*'s David Thigpen, "All my songs are therapy. I'm giving therapy to myself." After a splashy 1991 debut—including a Number One U.K. single and a top-selling album—he experienced several tumultuous and difficult years that caused him to confront the meaning of his sudden fame and, more importantly, his life.

Seal returned wiser and more assured with his 1994 sophomore effort, though in certain fundamental respects he was back where he began: with the same influential and supportive producer and the same title. Yet the variety of styles he enlisted—building on the already rich mixture of rock, soul, folk, and dance music that fills his first album—was, if anything, even greater. The journey to this achievement, as he told *Q,* necessitated a self-acceptance with which he struggled all his life. "You have to work out why you feel so undeserving," he insisted, adding "you have to start healing and you have to start saying to yourself, OK, I *am* worth it, I *do* deserve this."

Seal was born Sealhenry Olumide Samuel in London, England; his parents had moved there from Nigeria and divorced when he was still an infant. Raised first by foster parents and then by his own father, he had what he described to Rob Tannenbaum of *Rolling Stone* as "a rough childhood." In an interview with Mark Cooper of *Q* he called his father "a bitter person who'd missed a lot of opportunities in life. I think he loved me but was just incapable of showing it." Seal earned a degree in architecture and worked a variety of jobs, from electrical engineering to posting ads for London prostitutes; the latter occupation resulted in an arrest.

After trying to build a music career in London, Seal hooked up with a band called Push, playing funk music on tour in Japan. It was important more for geographical than for musical reasons: "I'd never been to that part of the equator before," he noted to Tannenbaum. "It was right up my alley. Every day was a new experience." After a jaunt with a Thailand blues group, he made his way to India and there had what he called "a few spiritual experiences." The happiness he felt there, he insisted, bestowed a calm and contentment about his future and allowed him to stop wanting a record deal so fervently. He believes this is why he soon got one.

Seal also became convinced that the half-moon scars under his eyes left by a skin ailment were a kind of omen of stardom. "I got really depressed about [the scars] at first, as you can understand," he recalled. "Now I really like them." The scars, he ultimately reasoned, would serve as a kind of insignia. "If I could design something, I don't think I could do it better." He did design the rest of his distinctive look: head-to-toe leather clothes and long dreadlocks, adding even more flash to his 6'4" frame.

Seal met producer Trevor Horn—who had made a fortune making records for the Art of Noise and Yes, among others, and had his own label, ZTT. "I thought he looked a bit frightening," Horn remembered to Tannenbaum. "I thought he was gonna like all kinds of music I wasn't gonna like. Then he told me he liked [folk-rockers] Crosby, Stills and Nash and Joni Mitchell. It was quite refreshing." Even so, he was disinclined to sign the fledgling artist.

Scored Hit With "Killer"

In 1990, however, Seal took his fate into his hands, achieving immediate success that would grab the attention of Horn and much of the pop world. He co-wrote a song called "Killer" with British keyboardist Adamski, and its mix of dance and rock—helped by heartfelt singing and lyrics—took it to the top of the U.K. charts. "I remember the first time we got to No. 1," he recollect-

ed in an interview with Giles Smith of *The Independent,* "Adamski and myself were in one of those family inn restaurants on a Sunday near Cambridge, [and] the week before we were No. 4 and [pop diva] Madonna was No. 1." When they realized that "Killer" had gained the top position, "I let out this huge roar. Honestly, families around us were going for their children—there was this six-foot-four black man gone wild in Cambridgeshire."

Seal was unprepared for what would follow. "I guess I was the epitome of the phrase 'meteoric success,'" he told Cooper of *Q.* "My kind of success was different because I had a hit record with something which wasn't immediately commercial in the pop sense. I took [my song] Crazy round to lots of record companies before Killer and although everybody really liked it, they wouldn't touch it. But if you manage to get a hit with a record like that, it's like you've broken through with something which allows you so much room." Soon ZTT found itself in competition with other labels that wanted to sign Seal; Horn's company recruited the young artist by offering him artistic freedom and, as Seal himself told Tannenbaum of *Rolling Stone,* "quite a bit of money, too."

Overwhelmed by Fame

Though Seal initially brought in various friends from the dance music world to help him produce the album, he eventually surrendered the reins to Horn. The producer told Tannenbaum that the singer's crowd "were very interested in Chicago house music. I thought that was absurd, when you have that much talent. It's limited—you don't sit and listen to it. You can't go to concerts and things like that." The resulting album, *Seal,* appeared on ZTT/Sire in 1991 and complemented the dance-floor grooves with acoustic guitars and an overall emphasis on melody and song structure.

Rolling Stone writer Thigpen called the Seal's debut album "a startlingly original synthesis that seemed to come from some undiscovered place along the axis of rock and soul." Seal's lyrics on this first album reflected what he later referred to in the *Independent* interview as a "very young, very idealistic" point of view: "if we only stick together we can save the world." His travels in the east had made him "unstoppable in that respect."

Seal was an international smash, thanks to "Killer" and "Crazy," an idealistic slice of pop-funk that was soon co-opted for a television commercial. And Seal himself was overwhelmed by fame. "You live one way for 26 years, and then suddenly there's a dramatic change," he reflected to Thigpen. "Five years ago I would get annoyed when my dole [unemployment] check arrived a day late. The next thing I know, I'm getting pissed off if my limo didn't turn up."

Indeed, as Seal told Cooper, the experience "was completely the opposite of what I'd imagined. If you're a sensitive person, like myself, you quickly realise that not everybody's intentions are genuine. And, yes, you have more people around you, lots more people around you, but your space becomes much smaller. People come up to you constantly in the street and they treat you like you're an alien." Most tragically, "I thought that the adoration would replace the attention that I sought from my father. I thought success or fame would bring me all these things." All of this led to "a very bad period when I had a lot of panic attacks." As he complained to *Rolling Stone*, "I wanted the money. I wanted to be a millionaire. But fame can be a pain in the ass."

Along with the anxiety, however, came laurels: the *Q* award for Best New Act of 1991, and three 1992 Brit Awards. Seal even performed at the Grammy Awards ceremony, though he took home no trophies. "The best thing that came out of the Grammys," he reflected to Smith of the *Independent,* "was that I did an interview for the *L.A. Times* and for the umpteenth time I was asked about my musical influences and for the umpteenth time I said I really like Joni Mitchell and reeled off this whole piece on why." On tour in France two months afterward, Seal received flowers and a note that said "Thanks for appreciating the work, love Joni." Seal had another brush with greatness when he joined British guitar legend Jeff Beck on a cover version of rock trailblazer Jimi Hendrix's "Manic Depression" for the Hendrix tribute album *Stone Free.*

Released Another Unique Album

After relocating to Los Angeles, Seal gradually began work on a follow-up album. Intent on a stylistic departure rather than a recreation of his debut, he selected a new producer. Steve Lillywhite, who'd worked with Irish rock superstars U2, among others, was his choice. But he soon asked Horn to take over. "Steve was wrong for all the reasons Trevor was the right producer," he commented to Thigpen. "Trevor's a musician first and foremost."

The resulting album—again called *Seal*—replaced the debut's pounding rhythms with slyer grooves, while Seal's singing moved away from the anthemic shouts of his earlier hits and became more nuanced and intimate. The first single, "Prayer for the Dying," a sober, reflective tune with an insistent funk beat, became a Top Ten hit. Jeff Beck played guitar on another track, "Bring It On," and Joni Mitchell joined Seal for a duet in the song "If I

Could." It was difficult for Seal to stop working on the project. "One time, I was going to the airport and I just turned round and came back to do more vocals," he confessed to Cooper. "I was dragged screaming from this record and so was Trevor. It was probably the most important thing about the whole record."

> *"You have to start healing and you have to start saying to yourself, OK, I am worth it, I do deserve this."*

Seal's new look—a shaved head—at once represented a concession to California temperatures and a clean break from the past. He'd lived through a number of losses and near catastrophes between the two albums. "I had a really heavy duty car crash in California," he told Cooper. "I nearly flew off a canyon on to a freeway a hundred feet below at peak hour. The car was completely written off and, miraculously, I walked away virtually unscathed. Then I got double pneumonia. The doctors said it was touch and go at one stage but I came out of that unscathed too, with no scarring on my lungs or anything. Then there was a shooting right in front of me on [Hollywood's] Sunset Boulevard."

Seal claimed that a London healer helped him recover from his illness and clarify his life; he appears on the cover of his second album in the nude, his newly shorn pate adding to the overall image of strength through vulnerability. "My whole approach to this record was one of openness," he told Cooper. He also emphasized in various interviews that the "idealistic" world-saving stance of his first album had neglected the necessity of healing oneself—spiritually and otherwise—before one could truly help others. Part of this healing meant putting fame in perspective, and allowing his "celebrity" self to surface when he needed to protect his private self. "The days I wanted to be noticed, wanted some feedback," he informed Smith in the *Independent,* "I could go out there and kind of *exude* and I'd get recognized," becoming "Seal, pop star, impervious to everything."

Seal the second was generally greeted with critical raves. "This British neo-soul singer's gift flows from his ability to transform dancefloor tracks into spine-tingling, magical experiences," enthused James Bernard of *Entertainment Weekly,* who gave the album an "A" grade. Reviewer Hobey Echlin of the Detroit *Metro Times* labeled the effort "Brilliant, subtle, indulgent and sentimental." Thigpen noted that "Seal's husky, expressive voice sounds even richer and more aged; the new record has an almost folky feel, with an undercurrent of melancholy and introspection that wasn't there before."

But it wasn't so much good reviews as good old fashioned radio airplay that helped the achievement sink in. "Somebody played the single on the radio the other day," Seal related to Smith. "I was speaking to my friend Oswald on the carphone. He said: 'They seem to be playing your record a lot.' I said, rather grumpily: 'Really? Cos I haven't heard it once.' Ironically enough as I said that, it came on the radio. I said: 'Oswald: I'm going to have to call you back.'"

Pulling over to the side of the road, Seal finally appreciated the finished product. "I'd been listening to it as *a song* and now I wanted to hear this thing that Trevor had always talked about: I wanted to hear *the record*. It sounded better on the radio than it did on the stereo at home. And the DJ said, 'That was the new one from Seal—well worth waiting for.'" The feeling, he noted, was one he'd felt only occasionally: "almost unquantifiable... just this rush."

Selected discography

"Killer" (single), 1990.
Seal (includes "Killer" and "Crazy"), ZTT, 1991.
(With Jeff Beck) "Crosstown Traffic," *Stone Free: A Tribute to Jimi Hendrix*, Reprise, 1993.
Seal (includes "Prayer for the Dying" and "If I Could"), ZTT, 1994.

Sources

Entertainment Weekly, June 3, 1994.
Guitar Player, October 1994.
The Independent, May 12, 1994.
Metro Times (Detroit), June 22, 1994.
Q, July 1994.
Rolling Stone, November 28, 1991; August 25, 1994.

—*Simon Glickman*

Shanice

Singer

Shanice Wilson learned about the demands and rewards of stardom at a very young age. She started singing when she was just a baby and was performing by the time most kids begin kindergarten. Her mother, who taught her the values of hard work and endurance and about the fickleness of fame and fortune, has encouraged—but never pushed—her daughter. Shanice told *USA Today,* "After I had signed with A&M records, my mom said 'Do you really want to do this? we can stop this now.' I said 'Mom, please, I want to do it.'"

Shanice was born into a musical family: her father, Carl Black, is a guitarist; her mother, Crystal Wilson, is a singer who has performed with the likes of Jennifer Holliday and Luther Vandross. Shanice showed great aptitude very early. "One of the first songs I ever sang was Chaka Khan's 'Tell Me Something Good' when I was seven months old," she remarked in *Essence* magazine. "My mom has the tape to prove it. I didn't know the words, but I knew the tune." She started performing while she was just a toddler. "My mom and aunt sang around the city, and mom would bring me on stage and let me sing a song in between their shows," she recalled in *USA Today.*

In 1979 Shanice's parents divorced, and shortly thereafter she moved with her mom and her aunt, Penny Wilson, to Los Angeles. With all three of them trying to break into show business, Shanice succeeded first. When she was just eight years old, she landed a television commercial for Kentucky Fried Chicken singing with legendary jazz vocalist Ella Fitzgerald. The adults were thrilled, but Shanice was a bit baffled by the excitement. "I had no idea who Ella Fitzgerald was," she told *People* magazine. "It was nice, but everyone around me was more excited than I was."

Shanice got more professional singing experience in the next few years as she performed in stage shows around the Los Angeles area. In 1985 an agent from A&M records saw her performing in *Get Happy* and signed her to a record deal. The same year, she appeared on television's *Star Search,* and won first prize. The record with A&M was slow in coming, but in 1988, it finally materialized. The album, *Discovery,* was a moderate success, but did not immediately lead to any further opportunities.

During the first few years following her debut album, the young Shanice's career did not advance much, so she used the time to grow a bit. She learned one valuable lesson in an exciting moment with superstar Michael Jackson. She described the meeting to *Newsday:* "I think Michael is the best entertainer ever. He called me

© Darlene Hammond/Archive Photos

213

For the Record . . .

Born Shanice Wilson in 1974 in Pittsburgh, PA; daughter of Carl Black and Crystal Wilson.

Sang in a television commercial for Kentucky Fried Chicken with Ella Fitzgerald, 1982; performed on stage in *Get Happy*, Los Angeles, 1985; signed first album deal, 1985; won first place on television program *Star Search*, 1985; released debut album, *Discovery*, A&M, 1988. Other television appearances include the *Tonight Show*, 1992; *Ebony/Jet Showcase*, 1992; and *Welcome Freshmen*, 1993.

Addresses: *Record company*—Motown Record Company, 6255 Sunset Blvd., Los Angeles, CA 90028.

up one day and asked if he could meet me. I guess he read in a magazine that I wanted to meet him. They picked me up in a limo and I watched him do his moonwalk video. It was an exciting day for me." Jackson advised Shanice to begin writing her own songs. "He told me how important it is to get into song writing," she told *USA Today*. "That's when he really became famous."

In the early 1990s Shanice's career picked up when she signed a new record deal with Motown. The company was happy to have her on their roster and vowed to catapult her into fame. "I tried to sign Shanice when I was at MCA," Jheryl Busby, president of Motown, told *Billboard*. "So when I had this second opportunity to work with her, I signed her immediately.... She's a cornerstone artist for us, and her project became a major priority the moment she signed with the company."

Shanice made other decisions and changes; she shortened her professional name from Shanice Wilson, to just Shanice. She explained this change to *USA Today:* "I used to hate my name Shanice. People used to say Chinese, Shannon, Charnice, instead of Sha-niece. I dropped Wilson so people would learn how to pronounce my name."

Deciding to take Jackson's advice, Shanice began to write songs with the help of her Motown producer, Narada Michael Walden. With suggestions and advice, Walden helped Shanice with over half of the songs on her first Motown release, *Inner Child*. "He really knows how to bring out the best in singers, and he's worked with some of the greats," she remarked in *Billboard*. "When we first met, he asked me to write down my ideas

and they became the titles for some of the songs we wrote together."

The song "I'm Crying" was born, Shanice noted, "when Narada asked me to pretend I was onstage and sing whatever came out. That's where the whole chorus came from." She described to *USA Today* how they came to write her biggest hit, "I Love Your Smile": "When I was working on my album, the Persian Gulf War was going on. Everybody was depressed. I wanted to bring out a song that would make people smile." Her album did indeed make lots of people smile. Upon the release of *Inner Child*, Shanice embarked on an international tour to promote the album and traveled to Hong Kong, Holland, England, Germany, and Canada. "I Love Your Smile" hit the Top Five in ten countries, and became Number One in the United States.

In 1994 Motown released Shanice's second album, *21 ... Ways to Grow*. As the title suggests, in this work, she shows just how much she has grown up from her teen years. "This album is a total opposite from my last," she explained in *Billboard*. "It fits me better because I was more involved; I co-wrote seven songs and co-produced three tracks. I did an album that the people would listen to and go, 'Hey now!'"

Motown's marketing strategy involved emphasizing Shanice's growth. "Her first album began to establish who she was and jell her image," Oscar Fields, executive vice president for Motown, stated in *Billboard*. "On this one, we want to show progression musically." He added that the company wanted all music video channels to showcase her work. Musically, the album is funkier than her previous ones, more rooted in rhythm and blues instead of mainstream pop, with more mature songs. "I'm not that little teenager anymore," she told *Essence*.

While her fame now seems assured with more records and even movie roles in her future, Shanice takes her success in stride like the seasoned veteran that she is. "My mother always told me that you should never take this business for granted," she explained to *Essence*. "You could be famous one day and gone tomorrow. I always keep a level head."

Selected discography

Discovery, A&M, 1988.
Inner Child, Motown, 1992.
21 ... Ways to Grow, Motown, 1994.

Sources

Billboard, November 30, 1991; April 23, 1994.

Chicago Tribune, December 12, 1991.

Ebony, September 1992; November 1993.

Essence, October 1994.

Jet, March 7, 1988; March 2, 1992.

Newsday, March 22, 1992.

New York Times, March 27, 1998.

People, April 20, 1992; August 8, 1994.

'Teen, August 1992.

Time, April 13, 1992.

USA Today, February 14, 1992; August 25, 1994.

Washington Post, January 29, 1992; August 31, 1994.

—Robin Armstrong

Johnny Shines

Guitarist

Truly a founding father of modern blues, Johnny Shines is regarded as the finest interpreter of Robert Johnson's immortal songs. Although Shines first heard guitar chording from Howlin' Wolf, he is embedded in blues mythology through his friendship and travels with Johnson, the archetypical cursed genius of the blues.

Shines was born on April 25, 1915, in Frazier, Tennessee. He worked on his father's farm as a boy, before wanderlust took him to Memphis and the sundry excitements found on Beale Street. Shines's interest in the blues was natural and began early; he recalled being inspired by Blind Lemon Jefferson after seeing him perform on Beale Street in 1925. As Shines told blues historian Peter Guralnick, "Anything there was, it was to be found on Beale Street. There were preachers, pimps, lawyers, gamblers, doctors, shysters, anything and everything."

It is not known under what circumstances Shines first encountered Howlin' Wolf, and later, Robert Johnson. Before Shines died in 1992, he completed his autobiography, *Success Was My Downfall,* but it remains unpublished. Shines recounted to Guralnick a 1932 sighting of the larger-than-life Howlin' Wolf: "I first met Wolf, I was afraid of Wolf. Because it was an old saying, you know, people thought about magic and all such things as that, and I come along and say, a guy that played like Wolf, he'd sold his soul to the devil. I mean the sound he was giving off—that's how great I thought Wolf was."

In 1935 Shines met Robert Johnson through a Memphis piano player named M&O. "Robert changed everything," Shines later told Guralnick. "Now I had Wolf's style in the beginning, and I was beginning to pick up on a few guys' different styles, and then I ran into Robert in Helena, Arkansas. Matter of fact I just began tagging along. Not that he wanted me along, I don't think, but Robert had a style that I liked, and I always felt if you wanted something you have to get right behind it and stay with it."

As they traveled together, Johnson and Shines often performed opposite one another, playing gin joints, country suppers and dances—any gig they could get. For three and a half years they rambled, going from the South to New Jersey, New York, Detroit, Canada, and finally, Chicago.

After Johnson's death in 1938, Shines traveled for a time with Robert Jr. Lockwood, Johnson's stepson. Eventually Shines settled in Chicago, where he cut sessions for both Columbia and the J.O.B. label, all while fronting the Dukes of Swing, an eight-piece jump blues group at the Apex Chateau in Robbins, Illinois.

Born April 25, 1915, in Frazier, TN; died in 1992 in Chicago, IL; married first wife, 1932; third wife's name, Hattie; eight children.

Began traveling to Memphis and Beale Street, 1925; learned guitar from Howlin' Wolf, 1932; traveled with Robert Johnson, 1935-38; led eight-piece band the Dukes of Swing; recorded for Columbia, 1946; recorded for J.O.B., 1953; worked in construction in Chicago, 1958-66; rediscovered by blues music world, 1966; toured with Willie Dixon's All Stars, 1969; recorded *Hey Ba Ba Re Bop,* Boston, MA, 1979.

The 1946 Columbia sessions were not released until the Testament label unearthed them in 1971. The album, titled *Chicago Blues—The Beginning,* reveals Shines as the embodiment of the great Delta country blues tradition, albeit somewhat displaced. The recordings were also highly portentous; with Muddy Waters, Shines foreshadowed the electric Chicago-style blues to come. Although the Dukes of Swing offered renditions of jazz and R&B tunes (anything by Count Basie or Duke Ellington was fair game), Shines soon drifted back to the blues for the J.O.B. sessions in 1953. In 1958 he gave music up entirely, selling his gear to a pawn shop for $100. Between 1958 and his rediscovery a decade later, Shines worked a construction job in Chicago.

In 1965, on the heels of the British infatuation with American blues, Shines was embraced by a young, white blues audience. British blues aficionado Mike Rowe brought Shines back into the international limelight; Rowe was impressed with Shines's personal history as much as he was with his affinity to African rhythms and voicings. Between the late 1960s and his death, Shines recorded for several labels and traveled with Willie Dixon's Blues All Stars, enjoying a reputation in the blues world as one of the living greats. Not only the keeper of Robert Johnson's flame, Shines also had a direct influence on modern bluesmen like Robert Cray and John Campbell. Shines died in 1992 at age 77. While his records display unmatched authenticity, great technical command, and an expressive candor, Shines will remain most famous for being the principal witness to Robert Johnson's mercurial talents and travels.

Selected discography

Chicago Blues: The Beginning, Testament, 1971.
Johnny Shines, Advent, 1974.
Hey Ba Ba Re Bop, Rounder, 1979.
(With Robert Jr. Lockwood) *Dust My Broom,* Flyright, c. 1979.
Johnny Shines, Hightone, 1989.
Last Night's Dream, Sire, 1993.

Sources

Guralnick, Peter, *Lost Highway,* Vintage Books, 1982.
Heilbut, Anthony, *The Gospel Sound,* fourth edition, Limelight, 1992.
Rees, Dafydd, and Luke Crampton, *Rock Movers and Shakers,* Billboard Books, 1991.
Rolling Stone Album Guide, edited by Anthony DeCurtis, James Henke, and Holly George-Warren, Straight Arrow, 1992.
Rolling Stone Encyclopedia of Rock & Roll, edited by Jon Pareles and Patricia Romanowski, Rolling Stone Press, 1983.
Rolling Stone Record Guide, edited by Dave Marsh, Rolling Stone Press, 1979.
Scott, Frank, *The Down Home Guide to the Blues,* A Capella Books, 1991.
Whitburn, Joel, *Top R&B Singles, 1942-88,* Billboard Books, 1990.

—Stewart Francke

Sir
Mix-A-Lot

Rap singer

The first successful rapper to come out of the Pacific Northwest, Sir Mix-A-Lot is often credited for putting Seattle, Washington, on the rap map. Part comedian, part storyteller, and part social satirist, Sir Mix-A-Lot is unique among hip-hop artists. By filling the void between pop rappers such as Hammer and the Fresh Prince and hard-core rappers like 2 Live Crew and Public Enemy, Mix created his own genre of rap and found multiplatinum success by blending hip-hop, humor, and social commentary.

With two platinum albums, one gold album, a Grammy Award, and an American Music Award under his belt, Sir Mix-A-Lot is one of the few rap artists to become an across-the-board success, appealing to both pop and hard-core rap fans. Mix believes his popularity lies in the fact that he thinks and feels the same things his fans do. "I'm not trying to be Malcolm X or Ice Cube," he explained in the *Detroit Free Press*. "I call myself a blue-collar rapper. I talk about what people are really thinking. They're not thinking about overthrowing the government or shooting [the president]. A lot of problem rap artists have had in the last two or three years is that they're either all gangster, all black activist or all goofy or pop. That's not me. I'm not all serious, and I'm not all funny. I'm a little of everything. I think that's what most people are like, too."

The son of a sheet metal worker, Sir Mix-A-Lot, whose real name is Anthony Ray, grew up in Seattle's Central District. He began rapping because he didn't like what most rappers were talking about in the early 1980s. "Nobody was talking back then about what was real," Mix told Dennis Hunt in the *Los Angeles Times*. "I was into funk back then, the Parliament/Funkadelic stuff. But rap seemed to have possibilities. I said to myself I can do better than this. So I tried."

Sir Mix-A-Lot formed Nastymix Records with Seattle businessman Ed Locke and deejay "Nasty" Nes Rodriguez, and he released his first single, "Square Dance Rap," in 1985. This comical tune that mixed Kraftwerk-inspired electronic bass-driven hip-hop rhythms with the hoe-down twang of a square dance caller caused some critics to dismiss Mix as a novelty act. But the fans didn't feel the same way. The single went on to become the number one song across the country.

Encouraged by the success of "Square Dance Rap," Sir Mix-A-Lot recorded and released his debut album, *Swass,* in 1987. The album, which featured everything from a rap/metal remake of Black Sabbath's "Iron Man" (backed by Seattle metal band Metal Church) to the gold-selling single "Posse on Broadway" (about the hilarious antics of Mix's band cruising Seattle's South

End district), was an immediate hit. With virtually no radio exposure, *Swass* achieved platinum status and spent over a year on both *Billboard's* Black Music and Pop Album charts. Mix achieved similar success with his second Nastymix release, 1989's *Seminar,* which went gold, selling over 700,000 copies.

Gained Creative Control

Legal battles with Nastymix over royalties and copyright infringements kept Sir Mix-A-Lot out of the rap scene for nearly two years. Finally, in 1991, Mix left Nastymix records after a dispute over creative control and formed his own label, Rhyme Cartel. "My main reason for leaving Nastymix was to get creative control over my product," he explained in *Spin.* "I have a difference of opinion with how most labels promote rap. People don't take it seriously. What's happening with rap is it's being all lumped together, and that's scary. Rap is more informative than any music ever was. So, the way these companies are going about promoting it is an injustice. You can't expect people to buy it because they show an African medallion or a profanity sticker."

Sir Mix-A-Lot signed a distribution deal with Rick Rubin's Def American Recordings and released his major label debut, *Mack Daddy,* in February of 1992. Mix recorded the album, with Rubin producing, in his home studio in Auburn, Washington, just outside Seattle. Like his previous albums, *Mack Daddy* burned up the charts.

It went gold in May and platinum in June. Also like his previous albums, *Mack Daddy* featured songs with witty, innuendo-laden lyrics rife with social commentary bordering on parody. The first single from the album, "One Time's Got No Case," was a sarcastic tale of suspicious police officers harassing him because he drove an expensive car. In a unique twist, rather than gunning the officers down, which Mix admitted most hard-core rappers would suggest, he gets his revenge in court.

Controversial Single Went Mainstream

Although Sir Mix-A-Lot had previously released two very successful albums, he was still a virtual unknown when *Mack Daddy* was released. The song that brought Mix out of the rap underground and into the pop spotlight was the second, and most controversial, single released from *Mack Daddy,* "Baby Got Back." A rollicking homage to plump female behinds, "Baby Got Back" went platinum, reigning at Number One on the *Billboard* Pop Singles chart for five consecutive weeks, and the accompanying video came in at Number One on MTV's *Top 20 Video Countdown.* Although "Baby Got Back" made Sir Mix-A-Lot the top-selling rap artist at the time, not everyone saw the humor in the song. Some complained the song was sexist, and because the record focused on black women, labeled Mix a racist. In the wake of the outcry, MTV pulled the video for "Baby Got Back" from regular rotation and would only show it after 9:00 p.m.

Sir Mix-A-Lot was surprised by the negative response to the song and countered by explaining the song was written to challenge the unattainable standard of the lean, "Barbie-doll" woman promoted by glamour magazines like *Cosmopolitan.* "The people who are complaining are missing my real message," Mix declared in the *Los Angeles Times.* "I'm on the side of the average woman who doesn't look like one of the bean-pole women in those magazines. I'm saying it's fine to have a big round rear end. That doesn't make you any less of a woman because you don't fit that stupid standard." Despite the controversy, or maybe because of it, "Baby Got Back" went on to become 1992's Number Two single, with over 2.5 million copies sold. Then, it earned Mix the 1993 American Music Award for favorite rap/ hip-hop artist and the 1993 Grammy Award for best rap solo act.

Riding high on his newfound fame, Sir Mix-A-Lot set out to help other Seattle rap artists break into the mainstream. In 1993 he produced and released *Seattle ... the Dark Side,* which featured performances by local Seattle rappers, including Kid Sensation and Jazz Lee

Aston. Explaining his reasons behind the album, Mix told Jody Benjamin of the *Seattle Times,* "My dream is to create 10 black millionaires right here in Seattle."

Sir Mix-A-Lot returned to the studio in 1994 to record and release his fourth album, *Chief Boot Knocka'.* In true Mix style, the album featured his trademark witty lyrics and quirky bass-driven electronic beats. Asked if he was concerned if the album would be as big a success as *Mack Daddy,* Mix replied in an American Recordings press release, "Once you start worrying about equaling your past success, the music gets weak." Eric Berman in *Spin* applauded *Chief Boot Knocka'* for its inspiration from dance music of the late 1970s and early 1980s and remarked, "Never the conformist, Mix continues to pioneer his eclectic Pacific Northwest sound."

The Lighter Side of Rap

Also in the mid-1990s, Sir Mix-A-Lot expanded his career to include television acting. He starred in a pop suspense anthology series set in Las Vegas called *The Watcher,* which premiered in January of 1995 on the United Paramount Network. Mike Duffy of the *Detroit Free Press* called his character, the Watcher, a "jive-talking host of sorts, portrayed with funkified energy."

Although some critics and rappers see Sir Mix-A-Lot as a novelty act because of his humorous approach to rap, Mix-A-Lot feels he is an important rap innovator because his lyrical style combats what is wrong with the genre. "It's too depressing," he told Stephanie Reader in the Tacoma, Washington *News Tribune.* "It's the same ... story every day. You know, boy meets girl, boy beats girl, boy calls girl bitch. Or someone goes looking

for respect and ends up spilling blood. Rap's been called the CNN [Cable News Network] of the streets, but it needs to find some new stories. If all the slaves did was sing about picking cotton, there would have been a lot of suicides."

Selected discography

"Square Dance Rap" (single), Nastymix, 1985.
Swass, Nastymix, 1987.
Seminar, Nastymix, 1989.
Mack Daddy, Rhyme Cartel/Def American, 1992.
Seattle ... The Dark Side, Rhyme Cartel/Def American, 1993.
Chief Boot Knocka', Rhyme Cartel/American, 1994.

Sources

Billboard, March 2, 1991; February 6, 1992; May 28, 1994.
Detroit Free Press, November 6, 1992; January 17, 1995.
Entertainment Weekly, March 13, 1992; July 29, 1994.
Los Angeles Times, July 19, 1992.
News Tribune (Tacoma, WA), July 19, 1994.
People, July 18, 1994.
Playboy, March 1991; June 1992; February 1994.
Rolling Stone, October 14, 1993.
Seattle Post-Intelligencer, November 23, 1990; February 6, 1992; November 27, 1993.
Seattle Times, August 1, 1993.
Source, August 1994.
Spin, May 11, 1991; September 1992; August 1994.
Vibe, fall 1992.

Additional information for this profile was obtained from American Recordings publicity materials, 1994.

—*Thaddeus Wawro*

The Smithereens

Rock band

B orn in 1956, Pat DiNizo, the lead singer and song-writer of the Smithereens and a self-described child of the 1960s, can remember exactly where he was when he first heard that other rock quartet, the Beatles: "I was standing on a stool, brushing my teeth in the mirror, with my little transistor radio that I would carry into the bathroom every morning," he noted in a 1986 *Rolling Stone* interview. Little did he know that he would grow up to form a band inspired by the 1960s "British Invasion" sound, a band that, according to Davis Schulps of *Musician,* "everyone with a typewriter compares to the Beatles."

Known for their devotion to traditional pop, the Smithereens have twice been described in *Rolling Stone* as "a course in Rock and Roll History, 101." The group adopts hokey rock-star theatrics on stage: walking down runway ramps during concerts; incessantly encouraging the audience to clap along; flailing guitars with Who guitarist Pete Townshend-style windmill strums; or performing garage-band thrash covers of the Beatles' "Why Don't We Do It in the Road" and the Who's

Courtesy of RCA Records

For the Record . . .

Members include **James Babjak,** lead guitar; **Pat DiNizo** (born in 1956; father ran a waste disposal company), rhythm guitar, vocals; **Michael Mesaros,** bass; and **Dennis Mikens,** drums.

Band formed in 1980; played 1960s cover tunes in New York before getting discovered, c. 1980-86; released *Especially for You,* Enigma, 1986; contributed single "Blood and Roses" to soundtrack *Dangerously Close;* dropped by Capitol, 1991; signed by RCA, 1993, and released *A Date With the Smithereens,* 1994.

Addresses: *Record company*—RCA, 1133 Avenue of the Americas, New York, NY 10036.

"Substitute." In pure postmodern form at a 1988 concert, the band performed a cover of a surf instrumental that segued into the theme from the *Batman* television show.

In the late 1970s however, DiNizo, far from a concert stage, was running a successful waste disposal company in New Jersey with his father. It was around that time that he saw *The Buddy Holly Story,* a rags-to-riches movie about a teenager that inspired him to start writing songs combining 1960s guitar rhythms and Hollyesque lyrics. DiNizo had been playing guitar since the age of seven and had studied the upright bass, saxophone, and drums with Tony Williams. While members of his peer group were hanging out in clubs like CBGB's in New York, DiNizo was commuting to Williams's Harlem brownstone and memorizing peradittles.

Not long after he saw the Buddy Holly movie, DiNizo answered a newspaper add for a local band that was looking for a lead singer. He met drummer Dennis Dikens, bassist Mike Mesaros, and lead guitarist Jim Babjak. The group soon became the Smithereens. "I think the strength of this band is that we're all so similar personality-wise and in temperament that we're almost like one person," DiNizo noted in *Musician.* Mesaros, Dikens, and Babjak grew up together and cite learning how to play music together as one of the reasons why the band has maintained its cohesion. "I started playing the summer I got out of high school," Mesaros recounted in *Musician.* "I borrowed a bass and Jimmy showed me 'I Can't Explain' by the Who. Everything I do came from the three notes of that chord progression. I learned how to play with Dennis and Jimmy, and so much of the way they play has influenced the natural instincts of how I play."

The Smithereen's sound is heavily influenced by other musicians and art genres; besides the more obvious Beatles and Buddy Holly comparisons, the Smithereens also point to unexpected and/or obscure pop and rock artists—as well as cinema performances—as inspirational. DiNizo pointed out in *Musician* that he had seen the rock band Black Sabbath 14 times; Dikens cited the Beach Boys as one of his great favorites; Mesaros named his New Jersey video store after the 1960s band the Flamin' Groovies; and a single off the Smithereens' 1988 release, *Especially for You,* was inspired by the 1950 film *In a Lonely Place,* which starred Humphrey Bogart and Gloria Grahame.

Six Years of Anonymity

Despite their verve and enthusiasm for rock nostalgia, the Smithereens played in the underground club scene for six years trying to get discovered. They even performed in a bar called the Dive, where all their equipment was stolen; for the following eight months they had to play on borrowed instruments. "We missed the boat entirely," DiNizo told David Frick of *Rolling Stone.* "The band started in March of 1980, but the whole New Wave CBGB thing had flown out the window by then. Nothing was going on there, nobody was getting signed.... By the time we started playing, that whole scene had died." Yet they continued to split $20 paychecks four ways and once worked as the backup band for 1950s songwriter Otis Blackwell in order to pay their rent.

The Smithereens's first EP was the self-produced maxi-single *Girls About Town* (released in 1980), which included a cover of the Beach Boys' "Girl Don't Tell Me" and three other songs about women and girlfriends. Jim Babjak felt so sure of the band's success that he quit college, even though he was only four credits shy of receiving a degree. The single was played on many college radio airwaves, but it would be three more years before they came out with their next album, *Beauty and Sadness,* produced by Alan Betrock. To fight the boredom of playing in covers-only bars, the Smithereens developed an eclectic repertoire of over 200 obscure 1960s tunes, as well as their own funky versions of surf-rock instrumentals. *Beauty and Sadness* was critically well received, but it failed to get the group a record contract or an agent.

What the album did get the Smithereens was a gig that ended in embarrassment. The band played at the Bottom Line club in Greenwich Village in a show that was attended by many professionals from the music industry. Word got back to the Smithereens that their music was received horribly, and the negative response created a cathartic low point for the group. Pat DiNizo revealed in *Musician:* "We'd been together for about four years and essentially they were telling us we should quit and acknowledge that there was no one interested in us professionally." DiNizo sold his bass, his saxophone, and his record collection; yet instead of quitting, the band strengthened its commitment, and, as DiNizo continued in his interview in *Musician,* "decided [that] we weren't going to give in, no matter what."

Signed by Enigma

By 1985 DiNizo felt that his songwriting had improved, but he had been rejected by so many labels that he had just about given up approaching them. The new songs were compiled on the LP *Especially for You,* and on a whim, DiNizo sent the cassette off to Enigma. The cassette fell in the hands of Scott Vanderbilt, a Smithereens fan who had played their earlier independent (indie) label EPs as a college radio deejay. "Apparently it was a struggle on his part even to get us signed," DiNizo told Dave Schulps of *Musician.* "I've heard that not too many other people at the label were knocked out by the sound of the band, but in keeping with Enigma's initial philosophy, they decided to release it if they thought it could sell 1000 or 2000 copies."

Before the album was released, the song "Blood and Roses" was selected by Cannon Pictures for part of the soundtrack for the teenage gore film, *Dangerously Close.* It was then that the band started getting its long-awaited breaks. They were employed to do a promotional video for the movie that was frequently played on MTV, and Enigma put a press packet together and promoted the single to radio stations. The album far exceeded the predicted sales.

Because of the success with Enigma, the Smithereens finally got an agent—the Premier Talent Agency, which also handled pop stars Lionel Richie and Madonna. By 1988 the band had released *Green Thoughts* on Capitol (on a joint-label deal with Enigma), and had played four sold-out shows at the Roxy theater in New York.

Reviewing that concert in *Rolling Stone,* Jeffrey Ressner described the band as playing tight, soaring harmonies and managing "to pay tribute to past rock masters without cloning specific styles." According to Ressner, the Smithereens still played some straight covers, yet much of their homage to rock greats lay in their chosen chord structures and the subtle echoes of familiar riffs. "DiNizo's catchy 'Something New,' sounded remarkably like the Kink's 'Stop Your Sobbing,'" the reviewer wrote, adding, "If imitation is indeed the sincerest form of flattery, the Smithereens must be considered extremely sincere."

"The sounds we use are thoroughly modern," Babjak told *Rolling Stone,* but added that "the song-writing approach is classic." Nevertheless, the Smithereens were often described by the press as self-taught copycats or a postmodern version of the Beatles, a comparison the group resented. "The live sound of the band bears no relationship to the Byrds' live sound or the Beatles' live sound," Babjak pointed out in *Rolling Stone.* In a later interview with Schulps he added, "if anything, we're just trying to recapture some of the spirit we feel has been lost." The band's style emulates what was "new" in the 1960s and what is now considered archaic: electric or acoustic guitars plugged into and played through Marshall amps, an equipment choice primarily of heavy metal bands. Yet, like the Beatles, DiNizo's early writing consisted mostly of light pop lyrics about love and relationships.

> *"The sounds we use are thoroughly modern, but the song-writing approach is classic."*
> —James Babjak

In 1989 the Smithereens released *11,* an LP produced by Ed Stasium, who tried to enlarge the band's sound until it reached the top output of the amplifiers used. "While hardly marking a retreat behind that wall of noise, Stasium and the group have built upon that solid foundation to make their next album, *Blow Up* (Capitol, 1991), a more versatile, fluid record," Wayne King wrote in *Rolling Stone.*

While *11* contained references to the mock rockumentary *Spinal Tap, Blow Up* alludes to Michelangelo Antonioni's 1966 cinematic portrayal of swinging London, which featured the band the Yardbirds. In keeping with their history of obscure music and cinematic allusions, on *Blow Up* the Smithereens included backup singing by the Cowsills ("Love American Style"), a move that King described as "either so warped it's cool or just plain pathetic." Later in the same review, King predicted that the Smithereens' appeal would soon be wearing thin, believing that the "progress shown from record to record has been too small," inevitably spelling doom for nonmetal groups, especially those that "recycle influences," and "wear their mid-Sixties rock and roll hearts on their sleeves."

King's review in *Rolling Stone* was somewhat prophetic; *Blow Up* never reached the commercial success that the Smithereens had hoped for. The band blamed the album's poor reception on the label's pressure to push them into the pop market. The results nonetheless left the Smithereens humiliated: because of low album sales, the group was dropped by Capitol Records, a situation that made DiNizo feel, he told *Billboard,* like he had gone "from Camelot to Smithereens."

In 1994 the Smithereens teamed up with former producer Don Dixon to try to recapture some of the success of their old live-sounding style. The result was *A Date With the Smithereens,* released on their new label, RCA. Don Dixon told *Billboard* that the RCA album was a more "roots-oriented rock n' roll project," similar to the successful sound of their first two albums in their club-playing days.

Toured and Recorded With Lou Reed

"I thought it was very important to recapture the essence of the band by using a lot of live stuff and picking songs that were less on the pop side and more on the darker side," Dixon continued. Many of the songs on the album reflect DiNizo's anger and frustration about the Capitol Records affair, and veer away from the traditional girl-friend-blaming love ballads. "War for My Mind," for example, explores mental anguish, and "Gotti" pokes fun at New York mobster Jon Gotti and the corrupt system that had him indicted.

The recording studio used for *A Date* was the same one used by Lou Reed, former lead singer of the Velvet Underground, for his album *Magic and Loss.* While the Smithereens were recording, Reed came by the studio and helped Jim Babjak write a guitar solo and added to the album's appeal by playing on a few more tracks. The group's acquaintance with Reed dates from the 1980s, when the Smithereens toured as his backup band.

In April of 1994, after the release of *A Date With the Smithereens,* the band was preparing to leave for a nine-month promotional club tour. "We're always prepared for the long haul," drummer Diken explained in *Billboard,* and judging from their rocky past, they seem to have proven themselves as a band that can't take short cuts to success. As Andre Odnitz wrote in a 1994 review in *Rolling Stone:* "Coming from the Smithereens, purveyors of classic pop, this is a statement: Trends fade, but successful methods from the past survive."

Selected discography

Girls About Town, 1980.
Beauty and Sadness, 1983.
Especially for You, Enigma, 1986.
Green Thoughts, Enigma /Capitol, 1988.
11, Capitol, 1989.
Blow Up, Capitol, 1991.
A Date With the Smithereens, RCA, 1994.

Also contributed song "Blood and Roses" to soundtrack *Dangerously Close.*

Sources

Billboard, April 2, 1988; August 20, 1988; January 11, 1992; March 13, 1994; May 7, 1994.
Creem, July 1988.
Melody Maker, December 20, 1986; February 27, 1988; September 17, 1988.
Musician, August 1988.
Rolling Stone, November 20, 1986; April 7, 1988; October 27, 1993; May 19, 1994.
Spin, September 1988.

—*Sarah Messer*

Spin Doctors

Rock band

The Spin Doctors' devil-may-care attitude toward music, the music business, and life in general has translated into some unholy platinum success for the four-member band. "Image *Schmimage* is my personal business motto," lead singer Chris Barron told *Rolling Stone*'s Jeff Giles in 1993 as their debut LP, *Pocket Full of Kryptonite,* was climbing the charts. Its tracks highlighted the band's funky blues-based rock, a sound that has sometimes been compared to a more-alive Grateful Dead. Another *Rolling Stone* writer, Alec Foege, termed them "the most successful of a recent crop of tie-dyed-in-the-wool neohippie groups [who] have tapped into the untroubled, feel-good vibe of a bygone era." The video for *Kryptonite*'s first single, "Little Miss Can't Be Wrong," pushed the Spin Doctors into heavy rotation on MTV nearly overnight, and with the LP's follow-up cut, "Two Princes," the songs became two of the most-requested radio tracks of 1993. By the end of 1994, the Spin Doctors were getting advice from former Who vocalist Roger Daltrey and opening mammoth stadium shows for the Rolling Stones.

Photograph by Paul LaRaia, © 1994 Sony Music

The Spin Doctors formed in New York City in the late 1980s when three of the four original members were students at the New School for Social Research. Vocalist Barron had been a military brat, spent several formative years in Australia, and then attended high school in Princeton, New Jersey. Original guitarist Eric Schenkman, who left the band in late 1994, was the progeny of two classical musicians and grew up in Toronto; he also relocated to New York to attend the New School. Drummer Aaron Comess, who hailed from Dallas, was enrolled, like Barron, in the New School's music program.

Earned a Dedicated Fan Base

At the time of the Spin Doctors' inception, Barron was rooming with high school friend John Popper. Popper was gaining success with his own band, an outfit called Blues Traveler. His growing commitments to it effectively grounded a second musical project called the Trucking Company that counted Barron and Schenkman as members. The two continued to work together without Popper anyway, and the Spin Doctors were formed in 1989 when Comess entered the scene. Comess, in turn, recruited bassist Mark White, its sole native New Yorker. White missed out on the group's first-ever gig, a fraternity party at Columbia University.

The group began writing original music and playing New York City clubs like CBGB, the Bottom Line, Night-

ingales, and the Cat Club. During these formative years the Spin Doctors built up a legion of dedicated fans around the Greenwich Village scene. They never played the same set twice, promoted bootlegging of their gigs, and returned the appreciation the fans showed them. "In the Eighties, everybody hated music," Barron told *Rolling Stone* reporter Giles in 1992 about what inspired them in those early days. "So we were trying to make this new kind of old kind of rock & roll. That whole aesthetic had been lost. Everything sounded like fake drummers and synthesized bullshit, and we wanted to make something human and real. We wanted to bake some pumpernickel, as opposed to all that presliced stuff."

It was at a New York bar called the Mondo Cane that the group attracted the attention of music-industry insider David Sonenberg, who once represented Meat Loaf. Sonenberg invited some record company people to hear the Spin Doctors. Despite the band's rather uncooperative nature on such nights—they often refused to play any of their more accessible tunes—they were signed to Epic Records in 1990. In 1991 the label put out the group's first release, a live EP called *Up for Grabs.* In the promotional materials accompanying the release, Epic enclosed a photo of, inexplicably, a six-member Spin Doctors, not realizing that there were actually only four of them. Later that year the full-length *Pocket Full of Kryptonite* was released. Initial sales were targeted at a modest 50,000, and Epic gave the group a corresponding promotion and tour budget.

The Tour That Wouldn't End

At the time, Epic was devoting its considerable resources to marketing Seattle grunge rock band Pearl Jam's debut release. The Spin Doctors began a road trip that literally went on for years, spending most of 1992 on tour. In London they traveled to shows by subway, and back in the States hooked up again with Popper and Blues Traveler for a HORDE (Horizons of Rock Developing Everywhere) summer tour. "A lot of the time we hid from Epic how hard this stuff was," Barron recalled in 1993 for *Rolling Stone* reporter Giles. "We'd be like 'We're out in the van! It's no problem at all!' We put up a front because we wanted to be their ... band. But the van was death, man. A slow form of death."

The Spin Doctors' numbing tour schedule, in its attempt to magnify their grassroots New York-scene success on a larger scale, eventually paid off. A Vermont radio station began playing "Little Miss Can't Be Wrong," and its program director even wrote to Epic, chastising them for virtually ignoring the band and its debut release. Things began to look up. The band funked it up on-camera for a "Little Miss" video shoot, sloshing buckets of bright paint all over themselves and a white sound-stage during the take. By the end of 1992 it had become one of MTV's five most-requested videos. *Homebelly Groove,* another live LP that communicated the band's well-honed performing persona, was released in November of 1992.

Success Surprised Everybody

Kryptonite eventually sold over six million copies—well above what management at Epic had ever imagined. Serious success on the U.S. charts and its perks—television appearances on the late-night shows of David Letterman and Jay Leno, Grammy and MTV Music Award nominations—were followed by respectable showings in Europe and Great Britain. Roger Daltrey, former lead singer of the Who, invited the Spin Doctors to play with him onstage for his Carnegie Hall show.

The Spin Doctors, however, remained rather unfazed by the success. "Don't be asking me no dumb questions, man," bassist Mark White told *Vox* interviewer Max Bell. "I wouldn't know anything except that we're exploiting the kids. I'm just a useless, talentless, no-good musician." White also likes to remind autograph-seekers that he used to work at McDonald's. Barron was also nonchalant. "I'm thankful that our world has the space for people like me, who aren't working in a field or a factory and don't put food on the table, but are good for morale. My position isn't necessary. We are lucky clowns," he told *Vox*'s Bell in 1994.

Still on the road through 1993, the band attempted to relax in a Memphis recording studio for a few days. This was unsuccessful, and they instead waited until March of 1994 to head back in front of the mixing boards for a follow-up to *Kryptonite.* An unusual blizzard in New York City helped ground them inside, and at the end of two days they had recorded 22 tracks. The resulting whittled-down LP, *Turn It Upside Down,* was released in June of 1994 to mixed reviews. *Stereo Review*'s Parke Puterbaugh contended that "Barron's capricious, stoned-cutup wordplay and the band's colorless, automatic funk quickly wear thin over the course of an album." On the other hand, John Swenson of *Rolling Stone* praised the sophomore effort, noting that the group's "popularity is based on universal rock & roll virtues—the tuneful grooves and the neohippie charm of vocalist Chris Barron. *Turn It Upside Down* delivers those qualities once again."

Unfortunately, the release meant that the long-suffering band was again back out on the road to support it. They spent the summer of 1994 in both the United States—where they played Woodstock in August—and Europe.

They returned stateside to open twelve dates for the Rolling Stones at the end of the year. "I have this theory that when you live on a bus travelling at 70mph, time goes by differently," the 26-year-old Barron told Bell in the *Vox* interview. "That's why I'm ageing quicker. I've spent a third of my life travelling at 70 miles an hour." The success of 1994 had one casualty for the Spin Doctors: guitarist Eric Schenkman, who left the group in September because of creative differences. He was replaced by New Jerseyite Anthony Krizan.

Throughout their career, taking the slower—albeit more grueling—road to success has seemed to pay off for the Spin Doctors. Sales for *Turn It Upside Down* climbed steadily, and the band remained philosophical about their image, or lack of it, as well as their future. *Rolling Stone* writer Foege queried Barron late in 1994 about the singer's attitude toward their success and general alternative-scene relevance. "We're just another rock band coming down the pike," Barron responded. "I don't know if we're a one-hit wonder or what. Six months from now, I may not even be able to get you on the phone. But I just want to carry the banner along for a little while—not by myself but with all these other great musicians. Just take this music down the street our little way and then give it up to some younger person."

Selected discography

Singles; on Epic

"Little Miss Can't Be Wrong," 1991.
"Two Princes," 1992.
"You Let Your Heart Go Too Fast," 1994.
"Cleopatra's Cat," 1994.

EPs; on Epic

Up for Grabs, 1991.

Albums; on Epic

Pocket Full of Kryptonite, 1991.
Homebelly Groove, 1992.
Turn It Upside Down, 1994.

Sources

Detroit Free Press, August 5, 1994.
Entertainment Weekly, June 17, 1994.
Guitar Player, February 1993.
Music Paper, August 1994.
People, June 20, 1994.

Q, July 1994.
Rolling Stone, May 28, 1992; January 7, 1993; June 16, 1994;
    July 14, 1994; November 17, 1994.
Stereo Review, October 1994.
Vox, July 1994.

Additional information for this profile was provided by Epic
Records publicity materials.

—Carol Brennan

Steel Pulse

Reggae band

Formed in 1975 by David Hinds and Selwyn Brown in the Handsworth section of Birmingham, England, Steel Pulse is most noted within reggae circles for being one of the first international bands to mix reggae's African, salsa, and calypso beats with pop and rock music. Steel Pulse established themselves as one of reggae's major forces throughout the 1980s and—at U.S. President Bill Clinton's request—was the first reggae band to perform for a presidential inauguration.

Although other reggae bands—such as the Wailers—fused rock with reggae in the 1970s, it was Steel Pulse who focused most intensely on the mix. When English reggae bands were gaining international attention in the mid-1970s, few of them allied themselves with England's punk rock movement. Steel Pulse, however, frequently opened concerts for punk rock bands like Ultravox, XTC, the Stranglers, and Generation X—and were as likely to be part of a punk rock concert as a reggae festival.

Photograph by Dennis Keeley, courtesy of MCA Records

229

For the Record...

Members include **Kevin Batchelor** (born December 19, 1960, in Missouri; joined group 1989), trumpet; **Selwyn "Bumbo" Brown** (born June 4, 1956, in London, England), keyboards, vocals; **Alvin Ewen** (born August 27, 1961, in Birmingham, England; joined group 1987), bass; **David Hinds** (born June 15, 1956, in Birmingham, England), rhythm guitar, lead vocals, songwriter; **Gerry Johnson** (born March 23, 1959, in New York; joined group 1990), saxophone; **Phonso Martin** (joined band in 1977; left group 1991), vocals, percussion; **Sidney Mills** (born January 15, 1959; joined group 1990), keyboards; **Steve "Grizzly" Nisbett** (born March 15, 1948, in Nevis, West Indies; joined band 1991), percussion; **Clifford "Moonie" Pusey** (born September 25, 1953, in Bridgeport, CT; joined group 1990), lead guitar.

Group formed in the Handsworth section of Birmingham, England, 1975; released first album, *Handsworth Revolution,* on Island/Mango label, 1978; switched to Elektra and released album *True Democracy,* 1982; signed with MCA and released album *State of Emergency,* 1988; recorded single "Can't Stand It" for film *Do the Right Thing,* 1989; played at U.S. President Bill Clinton's inauguration and appeared on the *Tonight Show,* 1993.

Awards: Grammy Award for best reggae album, 1986, for *Babylon the Bandit;* Grammy Award nominations, 1991, for *Victims,* and 1992, for *Rastafari Centennial: Live in Paris-Elysee Montmartre.*

Addresses: *Record company*—MCA Records, 1755 Broadway, New York, NY 10019.

Steel Pulse has consistently emphasized societal problems through their lyrics. Unlike the ethnically mixed, England-based ska groups that gained popularity in the late 1970s—like the Specials and the English Beat—Steel Pulse's members are all of Jamaican ancestry and have African-centered influences. In spite of this, Steel Pulse's first two albums on the Mango label in 1978 and 1979, *Handsworth Revolution* and *Tribute to the Martyrs,* have a ska beat and feel to them, which reflects the era in which they started.

Steel Pulse's first and second albums cemented their reputation as a reggae band with punk rock and ska undertones. Their lyrics shared an outrage with punk rock musicians, their confrontational style was borne of rock music, and their beat was a mixture of African reggae and England's "Two-Tone" ska music. While other reggae bands at the time were focusing on harmonic melody, heavy bass, and slow Rastafarian drum beats, Steel Pulse fused reggae with a faster, more confrontational rock-inspired delivery.

Although Steel Pulse's first two albums were well received, the songs on these albums were created more with live concerts in mind than for dancing. As a result, Steel Pulse had a tremendous audience base for touring but did not fare as well on radio or in dance halls. The singles "Handsworth Revolution," "Sound System," "Ku Klux Klan," and "Soldiers" from these first two albums would set the standards for their live performances for years to come and would prove to be the most enduring.

Reggae Fever—known as *Caught You* in England—was released in 1980 and was the band's last recording on the Mango label. The album's sales were disappointing. *Reggae Fever* was the result of an effort to smooth out Steel Pulse's rougher edges, characterized by a freewheeling style, and the album did not spark as much interest as their previous two albums. When Mango Records collected the best of Steel Pulse for its *Reggae Greats* album in 1985, the label focused primarily on Steel Pulse's early *Handsworth Revolution* album instead of their later material. Steel Pulse opened for the Talking Heads at Radio City Music Hall in 1980, which brought them further to the attention of the American audience.

Steel Pulse performed at the 1981 Reggae Sunsplash and won over the audience. *Reggae Report's* Lee O'Neill wrote, "Steel Pulse—according to all accounts—stunned the audience." Soon after the concert, Elektra released *Reggae Sunsplash '81* in 1982 with four Steel Pulse songs featured on the collection. That same year, Steel Pulse released *True Democracy* on the Elektra label. Their first album for a new label proved to be a redemptive effort: it was energetic, reminiscent of their early, lauded material and marked by a new, rigorous production style. *Rolling Stone's* Daisann McLane praised it as "the best album from one of the most important U.K.-based reggae bands of the '80s."

Earth Crises, released in 1984, was a turning point for Steel Pulse. For the first time, the band wrote a love song, incorporated soul and rhythm and blues melodies, emphasized bass and drums, and featured a new producer, Jimmy Haynes. Haynes—who often played lead guitar for the musician Aswad—attempted to repackage Steel Pulse into a more digestible, less hardcore, musical product. As a result, this was their first album that had an upbeat, danceable tempo.

In 1985 Steel Pulse released *Babylon the Bandit,* which was also experimental. The band won a best reggae album Grammy Award for this album in 1986. The lyrics weren't as fiery as they were in the band's early material, and the musical beat was broadened into a deep, soulful sound.

State of Emergency, released in 1988, had a different approach because Steel Pulse had a new producer and had switched over to the MCA label. They incorporated their previous hard-edged rock style with a rhythm and blues sound. After the release of *State of Emergency,* Steel Pulse recorded the single "Can't Stand It" in 1989 for director Spike Lee's film *Do the Right Thing,* which is available to date only on the film's soundtrack.

Steel Pulse released *Victims* on the MCA label in 1991; it featured both love songs and dance singles on one side and rock-influenced, political songs on the other. *Victims* was nominated for a Grammy Award. One of the album's tracks, "Taxi Driver," addresses the racism that people—particularly those with dreadlocks—face when trying to secure a cab in New York City. Steel Pulse's lead singer, David Hinds, embroiled himself in a million-dollar class-action lawsuit against New York City's Taxi & Limousine Commission. To draw attention to this plight, Hinds offered to demonstrate for the media—after the release of *Victims*—how arduous it was for him to hail a cab. As a dozen reporters and camera people crowded around him on a New York street, Hinds dramatically held out an arm for a cab. As a result of the crowd, cameras, and carnival atmosphere, a curious cab driver stopped immediately for Hinds.

In 1992 Steel Pulse released *Rastafari Centennial: Live in Paris-Elysee Montmartre,* which was nominated for a Grammy Award for best reggae album, marking Steel Pulse's third Grammy Award nomination. A live concert in France celebrated the 100th anniversary of the birth of Haile Selassie of Ethiopia—the spiritual leader of the Rastafarian movement—as well as other black leaders such as Steven Biko and Peter Tosh. In keeping with their tradition of addressing issues, the band released *Vex* in 1994, which *Billboard* praised for its balanced mix of political perceptions and "heartening fun." The reviewer also noted that the song "New World Order" from the album "has the potential to become a modern anthem for social justice in Britain."

Steel Pulse was the first reggae band to perform on the *Tonight Show.* They also made history as the first band to perform for a presidential inauguration when they played at the White House on January 20, 1993, for President Clinton.

Steel Pulse began as a band with a political message, and they may have been ahead of their time in that respect. "When I listen to bands like Public Enemy [or] Arrested Development," Hines told *Reggae Report's* Lee O'Neill, "it's like the flavor we were trying to come with in our heyday.... [They have] given us more encouragement, more insight into our next album, at least politically.... We can't sound like we're from the '80s, we have to move on."

Selected discography

Handsworth Revolution, Island/Mango, 1978.
Tribute to the Martyrs, Island/Mango, 1979.
Reggae Fever (released in England as *Caught You*), Island/ Mango, 1980.
True Democracy, Elektra, 1982.
Earth Crisis, Elektra, 1984.
Babylon the Bandit, Elektra, 1986.
State of Emergency, MCA, 1988.
Victims, MCA, 1991.
"Can't Stand It," *Do the Right Thing* (soundtrack), Motown, 1991.
Rastafari Centennial: Live in Paris-Elysee Montmartre, MCA, 1992.
Vex, MCA, 1994.

Sources

Billboard, November 5, 1994.
Detroit News and Free Press, December 5, 1992.
Ebony, September 1991.
New American, January 7, 1993.
New City/Chicago, March 4, 1992.
New York Daily News, May 14, 1993.
New York Newsday, July 12, 1994.
Reggae Report, November 1992.
Rolling Stone, February 24, 1994.
Washington Afro-American, January 30, 1993.

—B. Kimberly Taylor

Stone Temple Pilots

Rock band

The Stone Temple Pilots have spent much of their young career fighting the perception that they are a "Seattle" band. Their 1992 debut album, *Core,* invited comparisons to a host of other current alternative rock acts from the Pacific Northwest's burgeoning music scene, but the Stone Temple Pilots actually paid their proverbial dues in southern California. The group is often pejoratively lumped together with Seattle grunge rock success stories like Pearl Jam and Alice in Chains, but in reality all are part of a wave of new bands whose roots lie in a bizarre allegiance to both the power-chord arena rock of the 1970s and a modern-day punk rock aesthetic. James Rotondi of *Guitar Player* described STP's work as "memorable, tough rock songs backed by anvil-heavy grooves and rich, unflashy guitar parts."

Core spent over a year on the music charts, won a slew of awards, and eventually went triple platinum. The Stone Temple Pilots toured during most of 1993 and put in appearances as an opening act for heavy metal goliaths Megadeth as well as an *MTV Unplugged* show. In the summer of 1994, they released their sophomore

Photograph by Lisa Johnson, courtesy of Atlantic Records

Members include **Dean DeLeo** (born August 23, 1961, in New Jersey), guitar; **Robert DeLeo** (born February 2, 1966, in New Jersey), bass; **Eric Kretz** (born June 7, 1966, in Santa Cruz, CA), drums; and **Scott "Weiland" Weiland** (born October 27, 1967, in Santa Cruz, CA; married; wife's name, Janina), vocals.

Group formed c. 1987 in San Diego; originally named Mighty Joe Young; signed with Atlantic Records, April 1992; released first album, *Core,* September 1992; appeared on *MTV Unplugged,* 1993.

Awards: *Core* and *Purple* received Recording Industry Association of America triple-platinum certification; Grammy Award for best hard rock performance with vocal, 1993, for "Plush"; American Music awards for favorite new pop/rock artist and favorite new heavy metal/hard rock artist, both 1993; two *Billboard* Video awards and a *Billboard* Music Award for Number One rock track for "Plush," all 1993; MTV Music Video Award for best new artist of 1993; the band was voted best new artist and lead singer Scott Weiland was named best new male singer in a 1993 *Rolling Stone* readers' poll; a *Guitar Player* readers' poll voted Dean DeLeo best new talent of 1993.

Addresses: *Record company*—Atlantic Records, 75 Rockefeller Plaza, New York, NY 10020.

effort, *Purple,* another instant series of hits. Between the two albums, STP were a permanent fixture on the album rock charts. Despite their unparalleled success, the band members felt frustrated by the criticism that often accompanies such accomplishment, but album and concert ticket sales offered somewhat of a balm. "Being a musician, you're so used to what's going on in the industry," guitarist Dean DeLeo responded to the snarkiness in a 1993 *Rolling Stone* interview with Kim Neely, "but when you get fan mail and you read what real people are saying about you, that's what really counts."

Stone Temple Pilots formed around the Los Angeles-San Diego axis in the late 1980s. Two of its members, brothers Dean and Robert DeLeo, were transplanted New Jerseyites living in San Diego. They had played professionally once before, back home in a cover band called Tyrus. Robert came across singer Scott "Weiland" Weiland at a Black Flag concert; the two realized they had been dating the same woman. Nevertheless, a friendship developed and they started to mess around with their guitars and an eight-track recorder. Californian Eric Kretz, then playing drums in another band, soon joined them. Kretz and Robert DeLeo relocated to Los Angeles, and Dean followed after a few years to help out with a demo tape. The brother decided to stick around, and the band officially formed as Mighty Joe Young.

Hesitated Before Signing Contract

The first-ever show of Mighty Joe Young happened at the legendary Whiskey-A-Go-Go in Los Angeles. The band soon tired of the L.A. music scene and returned to San Diego, where they wrote music and schlepped equipment to local bars for the next two years. In 1992 a representative from Atlantic Records came to one of their shows and soon the label was expressing interest in signing them. Yet the quartet was leery of a big, juicy, major-label contract until they talked with industry-insider Danny Goldberg, then managing Seattle grunge-rockers Nirvana.

Mighty Joe Young signed the contract on April Fools' Day of 1992. They headed into the studio with Brendan O'Brien, erstwhile producer of such bands as the Red Hot Chili Peppers and Black Crowes. Shortly before their debut album's scheduled release, their lawyer discovered that the name Mighty Joe Young was already being used by an aged blues artist and they would need a new name. The "Stone Temple Pilots" moniker originated in the "STP" motor-oil logo sticker that the young Weiland's bike had sported. They invented the name from the letters.

Core began climbing the charts following its release in September of 1992. A video for the first single, "Sex Type Thing," made its first few appearances on the MTV metal showcase *Headbangers' Ball,* then garnered heavy rotation during the rest of the programming week. The Stone Temple Pilots arrived on the scene just as other up-and-coming bands—especially the Seattle triumvirate of Soundgarden, Pearl Jam, and Alice in Chains—also began rocking the alternative charts and stations with a similar edgy, guitar-based sound. Fans assumed the Pilots hailed from the Pacific Northwest, too.

Meanwhile, some critics assailed the overnight explosion of similar-sounding bands—for years the alternative scene had been a healthy industry unto itself with neither major-label interest nor support—but now the behemoths had stepped in and found a way to market one particularly accessible sound to a wider spectrum of youthful listeners. By mid-1993 the Pilots were fed up with the issue. "What is mainstream, and what's alternative?" fumed bassist Robert DeLeo in the *Rolling Stone* interview with Neely. "I mean, you can't really control who's gonna buy your album. You can't put an alternative sticker on it and say, 'This is for cool people only.'"

> *"What is mainstream, and what's alternative? You can't put an alternative sticker on an album and say, 'This is for cool people only.'"*
> —Robert DeLeo

The Stone Temple Pilots began a heavy tour schedule, making stops in both the United States and Europe. They turned down a slot as openers for Aerosmith in part because of the legendary act's traditional treatment of women as sex objects. *Core's* first single, "Sex Type Thing," was a strident message against date rape written by Weiland that nevertheless was sometimes read the wrong way as being *pro*-date-rape. The vocalist told *Rolling Stone* reporter Neely that he put himself in the frame of "the typical American macho jerk" as he was writing the song's lyrics from a first-person stance and was a bit stunned that some took his intent in a completely opposite way.

Demons of Success Came Calling

More criticism was heaped on the Stone Temple Pilots' second single, "Plus"; the track was easy to mistake for a Pearl Jam tune due to its riffs and Weiland's vocals. But *Guitar Player's* Rotondi tried to put the similarity in perspective, saying, "A generation that grew up discovering the joys of the Doors and Led Zeppelin in the wake of the punk explosion are bound to see and hear things similarly. If ... Weiland sounds like anybody, it's Jim Morrison, whose moody baritone has been appropriated by everyone from the Cult's Ian Astbury to Billy Idol to Glenn Danzig to Layne Staley to, well, Eddie Vedder—all, like Weiland, talented, charismatic figures."

The Stone Temple Pilots began racking up an impressive array of awards as their debut album was selling millions. "Plush" remained on the charts for a record-setting 77 weeks from 1993 to 1994, and won the Grammy for best hard rock performance with vocal as well as a *Billboard* award for Number One rock track;

indecisive American Music Award voters gave them honors for favorite new pop/rock artist and favorite new heavy metal/hard rock artist; *Rolling Stone* readers voted them the best new band and Weiland the best new male singer of 1994, and they also won an MTV Music Video Award for best new artist.

But the success as well as the pressure nearly dissolved the band, as Weiland admitted in retrospect to *RIP* reporter Mick Wall in early 1995. "A year ago, well, it just got to the point where we just really did not have the energy to communicate with each other," Weiland said of this period. "There were problems ... [like] the lack of respect that we had gotten from the music press, which we had always paid attention to." As a band they had been secure in their songwriting abilities, he explained, and at first were indifferent to what others were saying, but "then after a while I think it started running on us and we were thinking like, 'Maybe they're right,' you know? 'Maybe people are right. Maybe there's something wrong with what we're doing.'"

Critics Assail, Fans Adore

But the Stone Temple Pilots managed to keep their heads up long enough to duck back into a studio in Georgia in early 1994. Working again with Brendan O'Brien, they wrote much of the material for the next album in studio and got it down on tape in less than a month. The DeLeos wrote the music and Weiland the lyrics, and many of the twelve tracks on *Purple* could be termed somewhat brooding and introspective. "I guess I tend to find the darker shades of life more attractive than the yellows and oranges," Weiland told Neely in the *Rolling Stone* interview about his muses. "I know it's something that I relate to when I listen to music." Robert DeLeo looked forward to getting the album released in an effort to silence their critics. "I think the new album is going to be our only savior," he told Rotondi in *Guitar Player* in early 1994. "Hopefully, it will dispel a lot of the demons that are following us around."

Purple debuted at Number One on the *Billboard* 200 in June of 1994. Its first singles were "Vasoline" and "Interstate Love Song," each quickly becoming staples on both alternative and rock radio. Critical reaction was mixed. Reviewing it for *Entertainment Weekly,* David Browne called it "rock & roll utterly without roots or, despite the pseudo-underground sheen, a real, defined sense of time or place." *People* writer Tony Sinclair made the usual Pearl Jam comparison and also likened STP to a sort of modern-day Grand Funk Railroad. Lorraine Ali of *Rolling Stone* was less judgmental, however. She described *Purple's* lyrical content as "cryptic and sensitive" and lauded "mystical interludes and acoustic melodies [that] could be hokey but instead are naively pretty."

Critical barbs aside, *Purple* was an unqualified success. It went triple platinum in less than six months, and "Interstate Love Song" held at Number One for 15 weeks on *Billboard's* album rock charts, a rather rare feat. The Stone Temple Pilots began playing headlining dates around the country as well as sold-out shows overseas. By early 1995, they were working on a third album and planning a tour that would perhaps feature STP's own ticket distribution system. The band hoped to eliminate what they viewed as exorbitant service charges imposed on concertgoers by Ticketmaster, a national ticket distributor.

The Stone Temple Pilots remain nonchalant about their success and their detractors. "Before the Seattle thing happened, popular rock was stale," Robert DeLeo told *Guitar Player's* Rotondi. "Before we got into the whole alternative scene, things were fine. But bands that are in this so-called alternative scene are just trying to prove that 'Hey, my band's more underground than yours.' What's the point here? Are we trying to prove how underground we are, or are we trying to prove we can make good music? We're all making music, so why should we hack on each other? And why not look at the *differences* between bands? Everybody's got something to offer."

Selected discography

Singles; on Atlantic

"Sex Type Thing," 1992.
"Plush," 1993.
"Vasoline," 1994.
"Interstate Love Song," 1994.

Albums; on Atlantic

Core, 1992.
Purple, 1994.

Sources

Billboard, December 10, 1994; January 14, 1995; March 4, 1995.
Entertainment Weekly, June 10, 1994.
Guitar Player, August 1993; February 1994.
People, June 13, 1994.
RIP, February 1995.
Rolling Stone, August 5, 1993; February 10, 1994; July 17, 1994.

Additional information for this profile was provided by Atlantic Records publicity materials.

—*Carol Brennan*

SWV

Rhythm and blues trio

SWV, an acronym that stands for Sisters With Voices, has both an immediate and a general reference. The trio of rhythm and blues women vocalists who use it as their official moniker have won the praise and money of a large portion of the record-buying public. The broader reference, however, notes the group's history—its place in a long line of what music critics and students call the "girl groups" of the 1960s. Although the formula is enjoying a revival with such ensembles as En Vogue and Jade, SWV has set itself apart through a particularly 1990s style of self-presentation. Consequently, critics acclaim the trio as the best of the old and the new.

After En Vogue set the trend in the music industry in the early 1980s, a slew of similarly fashioned female groups followed, saturating the market in a brief period of time. That saturation, of course, meant that a certain number would fade from sight fairly quickly. The combined voices of Cheryl "Coko" Gamble, Leanne "Lelee" Lyons, and Tamara "Taj" Johnson introduced SWV in the spring of 1993, when *Billboard*'s Janine McAdams caught

them "emerging from the pack of En Vogue inspired
female groups." The trio quickly rose to the top, some
critics even arguing that they eclipsed their forerunners.

Gamble, Lyons, and Johnson were all born within three
years of one another in the early 1970s. Gamble and
Johnson grew up in Brooklyn's Bedford-Stuyvesant
neighborhood, where both sang in church, consuming
a steady diet of gospel music. By the time they were 13,
they had become regulars on the local talent-show
circuit. They were also "known locally for breaking out
into song on every corner from the school yard to the
grocery store," according to Deborah Gregory in *Essence.*

Female Edition

Gamble and Johnson's passion, however, was the R&B
sound epitomized at the time by the teenage crew of
New Edition, a group of male vocalists outrageously
popular with adolescent girls like Gamble and Johnson.
The two expressed their devotion by naming their earliest attempt at a group Female Edition, in honor of their
heros. "We were in love with them," Johnson told *Rap
Masters.* "The plan was to form a group, so that we could
meet them. We used to get together in the hallways in
school and sing all of the New Edition tunes, and fight
over who would be [lead singer] Bobby Brown."

The pair became a threesome when Gamble's mother
moved to the South Bronx, where Gamble met Lyons. At
first, Lyons and Gamble joined their singing talents in a
gospel group with several other girls, but they soon

shifted to R&B. In 1990 Johnson rejoined her earlier
singing partner and the trio became SWV.

Maureen Singleton, SWV's manager, secured them a
contract with RCA in 1992 after presenting a demo tape
to Kenny Ortiz, an executive at the company. Ortiz had
already decided that the label needed a way to break
into the girl group revival that was taking place; when he
heard SWV, he believed they could do it. As Christian
Wright told the story in *Vibe,* Ortiz thought that "the
female strength implicit in many of the smooth, sexy
ballads would distinguish SWV from their peers, the
seemingly endless blur of girl groups from En Vogue to
Express." With this in mind, RCA released *It's About
Time* at the end of October, 1992.

Championed on Black Radio

The album rode in easily on the success of the first
single, "Right Here," which broke the Top 100 on *Billboard's* singles charts and made the Top 20 in the R&B
category. Ironically, however, the album's success happened despite the mainstream airwaves and the music
press, neither of which took much notice. But a few radio
stations with large black audiences, particularly in St.
Louis, Missouri, and Detroit, embraced the single, ex-
posing their listeners to it at every turn.

While airplay mainly on black stations might once have
meant a permanent following on the margins, in the
early 1990s it meant increasing attention from mainstream pop markets. "Black radio wields more and
more influence over pop as more black music crossed
over to the Top 10," explained Wright. "Pop radio has
even started looking for urban product earlier than
black stations do," RCA executive Ronald Edison told
Vibe's Wright. SWV came along at a critical moment,
when they could benefit from this trend and contribute
to it.

After the success of the group's second single, "I'm So
Into You," the following spring, RCA knew that SWV was
their ticket into the burgeoning R&B market. Company
executives hoped that SWV could help them in their
quest to "actively turn around [RCA's] fortunes with the
R&B market," as *Billboard's* McAdams wrote. Skip
Miller, an executive in RCA's black music division,
elaborated on the label's sense of the group's success;
he told McAdams that SWV's output was "indicative of
the music we want to make. We're in the building stage
of making music and SWV is our flagship."

The flagship built up speed when a second single,
"Weak," followed "I'm So Into You" into the upper-
stratosphere of the R&B singles chart by the fall of 1993,

at which time both singles went gold and the album went platinum. Wright noted that "Weak" sold 50,000 copies in one day, ultimately eclipsing both preceding singles and topping the charts. Not surprisingly, the strength of the singles from the debut album carried the group through 1993 and 1994.

A Real New York Vibe

"What distinguishes SWV," wrote McAdams in *Billboard*, "is street-level imaging and aggressive, swing-style harmonies, which place them in the burgeoning 'ghetto soul' category." Kenny Ortiz, the executive who first tagged SWV for RCA, described them further for McAdams. "They have to be the first female group out there that has a real soulful, nonbubblegum sound," he commented. "They have a real New York vibe to them in the way they act and look." Speaking with Wright in *Vibe*, Ortiz characterized it as "an aggressive edge." Nelson George, a prominent black culture critic who appears regularly in the pages of the *Village Voice*, described the new phenomenon in his column. He specifically lauded the power of SWV's "hard-eyed, I'm-going-for-mine edge that is so authentically New York it makes females from any other city seem too coy to be taken seriously."

Nothing exemplified this in the SWV repertoire so much as the cut "Downtown," which *Vibe's* Wright described as "a sexy, forthright confrontation with a black male taboo: oral sex." Johnson explained the trio's purpose in just as forthright a manner, telling Wright, "We're taking a stand for the ladies, telling the guys that this is the '90s. We're allowed to ask for what we want. And we're allowed to get what we want." Lyons told *People's* Janice Min, "Some guys call us nasty dirty whores because of the songs. But the people doing all the talking, I'm sure they've done it once in their lives." Certainly, the song had enthusiastic listeners who put it at the top of the R&B charts. SWV elaborated on the theme with a cut called "Blak Pudd'n."

SWV has earned the adulation of their audience, often to the point of adoration. "Sometimes it gets real bad," Johnson told Min, "and we have to let security handle it. They mostly give us the usual 'we love you, I love you, I want to marry you.'" The group quickly consolidated a general media reputation, but they became icons in venues focusing on black audiences. Teenage girls embraced them as role models, bringing them regularly to the pages of magazines like *Hype Hair, Right On!,* and *Sister 2 Sister.*

Billboard's McAdams noted that SWV has made national tours of radio programs and college campuses, as well as the usual concert tours, and that they have appeared before television audiences on many programs, including *Showtime at the Apollo,* MTV's *Fade to Black,* and Black Entertainment Television's (BET) *Video Soul.* By 1993 they had become one of the main attractions of the massive entourage of the Budweiser Superfest, the longest-running and most reputable rhythm and blues music festival in the country. And they were, of course, contenders for best new artist at the 1994 Grammy Awards ceremony.

Selected discography

It's About Time (includes "Right Here," "I'm So Into You," "Weak," "Downtown," and "Blak Pudd'n"), RCA, 1992.
"I'm So Into You" (maxi single), RCA, 1994.
"Always on My Mind" (maxi single), RCA, 1994.
"Anything" (maxi single), RCA, 1994.
The Hits Re-Mixed, RCA, 1994.

Sources

Billboard, January 30, 1993; March 13, 1993; July 24, 1993.
Essence, March 1994.
People, September 6, 1993.
Rap Masters, spring 1994.
Right On!, March 1994.
Source, January 1994.
USA Today, March 1, 1994.
Vibe, September 1993.
Village Voice, August 24, 1993.

Additional information for this profile was obtained from RCA Records publicity materials.

—*Ondine E. Le Blanc*

Arturo Toscanini

Conductor

Archive Photos

For more than half a century, Arturo Toscanini was one of the world's most respected conductors, a musical powerhouse whose performances packed orchestra halls—and filled the radio waves—in every major city in the United States. Toscanini dominated the classical music world, leading the debut performances of numerous important operas and symphonies. In a time when the majority of Americans craved popular music and novel trends, Toscanini did more than any other artist to increase the audience for classical symphonies and operatic works. A *New York Times* reporter noted that the fiery conductor "represented absolute, uncompromising integrity. He strove earnestly to realize as exactly as possible the composer's intentions as printed in the musical score. To achieve perfection he drove musicians relentlessly, himself hardest of all."

Toscanini conducted entirely from memory. Nearsighted from childhood, he memorized hundreds of intricate operas, symphonies, and concertos and then—in performance and often in rehearsals as well—led without ever consulting the score. The temperamental former cellist kept a full schedule of touring, recording, and performing until well into his eighties, finally retiring just three years before his death. The *New York Times* praised Toscanini for his "judgment, experience, vast musical knowledge, uncompromising standards and the touch of incandescent brilliance he infused into every performance he conducted."

Began Conducting at 19

Toscanini was born in 1867 and grew up in Parma, Italy. His father was a tailor, and as a youth Arturo, too, wanted to make clothes. His ambitions changed at the age of nine when he began cello lessons at the Parma Conservatory of Music. He was fascinated by the instrument and by classical music in general. Within two years he won a full scholarship to the conservatory, where he was known to sell his lunch in order to buy more sheet music.

After graduating from the conservatory in 1885, Toscanini immediately found work with travelling orchestras in Italy. In 1886 he joined a company that journeyed to Rio de Janeiro, Brazil, to stage some operas. On that particular trip the company conductor one day refused to lead a performance. The musicians persuaded Toscanini to step in as conductor—his penchant for memorizing whole scores had already marked him as extraordinary. Toscanini reluctantly accepted the assignment and, with no prior preparation, made his conducting debut on June 25, 1886. He was 19 at the time.

Word soon spread in Italy of the young cellist who

For the Record . . .

Born March 25, 1867, in Parma, Italy; died of complications from a stroke, January 16, 1957, in Riverdale, the Bronx, NY; son of Claudio and Paola (Montani) Toscanini; married Carla dei Martini, 1897; children: Walter, Wally, Wanda. *Education:* Studied music at Parma Conservatory of Music, 1876-85.

Cellist with touring orchestras in Italy, 1885-87; conductor of orchestras in Italy, 1887-1908; conductor of Metropolitan Opera orchestra, New York City, 1908-15; conductor in Italy, 1915-26; conductor of New York Philharmonic-Symphony Orchestra, 1926-36; conductor of Palestine Symphony Orchestra, 1936; conductor of NBC Symphony Orchestra, 1937-54; guest conductor of numerous symphony orchestras in U.S. and Europe. Made numerous recordings on RCA Victor label.

conducted whole operas from memory. Toscanini found himself invited to the podium on numerous occasions with local opera companies, and he conducted the world premieres of Ruggiero Leoncavallo's *Pagliacci* in 1892 and Giacomo Puccini's *La Boheme* in 1896. Both productions were highly successful, and the young musician was invited to conduct at La Scala in Milan—Italy's most important opera house. By 1898 Toscanini was named chief conductor and artistic director at La Scala, and he became well known there for introducing new operas and symphonic works. He also gained a reputation for his unorthodox attitudes; he was dismissed in 1903 for refusing to permit encores.

Toscanini brought his talents to America in 1908 as conductor for the Metropolitan Opera. He proved quite popular in New York City—as a *New York Times* contributor put it, his "success was instantaneous ... one triumph after another." After opening with Verdi's *Aida* on November 16, 1908, Toscanini stayed with the Metropolitan Opera for seven seasons. He returned to Italy at the outbreak of World War I to conduct benefit performances for the country's soldiers. At the end of the war, he received a decoration for bravery for leading an army band in the midst of a battle between the Italians and the Austrians.

After World War I Toscanini returned to America with an orchestra that he had engaged himself. It was with this orchestra that he made his first recordings on the Victor label in 1921. Some five years later he accepted the post of conductor with the New York Philharmonic Orchestra. That group merged with the New York Symphony Soci-

ety in 1928 as the New York Philharmonic-Symphony Orchestra. Toscanini was its principal conductor for ten years. He also found time to serve as a guest conductor at festivals and concerts in Germany, France, Austria, and London.

Spoke Out Against Fascism

Never one to shun politics, Toscanini was appalled by the fascist movement in Italy. He was an outspoken opponent of the fascists and was once badly beaten during a concert appearance when he refused to conduct the fascist anthem. He also severed ties with the Wagner festival at Bayreuth, Germany, and the Salzburg festival in Austria when Adolf Hitler took power. Toscanini spent the years of World War II in America, at the helm of the orchestra that he would lead for the rest of his life.

In 1937 Toscanini accepted a position as director of the newly formed National Broadcasting Company (NBC) Symphony Orchestra. The NBC Symphony was the first classical orchestra ever commissioned and subsidized by a broadcasting company. Toscanini was paid a then-fabulous salary of $40,000 as its conductor.

Some of the new symphony orchestra's performances were held at Radio City Music Hall, and most were broadcast nationwide on radio. This exposure increased Toscanini's popularity immensely. When he led the NBC Symphony Orchestra on a transcontinental trip in 1950, he was hailed by enthusiastic fans in major metropolitan areas and small towns alike. "Seldom in the history of America had a musician received such warm and widespread veneration," wrote a *New York Times* reporter.

"The Maestro"

Toscanini worked tirelessly until he was 87 years old. During his last years with the NBC Symphony Orchestra he engaged in a hectic schedule of recording, making some 30 albums with RCA Victor, including all nine of Beethoven's symphonies and the four symphonies by Brahms. The energetic conductor formally retired on April 4, 1954, immediately following a concert at Carnegie Hall. He died three years later following a severe stroke, just months before his ninetieth birthday.

In his day Toscanini was treated with an awe and reverence reserved for a select few. More than once the New York police had to barricade his concerts to keep out throngs of fans. Musicians and singers endured his temperamental outbursts, and audiences respected his eccentric notions about applause and encores. Throughout his career Toscanini was affectionately known as "The Maestro." His passing was mourned by political leaders and classical musicians all over the world.

Responding to the conductor's death on January 17, 1957, David M. Keiser, then president of the New York Philharmonic-Symphony, told the *New York Times* that Toscanini, "more than any other person in our time, has symbolized the supreme peak in musical perfection." *New York Times* correspondent Olin Downes offered a similar sentiment, writing of Toscanini: "There has never been a more gallant and intrepid champion of great music, or a spirit that flamed higher, or a nobler defender of the faith."

Selected discography

Toscanini and the NBC Symphony, Melogram, 1989.

Toscanini at La Scala, SRO, 1993.
Toscanini Conducts Music by His Contemporaries, dell'Arte, 1993.
The Toscanini Collection, 71 volumes, RCA, 1994.
Toscanini and the Philharmonic-Symphony Orchestra: Great Recordings 1926-1936, 3 volumes, Pearl 3.

Sources

American Record Guide, September/October 1988; September/October 1990.
Musical America, November 1989; July 1990.
New York Times, April 5, 1954; January 15, 1957.
New York Times Magazine, November 8, 1953; December 27, 1953.

—*Anne Janette Johnson*

Merle Travis

Guitarist, singer, songwriter

MICHAEL OCHS ARCHIVES/Venice, CA

The name Merle Travis stands solidly on its own, the symbol of an era that witnessed some of the greatest innovations in modern country music. Along with other legendary pickers like Chet Atkins, Doc Watson, and Roy Clark, Travis was both a traditionalist and an inventor on the guitar. In songs such as "Dark as a Dungeon" and "Sixteen Tons" he fashioned emotive vignettes of scenes from American life; from his roots in folk culture he moved on to define classic honky-tonk music with his hits "Divorce Me C.O.D." and "Three Times Seven."

While preserving the best of country music tradition, Travis's talents extended the instrumental limits of country music styling. His development of the technique that became known as "Travis Picking" made a lasting impact on generations of Nashville pickers who would follow. In addition, he is credited with developing one of the first solid-body guitar prototypes; his early design was the inspiration for Leo Fender and the Fender guitars that became a mainstay of rock music.

Travis was born on November 29, 1917, in Rosewood, Muhlenberg County, Kentucky. The youngest of four children, Merle and his family moved to nearby Ebenezer when his father left tobacco farming behind for the better pay offered by the coal mines. Merle's first instrument was a cast-off five-string banjo that he played alongside his father, an enthusiastic banjo picker. When he was 12, his talented older brother Taylor gave him a guitar that he had made himself.

Playing music was a popular pastime in the area, and the Travis family often got together to jam with neighbors like Ike Everly, father to the same Phil and Don who would one day be one of the most popular vocal duos in America. It was from his neighbor Mose Rager that young Merle learned the basics of the right-hand guitar technique that would eventually bear his name. Rager, in turn, had been heavily influenced by the playing of a local railroad hand, African-American fiddler and guitarist Arnold Shultz.

During a time when most country guitar was a flat-picked rhythmic backup for vocals, Travis used the thumb of the right hand to create a syncopated bass-note accompaniment to the melody line created by the first two fingers of his right hand. His was a more complex arrangement than that shown him by his coal-miner neighbors because of Merle's background as a banjo picker. The sound Travis obtained on a single guitar would never require backup by a rhythm section.

After grade school, Travis began to earn money by playing for square dances, town get-togethers, and whatever else he could find. Music was his path away

Born Merle Robert Travis, November 29, 1917, in Rosewood, KY; died of a heart attack, October 20, 1983; son of Robert Travis (a coal miner); married, 1937 (divorced); married June Hayden (a singer; divorced); married Bettie Morgan, c. 1954 (divorced); married Dorothy Thompson; children: Dennis, Mildred, Pat, Cindy, Merlene.

Began playing with Tennessee Tomcats, Evansville, IL, 1935; joined Georgia Wildcats, 1936; joined Drifting Pioneers and performed on WLW, Cincinnati, 1937-44; signed with Capitol Records, 1946-69; co-host of television show *Merle Travis and Company*, c. 1953; performed with other legendary country stars on *Will the Circle Be Unbroken*, 1972; signed with CMH. Appeared in films, including *From Here to Eternity*, 1953, and *Honky Tonk Man*, 1982. *Military service:* U.S. Marine Corps, 1942-44.

Awards: Inducted into Nashville Songwriters Hall of Fame, 1970; Grammy Award (with Chet Atkins) for best country instrumental performance, 1974, for *The Atkins-Travis Traveling Show;* inducted into the Country Music Hall of Fame, 1977.

career. With Pappy's help, in less than a year the young guitarist was performing with the Drifting Pioneers on WLW-Cincinnati's *Boone County Jamboree,* a popular radio show that would become even more well known as the *Midwestern Hayride.*

The 50,000-watt signal generated by the station let Travis popularize his finger-style guitar technique nationwide during WLW broadcasts. Among his many national listeners was an asthmatic teenager from rural Georgia who was teaching himself to play the guitar in opposition to parents, who desired him to pursue a career as a violinist. Sitting by his radio, the teen leaned forward to hear every note of Travis's intricate finger-picked guitar breaks —unique because of their degree of complexity and the bluesy sound they brought to country music—and was inspired to develop a style like it himself. The young man's name was Chet Atkins; he would cross paths with Travis many years later when the two met in the recording studio to begin work on an award-winning collaboration titled *The Atkins-Travis Traveling Show.*

During World War II Travis joined the Marine Corps but found that its severe discipline clashed with his independent nature. After two years he returned to WLW, but problems with alcohol and pills caused his second marriage to come apart. Unable to deal with either his personal or marital problems, Travis blamed his dissatisfaction on the dismal Midwest winters. He moved to California in 1944.

from the hard life in the mines, a way of living with which he had become all too familiar during his childhood and about which he would write extensively in his later songs. He got a job with the Civilian Conservation Corps until he saved $30, enough money to buy a Gretch guitar. With new guitar in hand, he and a friend hitchhiked around the country, playing on street corners for the money they needed to continue their travels.

Linked Up With the Skillet Lickers

In 1935, the year Travis turned 18, his ramblings had led him to Evansville, Indiana, where his brother Taylor lived. While attending a local dance marathon, he gave a performance of "Tiger Rag" that showcased his upbeat new style. Travis's innovative guitar work caught the ear of the members of a local band, the Tennessee Tomcats, who quickly hired the newcomer. In late 1936 Travis left the Tomcats to begin touring with the popular Georgia Wildcats. Wildcatter Clayton "Pappy" McMitchen, also a member of the Skillet Lickers and one of the most highly praised American fiddlers of the 1930s, would prove to be a great help in promoting Travis's

Penned Hits; Popularity Soared

Supporting himself by acting in minor roles in a few western films and playing with Ray Whitley's Western Swing Band, Travis helped fellow musicians Tex Ritter and Cliffie Stone get a recording contract with the newly formed Capitol Records in 1946. There he became one of the most sought-after stars on the young label. Honky-tonk hits like "So Round, So Firm, So Fully Packed," a take-off on advertising slogans of the day, was a radio favorite in 1947. Travis wrote or cowrote all of his songs; "No Vacancy," lamenting the housing shortage facing the soldiers returning stateside after World War II, was a collaboration with Stone, and Tex Williams helped on "Smoke! Smoke! Smoke! (That Cigarette)." A song that grew to the stature of an American folk classic, "Dark as a Dungeon" was written under the glow of a street light as Travis stopped to jot down the lyrics on a motorcycle ride home from Redondo Beach.

With a great talent for both language and music, Travis was able to create new songs almost on demand. His witty lyricism was peppered with the easygoing slang that made his songs instantly popular. "Divorce Me C.O.D." held the Number One spot for 14 weeks through the end of 1946. With songs like "Dark as a Dungeon" and "Sixteen Tons," both released on *Folk Songs of the Hills* in 1947, Travis proved to be tough competition for other record labels. In 1947 rival RCA Victor hired budding guitar virtuoso Atkins to compete head-to-head with Merle; Travis was unbeatable, however, and Atkins temporarily returned to the performance circuit after only one recording.

"Reenlistment Blues" and the Bottle

By 1950 Travis had become a familiar face on Stone's *Hometown Jamboree* and *Town Hall Party,* two Los Angeles-based television music shows; he and his second wife, singer June Hayden, also hosted *Merle Travis and Company* through several seasons. In addition, Travis appeared as a guitar-playing sailor in the 1953 film *From Here to Eternity,* swapping vocals with Frank Sinatra in the catchy "Reenlistment Blues."

In the fall of 1955 Travis's friend Tennessee Ernie Ford recorded "Sixteen Tons"; by working the song into his NBC-TV shows Ford made the song so popular that demand for it would make the Travis-penned saga of the coal-miner's plight the best-selling 45 rpm single of all time. Its author soon attained celebrity status as well; unfortunately, not all mentions of the songwriter in the media were positive. One night in early 1956 he struck his third wife, Bettie, forcing her to flee their home. News accounts would embellish the details of Travis's drunken threats and his final surrender to police. But by June the event was eclipsed as the musician returned to his hometown of Ebenezer, Kentucky, to be honored with a memorial and "Merle Travis Day."

Unfortunately, hard drinking and drug use would continue to plague Travis throughout his life. In the early 1960s the musician was hospitalized for a period after his arrest on the charge of driving under the influence of narcotics. Although he moved to Nashville during the 1960s and appeared regularly on the stage of the famed Grand Ole Opry, Travis's technique began to suffer from his taxing lifestyle. He recorded two more records, including another album of mining songs, before his association with Capitol ended in 1969. A recording project with producer Atkins, *The Atkins-Travis Traveling Show,* won the pair a Grammy Award in 1974. Shortly thereafter, Travis returned to the West Coast, where he played occasional concerts and recorded for CMH Records.

At this point in his life, newly remarried, Travis slowly began to get control of his life. His performance skills began to return to their former level, as evidenced by 1981's *Travis Pickin',* which earned Travis a Grammy nomination. Tragically, in October of 1983, a month shy of 66, Travis suffered a massive heart attack, which proved fatal. His film appearance in Clint Eastwood's *Honky Tonk Man* a year earlier was his last.

Revered by countless musicians as country's consummate Renaissance Man, Travis is acknowledged as one of the most influential guitarists of the twentieth century. Indeed, he has been an inspiration to many—like a young Gene Autry—who first heard his unique guitar stylings via the radio shows of the early 1940s. Noted performers Doc Watson and Chet Atkins both named their sons Merle—after the man they counted among their personal heroes.

Selected discography

Folk Songs of the Hills (includes "Nine-Pound Hammer," "I Am a Pilgrim," and "Sixteen Tons"), Capitol, 1947, reissued, Bear Family.
Back Home, Capitol, 1957.
Travis!, Capitol, 1962.
Walkin' the Strings, Capitol, 1962.
Songs of the Coal Miners, Capitol, 1963.
Guitar Standards, Capitol, 1968.
(With the Nitty Gritty Dirt Band and others) *Will the Circle Be Unbroken,* United Artists, 1972.
(With Chet Atkins) *The Atkins-Travis Traveling Show,* RCA, 1974.
Travis Pickin', CMH, 1981.
The Best of Merle Travis, Rhino, 1990.
(With Joe Maphis) *Merle Travis and Joe Maphis,* Capitol.

Sources

Books

Malone, Bob C., and Judith McCulloch, *Stars of Country Music,* University of Illinois Press, 1975.
Shestack, Melvin, *Country Music Encyclopedia,* Crowell, 1973.
Stambler, Irwin, *Encyclopedia of Folk, Country and Western Music,* St. Martin's, 1983.

Periodicals

Country America, March 1994.
Guitar Player, June 1969.

Additional information for this profile was obtained from liner notes by Rich Kienzle, *The Best of Merle Travis,* Rhino, 1990.

—*Pamela L. Shelton*

Narada Michael Walden

Producer, songwriter, percussionist

Drummer-turned-songwriter-turned-producer Narada Michael Walden is something of a pop music Midas—the singles and albums he touches often turn to gold, or even platinum. A Walden song—whether performed by Lionel Ritchie, Whitney Houston, Aretha Franklin, or Barbra Streisand—is characterized by a memorable tune and lavish production values. The man described by *San Francisco* magazine as "vivacious, impish [and] vastly affable" has reached the top, both commercially and artistically, since the early 1980s.

In interviews, Walden (born Michael Walden; the moniker *Narada*—meaning "supreme musician"—was bestowed on the artist by his spiritual mentor) likes to point out that he grew up near Kalamazoo, Michigan—halfway between Detroit and Chicago, affording Walden the influences of both Motown soul and Windy City rhythm and blues. But the musical influences reached even farther: "God planted me in Michigan for a reason—to hear everything. And I did, from classical to country," Walden told *San Francisco* magazine writer John Mendelssohn. "I always knew music was my thing," Walden continued. "I'm blessed in that way—I never had to search for what I wanted to do. As a kid, I'd put records on a turntable and just watch them spin, or study the album covers. I'd take my little Gretsch catalogue with me to Mass every morning, pick out a drum set I wanted, and pray for it."

Walden was born in 1952 and grew up in Plainwell, Michigan, where he was voted the most popular, best-dressed, and most creative graduate of his rural high school. Publicity materials from Walden's production company noted that Walden started performing as a young teen. Walden recalled, "There was a lounge on the north side of Kalamazoo where all the blues musicians hung out, called the Ambassador Lounge. And the guy I was working with—an unbelievable piano player, who seemed to come out of his mother's womb playing the blues—his uncle owned this lounge, so we became the opening act." Walden went on to attend Western Michigan University, where he studied music and joined a soul ensemble that eventually was based out of Fresno, California. Youthful experimentation with mind-expanding drugs led Walden to believe that a higher consciousness could be obtained without the use of pharmaceuticals. He took up meditation, then found his niche under the tutelage of Indian guru Sri Chimoy—"When [he] smiled at me, I felt I'd found a home for myself," Walden declared in the *San Francisco* profile.

At the same time, Walden was making a name for himself as the drummer with the pop-soul-fusion group Mahavishnu Orchestra, fronted by guitar legend John

For the Record . . .

Born Michael Walden, April 23, 1952, in Plainwell, MI; married Lisa Coles (later named Anukampa; a health food store owner), 1979. *Education:* Attended Western Michigan University, 1970-72.

Began career as musician (sideman for various artists) and songwriter, c. 1975; worked as a Warner Bros. recording artist; founder and president, Perfection Light Productions, beginning in 1976. Independent producer/songwriter for artists including Lionel Ritchie, Aretha Franklin, and Whitney Houston.

Awards: Named outstanding black contemporary artist, Bay Area Music Awards, 1982; Grammy awards for best rhythm and blues song, 1985, for "Freeway of Love"; for producer of the year, 1987; and for best album, 1993, for *The Bodyguard;* named producer of the year, 1986, *Billboard.* Produced numerous gold records.

Addresses: *Office*—Perfection Light Productions, 1925-G Francisco Blvd., San Rafael, CA 94801.

McLaughlin. Walden joined the group in time to record Mahavishnu's best-known work, the *Apocalypse* LP, which was produced by ex-Beatles producer George Martin and went on to gain cult status. Walden later wrote songs and played on ex-Yardbirds guitarist Jeff Beck's 1976 release *Wired,* and also performed as a sideman with the likes of musicians Jaco Pastorius and Alphonso Johnson. From there it was on to his own albums—at least nine that bear his name, including the Atlantic releases *Garden of Love Light, I Cry—I Smile, Victory, Confidence, The Dance of Life,* and *Awakening.*

While some of Walden's singles—most notably his Number One rhythm and blues hit "I Don't Want Nobody Else to Dance With You"—were well received by listeners. The "crossover" success that eluded him as a performer arrived later when he became a top mainstream producer. Walden's solo albums, though, do have their fans among critics. For example, Mendelssohn declared Walden's late 1980s album *Divine Emotions* "very agreeable indeed—not only soulfully sung, but drolly too, tuneful and nearly impossible not to dance to."

Through his production company, Perfection Light Productions, of San Rafael, California, Walden embarked on his main career as independent producer. The singles Walden supervised became better known than any song he performed himself: Starship's "Nothing's

Gonna Stop Us Now," George Michael's "I Knew You Were Waiting for Me" (both back-to-back Number One hits from 1987), and Whitney Houston's "I Wanna Dance with Somebody." Walden also wrote and produced Aretha Franklin's Grammy-winning hit "Freeway of Love," and can be seen at the drum kit in the video. *Who's Zoomin' Who,* the album containing the single, was Franklin's first Number One LP in her long career and earned Walden producer of the year honors from *Billboard.*

Working with young talent is also a Walden trademark. He was involved in the early success of teenage popsters Stacy Lattisaw, Tevin Campbell, and Shanice, and in 1994 announced a project with "a 13-year-old vocalist named Princess K," according to a *Billboard* report. Walden told the magazine's J. R. Reynolds that he enjoys working with growing artists: "Kids are so innocent and are less set in their ways."

While in the 1980s Walden was an A-list producer whose stream of hits never seemed to stem, his Midas touch "cooled" a bit in the 1990s, as Reynolds noted. In 1993 he produced only one Top Five rhythm-and-blues hit, Houston's "I'm Every Woman." But that single came off Houston's *Bodyguard* soundtrack, which won the Grammy Award for best album that year. Still, continued Reynolds, "In the pressure-packed world of R&B, Walden must score big in '94 if he wants to continue being regarded as among the producer-elite."

Walden took steps to that end by contributing to the reemergence of former teen idols New Kids on the Block. Now older and renamed NKOTB, their comeback album, *Face the Music,* was coproduced by Walden and was subsequently hailed by *Time* magazine's Guy Garcia as "the most polished album the Kids have ever made." Walden also produced music for filmmaker Spike Lee's movie *Crooklyn,* supervising a remake of "People Make the World Go Round."

Walden's spirituality guides his career; it also guides his personal life. His wife, Anukampa (born Lisa Coles), owns the San Francisco-based Perfect Health Joy Songs health food store, according to *Ebony.* The same article quoted Narada as saying: "You learn what team effort means, that it is something to work at. And we do work at our marriage. It takes a conscious effort on both our parts. Marriage has to be a priority." Regular trips to a retreat in Hawaii also serve to uplift him. Walden keeps in good physical shape by weightlifting and running—in 1987 he was a spokesperson for "The Peace Run," a worldwide relay on behalf of peace.

"I'm an artist," Walden told *San Francisco's* Mendelssohn, "but I'm a producer too. I'm a dreamer, but also very real. My head's in the sky, and my feet are firmly planted on the ground. When someone pays me X amount of dollars to produce their album, the reason they're coming to me is to guarantee them a hit record. That's my job." Walden is not shaken by working with the big names. "The human might be a little intimidated at first by Lionel [Ritchie] or Aretha [Franklin] or Whitney [Houston], because they've done so much more than I could dream of doing. But when the music comes on, the divine, Narada side, the one that knows art is greater than the artist, takes over. And from there I feel completely comfortable."

Selected discography

As performer

(With Mahavishnu Orchestra) *Apocalypse,* 1974.
Jeff Beck, *Wired,* 1976.
Garden of Love Light, Atlantic.
I Cry—I Smile, Atlantic.
Victory, Atlantic.

Confidence.
The Dance of Life, Atlantic.
Awakening, Atlantic.
Divine Emotions.

Also producer/songwriter for numerous artists, including Barbra Streisand, Aretha Franklin, Whitney Houston, Lionel Ritchie, Angela Bofill, Stacy Lattisaw, Mariah Carey, New Kids on the Block (NKOTB), and Tevin Campbell.

Sources

Billboard, April 16, 1994.
Ebony, December 1987; February 1991.
San Francisco, June 1988.
Time, February 7, 1994.
USA Today, April 29, 1988.

Additional information for this profile was obtained from Perfection Light Productions publicity materials.

—*Susan Salter*

War

Rock band

War, a nine-member, Los Angeles-based group noted throughout the 1970s for their fusion of rock, Latin jazz, funk, and rhythm and blues, released their first major label album, *Peace Sign,* in June of 1994 after a 13-year recording hiatus. Hip-hop music and rap samples of War's material from the 1970s revived an interest in the group in the 1990s, as did brief snippets of War's music heard briefly on film soundtracks and on television commercials. War's most sampled hit songs are "Why Can't We Be Friends?," "The World Is a Ghetto," "Low Rider," and "Cisco Kid."

Although War occasionally toured clubs and festivals during the 1980s and early 1990s, recording an album proved difficult because the band struggled with the loss of many of its original members. War is comprised of Kerry Campbell (saxophone), Sal Rodriguez (percussion), Tetsuya "Tex" Nakamura (harmonica), Charles Green (saxophone), Rae Valentine (keyboards), Lonnie Jordan (keyboards, bass, vocals), Howard Scott (guitar, vocals), Ron Hammon (drums, vocals), and Harold Brown (drums, vocals). Founding member Lee Oskar

Photograph by Jeffrey Mayer, courtesy of Avenue Records

For the Record . . .

Original members include **Papa Dee Allen** (born July 19, 1931; died of a brain aneurysm, 1989), vocals and percussion; **Harold Brown,** (born March 17, 1946; left band, 1983; rejoined, 1993) vocals and percussion; **B. B. Dickerson** (born August 3, 1949; left band, 1979); **Jerry Goldstein,** cowriter and producer; **Lonnie Jordan** (born November 21, 1948), vocals and keyboards; **Charles Miller** (born June 21, 1939; died, 1980; left band, 1979), flute and saxophone; **Lee Oskar** (born March 24, 1948, in Copenhagen, Denmark; left group, 1993), harmonica; **Peter Rosen** (died of a drug overdose, early 1960s); **Howard Scott** (born March 15, 1946), vocals and guitar.

Later members include **Kerry Campbell** (joined band, 1994), saxophone; **Charles Green** (joined band, 1994), saxophone; **Ron Hammon** (joined band, 1978), drums; **Tetsuya "Tex" Nakamura** (joined band, 1994), harp and harmonica; **Sal Rodriguez** (joined band, 1994), percussion; **Tweed Smith** (bandmember 1982-83), vocals; **Rae Valentine** (born Harold Rae Brown, Jr.; son of bandmember Harold Brown; joined band, 1994), keyboards.

Group formed as the Creators, Los Angeles, 1960; re-formed as the Night Shift, 1968; re-formed again as War with Eric Burdon, 1969; released first albums with Burdon on MGM, 1970; released first solo album, *War,* on United Artists, 1971; released 12 albums, including one more with Burdon, 1970s; released three more albums, early 1980s; returned with *Rap Declares War,* Avenue, 1992.

Addresses: *Publicist*—Sandy Friedman, Rogers & Cowan, 10000 Santa Monica Blvd., #400, Los Angeles, CA 90069. *Record company*—Avenue Records, 11100 Santa Monica Blvd., Suite 2000, Los Angeles, CA 90025.

left the band in December of 1993—after 24 years with the group—and was replaced by harmonica player Tetsuya "Tex" Nakamura, a blues harpist from Japan. Original band member Papa Dee Allen collapsed on stage while playing "Gypsy Man" during a concert in 1989 and died shortly thereafter of a brain aneurysm; founding band member Charles Miller left the band in 1979.

Remaining original War bandmembers include guitarist Howard Scott, drummer Harold Brown, drummer Ron Hammon (who joined in 1978), and keyboard player Lonnie Jordan. Percussionist Sal Rodriguez played in the bands Tierra and El Chicano before joining. War keyboardist Rae Valentine is Harold Brown's son, a legacy Brown passed on to the next generation of War enthusiasts. Brown left the band from 1983 to 1993.

Began With Eric Burdon

In 1962 original War members Scott and Brown formed a rhythm and blues cover band called the Creators and eventually added Jordan, Dickerson, and Miller. The Creators often opened for Ike and Tina Turner when they played in Los Angeles. The Creators were forced to dissolve when guitarist Scott was drafted; he was called for military duty in the mid-1960s for two years. When Scott returned to Los Angeles after his tour of duty, the Creators reunited briefly.

In 1968 Scott, Brown, Miller, and Jordan formed a new band called the Night Shift. Producer and songwriter Jerry Goldstein heard the band play during one of their rehearsals and decided the band would complement the vocal style of Eric Burdon, formerly of the Animals. The Night Shift became War in early 1969. The name "War" was chosen for the band to offset the fact that the word "peace" was bandied about constantly in pop culture.

Burdon liked the band and decided to tour with them in 1969. Their first concert was at the Devonshire Pop Festival, a three-day event in the Los Angeles area that attracted 100,000 people. Eric Burdon and War followed Credence Clearwater at the festival. Burdon and War released an album in 1970 titled *Eric Burdon Declares "War."* The gold-selling album reached Number 18 on the music charts and its single "Spill the Wine" reached Number Three. War played Ronnie Scott's London jazz club in 1970 with Jimi Hendrix—Hendrix's last concert before his death. Hendrix and War played the Memphis Slim song "Mother Earth" together. War recorded three albums with Eric Burdon in 1970 and 1971, one of which was not released for five years. *Love Is All Around* was recorded in 1971 and released in 1976.

Multiple Top 40 Hits

In 1971 War and Eric Burdon divided to become solo acts. The move was prompted by an experience War band members had with Burdon. In 1970 Burdon vanished in the middle of a European tour, and War was forced to appear without him, hoping audience members at concerts wouldn't demand refunds. War's solo shows sold out, much to their delight, and the band knew they would be well received on their own.

War's breakthrough album, *All Day Music,* which sold almost two million copies and reached Number 16 on the *Billboard* pop music chart, was released in 1971. Two of the album's singles became Top 40 hits: "All Day Music" and "Slippin' Into Darkness." In 1972 War released *The World Is a Ghetto.* This album became the best-selling album of 1973. The singles "Cisco Kid" and "The World Is a Ghetto" both went gold, and War was established as a major musical force. The double album *War Live* was released in 1974, featuring the Top 40 single "Ballero." From 1975 to 1981 War released seven more albums, including *Why Can't We Be Friends?,* each meeting with acclaim and enthusiastic response.

War and Peace

Avenue Records CEO Jerry Goldstein is credited with having urged War back into the recording realm. War's cowriter since the band's inception, Goldstein produced all of the band's major hits in the 1970s and then gained possession of the band's copyrights and masters in the mid-1980s. Avenue Records reissued much of War's back catalog on CD in the 1990s, which fueled a renewed interest in the band. The fact that War was sampled so liberally by the rap and hip-hop community in the 1990s create mixed feelings for War's bandmembers, who alternately felt flattered and robbed. War bandmember Howard Scott told *Billboard's* Jon Cummings, "Instead of suing, we decided to do that record and make peace with the rap community."

Avenue Records released a compilation record in 1992 titled *Rap Declares War,* which featured War bandmembers with the rap musicians who had sampled their music. Some of the War-struck rappers on the album included De La Soul, Poor Righteous Teachers, Brand Nubian, Nice 'N Smooth, Beastie Boys, Ice-T, Wreckx-N-Effect, Kid Frost, and 2Pac. This album cemented War's tie-in with the hip-hop and rap community and highlighted how much the band had in common with the musicians who had sampled War's music.

South Central Environs

In its early days, War drew its flavor from South Central Los Angeles. South Central also inspired a lion's share of later rappers, such as N.W.A. and Ice-T. War's message, however, is decidedly different than that of the "gangsta" rappers from the same environment. Anger, urban violence, and despair are replaced with optimism, understanding, peace, and hope in War's music. The band provides positive messages, as evidenced in the singles "Peace Sign," "What If," and "Let Me Tell Ya." "Instead of throwing up gang signs, we're throwing up peace signs," Scott told Cummings.

War aims to be multifaceted and to provide varying formats for its music. The band is equal parts Latino, black, and white, so War hopes to be able to appeal to a wide range of listeners. *Vibe* magazine's Richard Torres described War and its music as "user-friendly funk for the '90s ... light on the feet and easy on the hips," and "a laid-back groove factory with a conscience." Jazz, rhythm and blues, rock, and Latin melodies are frequently combined in War's songs to create a distinctive multilayered sound, slightly reminiscent of each style.

After a 13-year absense from the recording studio, War released *Peace Sign* in 1994—the band's eighteenth major label album—produced by Jerry Goldstein and War band member Lonnie Jordan. The single "East L.A." is a West Coast version of Ben E. King's "Spanish Harlem" with Jose Feliciano contributing vocals. Some of the album's singles are beautiful ballads, others are reminiscent of War's previous hits in the 1970s, and others reveal experimentation and an unbridled, fresh approach to their music.

War released *Peace Sign* in 1994 because the band still has much to say about American society. In "Homeless Hero" on *Peace Sign,* War sings about a Vietnam War veteran who grapples with drugs, alcohol, and a society that no longer finds him useful. War's Harold Brown told *Goldmine's* Steve Roeser "We're more 'street.'... We're more ground-zero, more ground level. We're the kind of guys who can go into south Los Angeles or go to the projects or the barrio ... and every day that we live ... it's because of music."

Selected discography

As the Creators

Little Johnny Hamilton and the Creators, Dore Records, 1965.

With Eric Burdon

Eric Burdon Declares War (includes "Spill The Wine"), MGM, 1970.
The Black Man's Burdon, MGM, 1970.
Love Is All Around, ABC, 1976.

Without Eric Burdon

War, United Artists, 1971.
All Day Music, Far Out/UA, 1971.
The World Is a Ghetto, Far Out/UA, 1972.
Deliver the Word, UA, 1973.
Radio Free War, UA, 1973.
War Live, Far Out/UA, 1974.
Why Can't We Be Friends?, Far Out/UA, 1975.
War's Greatest Hits, Far Out/UA, 1977.
Platinum Jazz, Blue Note, 1977.
Galaxy, MCA, 1977.
Youngblood (soundtrack), UA, 1978.
The Music Band, MCA, 1978.
The Music Band, Part 2, MCA, 1979.
Best of the Music Band, MCA, 1981.
Outlaw, RCA, 1982.
Life Is So Strange, RCA, 1983.

The Best of War ... And More, Avenue, 1987.
Rap Declares War, Avenue, 1992.
War, Avenue, 1992.
Peace Sign, Avenue/Rhino, 1994.
Anthology 1970-1994, Avenue, 1994.

Sources

Billboard, June 14, 1994.
Goldmine, September 2, 1994.
Vibe, August 1994.

Additional information for this profile was provided by Avenue Records publicity materials.

—B. Kimberly Taylor

Chick Webb

Drummer, bandleader

MICHAEL OCHS ARCHIVES/Venice, CA

At the helm of one of the most outstanding jazz bands of the 1930s, Chick Webb emerged as both a tremendously influential drummer and orchestra leader. Webb was the first jazz drummer to become a nationally recognized bandleader and helped transform traditional Dixieland-style percussion into a modern swing idiom. Dwarfed by a deformity of the spine that left him hunchbacked and less than five feet tall, Webb produced innovative rhythms that remained unencumbered by physical limitations. Though nearly obscured behind his 28-inch bass drum, Webb drove his orchestra with an innate sense of swing that brought accolades from jazz great Duke Ellington to young drummer Gene Krupa, whose musical style and a drum-led ensemble would remain deeply indebted to Webb's musical legacy. Webb is a pivotal figure in the history of jazz; his later obscurity fails to overshadow his role in defining the art of modern drumming and its integration and conceptual definition within the jazz orchestra.

William Henry Webb was born on February 10, 1909, in Baltimore, Maryland. A member of a poor family, he was raised by his mother and spent most of his childhood at the home of his grandfather, a porter employed at a downtown Baltimore shoe store. At a young age, Webb, inflicted with spinal tuberculosis, underwent an operation at Johns Hopkins Hospital in Baltimore. Although the operation enabled him to walk, it resulted in the limited use of his legs and shoulders. Webb refused to let his physical deformity hinder his dream of becoming a drummer. By age three he played on pots and pans and later practiced rhythms on iron railings and marble steps around his neighborhood. With money earned from selling newspapers, he purchased a secondhand drum set and began to perform with local aspiring musicians.

Harlem: The Great Jazz Oasis

Webb's first professional engagement came about when he joined the Jazzola Orchestra, playing drums with the band on excursion boats that crossed Sheepshead Bay. In the Jazzola Orchestra, he met lifelong friend and musical sideman John Truehart, a talented Baltimore-born banjo player and guitarist. When Truehart returned from an unsuccessful trip to find musical employment in New York City, he left once again in 1924, this time accompanied by Webb, who longed to explore the musical nightlife of Harlem.

In Harlem Webb played with saxophonists Tony Hardwick, Johnny Hodges, and Benny Carter, and pianist Duke Ellington in the legendary Sunday jam sessions held at Small's Paradise. Webb's association with trum-

For the Record . . .

Born William Henry Webb, February 10, 1909, in Baltimore, MD; died June 16, 1939, in Baltimore.

Professional drummer with Jazzola Orchestra, Baltimore, MD, early 1920s; moved to New York City, 1924, and played in clubs around Harlem; bandleader, beginning in 1926; leader of Savoy Ballroom's house band, beginning in 1931; recorded for Columbia and Decca labels, beginning in 1934; hired singer Ella Fitzgerald, 1935.

Awards: The city of Baltimore dedicated a memorial recreational center to Webb, 1947.

peter Bobby Stark, a member of Edgar Dowell's band, resulted in his first musical job in New York. While visiting a club where Dowell's band was auditioning, Webb, through the urging of Stark, was allowed to sit in for the group's absent drummer. Impressed with Webb's stage presence and musicianship, the club owner agreed to hire the band, with the guarantee that Dowell would feature the unknown drummer.

Eventually Ellington, one of Webb's most outspoken admirers, booked him and four sidemen at the Black Bottom Club. Although the group fell under Webb's nominal leadership, the drummer possessed no desire to become a bandleader. "At that time," Ellington explained in *Hear Me Talkin' to Ya,* "Chick wasn't thinking anything about getting along on his own, his mind was all on the drums." Following a five-month stint at the Black Bottom Club, Ellington booked Webb at the Paddock Club—an engagement that resulted in the expansion of the band to eight members. At the Paddock Club, located below Carroll's Theater on Seventh Avenue, Webb and his band found steady employment until a fire forced the closing of the club in 1926.

King of the Savoy

Despite his persistent reluctance to become a bandleader, Webb followed the advice of cousin and bandmember Johnny Hodges and took his band to the Savoy Ballroom in 1927. The Savoy was a ballroom that stretched the entire length of 140th and 141st Streets. According to David Levering Lewis in *When Harlem Was in Vogue,* the club was "architecturally ... dazzled with a spacious lobby framing a huge cut-glass chandelier and marble staircase, an orange and blue dance hall with soda fountain, and heavy carpeting covering

half its area, the remainder a burnished dance floor 250 feet by 50 feet with two bandstands." Known by Harlemites as "the Track," the Savoy accommodated 4,000 dancers and some of the best jazz orchestras of the period.

At the Savoy's battle of the band contests, Webb's Harlem Stompers reigned victorious against the ensembles of Fletcher Henderson, Fess Williams, Lloyd Scott, and Alex Jackson. One such battle in May of 1927 inspired a *Down Beat* critic to write, as quoted in the book *Ella Fitzgerald,* "Chick had such amazing musicians in his band and they played with so much feeling and fervor that they swung the crowd right over to them, astounding everybody."

A Little Girl Named Ella

After his contract expired at the Savoy, Webb booked his band at the Rose Danceland on 125th Street in December of 1927. Instead of staying at the Rose Danceland, however, Webb took a job playing behind vaudeville dancers. Ill-suited for the engagement, the band not only lost the job, but outraged the owners of the Rose Danceland, who became embittered at the financial loss incurred by Webb's sudden departure. The lack of steady work and the erratic management by Webb forced several musicians to leave the band. Among them were key soloists like Hodges, who joined Ellington, and Stark, who periodically left for employment with Fletcher Henderson.

Webb's return to the Savoy in 1931 proved triumphant. Steady employment at the Savoy enabled Webb to assemble a formidable musical lineup with trombonist Jimmy Harrison and saxophonists Benny Carter, Edgar Sampson, and Don Redman. Described by Ellington as "battle mad," Webb took on the best ensembles of the day, winning legendary victories against the Benny Goodman Orchestra in 1937 and Count Basie in 1938. Webb's band emerged successful on record as well. In 1934 they released an album for Columbia under the name Chick Webb's Savoy Orchestra and later that year signed with Decca, producing the Edgar Sampson compositions "Blue Lou," "Blue Minor," "Stompin' at the Savoy," and "Don't Be That Way."

In 1935 Savoy manager Charlie Buchanan called upon Webb to find a popular singer to boost the commercial potential of his group. Though Webb had featured several singers, including handsome balladeer Charles Linton, Buchanan pressured him to find a young female vocalist versed in the modern swing style. Linton learned of a 17-year-old singer, Ella Fitzgerald, who had won first prize at the Apollo Theater's amateur show.

At first reluctant to hire the young singer, Webb soon added Fitzgerald to the band's payroll. The singer became an instant success with Harlem crowds and within a few weeks of joining the band—in June of 1935—she recorded the sides "Are You Here to Stay" and "Love and Kisses." Many of the Webb/Fitzgerald recordings bordered on commercial novelty numbers, but the pair did bring the band nationwide fame and first-rate bookings. "Despite the trite material Ella chose (or was obliged) to sing," wrote Gunther Schuller in *The Swing Era,* "her innate talent shone through. Indeed, she lifted these banal songs to heights they did not deserve by her impeccable pitch."

For the next three years, Webb recorded 60 numbers featuring Fitzgerald, while only producing 14 instrumental recordings, including the critically acclaimed "Clap Hands! Here Comes Charlie" and "Harlem Congo," arranged by guitarist Charlie Dixon. These instrumentals exhibit Webb's flawless drumming—his complete control over timing and the tasteful use of fills. On these recordings one can hear his use of cowbell, cymbal, wood block, snare-drum, tom-toms, and bass drum, on which he pounded out steady four-four time.

A Musical Father Figure

As his band found fame, however, Webb's health worsened. Refusing to allow his illness to stand in the way of his musical career, he continually booked the band to play extensive tours and theater engagements. As Barry Ulanov noted in *A History of Jazz,* Webb was wholly devoted to playing the drums and leading his band and countered the effects of his illness by explaining, "I've gotta keep my boys working."

In the early months of 1939, Webb began to collapse after shows, his face often bearing a grayish, sickly complexion. While playing on a riverboat outside Washington, D.C., he fell ill and had to be rushed to Johns Hopkins—the same Baltimore hospital where he had received treatment some 25 years earlier. Following an operation in June of 1939, he fell into an extremely weak state. As Ulanov wrote in *A History of Jazz,* "At eight o'clock in the evening of the sixteenth, with his relatives and close friends around him, Chick asked his mother to raise him up. Raised, he faced everybody in the room, grinned, jutted his jaw, and announced cockily, 'I'm sorry I got to go!'—and died."

To jazz artists of the Swing Era, Chick Webb was a musical father figure. In dance halls throughout the United States musicians such as Gene Krupa crowded around bandstands to study Webb's drum style. Per-

haps Krupa best summed up his mentor when he exclaimed in *Modern Drummer,* "He had style!" For it was Webb's tasteful control and use of the drum kit that enabled him to help modernize the whole concept of jazz percussion. Years later, music writer Helen Oakley Dance recalled in *Drummin' Men: The Heartbeat of Jazz, the Swing Years* how Webb would boast that "ain't nobody gonna cut me or my band." In his short 30 years, he more that lived up this pronouncement, leaving behind a musical legacy that continues to awe jazz historians and listeners who recall a time when the "King of the Savoy" reigned.

Selected discography

Stompin' at the Savoy (recorded 1936), Circle, 1985.
Spinnin' the Webb, Decca Jazz, 1994.
Chick Webb Volume 1—A Legend: 1929-1936, MCA.
Chick Webb Volume 2—King of the Savoy: 1937-1939, Decca.
Rhythm Man: 1934-35, Hep.
Strictly Jive 1936-1938, MCA.
1939 Radio Recordings, Tax.

With Ella Fitzgerald

Ella Fitzgerald With Chick Webb, Ace of Hearts.
Ella Swings the Band, MCA.

Sources

Books

Korall, Burt, *Drummin' Men: The Heartbeat of Jazz, the Swing Years,* Shirmer Books, 1990.
Lewis, Levering David, *When Harlem Was in Vogue,* Oxford University Press, 1989.
Nicholson, Stuart, *Ella Fitzgerald,* Victor Gollanez, 1993.
Schuller, Gunther, *The Swing Era: The Development of Jazz, 1930-1945,* Oxford University Press, 1989.
The Story of Jazz by the Men Who Made it, edited by Nat Shapiro and Nat Hentoff, Dover Publications, 1966.
Ulanov, Barry, *A History of Jazz in America,* Viking Press, 1952.

Periodicals

Modern Drummer, January 1988.
Jazz Journal International, April 1986; February 1989.

—John Cohassey

Paul Weller

Singer, songwriter

Photograph by Lawrence Watson, courtesy of Polygram Label Group

Rock icons are often and easily trapped within the legend that they and the media create around them, but not in the case of Paul Weller. The singer-songwriter jumped to the forefront of English alternative rock fame in the late 1970s via the Jam, which Vic Garbarini of *Musician* later dubbed "*the* British pop phenomenon of the early 80s." Weller then effected an impressive escape from the demands and expectations of this first public persona, reinventing himself in the context of a very different but also very successful soul-oriented duo, the Style Council. With both bands, he scored a remarkable string of Top Ten singles and earned a reputation for a commitment to his music and his politics. He also later embarked on a solo career, pursuing a rigorous touring schedule and achieving commercial and critical success.

Weller grew up in a working-class home in the town of Woking in Surrey, England, where he was born on May 25, 1958. Years later, Weller would wax poetic about the sense of community that reigned in that neighborhood. In an interview with *Melody Maker* he told Paolo Hewitt about "Stanley Road in Woking, which is all terraced houses, and you could leave your back door open and no-one would rip you off. The neighbours would be walking in and out and there's a general working-class integrity which has now vanished."

Without an environment that offered him any formal training, Weller was nonetheless drawn into music at an early age, inspired by the then-emerging rock that he heard around him. "The whole reason I started playing music when I was 12 or 13 was because of the Beatles," he told Adam Sweeting of *Melody Maker* in 1984, "so I was brought up on all that and I did believe in it."

Created the Jam

Hewitt, writing for *Melody Maker* in October of 1982, right after the Jam announced that it was disbanding, traced the roots of group to 1972, when Weller played sets with his school friend Steve Brookes at local working men's clubs. By 1973 the duo had expanded with the addition of Nigel Harris and Dave Waller. In 1975 and 1976, however, the lineup gradually shifted and Weller was the only remaining original member; Brookes, Harris, and Waller left and were replaced by Rick Buckler and Bruce Foxton. This trio would constitute the Jam for the next six years.

By the end of 1976 the band had coalesced around Weller, who performed most of the lead guitar and vocals and wrote most of the songs. That year, the trio headed for London, where they broke into the circuit of

Born Paul Weller, May 25, 1958, in Woking, Surrey, England; married Dee C. Lee, 1986; children: John.

Began playing sets with Steve Brookes as the Jam at working men's clubs in England, early 1970s; Nigel Harris and Dave Waller joined group, 1973; Brookes, Harris, and Waller left group, c. 1975 and 1976; Rick Buckler and Bruce Foxton joined Weller, c. 1976; group signed with Polydor Records and released debut album, *In the City,* 1977; founded *Jamming* magazine, 1981; founder and owner of Respond Records, 1981-86; the Jam dissolved, 1982; Weller formed duo Style Council with keyboardist Mick Talbot, 1983; released debut single, "Speak Like a Child," Polydor, 1983; released U.S. debut, *Introducing the Style Council,* Polygram, 1983; released U.K. debut, *Café Bleu,* Polydor, 1984; formed and disbanded Paul Weller Movement, 1990; Weller released debut solo album, *Paul Weller,* Go! Discs, 1992.

Addresses: *Record company*—Go! Discs, 825 Eighth Ave., New York, NY 10019.

clubs that nurtured the punk scene. "The Jam's first London gigs collided with the emergence of punk," Paolo Hewitt wrote in *Melody Maker,* "and the group, sporting mohair suits, soon gained a following thanks to Weller's fast, energetic songs." Garbarini later described this earliest incarnation of the band as "a sinewy, somewhat brittle punk version of the Who in hyperdrive."

Early in 1977, the Jam had secured a contract with Polydor Records. The group's first recording, a single released in the spring of 1977 called "In the City," just cracked the British Top 40. It was, at the very least, an auspicious beginning. The debut album, also called *In the City,* claimed the Number 20 position. By August a second single, "All Around the World," rose to Number 13. The album release preceded the band's pair of first serious tours: the U.K. tour introduced the Jam to an already enthusiastic audience, while the U.S. tour—characteristic of the band's relationship to American audiences—was not particularly successful.

Back at home, however, the Jam was already solidly ensconced on the "mod revival" landscape. In December of 1977, the band's second album, *This Is the Modern World,* almost made the Top 20 and kicked off

another English tour. The next few years witnessed a very regular output from the trio, including their first world tour in 1979 and a consistently enthusiastic reception from the English market. Their chart hits included a long list of singles, among them "Down in the Tube Station at Midnight," "Strange Towns," and "The Eton Rifles" in 1978 and 1979. In 1980 they were graced with another string of hit singles, including "Going Underground" and "Start." When "Going Underground" topped the charts upon its release, *Melody Maker's* Hewitt described the event as "reminiscent of the Beatles at their height." The Jam's albums were also making it into the British Top Five and finally beginning to edge into the U.S. Top 200.

Weller's Politics Integral to Band

Weller's public persona seemed to embody the Jam's angry, nonconformist attitude; he rejected even the usual pretensions of rock star rebels. Discussing a song from *The Gift* in *Melody Maker,* Weller celebrated it as "a smack in the face to all those shitty groups I detest," which he characterized as "showbiz and escapist." Weller would later express a similar contempt to *Musician's* Garbarini, explaining his sense that "rock culture's a myth, it's not part of reality. From a historical point of view, it's always been a way to escape and live out your fantasies."

Weller's politics also played a vital role in shaping his music. He maintains an uncompromising anticapitalist criticism of government. Explaining his political beliefs to Hewitt in March, Weller expressed himself with a vehemence that the public by then considered characteristic of the singer: "Obviously the first thing you have to do is get rid of this government, but I'd like to get rid of all governments really and replace them with people's councils that are re-elected every six months. It's something that you'd have to implant now and you'd only see the fruits in 100 years time or something. But unless you start doing something now it's just f——ed." He was notorious for declaring such opinions to the press, but his convictions also showed through in his activities and in his song lyrics, which were as much about the struggles of the working-class as about the romantic longings of classless teenagers.

As the band's reputation and production cycle became stable, Weller allowed himself to expand into other venues. In 1981 he started a magazine called *Jamming* and his own label, Respond Records. A breakdown early in 1982 prompted him to swear off alcohol, which further increased his restlessness. Since his rebel stance was actually less about image than about politics, Weller became uncomfortable with the band's security; he began tinkering with it, altering the Jam's music to suit his own need to experiment and take risks. The 1982 release *The Gift* featured an infusion of some retro-soul into the alternative rock sound.

Moved On to the Style Council

During the summer of 1982 Weller's sense of stasis had become so profound that he decided to disband the Jam, despite the band's unmitigated reign on the British alternative rock scene. The group announced the breakup in October of 1982, promising to complete one last tour before parting for good in 1983. Explaining that he wanted the group to "finish with dignity," as quoted by Paolo Hewitt in *Melody Maker,* Weller declared, "We have achieved all we can together as a group ... both musically and commercially." The Jam went out with a bang, their last performances accompanied by the reissue of all of the band's singles and several albums. They were back on the U.K. charts.

Weller acknowledged the sense of shock that Jam fans felt, noting in an interview in November of 1982 with *Melody Maker*'s Hewitt that the band had "become such an institution, such an establishment." Trying to explain his motivation in breaking up the band, Weller confessed to Hewitt that he "was frightened by the security of the Jam." Furthermore, as Hewitt argued, Weller's critics "fail to comprehend ... the enormous faith Weller has in music as a positive force and his breaking up of the group is perhaps the finest example of this belief."

Although Weller had briefly toyed with the idea of pursuing a solo career, he formed the Style Council with keyboardist Mick Talbot only a year after the Jam disbanded. Signed with Polydor, the duo became a vehicle for the soul-based sound that Weller had begun exploring in the Jam's last years. Weller found a more amenable atmosphere for that work with Talbot, and the two began recording cuts with pronounced soul, jazz, and R&B inflections. "I think the time is right for a new way of presenting music without the usual bullshit," Weller told Brian Harrigan of *Melody Maker* on the dawn of the Style Council early in 1983.

"I wanted Mick Talbot in my new group because I believe him to be the finest young jazz/soul organist in the country," Weller explained in *Melody Maker,* "and also because he too shares a hatred of the rock myth and rock culture." Although the sound had shifted, Weller stressed that his motives as a public figure remained largely the same. That summer, he told *Melody Maker* that "the level of commitment in the Style Council is higher, actually ... in the six months we've been going we've done more than I've ever done in the past."

In particular, the Style Council played regularly at charity venues, with proceeds generally going to working-class causes; Weller also earmarked the profits for certain singles, including "The Money-Go-Round," to benefit specific causes. The Style Council announced its political commitment with its first live performance at the May Day Show for Peace and Jobs, a music festival supporting leftist politics. By 1985 *Melody Maker*'s Barry McIlheney would dub the band "Europe's leading social workers." The Style Council also demonstrated their support for the Labour Party in 1986, taking part in the "Red Wedge" tour and hoping to spark political interest in young Brits.

> "Music has a lot of responsibility to live up to—it has to supply the fight which is missing in our culture."

The Style Council's first singles demonstrated quite soundly that Weller had not sacrificed commercial success in his search of a new sound: "Speak Like a Child," the duo's first single, went to Number Four on the British charts. It was followed by a pair of Number 11 hits, "The Money-Go-Round" and "Solid Bond in Your Heart." A first EP, *Paris,* rose to the Number Three spot, where it was eventually eclipsed by 1984's official debut album, *Café Bleu,* which peaked at Number Two. "My Ever Changing Moods" emerged as one of the strongest cuts from the album, taking a solid Number Five spot on U.K. charts.

While the Style Council's first U.S. release, *Introducing the Style Council,* did about as well as Jam albums ever did with U.S. audiences, the second U.S. album, called *My Ever Changing Moods,* actually broke the Top 100 in 1984, rising to the Number 56 spot. *High Fidelity*'s Steven Rea noted, "Weller ... has refined and, to some extent, redefined his style and music with his new combo," but concluded that "whether it will win where the Jam did not—in America—remains to be seen. My bet is no: Paul Weller is still Paul Weller no matter what band he's fronting." While Weller's new experiments went over well with English buyers, the American market was not especially receptive. The Style Council's video for "Long Hot Summer" couldn't win airplay on MTV, because, as Weller told Garbarini, "it's too R&B."

After the release of *My Ever Changing Moods, Musician*'s Gabarini placed the Style Council within a broader movement to return to rock music roots. He mused, "So far it's only been Weller and a few others who understand the implications of what's happening, who see clearly that this is a necessary therapeutic step towards the formulations of new values, not just another fad." Garbarini also speculated that "being the singleminded, intense lad that he is, Weller has extended his search back beyond Motown to black pop's real roots, gospel music."

For Weller, as Garbarini suggested, the meaning was ultimately not about market, but about politics. "There was an English soul group in the '60s," Weller told Garbarini, "who referred to music as the new religion, and that's how it is. Music has a lot of responsibility to live up to—it has to supply the fight which is missing in our culture right now. As far as I'm concerned, religion is pretty much dead on its feet, and politics is just a waste of time at the moment, so young people have nowhere else to put their faith."

Weller maintained his usual level of involvement in political activism, taking part in another "Aid" concert in the fall of 1984, this one in support of coal miners on strike, and participating in the international Live Aid concerts before the Red Wedge. In the meantime, the Style Council added more titles to their list of U.K. chart hits: 1984 saw "You're the Best Thing" reach Number Five and "Shout to the Top" climb to Number Seven. In 1985 "Walls Come Tumbling Down" claimed the Number Six spot, and *Our Favorite Shop* spent a week in the Number One position on British charts. McIlheney, commenting on the "considerable acclaim" that greeted the album, predicted that the Style Council were likely to be "going on and moving up for some time to come."

Dissolved Style Council

Weller made some major changes in 1986, including closing down Respond Records. He also married a former singing partner, Dee C. Lee, in December; their son John was born two years later in June. The Style Council remained a productive band until 1990; they recorded several more albums and many more hit singles along the way, although they didn't perform live after 1988. By 1990, however, Weller would decide that he needed to catalyze another change in his music career: he dissolved the Style Council at the beginning of the year and by the fall of 1990, announced the formation of the Paul Weller Movement. The band proved to be only a brief experiment and had no releases. Following that tepid effort, Weller receded from public life and the music business, his first real break.

In an interview with Gary Graff of the *Detroit Free Press,* Weller articulated what those intervening years were like for him. "There was a lot of change for me at that time. I was turning 30, and that freaked me out.... I always figured that was the end of the road when you hit 30. So I definitely had a couple of years of being quiet, just kind of finding myself. It was a period to sit back and reassess what I was doing, what I wanted to do in the future. I started thinking about whether I wanted to continue doing music. I was looking at *why* I was doing it, what were my motives for wanting to do music?"

Encountered First Flop

When his first solo album, *Paul Weller,* hit the market in 1992, the artist encountered the first flop in a 16-year career. Not only did many reviewers pan the album, but some even perceived Weller as letting go of the principles that had set him apart earlier in his career. "I can't find Weller here," declared Steve Sutherland of *Melody Maker*. "Weller, who once gnashed and growled and writhed against the system like a mad dog in a muzzle," he elaborated, "is now making music out of habit, just for the sake of it."

Of course, Weller had originally put to rest the phenomenal career of the Jam because he didn't want to be making music for the routine of it. Ultimately, Sutherland felt that the album was "utterly bereft of virtue." Critical of Weller's "obsession" with soul music, Thom Jurek wrote in Detroit's *Metro Times* that the album "comes off sounding like little more than a white boy fantasy of a time that—for him—never was." In addition, *Rolling Stone* reviewer Kara Manning labeled Weller "a thirtysomething Brit with an identity crisis," and she noted with regret that the album's "moments of coherent beauty are countered by episodes of confused ingenuity."

Spin, however, summarized the very different critical reception that greeted Weller's second solo effort, released in 1994. Announcing that "the breadth of material on *Wild Wood* puts Weller back at the top of his game," Jonathan Bernstein also noted that the British public concurred, receiving the album "with fulsome praise and brisk across-the-counter activity." Scott Schinder in *Pulse!* reported that the album "reestablished Weller as a major star in the U.S. and Europe." Bernstein also heaped praise on Weller, whom he saw as "maturing like fine wine" as he produced "the most accomplished and affecting songs of his career." With the success of *Wild Wood,* Weller admitted to Schinder, "I kind of ignored America for a long time, but I'm quite interested in making it in the States now. I'm not sure why, but it just feels like it's the right time now."

Selected discography

Singles, with the Jam; on Polydor

"In the City," 1977.
"All Around the World," 1977.
"The Modern World," 1977.
"Down in the Tube Station at Midnight," 1978.
"Strange Towns," 1979.
"Eton Rifles," 1979.
"Going Underground," 1980.
"Start," 1980.

Singles, with the Style Council; on Polydor

"Speak Like a Child," 1983.
"The Money-Go-Round," 1983.
"My Ever Changing Moods," 1984.
"You're the Best Thing," 1984.
"Shout to the Top," 1984.
"Walls Come Tumbling Down," 1985.
"Solid Bond in Your Heart."

Albums; with the Jam; on Polydor

In the City, 1977.
This Is the Modern World (includes "The Modern World" and "All Around the World"), 1977.
All Mod Cons (includes "Down in the Tube Station at Midnight"), 1978.
Setting Sons (includes "Eton Rifles" and "Strange Towns"), 1980.
Sound Affects (includes "Start"), 1980.
The Gift, 1982.
Dig the New Breed, 1982.
Snap!, 1983.
Live Jam, 1994.

Albums; with the Style Council

Paris (EP), Polydor, 1983.
Introducing the Style Council (includes "Long Hot Summer," "Money-Go-Round," and "Speak Like a Child"), Polygram, 1983.
Café Bleu, Polydor, 1984.
My Ever Changing Moods (includes "My Ever Changing Moods"), Geffen, 1984.
Our Favorite Shop, Polydor, 1985.
Internationalists, Geffen, 1985.
Home and Abroad, Polydor, 1986.
The Cost of Loving, Polydor, 1987.
Confessions of a Pop Group, Polydor, 1988.
Singular Adventures of the Style Council (includes "You're the Best Thing," "Walls Come Tumbling Down," "Shout to the Top," and "Solid Bond in Your Heart"), Polydor, 1989.

Solo albums

Paul Weller, Go! Discs, 1992.
Wild Wood, Go! Discs, 1994.

Sources

Books

Rock Movers and Shakers, edited by Dafydd Rees and Luke Crampton, Billboard Books, 1991.

Periodicals

Detroit Free Press, November 13, 1992.
High Fidelity, January 1994.
Melody Maker, March 13, 1982; October 30, 1982; November 6, 1982; February 19, 1983; August 13, 1983; March 24, 1984; February 23, 1985; July 20, 1985; November 17, 1990; August 28, 1992.
Metro Times (Detroit), October 28, 1992.
Modern Drummer, July 1993.
Musician, April 1984; October 1992.
People, January 18, 1993.
Pulse!, September 1992; July 1994.
Rolling Stone, November 26, 1992.
Spin, October 1992; April 1994.

Additional information for this profile was obtained from Go! Discs publicity materials.

—Paul E. Anderson

Nancy Wilson

Singer

Courtesy of John Levy Enterprises, Inc.

Self-taught jazz, pop, and rhythm and blues vocalist Nancy Wilson released her first album, *Like in Love,* in April of 1960 and went on to record 55 more albums between 1960 and 1994. Wilson's unique vocal style melds a jazzy elegance with an earthy, heartfelt blues timbre, and more than 30 of her LPs between 1960 and 1976 were prominent on the *Billboard* music charts.

Wilson is noted for choosing songs with lyrics that tell a compelling tale as well as provide melodic pleasure. The singer strives to avoid being categorized into a particular musical slot—such as jazz, pop, or blues—and prefers to be classified only as a "song stylist." Adept at creating an array of musical moods, she upholds in her songs the theme of timeless love. Wilson balks at being dubbed a jazz singer, telling Zan Stewart of the *Los Angeles Times,* "I don't scat ... I just sing my songs." She added, "If the material doesn't have feeling and warmth, I don't want to do it.... My strongest suit is the big ballad."

In the course of her long career, Wilson has also ventured into the realm of television, garnering an Emmy Award for NBC's *The Nancy Wilson Show: Red, Hot, & Cool,* which was televised in 1967 and 1968. On the Fox television comedy *Sinbad,* Wilson portrayed the comedian's mother, Louise, in 1993 and 1994. She has also enjoyed cameo appearances on *The Tonight Show, I Spy, The Cosby Show, The Ed Sullivan Show, The Carol Burnett Show, Hawaii Five-O, The Today Show,* and *Police Story.* Wilson gave talk-show host Arsenio Hall his first break when she asked him to open for her during a concert tour. As a result, she was a frequent guest on *The Arsenio Hall Show.*

Nancy Wilson was born in Chillicothe, a small town in southern Ohio, and was raised in Columbus, Ohio. She knew by the age of four that she had a strong singing voice. She sang in church choirs throughout her childhood, attempting to emulate such early influences as Dinah Washington, Nat King Cole, Billie Holiday, Ruth Brown, Louis Jordan, Billy Eckstine, and Jimmy Scott. By the time Wilson was in her mid-teens, she was performing in theater clubs in the Columbus area and perfecting her sultry signature style. She also appeared on the local television show *Skyline Melody.*

Two of Wilson's grounding influences were her mother and stepmother, both of whom provided constant encouragement and unflagging emotional support. By the time she was a teen, Wilson had moved in with her father, Olden, and stepmother, Bertha. Wilson's mother lived only a few blocks away, and along with her six younger siblings, Nancy was raised in an atmosphere of strong family unity and community ties.

For the Record . . .

Born February 20, 1937, in Chillicothe, OH; daughter of Olden (an iron foundry worker) and Lillian (a housekeeper) Wilson; married Kenny Dennis (a drummer), 1960 (divorced 1970); married Reverend Wiley Burton; children: (first marriage) Kenneth "Kacy" Dennis Jr. Wilson; (second marriage) Samantha, Sheryl. *Education:* Attended Central State College in Ohio.

Began singing in church choirs as a child; performed in theater clubs in Columbus, OH, area and appeared on local television show *Skyline Melody* as a teen; toured U.S. and Canada with Rusty Bryant's Carolyn Club Band; New York Institute of Technology, New York City, secretary, beginning in 1959; signed with Capitol Records, 1959, and released debut album, *Like in Love,* 1960. Television appearances include *The Nancy Wilson Show: Red, Hot, & Cool,* 1967-68; *Sinbad,* 1993-94; and guest spots on *The Tonight Show, I Spy, The Cosby Show, The Ed Sullivan Show, The Carol Burnett Show, Hawaii Five-O, The Today Show,* and *Police Story.*

Selected awards: Grammy Award, 1964, for *How Glad I Am;* Grammy Award nominations, 1965, for *Gentle Is My Love,* 1988, for *Forbidden Lover,* and 1994, for *With My Lover Beside Me;* Emmy Award for *The Nancy Wilson Show: Red, Hot, & Cool;* winner of Tokyo Song Festival, 1983; received star on Hollywood Walk of Fame, 1990; Image Award, National Association for the Advancement of Colored People (NAACP); Essence Award, 1992; Martin Luther King Center for Social Change award, 1993; Turner Broadcasting Trumpet Award for Outstanding Achievement, 1994; Whitney M. Young Award; honorary doctorate from Berkeley College of Music.

Addresses: *Management*—Lynn Coles Productions, P.O. Box 93-1198, Los Angeles, CA 90093.

After Wilson graduated from high school in Ohio, she attended Central State College, planning to be a teacher. She left school, however, in favor of touring with Rusty Bryant's Carolyn Club Band in Columbus and performed for three years throughout the United States and Canada. While touring, Wilson met jazz saxophonist Julian "Cannonball" Adderley, who became a close friend and would later record an album with her.

Adderley helped Wilson define her professional goals, which were to remain a solo recording artist, record albums for Capitol Records, and to persuade Adderley's manager, John Levy, to work with her. Upon moving to New York City in 1959, the singer gave herself six months to reach these goals. She worked as a secretary by day at the New York Institute of Technology and sang four evenings a week in nightclubs. Within only three weeks, Wilson attained all three of her goals: she recorded two solo demos, John Levy became her manager, and she signed with Capitol Records.

In 1960 Wilson married drummer Kenny Dennis and had a son, Kenneth "Kacy" Dennis Jr. Wilson. After ten years together, the couple divorced in 1970; Wilson would eventually marry Reverend Wiley Burton of Pittsburgh and have two daughters, Samantha Burton and Sheryl Burton.

Also in 1960, Wilson released her debut album, *Like in Love.* The singer's first recorded single was a heartrending version of "Guess Who I Saw Today?" Her second album, *Something Wonderful,* followed six months later. In early 1961, she released *The Swingin's Mutual,* and her first big rhythm and blues hit, "Save Your Love for Me," was put out in 1962.

In 1964 Wilson received a Grammy Award for *How Glad I Am* and a year later earned a Grammy nomination for *Gentle Is My Love.* Wilson's third Grammy nomination came in 1988 for *Forbidden Lover,* and her fourth followed in 1992 for *With My Lover Beside Me.*

Wilson learns songs by listening to the melody as opposed to learning how to read music. A large part of her success is due to two factors: instinctually knowing which songs best set off her rich, flexible voice and choosing memorable, classic songs to record. The Duke Ellington/Billy Strayhorn composition "Day Dream," Bonnie Raitt's "I Can't Make You Love Me," and Stephen Sondheim's "I Remember" are examples of songs that Wilson successfully chose to showcase her vocal talents. Other works, including Wilson's 1991 album *With My Lover Beside Me,* which features a collection of previously unpublished lyrics written by Johnny Mercer set to music by Barry Manilow, were further evidence of her distinctive taste.

In 1994 Wilson released her fifty-fifth album, *Love, Nancy.* Reviewer Harry Allen commented in *Vibe,* "With naked emotion as her fuel, Wilson's voice usually blasts through her orchestral ballads like a blowtorch through candle wax." Wilson expressed to Allen that she values popular singers like Anita Baker and Regina Belle, noting, "They've got emotion ... very much like me." She continued, "There are some really phenomenal voices out there. We just need people to write material that matters."

In addition to her active recording career, Wilson has an abiding interest in charity work and has contributed generously to the Martin Luther King Center for Social Change, the National Heart Association, the Cancer Society, and the United Negro College Fund. She was given a star on the Hollywood Walk of Fame in 1990, and has received awards such as the National Association for the Advancement of Colored People (NAACP) Image Award, a 1994 Trumpet Award for outstanding achievement from the Turner Broadcasting Company, the 1992 Essence Award, the Whitney M. Young Award, and an honorary doctorate from the Berkeley College of Music. She was also the winner of the 1983 Tokyo Song Festival. In addition to her philanthropic endeavors, Wilson successfully—and tirelessly—divides her time between family, concert tours, and television work.

Selected discography

On Capitol Records

Like in Love, 1960.
Something Wonderful, 1960.
The Swingin's Mutual, 1961.
Nancy Wilson/Cannonball Adderley Quintet, 1962.
Hello Young Lovers, 1962.
Broadway—My Way, 1963.
Hollywood—My Way, 1963.
Yesterday's Love Songs, Today's Blues, 1963.
Today, Tomorrow, Forever, 1964.
How Glad I Am, 1964.
The Nancy Wilson Show at the Coconut Grove, 1965.
Nancy Wilson Today—My Way, 1965.
Gentle Is My Love, 1965.
From Broadway With Love, 1966.
A Touch of Love Today, 1966.
Tender Loving Care, 1966.
Nancy—Naturally, 1966.
Just for Now, 1967.
Lush Life, 1967.
Welcome to My Love, 1968.
Easy, 1968.
The Best of Nancy Wilson, 1968.
Sound of Nancy Wilson, 1968.
Nancy, 1969.
Son of a Preacher Man, 1969.
Close Up, 1969.
Hurt So Bad, 1969.

Can't Take My Eyes off You, 1970.
Now I'm a Woman, 1970.
Double Play, 1971.
Right to Love, 1971.
But Beautiful, 1971.
I Know I Love Him, 1973.
All in Love Is Fair, 1974.
Come Get to This, 1975.
This Mother's Daughter, 1976.
I've Never Been to Me, 1977.
Music on My Mind, 1978.
Life, Love & Harmony, 1979.
Take My Love, 1980.

Other

At My Best, A.S.I., 1981.
Echoes of an Era, Elektra, 1982.
What's New, EMI (Japan), 1982.
Your Eyes, Nippon Columbia, 1983.
I'll Be a Song, Interface (Japan), 1983.
Godsend, Interface (Japan), 1984.
(With Ramsey Lewis) *The Two of Us,* Columbia, 1986.
(With the Crusaders) *The Good and Bad Times,* MCA, 1986.
Keep You Satisfied, Columbia, 1986.
Forbidden Lover, Columbia, 1987.
Nancy Now!, Columbia, 1988.
A Lady With a Song, Columbia, 1990.
With My Lover Beside Me, Columbia, 1991.
Love, Nancy, Columbia, 1994.

Sources

Books

Gillett, Charlie, *The Sound of the City: The Rise of Rock and Roll,* Dutton, 1970.

Periodicals

Black Voice News, April 24, 1994.
Ebony, June 1992; January 1993; July 1994.
Essence, May 1992.
Jet, February 24, 1992; April 20, 1992.
Los Angeles Times, March 27, 1994; December 17, 1993.
Maclean's, August 12, 1991.
People, November 22, 1993.
Rexburg Standard Journal, April 14, 1994.
San Francisco Examiner, December 19, 1993.
Time, January 17, 1994.
Vibe, March 1995.

—B. Kimberly Taylor

Lester Young

Saxophonist

Saxophonist Lester Young had one of the memorable styles in twentieth-century jazz. Prez, or the President, as Young was nicknamed by singer Billie Holiday, played a spare and cerebral saxophone, though often a melancholy one. His tenor sax technique counterbalanced his peer Coleman Hawkins's lush, heavily ornamented tone. In his book *The Reluctant Art: The Growth of Jazz,* Benny Green described the difference between the two artists: "Where Hawkins is profuse, Lester is pithy; where Hawkins is passionate, Lester is reflective."

Young's presence on the bandstand, with his horn up and out at a 45 degree angle, was striking. Six feet tall with green eyes and reddish hair, Young was the archetypal hipster, wearing flashy double-breasted suits and pork-pie hats. His phrases, both in words and music, became legendary among other musicians. With the Count Basie Orchestra in the 1930s, Young defined the ideal for solo improvisations. In the 1950s he associated with the bebop innovators, such as alto saxophonist Charlie Parker, but he remained singular, a bridge between the hot jazz and the cool. Critic John Hammond, writing for *Down Beat* magazine in 1937, called Young "without a doubt the greatest tenor player in the country ... the most original and inventive saxophonist I have ever heard."

Born on August 27, 1909, in Woodville, Mississippi, Young soon moved to Algiers, across the river from New Orleans. His mother was a Creole who taught school; Young's father, Willis Handy, whom Young hardly knew, was an itinerant musician. Young grew up during the period in New Orleans when King Oliver, Louis Armstrong, Jelly Roll Morton, and Sidney Bechet were creating jazz. Young remembered chasing after wagons loaded with players and distributing the musicians' handbills to the gathering crowds. Other jobs included shining shoes and delivering newspapers. When he turned ten, Young's existence drastically changed. His father returned and his parents divorced. Lester and his siblings, Irma and Lee, went with their father on the road, moving to Memphis, Tennessee, then to Minneapolis, Minnesota. Everyone in the family was a member of Willis Handy's band; Lester played drums and, later, alto saxophone.

Willis Handy was a stern taskmaster who demanded that his children learn to read music and who punished missteps. As a teenager, Lester evidenced a whimsical nature that often brought him into conflict with his father. Young split with his family as they were embarking on a tour through Texas and New Mexico in 1927. He then joined a succession of other bands. In 1928, while traveling with Art Bronson's Bostonians, Young made

Born Lester Willis Young, August 27, 1909, in Woodville, MS; died March 14, 1959, in New York, NY; son of Willis Handy (a bandleader) and Lizetta; married first wife, Beatrice (marriage ended); lived with common law spouse, Mary, 1937-46; married second wife, also named Mary, 1948; children: Lester, Jr., Yvette.

Played with family band, 1919-27; toured with Art Bronson's Bostonians and other bands, 1928-34; joined Count Basie Orchestra, then groups led by Fletcher Henderson and Andy Kirk; tenor saxophonist for Count Basie, 1936-40; played with brother Lee in Los Angeles, 1941; guest soloist for bands in New York City, 1941-44; recorded *Jumpin' With Symphony Sid*, 1947; performed at Charlie Parker's Birdland club, 1949 and 1951-54; toured United States and Europe 1952-57. *Military service:* U.S. Army, 1944-45.

Awards: Named greatest tenor saxophonist ever, Leonard Feather poll, 1956; elected posthumously to *Down Beat* Hall of Fame, 1959.

the tenor sax his primary instrument, apparently because the band's tenor player was too slow dressing for performances. Young also preferred the larger sax's deeper tone, although the alto more commonly got the solo part.

The Bostonians folded in September of 1930, and Young joined Walter Page's Blue Devils. An unpaid hotel bill in Beckley, West Virginia, left Young and the other musicians stranded and their equipment confiscated. Young managed to get back to Minneapolis, where he played at the Nest Club, and then moved to jazz capital Kansas City. William Basie, who became known as "Count," played in Kansas City, as did Mary Lou Williams, Ben Webster, and, later, Charlie Parker. Young met Bennie Moten through mutual friend and saxophonist Herschel Evans. With Moten's group, Young slipped easily into the "Kaycee" jazz style, which emphasized the second and fourth beats, as in the blues, and displayed short riffs repeated in different variations. The saxophonist became known for quiet bursts of invention that stunned listeners with their succinct power.

Young dueled Coleman Hawkins of the Fletcher Henderson Orchestra in a marathon "jam" session in 1933, an event that cemented his growing reputation. He joined

Count Basie in 1934 and worked with him on and off for the next six years. During this period, he made his first recordings in Chicago, including *Lady Be Good*. By 1938 Young was celebrated enough to perform with Benny Goodman at Carnegie Hall, and he joined Count Basie at the Famous Door and the Southland Cafe. Leaving Basie in December of 1940, Young went to Los Angeles to play with his brother Lee. World War II was looming, but Young was not interested in becoming a soldier. Eventually, a Federal Bureau of Investigations agent served induction notices on Jo Jones, the drummer, and Young at the Plantation Hotel in Los Angeles.

Young's experience in the army was a disaster. Shortly after his entrance, he was arrested for drug possession: barbiturates that he had received for an obstacle course injury and marijuana. Young did not use hard drugs but smoked marijuana and drank alcohol more and more heavily throughout his life. He was sentenced to a year's imprisonment at Fort Gordon, Georgia, and was dishonorably discharged on December 1, 1945.

Opinions are mixed on whether Young was effective as a saxophonist after the war. Some critics thought that he became less creative and more eccentric. His popularity, however, increased steadily in the late 1940s, until he was making as much as $50,000 a year. His idiosyncrasies while performing became more pronounced. He would approach the bandstand in tiny baby steps and referred to everyone by the names "Prez" or "Lady." He reportedly became paranoid, feeling as if no one liked him, and apparently resented his own success, which made his most original solos standard fare. Young played at the opening of Charlie Parker's Birdland in 1949 and toured Europe with Birdland groups and with Count Basie. In 1956 he was voted greatest tenor saxophonist ever by his fellow jazz musicians in a Leonard Feather poll.

Young was hospitalized several times in the 1950s for medical problems related to his drinking. By February of 1958 he had recovered enough to attempt recording again, but the results were weak. In the spring, he moved out of his house and into the Alvin Hotel on 52nd Street in New York City, across from Birdland. A woman named Elaine Swain nursed him there, and he gradually regained strength. He soon made an appearance with Jack Teagarden at the Newport Jazz Festival and arranged for new promotional materials. As a sign of his recovery, he made an engagement to play the Blue Note Club in Paris, France. The run proved to be his last—he started drinking again and was forced to return to New York. Young died at his hotel on March 15, 1959.

Many saxophone players have credited Young as their inspiration. Young noted that his style was much like

Billie Holiday's singing. In Holiday's autobiography, *Lady Sings the Blues,* Young is quoted as saying that he would listen to records of Holiday in duets with himself, and they would "sound like two of the same voices, if you don't be careful, you know—or the same mind or something like that." His personal and musical imagination are embedded in the textures of modern jazz.

Selected discography

(With others) *The Jazz Giants,* Verve, 1986.

The Complete Lester Young on Keynote (recorded 1944), Mercury, 1987.

(With others) *Lester Young and the Piano Giants,* Verve, 1988.

Live at Birdland 1951, Bandstand, 1992.

Jazz Immortal Series (reissue), Savoy Jazz, 1993.

The Master's Touch (reissue), Savoy Jazz, 1993.

(With others) *Rarities* (recorded 1941), Moon, 1993.

(With others) *Lester Young in Washington, D.C.* (recorded 1979), Fantasy/OJC, 1993.

(With others) *The Lester Young Trio* (reissue), Verve, 1994.

The Best of Lester Young, Pablo.

The Lester Young Story (Volumes 1-5), Columbia.

Count Basie: The Complete Collection of Count Basie Orchestra on Decca, MCA.

Kansas City Six and Five: Commodore Classics in Jazz, Commodore.

Prez and Friends, Commodore.

Saxophone Giants, RCA.

Pres: The Complete Savoy Recordings, Savoy.

Jazz at the Philharmonic: Bird and Pres the 46 Concerts, Verve.

Jazz at the Philharmonic: Lester Young Carnegie Blues, Verve.

The Sound of Jazz, Columbia.

Sources

Books

Delannoy, Luc, *Pres, The Story of Lester Young,* University of Arkansas Press, 1993.

Green, Benny, *The Reluctant Art: The Growth of Jazz,* Horizon Press, 1963.

Hammond, John, *John Hammond on Record: An Autobiography,* Ridge Press, 1977.

Holiday, Billie, with William Dufty, *Lady Sings the Blues,* Doubleday, 1956.

Porter, Lewis, *Lester Young,* Twayne, 1985.

Simon, George T., *The Big Bands,* Macmillan, 1967.

Stearns, Marshall, *The Story of Jazz,* Oxford Press, 1962.

Wilson, John S., *Jazz: The Transition Years,* Appleton, 1966.

Periodicals

Down Beat, November 2, 1955; March 7, 1956; March 1, 1962.

—*Paul E. Anderson*

Zap
Mama

Vocal group

Photograph by Marla Dawlat, © 1994 Luaka Bop

In 1993 Zap Mama—five European women vocalists of African descent—was offered the opportunity to do a Coca-Cola commercial; at first, the group resisted. "But we do like Robin Hood," Marie Daulne, the group's founder, told Melinda Newman of *Billboard* in 1994. "I thought there is money there that can go to help people. I see poor people and think, 'Maybe one day when Zap Mama is over, I can help people.' Then I thought, I can help people now."

The women in Zap Mama decided that they would use the income the commercial generated to build a school in Africa. That opportunity and its resolution is typical of the group, an *a capella* world music outfit that has helped the genre in its movement toward mainstream recognition. While Zap Mama was born from a desire for cultural preservation rather than profit, it has won success at a business level: for eleven weeks, their United States debut album held the Number One position on *Billboard*'s world music chart. But the surplus of that success has gone back into furthering their initial motive, as the Coca Cola commercial demonstrated.

When Zap Mama was formed in 1990, Marie Daulne was the force behind it. Although all of the women in the original line-up considered Belgium their home, Daulne's complicated past exemplified the hybrid national identity that characterizes the group. In fact, that background became the subject of a 1991 documentary film, *Miziké Mama,* that went on to impress a wide audience in Europe and America, receiving awards at film festivals on both continents.

The daughter of a Belgian father and an African mother, Daulne was born in Zaire in the early 1960s, soon after the country threw off the fetters of Belgian imperialism. Daulne would have entered the world via a middle-class home in a major African city, except that uprisings in Zaire forced the family to flee after her father's death.

Daulne's mother took refuge at a nearby village of Pygmies. "My mother is Bantu," she told Larry Birnbaum in *Pulse!,* "but she is from the forest in the northeast near Sudan, not far from the pygmies. The rebel group killed the white people and threw them in the river, but the pygmies saved a lot of people." There is some confusion about the exact circumstances of Daulne's birth: Deborah Kirk recorded in *Harper's Bazaar* that Daulne was born before her mother fled into jungle; other reporters have generally claimed that Daulne was actually born in the Pygmy village. Nonetheless, it was that location that kept them safe.

"The rebels were terrified of the Pygmies," Daulne told Kirk, "because they were always singing. But they—

and the noises they made—protected us until my mother could take us to Belgium. The Pygmies who gave them refuge not only guaranteed Daulne's safety, but also provided her with the musical influence that would set her apart from other world music aspirants. When Daulne first created Zap Mama, she made the Pygmy chants an integral part of their sound. "The way the Pygmies sing is very spiritual," she told Kirk. "They repeat sounds over and over, and the vibration creates a trancelike state."

Once it was safe to do so, Daulne's mother moved the family to Belgium, where Daulne, her mother, five other sisters, and an aunt continued to sing the traditional music of Zaire and the pygmies. While in college, Daulne studied jazz before deciding that she wanted to focus on a different kind of sound—a sound that gathered and blended musical traditions from around the globe. The Antwerp School of Jazz provided her a brief period of formal training; Gene Santoro noted in the *Nation* that she also "studied Arab, Asian and African polyphony."

Zap Mama Founded

In 1989 Daulne was preparing music for a solo album when she decided to return to the jungle in Africa where she had started life to meet the Pygmies again. She discovered something else there as well—her musical vocation. "When I heard them chanting," she told Kirk, "I suddenly understood the sheer power of the human voice. I knew right then that I wanted to sing, too, to convey as much with my voice as I can."

Daulne also discovered that she couldn't work as a solo artist. "I saw in Zaire that I have to mix with other people," she told Birnbaum, "because with me alone, the polyphony is not there. I knew there must be singers in the world I could mix with, and I found them."

In 1990, Daulne started singing with Sabine Kabongo and Sylvie Nawasadio, neither of whom had a professional background. After the ensemble gathered four other women, they began performing in venues around their home city. The original group, like Daulne, displayed a mixed heritage. Daulne told Birnbaum, "We have a Zairean memory and a European memory, and together we find the same vibration, because we have European and Zairean music inside." She explained further her belief that that kind of hybrid could transcend differences by recognizing and playing with them: "We have French, English, Spanish, Arabic, Swahili, Zulu, Lingala, and Baboudou. And we invent a language—onomatopoeia. It's the language of humans, because every human makes the same sounds."

Gained a Following Abroad

Zap Mama received some of its initial support from the French Belgian Community Government's cultural department. Soon, however, the group came to the attention of Teddy Hillaert, a manager, through performances at the Ancienne Belgique in Brussels, where they made a strong impression on him. "It's a mixture of humor, dance, color; it's really powerful," Hillaert told *Billboard* writer Thom Duffy in 1993. "Their show sold out so quickly, I said 'This is amazing.'"

Hillaert decided to become a part of the phenomenon, signing on as Zap Mama's manager. Marc Hollander, the managing director of Crammed Discs, a Belgian label, also saw the quintet in 1991 and decided that he, too, wanted a contract with them. "Their mixed Afro-European orgins enable them to bridge the gap between both cultures," Hollander explained to Duffy. "They present Western audiences with an impression of Africa which is half-real and half-imaginary.... They research and reinterpret certain forms of traditional music, but from a semi-European standpoint, with a lot of humor, and a vision which doesn't lack social and political content." By the summer of 1991, Zap Mama was in the studio recording, and their self-titled debut album followed soon after in October of 1991. The European sales were impressive, and the album eventually went gold.

Zap Mama continued to pick up fans at a gradually accelerating pace, thanks to the Crammed Disc recording and their live performances. While the group's European following grew, Americans also began discovering the debut disc in import bins. The ensemble earned some of their early U.S. exposure through insightful deejays at a college radio station at the University of Santa Monica, where the album topped the station's unofficial charts for several weeks.

"We have a Zairean memory and a European memory, and together we find the same vibration, because we have European and Zairean music inside."
—Marie Daulne

A few astute reviewers began to take note of the quiet phenomenon. Marc Maes, writing for *Billboard* in the summer of 1992, dubbed Zap Mama "flavor of the month on the international circuit." Randall Grass heard the import disc in 1992 and spotlighted it in the *Village Voice*. "A circular close harmony pattern presents an extraterrestrial backdrop for a dreamy, at times Sam Cooke-ian lead melody," he noted. He praised their "positively ground-breaking amalgams of African, Arabic, and European melody, and snatches of South African *mbube* amidst a little Bulgarian *mystère*."

By 1992, Zap Mama was being watched by several American labels, including a new one created by David Byrne—the force that drove new wave supergroup the Talking Heads in the 1970s and 1980s—and his business partner, Yale Evelev. The offices at Luaka Bop, Byrne's label, received a Zap Mama video and CD that winter or spring, sent on from the French Music Office in New York. Executives from Luaka Bop and other companies came to New York City for a few weeks in July, when Zap Mama performed several engagements for the New Music Seminar, the annual convention for cutting-edge trends in the music industry.

Byrne and Evelev determined that Zap Mama would be the appropriate vehicle to launch the new label, while Daulne decided that Byrne would be a fitting sponsor of their U.S. career. "I don't know the music of this man, but I know this man is good," she told Duffy. "We have the same passion." Evelev informed Duffy that the quintet made a similar impression on him and Byrne; he noted, "It's very popular music but there's a real artistic underpinning to it. It's not somone saying, 'What can I do to be successful?' It's someone saying, 'This is the music I

want to do.'" *Adventures in Afropea 1: Zap Mama* repackaged the first Crammed Discs release for American listeners in 1993; *Billboard* would eventually declare it the best-selling world music album of the year.

As the line-up of the ensemble shifted in its first couple of years, before they had solid American marketing, reporters often offered conflicting lists of names. In the summer of 1993, *Billboard* recorded the vocalists as Daulne, Kabongo, Nawasadio, and Cécilia Kakonda. Larry Birnbaum, on the other hand, had a member list that consisted of Daulne, Kabongo, Nawasadio, Cecilia Kankonda, and Marie Cavenaile—the only member of solely Belgian descent. By the time Luaka Bop had the group's second album prepared for release, however, the line-up appeared to have solidified, Kabongo and Nawasadio staying with Daulne, while Sally Nyolo and Marie Afonso came on board.

Like the group's debut, *Sabsylma* met with very positive critical response and strong sales for its category. "Zap Mama is riding the crest of world music's growing wave of domestic and international acceptance," *Billboard's* Duffy wrote. "Previously," reported Daisann McLane in *Rolling Stone,* "other groups have attempted a poly-global sound, but the a capella women of Zap Mama are the first who have made this concept work—perhaps because they focus on the one instrument common to all world music"—the human voice. Amy Linden argued in *People* that Zap Mama "artfully and beautifully blurs cultural and linguistic distinctions." The *Nation's* Santoro was struck by the group's "lapping vocals and dazzlingly varied array of technical and sonic approaches."

Challenged Boundaries of Music Genres

Byrne and Evelev saw Zap Mama as an opportunity to challenge the boundaries of music categories, hoping that Zap Mama's appeal could seep over from world music into other genres. In particular, the label increased the group's U.S. exposure early in 1993, when the band travelled with the well-established alternative rock outfit 10,000 Maniacs. "We have tried to give Zap Mama the approach of a pop band, not a world music band," Hillaert told Duffy.

More pop music tours followed the release of *Sabsylmo,* including dates with jazz artist Bobby McFerrin and on David Byrne's own tour. The promoters made a special effort to draw on Zap Mama's strong stage performances. "The way to really understand Zap Mama," Peter Standish, a manager at Warner Bros., told *Billboard's* Newman, "is to see them [perform]. They are mesmerizing. That's how we got them on [television show]

'Arsenio Hall.' People from the show came down to a concert and were blown away. They really know how to work a crowd."

More than in U.S. sales, however, the members of Zap Mama feel their success lies in their reputation in Zaire, where bootleg tapes are distributed through an underground market. Here, rather than entertaining Western audiences and earning money, they can restore a sense of pride and history to Africans and Westerners of African descent. Daulne explained to Birnbaum that, "In Africa they want to change, to become like white people, but I tell them, 'Stay like you are.' In the beginning my mother didn't understand why I always asked her about traditional music, because everybody wants to do American-style music.... Colonization changed the mentality of our parents. After Zap Mama, my mother and my aunt began to sing together again, and now my aunt says, 'Thank you.'"

Selected discography

Zap Mama, Crammed Discs, 1991.

Adventures in Afropea 1: Zap Mama, Luaka Bop, 1993.
Sabsylma, Luaka Bop, 1994.

Sources

Billboard, June 20, 1992; August 7, 1993; April 2, 1994.
Down Beat, June 1993.
Harper's Bazaar, April 1993.
Nation, April 26, 1993.
People, March 22, 1993.
Pulse!, June 1993.
Rolling Stone, February 18, 1993.
Spin, February 1993.
Village Voice, December 29, 1992.

Additional information for this profile was obtained from Luaka Bop/Warner Bros. publicity materials.

—*Ondine E. Le Blanc*

Cumulative Indexes

Cumulative Subject Index

Volume numbers appear in **bold**.

273

Alpert, Herb **11**
Anka, Paul **2**
Atkins, Chet **5**
Bacharach, Burt **1**
Benson, George **9**
Berlin, Irving **8**
Bernstein, Leonard **2**
Bley, Carla **8**
Bley, Paul **14**
Braxton, Anthony **12**
Brubeck, Dave **8**
Burrell, Kenny **11**
Byrne, David **8**
    Also see Talking Heads
Cage, John **8**
Cale, John **9**
Casals, Pablo **9**
Clarke, Stanley **3**
Coleman, Ornette **5**
Cooder, Ry **2**
Cooney, Rory **6**
Copeland, Stewart **14**
Copland, Aaron **2**
Crouch, Andraé **9**
Davis, Chip **4**
Davis, Miles **1**
de Grassi, Alex **6**
Dorsey, Thomas A. **11**
Elfman, Danny **9**
Ellington, Duke **2**
Eno, Brian **8**
Enya **6**
Foster, David **13**
Gillespie, Dizzy **6**
Glass, Philip **1**
Gould, Glenn **9**
Grusin, Dave **7**
Guaraldi, Vince **3**
Hamlisch, Marvin **1**
Hancock, Herbie **8**
Handy, W. C. **7**
Hartke, Stephen **5**
Herrmann, Bernard **14**
Hunter, Alberta **7**
Isham, Mark **14**
Jarre, Jean-Michel **2**
Jarrett, Keith **1**
Jones, Quincy **2**
Joplin, Scott **10**
Jordan, Stanley **1**
Kenny G **14**
Kern, Jerome **13**
Kitaro **1**
Kottke, Leo **13**
Lee, Peggy **8**
Lewis, Ramsey **14**
Lincoln, Abbey **9**
Lloyd Webber, Andrew **6**
Loewe, Frederick
    See Lerner and Loewe
Mancini, Henry **1**
Marsalis, Branford **10**
Marsalis, Ellis **13**
Masekela, Hugh **7**
Menken, Alan **10**

Metheny, Pat **2**
Mingus, Charles **9**
Monk, Meredith **1**
Monk, Thelonious **6**
Morton, Jelly Roll **7**
Nascimento, Milton **6**
Newman, Randy **4**
Ott, David **2**
Parker, Charlie **5**
Peterson, Oscar **11**
Ponty, Jean-Luc **8**
Porter, Cole **10**
Puente, Tito **14**
Reich, Steve **8**
Reinhardt, Django **7**
Ritenour, Lee **7**
Roach, Max **12**
Rollins, Sonny **7**
Rota, Nino **13**
Satriani, Joe **4**
Schickele, Peter **5**
Schuman, William **10**
Shankar, Ravi **9**
Shaw, Artie **8**
Shorter, Wayne **5**
Solal, Martial **4**
Sondheim, Stephen **8**
Sousa, John Philip **10**
Story, Liz **2**
Strayhorn, Billy **13**
Summers, Andy **3**
Sun Ra **5**
Takemitsu, Toru **6**
Talbot, John Michael **6**
Taylor, Billy **13**
Taylor, Cecil **9**
Thielemans, Toots **13**
Threadgill, Henry **9**
Tyner, McCoy **7**
Washington, Grover, Jr. **5**
Weill, Kurt **12**
Williams, John **9**
Wilson, Cassandra **12**
Winston, George
Winter, Paul **10**
Worrell, Bernie **11**
Yanni **11**
Zimmerman, Udo **5**

Conductors
Bacharach, Burt **1**
Bernstein, Leonard **2**
Casals, Pablo **9**
Copland, Aaron **2**
Domingo, Placido **1**
Fiedler, Arthur **6**
Herrmann, Bernard **14**
Jarrett, Keith **1**
Levine, James **8**
Mancini, Henry **1**
Marriner, Neville **7**
Masur, Kurt **11**
Mehta, Zubin **11**
Menuhin, Yehudi **11**
Rampal, Jean-Pierre **6**

Schickele, Peter **5**
Solti, Georg **13**
Toscanini, Arturo **14**
von Karajan, Herbert **1**
Welk, Lawrence **13**
Williams, John **9**
Zukerman, Pinchas **4**

Contemporary Dance Music
Abdul, Paula **3**
Aphex Twin **14**
Bee Gees, The **3**
B-52's, The **4**
Brown, Bobby **4**
Brown, James **2**
Cherry, Neneh **4**
Clinton, George **7**
Deee-lite **9**
De La Soul **7**
Depeche Mode **5**
Earth, Wind and Fire **12**
English Beat, The **9**
En Vogue **10**
Erasure **11**
Eurythmics **6**
Exposé **4**
Fox, Samantha **3**
Gang of Four **8**
Hammer, M.C. **5**
Harry, Deborah **4**
Ice-T **7**
Idol, Billy **3**
Jackson, Janet **3**
Jackson, Michael **1**
James, Rick **2**
Jones, Grace **9**
Madonna **4**
New Order **11**
Pet Shop Boys **5**
Prince **14**
    Earlier sketch in CM **1**
Queen Latifah **6**
Rodgers, Nile **8**
Salt-N-Pepa **6**
Simmons, Russell **7**
Summer, Donna **12**
Technotronic **5**
Village People, The **7**
Was (Not Was) **6**
Young M.C. **4**

Contemporary Instrumental/New Age
Ackerman, Will **3**
Clinton, George **7**
Collins, Bootsy **8**
Davis, Chip **4**
de Grassi, Alex **6**
Enigma **14**
Enya **6**
Hedges, Michael **3**
Isham, Mark **14**
Jarre, Jean-Michel **2**
Kitaro **1**
Kronos Quartet **5**
Story, Liz **2**

Summers, Andy **3**
Tangerine Dream **12**
Winston, George **9**
Winter, Paul **10**
Yanni **11**

Cornet
Cherry, Don **10**
Handy, W. C. **7**

Country
Acuff, Roy **2**
Alabama **1**
Anderson, John **5**
Arnold, Eddy **10**
Asleep at the Wheel **5**
Atkins, Chet **5**
Auldridge, Mike **4**
Autry, Gene **12**
Bellamy Brothers, The **13**
Black, Clint **5**
Bogguss, Suzy **11**
Boone, Pat **13**
Brooks, Garth **8**
Brooks & Dunn **12**
Brown, Clarence "Gatemouth" **11**
Brown, Marty **14**
Brown, Tony **14**
Buffett, Jimmy **4**
Byrds, The **8**
Campbell, Glen **2**
Carpenter, Mary-Chapin **6**
Carter, Carlene **8**
Carter Family, The **3**
Cash, Johnny **1**
Cash, June Carter **6**
Cash, Rosanne **2**
Chesnutt, Mark **13**
Clark, Roy **1**
Cline, Patsy **5**
Coe, David Allan **4**
Cooder, Ry **2**
Cowboy Junkies, The **4**
Crowe, J. D. **5**
Crowell, Rodney **8**
Cyrus, Billy Ray **11**
Daniels, Charlie **6**
DeMent, Iris **13**
Denver, John **1**
Desert Rose Band, The **4**
Diamond Rio **11**
Dickens, Little Jimmy **7**
Diffie, Joe **10**
Dylan, Bob **3**
Flatt, Lester **3**
Ford, Tennessee Ernie **3**
Frizzell, Lefty **10**
Gayle, Crystal **1**
Gill, Vince **7**
Gilley, Mickey **7**
Gilmore, Jimmie Dale **11**
Greenwood, Lee **12**
Griffith, Nanci **3**
Haggard, Merle **2**
Hall, Tom T. **4**

Harris, Emmylou **4**
Hartford, John **1**
Hay, George D. **3**
Hiatt, John **8**
Highway 101 **4**
Hinojosa, Tish **13**
Jackson, Alan **7**
Jennings, Waylon **4**
Jones, George **4**
Judd, Wynonna
   See Wynonna
Judds, The **2**
Kentucky Headhunters, The **5**
Ketchum, Hal **14**
Kristofferson, Kris **4**
Lang, K. D. **4**
Lawrence, Tracy **11**
LeDoux, Chris **12**
Lee, Brenda **5**
Little Feat **4**
Little Texas **14**
Louvin Brothers, The **12**
Loveless, Patty **5**
Lovett, Lyle **5**
Lynn, Loretta **2**
Lynne, Shelby **5**
Mandrell, Barbara **4**
Mattea, Kathy **5**
McBride, Martina **14**
McClinton, Delbert **14**
McEntire, Reba **11**
Miller, Roger **4**
Milsap, Ronnie **2**
Monroe, Bill **1**
Montgomery, John Michael **14**
Morgan, Lorrie **10**
Murphey, Michael Martin **9**
Murray, Anne **4**
Nelson, Willie **11**
   Earlier sketch in CM **1**
Newton-John, Olivia **8**
Nitty Gritty Dirt Band, The **6**
Oak Ridge Boys, The **7**
O'Connor, Mark **1**
Oslin, K. T. **3**
Owens, Buck **2**
Parsons, Gram **7**
   Also see Byrds, The
Parton, Dolly **2**
Pearl, Minnie **3**
Price, Ray **11**
Pride, Charley **4**
Rabbitt, Eddie **5**
Raitt, Bonnie **3**
Reeves, Jim **10**
Restless Heart **12**
Rich, Charlie **3**
Robbins, Marty **9**
Rodgers, Jimmie **3**
Rogers, Kenny **1**
Rogers, Roy **9**
Sawyer Brown **13**
Scruggs, Earl **3**
Seals, Dan **9**
Skaggs, Ricky **5**

Sonnier, Jo-El **10**
Statler Brothers, The **8**
Stevens, Ray **7**
Stone, Doug **10**
Strait, George **5**
Stuart, Marty **9**
Sweethearts of the Rodeo **12**
Texas Tornados, The **8**
Tillis, Mel **7**
Tillis, Pam **8**
Tippin, Aaron **12**
Travis, Merle **14**
Travis, Randy **9**
Tritt, Travis **7**
Tubb, Ernest **4**
Tucker, Tanya **3**
Twitty, Conway **6**
Van Shelton, Ricky **5**
Van Zandt, Townes **13**
Wagoner, Porter **13**
Walker, Jerry Jeff **13**
Watson, Doc **2**
Wells, Kitty **6**
West, Dottie **8**
Whitley, Keith **7**
Williams, Don **4**
Williams, Hank, Jr. **1**
Williams, Hank, Sr. **4**
Willis, Kelly **12**
Wills, Bob **6**
Wynette, Tammy **2**
Wynonna **11**
   Also see Judds, The
Yearwood, Trisha **10**
Yoakam, Dwight **1**
Young, Faron **7**

Dobro
Auldridge, Mike **4**
   Also see Country Gentlemen, The
   Also see Seldom Scene, The
Burch, Curtis
   See New Grass Revival, The
Knopfler, Mark **3**

Drums
   See **Percussion**

Dulcimer
Ritchie, Jean **4**

Fiddle
   See **Violin**

Film Scores
Anka, Paul **2**
Bacharach, Burt **1**
Berlin, Irving **8**
Bernstein, Leonard **2**
Blanchard, Terence **13**
Byrne, David **8**
   Also see Talking Heads
Cafferty, John
   See Beaver Brown Band, The
Cahn, Sammy **11**
Cliff, Jimmy **8**

Copeland, Stewart **14**
Copland, Aaron **2**
Crouch, Andraé **9**
Dibango, Manu **14**
Dolby, Thomas **10**
Donovan **9**
Eddy, Duane **9**
Elfman, Danny **9**
Ellington, Duke **2**
Ferguson, Maynard **7**
Gershwin, George and Ira **11**
Gould, Glenn **9**
Grusin, Dave **7**
Guaraldi, Vince **3**
Hamlisch, Marvin **1**
Hancock, Herbie **8**
Harrison, George **2**
Hayes, Isaac **10**
Hedges, Michael **3**
Herrmann, Bernard **14**
Isham, Mark **14**
Jones, Quincy **2**
Knopfler, Mark **3**
Lennon, John **9**
    Also see Beatles, The
Lerner and Loewe **13**
Mancini, Henry **1**
Marsalis, Branford **10**
Mayfield, Curtis **8**
McCartney, Paul **4**
    Also see Beatles, The
Menken, Alan **10**
Mercer, Johnny **13**
Metheny, Pat **2**
Nascimento, Milton **6**
Nilsson **10**
Peterson, Oscar **11**
Porter, Cole **10**
Reznor, Trent **13**
Richie, Lionel **2**
Robertson, Robbie **2**
Rollins, Sonny **7**
Rota, Nino **13**
Sager, Carole Bayer **5**
Schickele, Peter **5**
Shankar, Ravi **9**
Taj Mahal **6**
Waits, Tom **12**
    Earlier sketch in CM **1**
Weill, Kurt **12**
Williams, John **9**
Williams, Paul **5**
Willner, Hal **10**
Young, Neil **2**

Flute
Anderson, Ian
    See Jethro Tull
Galway, James **3**
Rampal, Jean-Pierre **6**
Ulmer, James Blood **13**
Wilson, Ransom **5**

Folk/Traditional
Arnaz, Desi **8**
Baez, Joan **1**
Belafonte, Harry **8**

Blades, Ruben **2**
Bloom, Luka **14**
Brady, Paul **8**
Bragg, Billy **7**
Buckley, Tim **14**
Bulgarian State Female Vocal
    Choir, The **10**
Byrds, The **8**
Carter Family, The **3**
Chapin, Harry **6**
Chapman, Tracy **4**
Cherry, Don **10**
Chieftains, The **7**
Childs, Toni **2**
Clegg, Johnny **8**
Cockburn, Bruce **8**
Cohen, Leonard **3**
Collins, Judy **4**
Colvin, Shawn **11**
Crosby, David **3**
    Also see Byrds, The
Cruz, Celia **10**
de Lucia, Paco **1**
DeMent, Iris **13**
Donovan **9**
Dr. John **7**
Dylan, Bob **3**
Elliot, Cass **5**
Enya **6**
Estefan, Gloria **2**
Feliciano, José **10**
Galway, James **3**
Gilmore, Jimmie Dale **11**
Gipsy Kings, The **8**
Griffith, Nanci **3**
Guthrie, Arlo **6**
Guthrie, Woodie **2**
Harding, John Wesley **6**
Hartford, John **1**
Havens, Richie **11**
Hinojosa, Tish **13**
Iglesias, Julio **2**
Indigo Girls **3**
Ives, Burl **12**
Khan, Nusrat Fateh Ali **13**
Kingston Trio, The **9**
Kottke, Leo **13**
Kuti, Fela **7**
Ladysmith Black Mambazo **1**
Larkin, Patty **9**
Lavin, Christine **6**
Leadbelly **6**
Lightfoot, Gordon **3**
Los Lobos **2**
Makeba, Miriam **8**
Masekela, Hugh **7**
McLean, Don **7**
Melanie **12**
Mitchell, Joni **2**
Morrison, Van **3**
Morrissey, Bill **12**
Nascimento, Milton **6**
N'Dour, Youssou **6**
Near, Holly **1**
Ochs, Phil **7**
O'Connor, Sinead **3**

Odetta **7**
Parsons, Gram **7**
    Also see Byrds, The
Paxton, Tom **5**
Peter, Paul & Mary **4**
Pogues, The **6**
Prine, John **7**
Proclaimers, The **13**
Redpath, Jean **1**
Ritchie, Jean, **4**
Rodgers, Jimmie **3**
Sainte-Marie, Buffy **11**
Santana, Carlos **1**
Seeger, Pete **7**
    Also see Weavers, The
Shankar, Ravi **9**
Simon, Paul **1**
Snow, Pheobe **4**
Story, The **13**
Sweet Honey in the Rock **1**
Taj Mahal **6**
Thompson, Richard **7**
Tikaram, Tanita **9**
Van Ronk, Dave **12**
Van Zandt, Townes **13**
Vega, Suzanne **3**
Wainwright III, Loudon **11**
Walker, Jerry Jeff **13**
Watson, Doc **2**
Weavers, The **8**

French Horn
Ohanian, David
    See Canadian Brass, The

Funk
Bambaataa, Afrika **13**
Brand New Heavies, The **14**
Brown, James **2**
Burdon, Eric **14**
    Also see War
Clinton, George **7**
Collins, Bootsy **8**
Fishbone **7**
Gang of Four **8**
Jackson, Janet **3**
Khan, Chaka **9**
Mayfield, Curtis **8**
Meters, The **14**
Parker, Maceo **7**
Prince **14**
    Earlier sketch in CM **1**
Red Hot Chili Peppers, The **7**
Stone, Sly **8**
Toussaint, Allen **11**
Worrell, Bernie **11**

Fusion
Anderson, Ray **7**
Beck, Jeff **4**
    Also see Yardbirds, The
Clarke, Stanley **3**
Coleman, Ornette **5**
Corea, Chick **6**
Davis, Miles **1**
Fishbone **7**

Robertson, Robbie **2**
Robillard, Duke **2**
Rodgers, Nile **8**
Rush, Otis **12**
Saliers, Emily
  See Indigo Girls
Santana, Carlos **1**
Satriani, Joe **4**
Scofield, John **7**
Segovia, Andres **6**
Shines, Johnny **14**
Skaggs, Ricky **5**
Slash
  See Guns n' Roses
Springsteen, Bruce **6**
Stewart, Dave
  See Eurythmics
Stills, Stephen **5**
Stuart, Marty **9**
Summers, Andy **3**
Taylor, Mick
  See Rolling Stones, The
Thielemans, Toots **13**
Thompson, Richard **7**
Tippin, Aaron **12**
Townshend, Pete **1**
Travis, Merle **14**
Tubb, Ernest **4**
Ulmer, James Blood **13**
Vai, Steve **5**
Van Halen, Edward
  See Van Halen
Van Ronk, Dave **12**
Vaughan, Jimmie
  See Fabulous Thunderbirds, The
Vaughan, Stevie Ray **1**
Wagoner, Porter **13**
Waits, Tom **12**
  Earlier sketch in CM **1**
Walker, Jerry Jeff **13**
Walker, T-Bone **5**
Walsh, Joe **5**
  Also see Eagles, The
Watson, Doc **2**
Weir, Bob
  See Grateful Dead, The
Weller, Paul **14**
Wilson, Nancy
  See Heart
Winston, George **9**
Winter, Johnny **5**
Yamashita, Kazuhito **4**
Yarrow, Peter
  See Peter, Paul & Mary
Young, Angus
  See AC/DC
Young, Malcolm
  See AC/DC
Young, Neil **2**
Zappa, Frank **1**

Harmonica
Dylan, Bob **3**
Guthrie, Woodie **2**
Lewis, Huey **9**
Little Walter **14**

McClinton, Delbert **14**
Musselwhite, Charlie **13**
Thielemans, Toots **13**
Waters, Muddy **4**
Williamson, Sonny Boy **9**
Wilson, Kim
  See Fabulous Thunderbirds, The

Heavy Metal
AC/DC **4**
Aerosmith **3**
Alice in Chains **10**
Anthrax **11**
Black Sabbath **9**
Danzig **7**
Deep Purple **11**
Def Leppard **3**
Faith No More **7**
Fishbone **7**
Ford, Lita **9**
Guns n' Roses **2**
Iron Maiden **10**
Judas Priest **10**
King's X **7**
Led Zeppelin **1**
L7 **12**
Megadeth **9**
Metallica **7**
Mötley Crüe **1**
Motörhead **10**
Nugent, Ted **2**
Osbourne, Ozzy **3**
Pantera **13**
Petra **3**
Queensrÿche **8**
Reid, Vernon **2**
  Also see Living Colour
Reznor, Trent **13**
Roth, David Lee **1**
  Also see Van Halen
Sepultura **12**
Slayer **10**
Soundgarden **6**
Spinal Tap **8**
Stryper **2**
Whitesnake **5**

Humor
Coasters, The **5**
Jones, Spike **5**
Lehrer, Tom **7**
Pearl, Minnie **3**
Russell, Mark **6**
Schickele, Peter **5**
Shaffer, Paul **13**
Spinal Tap **8**
Stevens, Ray **7**
Yankovic, "Weird Al" **7**

Inventors
Fender, Leo **10**
Paul, Les **2**
Scholz, Tom
  See Boston
Teagarden, Jack **10**

Jazz
Allen, Geri **10**
Anderson, Ray **7**
Armstrong, Louis **4**
Bailey, Mildred **13**
Bailey, Pearl **5**
Baker, Anita **9**
Baker, Chet **13**
Basie, Count **2**
Belle, Regina **6**
Benson, George **9**
Berigan, Bunny **2**
Blakey, Art **11**
Blanchard, Terence **13**
Bley, Carla **8**
Bley, Paul **14**
Blood, Sweat and Tears **7**
Brand New Heavies, The **14**
Braxton, Anthony **12**
Brown, Ruth **13**
Brubeck, Dave **8**
Burrell, Kenny **11**
Burton, Gary **10**
Calloway, Cab **6**
Canadian Brass, The **4**
Carter, Benny **3**
Carter, Betty **6**
Carter, Ron **14**
Charles, Ray **1**
Cherry, Don **10**
Christian, Charlie **11**
Clarke, Stanley **3**
Clooney, Rosemary **9**
Cole, Nat King **3**
Coleman, Ornette **5**
Coltrane, John **4**
Connick, Harry, Jr. **4**
Corea, Chick **6**
Davis, Miles **1**
DeJohnette, Jack **7**
Di Meola, Al **12**
Eckstine, Billy **1**
Eldridge, Roy **9**
Ellington, Duke **2**
Ferguson, Maynard **7**
Fitzgerald, Ella **1**
Fleck, Bela **8**
  Also see New Grass Revival, The
Fountain, Pete **7**
Galway, James **3**
Getz, Stan **12**
Gillespie, Dizzy **6**
Goodman, Benny **4**
Gordon, Dexter **10**
Grappelli, Stephane **10**
Green, Grant **14**
Guaraldi, Vince **3**
Haden, Charlie **12**
Hampton, Lionel **6**
Hancock, Herbie **8**
Hawkins, Coleman **11**
Hedges, Michael **3**
Henderson, Joe **14**
Herman, Woody **12**
Hines, Earl "Fatha" **12**

Leiber and Stoller **14**
Lemper, Ute **14**
Lennon, John **9**
    Also see Beatles, The
Lennon, Julian **2**
Lewis, Huey **9**
Liberace **9**
Lightfoot, Gordon **3**
Loggins, Kenny **3**
Lovett, Lyle **5**
Lowe, Nick **6**
Lush **13**
Lynne, Jeff **5**
MacColl, Kirsty **12**
Madonna **4**
Mancini, Henry **1**
Manhattan Transfer, The **8**
Manilow, Barry **2**
Marley, Bob **3**
Marley, Ziggy **3**
Marsalis, Branford **10**
Martin, Dean **1**
Martin, George **6**
Marx, Richard **3**
Mathis, Johnny **2**
McCartney, Paul **4**
    Also see Beatles, The
McFerrin, Bobby **3**
McLachlan, Sarah **12**
McLean, Don **7**
Medley, Bill **3**
Melanie **12**
Michael, George **9**
Midler, Bette **8**
Miller, Mitch **11**
Miller, Roger **4**
Milli Vanilli **4**
Mills Brothers, The **14**
Mitchell, Joni **2**
Monkees, The **7**
Montand, Yves **12**
Morrison, Jim **3**
Morrison, Van **3**
Morrissey **10**
Mouskouri, Nana **12**
Moyet, Alison **12**
Murray, Anne **4**
Myles, Alannah **4**
Neville, Aaron **5**
    Also see Neville Brothers, The
Neville Brothers, The **4**
New Kids on the Block **3**
Newman, Randy **4**
Newton, Wayne **2**
Newton-John, Olivia **8**
Nicks, Stevie **2**
Nilsson **10**
Nitty Gritty Dirt Band **6**
Nyro, Laura **12**
Oak Ridge Boys, The **7**
Ocasek, Ric **5**
Ocean, Billy **4**
O'Connor, Sinead **3**
Osmond, Donny **3**
Page, Jimmy **1**
    Also see Led Zeppelin
    Also see Yardbirds, The

Page, Patti **11**
Parsons, Alan **12**
Parton, Dolly **2**
Pendergrass, Teddy **3**
Penn, Michael **4**
Pet Shop Boys **5**
Peter, Paul & Mary **4**
Phillips, Sam **12**
Piaf, Edith **8**
Plant, Robert **2**
    Also see Led Zeppelin
Pointer Sisters, The **9**
Porter, Cole **10**
Presley, Elvis **1**
Prince **14**
    Earlier sketch in CM **1**
Proclaimers, The **13**
Queen **6**
Rabbitt, Eddie **5**
Raitt, Bonnie **3**
Rea, Chris **12**
Redding, Otis **5**
Reddy, Helen **9**
Reeves, Martha **4**
R.E.M. **5**
Richard, Cliff **14**
Richie, Lionel **2**
Riley, Teddy **14**
Robbins, Marty **9**
Robinson, Smokey **1**
Rogers, Kenny **1**
Rolling Stones **3**
Ronstadt, Linda **2**
Ross, Diana **1**
Roth, David Lee **1**
    Also see Van Halen
Ruffin, David **6**
Sade **2**
Sager, Carole Bayer **5**
Sainte-Marie, Buffy **11**
Sanborn, David **1**
Seal **14**
Seals, Dan **9**
Seals & Crofts **3**
Secada, Jon **13**
Sedaka, Neil **4**
Shaffer, Paul **13**
Sheila E. **3**
Shirelles, The **11**
Shonen Knife **13**
Siberry, Jane **6**
Simon, Carly **4**
Simon, Paul **1**
Sinatra, Frank **1**
Smiths, The **3**
Snow, Pheobe **4**
Spector, Phil **4**
Springfield, Rick **9**
Springsteen, Bruce **6**
Squeeze **5**
Stansfield, Lisa **9**
Starr, Ringo **10**
Steely Dan **5**
Stevens, Cat **3**
Stewart, Rod **2**
Stills, Stephen **5**
Sting **2**

Story, The **13**
Streisand, Barbra **2**
Summer, Donna **12**
Supremes, The **6**
Sweat, Keith **13**
Sweet, Matthew **9**
SWV **14**
Talking Heads **1**
Taylor, James **2**
Tears for Fears **6**
Teenage Fanclub **13**
Temptations, The **3**
10,000 Maniacs **3**
They Might Be Giants **7**
Three Dog Night **5**
Tiffany **4**
Tikaram, Tanita **9**
Timbuk 3 **3**
Toad the Wet Sprocket **13**
Tony! Toni! Toné! **12**
Torme, Mel **4**
Townshend, Pete **1**
    Also see Who, The
Turner, Tina **1**
Valli, Frankie **10**
Vandross, Luther **2**
Vega, Suzanne **3**
Vinton, Bobby **12**
Walsh, Joe **5**
Warnes, Jennifer **3**
Warwick, Dionne **2**
Was (Not Was) **6**
Washington, Dinah **5**
Watley, Jody **9**
Webb, Jimmy **12**
"Weird Al" Yankovic **7**
Weller, Paul **14**
Who, The **3**
Williams, Andy **2**
Williams, Deniece **1**
Williams, Joe **11**
Williams, Lucinda **10**
Williams, Paul **5**
Williams, Vanessa **10**
Wilson, Jackie **3**
Wilson Phillips **5**
Winwood, Steve **2**
Womack, Bobby **5**
Wonder, Stevie **2**
XTC **10**
Young, Neil **2**
Young M.C. **4**

Producers
Ackerman, Will **3**
Alpert, Herb **11**
Baker, Anita **9**
Bogaert, Jo
    See Technotronic
Brown, Tony **14**
Browne, Jackson **3**
Burnett, T Bone **13**
Cale, John **9**
Clarke, Stanley **3**
Clinton, George **7**
Collins, Phil **2**
Costello, Elvis **2**

Fabulous Thunderbirds, The **1**
Four Tops, The **11**
Fox, Samantha **3**
Franklin, Aretha **2**
Gaye, Marvin **4**
Gordy, Berry, Jr. **6**
Green, Al **9**
Hall & Oates **6**
Hayes, Isaac **10**
Holland-Dozier-Holland **5**
Ingram, James **11**
Isley Brothers, The **8**
Jackson, Freddie **3**
Jackson, Janet **3**
Jackson, Michael **1**
Jackson, Millie **14**
Jacksons, The **7**
Jam, Jimmy, and Terry Lewis **11**
James, Etta **6**
Jodeci **13**
Jones, Booker T. **8**
Jones, Grace **9**
Jones, Quincy **2**
Jordan, Louis **11**
Khan, Chaka **9**
King, Ben E. **7**
Knight, Gladys **1**
Kool & the Gang **13**
LaBelle, Patti **8**
Los Lobos **2**
Mayfield, Curtis **8**
Medley, Bill **3**
Meters, The **14**
Milli Vanilli **4**
Moore, Melba **7**
Morrison, Van **3**
Neville, Aaron **5**
    Also see Neville Brothers, The
Neville Brothers, The **4**
Ocean, Billy **4**
O'Jays, The **13**
Pendergrass, Teddy **3**
Pickett, Wilson **10**
Pointer Sisters, The **9**
Prince **14**
    Earlier sketch in CM **1**
Redding, Otis **5**
Reese, Della **13**
Reeves, Martha **4**
Richie, Lionel **2**
Riley, Teddy **14**
Robinson, Smokey **1**
Ross, Diana **6**
    Also see Supremes, The
Ruffin, David **6**
    Also see Temptations, The
Sam and Dave **8**
Scaggs, Boz **12**
Secada, Jon **13**
Shanice **14**
Shirelles, The **11**
Stansfield, Lisa **9**
Staples, Mavis **13**
Staples, Pops **11**
Stewart, Rod **2**

Stone, Sly **8**
Supremes, The **6**
    Also see Ross, Diana
Sure!, Al B. **13**
Sweat, Keith **13**
SWV **14**
Temptations, The **3**
Third World **13**
Tony! Toni! Toné! **12**
Toussaint, Allen **11**
Turner, Tina **1**
Vandross, Luther **2**
Was (Not Was) **6**
Watley, Jody **9**
Williams, Deniece **1**
Williams, Vanessa **10**
Wilson, Jackie **3**
Winans, The **12**
Womack, Bobby **5**
Wonder, Stevie **2**

Rock
AC/DC **4**
Adam Ant **13**
Adams, Bryan **2**
Aerosmith **3**
Alexander, Arthur **14**
Alice in Chains **10**
Allman Brothers, The **6**
Anthrax **11**
Band, The **9**
Basehead **11**
Beach Boys, The **1**
Beastie Boys, The **8**
Beatles, The **2**
Beaver Brown Band, The **3**
Beck, Jeff **4**
    Also see Yardbirds, The
Belew, Adrian **5**
Benatar, Pat **8**
Berry, Chuck **1**
Black, Frank **14**
Black Crowes, The **7**
Black Sabbath **9**
Blondie **14**
Blood, Sweat and Tears **7**
BoDeans, The **3**
Bon Jovi **10**
Boston **11**
Bowie, David **1**
Bragg, Billy **7**
Brickell, Edie **3**
Browne, Jackson **3**
Buckingham, Lindsey **8**
    Also see Fleetwood Mac
Buckley, Tim **14**
Burdon, Eric **14**
    Also see War
Burnett, T Bone **13**
Buzzcocks, The **9**
Byrds, The **8**
Byrne, David **8**
    Also see Talking Heads
Cale, John **9**
Captain Beefheart **10**

Cave, Nick **10**
Charlatans, The **13**
Cheap Trick **12**
Cher **1**
Chicago **3**
Church, The **14**
Clapton, Eric **11**
    Earlier sketch in CM **1**
    Also see Cream
    Also see Yardbirds, The
Clash, The **4**
Clemons, Clarence **7**
Clinton, George **7**
Coasters, The **5**
Cocker, Joe **4**
Collins, Phil **2**
Cooder, Ry **2**
Cooke, Sam **1**
    Also see Soul Stirrers, The
Cooper, Alice **8**
Costello, Elvis **12**
    Earlier sketch in CM **2**
Cougar, John(ny)
    See Mellencamp, John "Cougar"
Cracker **12**
Cranberries, The **14**
Crash Test Dummies **14**
Cream **9**
Crenshaw, Marshall **5**
Crosby, David **3**
    Also see Byrds, The
Crowded House **12**
Cure, The **3**
Curry, Tim **3**
Curve **13**
Dale, Dick **13**
Daltrey, Roger **3**
    Also see Who, The
Daniels, Charlie **6**
Danzig **7**
D'Arby, Terence Trent **3**
Dave Clark Five, The **12**
Davies, Ray **5**
Deep Purple **11**
Def Leppard **3**
Depeche Mode **5**
Devo **13**
Diddley, Bo **3**
Dinosaur Jr. **10**
Doc Pomus **14**
Doobie Brothers, The **3**
Doors, The **4**
Duran Duran **4**
Dylan, Bob **3**
Eagles, The **3**
Eddy, Duane **9**
Einstürzende Neubauten **13**
Electric Light Orchestra **7**
Elliot, Cass **5**
Emerson, Lake & Palmer/Powell **5**
English Beat, The **9**
Eno, Brian **8**
Etheridge, Melissa **4**
Eurythmics **6**
Extreme **10**

Stevens, Cat **3**
Stewart, Rod **2**
Stills, Stephen **5**
Sting **2**
Stone, Sly **8**
Stone Temple Pilots **14**
Stray Cats, The **11**
Stryper **2**
Sugarcubes, The **10**
Summers, Andy **3**
Tears for Fears **6**
Teenage Fanclub **13**
10,000 Maniacs **3**
Texas Tornados, The **8**
They Might Be Giants **7**
Thin Lizzy **13**
Thompson, Richard **7**
Three Dog Night **5**
Timbuk 3 **3**
Toad the Wet Sprocket **13**
Townshend, Pete **1**
   Also see Who, The
T. Rex **11**
Turner, Tina **1**
U2 **12**
   Earlier sketch in CM **2**
Ulmer, James Blood **13**
Vai, Steve **5**
Valli, Frankie **10**
Van Halen **8**
Vaughan, Stevie Ray **1**
Velvet Underground, The **7**
Violent Femmes **12**
Waits, Tom **12**
   Earlier sketch in CM **1**
Walsh, Joe **5**
   Also see Eagles, The
War **14**
Weller, Paul **14**
Whitesnake **5**
Who, The **3**
Winter, Johnny **5**
Winwood, Steve **2**
X **11**
Yardbirds, The **10**
Yes **8**
Young, Neil **2**
Zappa, Frank **1**
Zevon, Warren **9**
ZZ Top **2**

Rock and Roll Pioneers
Berry, Chuck **1**
Clark, Dick **2**
Darin, Bobby **4**
Didley, Bo **3**
Dion **4**
Domino, Fats **2**
Eddy, Duane **9**
Everly Brothers, The **2**
Francis, Connie **10**
Haley, Bill **6**
Hawkins, Screamin' Jay **8**
Holly, Buddy **1**
James, Etta **6**

Jordan, Louis **11**
Lewis, Jerry Lee **2**
Little Richard **1**
Nelson, Rick **2**
Orbison, Roy **2**
Paul, Les **2**
Perkins, Carl **9**
Phillips, Sam **5**
Presley, Elvis **1**
Professor Longhair **6**
Sedaka, Neil **4**
Shannon, Del **10**
Shirelles, The **11**
Spector, Phil **4**
Twitty, Conway **6**
Valli, Frankie **10**
Wilson, Jackie **3**

Saxophone
Braxton, Anthony **12**
Carter, Benny **3**
Clemons, Clarence **7**
Coleman, Ornette **5**
Coltrane, John **4**
Dibango, Manu **14**
Dorsey, Jimmy
   See Dorsey Brothers, The
Getz, Stan **12**
Gordon, Dexter **10**
Hawkins, Coleman **11**
Henderson, Joe **14**
Herman, Woody **12**
Kenny G **14**
Kirk, Rahsaan Roland **6**
Lopez, Israel "Cachao" **14**
Lovano, Joe **13**
Marsalis, Branford **10**
Morgan, Frank **9**
Parker, Charlie **5**
Parker, Maceo **7**
Redman, Joshua **12**
Rollins, Sonny **7**
Sanborn, David **1**
Shorter, Wayne **5**
Threadgill, Henry **9**
Washington, Grover, Jr. **5**
Winter, Paul **10**
Young, Lester **14**

Songwriters
Acuff, Roy **2**
Adams, Bryan **2**
Alexander, Arthur **14**
Allen, Peter **11**
Alpert, Herb **11**
Amos, Tori **12**
Anderson, Ian
   See Jethro Tull
Anderson, John **5**
Anka, Paul **2**
Armatrading, Joan **4**
Atkins, Chet **5**
Autry, Gene **12**
Bacharach, Burt **1**
Baez, Joan **1**

Baker, Anita **9**
Balin, Marty
   See Jefferson Airplane
Barrett, (Roger) Syd
   See Pink Floyd
Basie, Count **2**
Becker, Walter
   See Steely Dan
Belew, Adrian **5**
Benton, Brook **7**
Berlin, Irving **8**
Berry, Chuck **1**
Black, Clint **5**
Black, Frank **14**
Blades, Ruben **2**
Bloom, Luka **14**
Bono
   See U2
Brady, Paul **8**
Bragg, Billy **7**
Brickell, Edie **3**
Brooke, Jonatha
   See Story, The
Brooks, Garth **8**
Brown, Bobby **4**
Brown, James **2**
Brown, Marty **14**
Browne, Jackson **3**
Buck, Peter
   See R.E.M.
Buck, Robert
   See 10,000 Maniacs
Buckingham, Lindsey **8**
   Also see Fleetwood Mac
Buckley, Tim **14**
Buffett, Jimmy **4**
Burdon, Eric **14**
   Also see War
Burnett, T Bone **13**
Bush, Kate **4**
Byrne, David **8**
   Also see Talking Heads
Cahn, Sammy **11**
Cale, John **9**
Calloway, Cab **6**
Captain Beefheart **10**
Carpenter, Mary-Chapin **6**
Carter, Carlene **8**
Cash, Johnny **1**
Cash, Rosanne **2**
Cetera, Peter
   See Chicago
Chapin, Harry **6**
Chapman, Tracy **4**
Charles, Ray **1**
Childs, Toni **2**
Chilton, Alex **10**
Clapton, Eric **11**
   Earlier sketch in CM **1**
   Also see Cream
   Also see Yardbirds, The
Cleveland, James **1**
Clinton, George **7**
Cockburn, Bruce **8**
Cohen, Leonard **3**

Cumulative Musicians Index

Volume numbers appear in **bold**.

Abba **12**
Abbruzzese, Dave
  See Pearl Jam
Abdul, Paula **3**
Abrahams, Mick
  See Jethro Tull
Abrantes, Fernando
  See Kraftwerk
AC/DC **4**
Ackerman, Will **3**
Acland, Christopher
  See Lush
Acuff, Roy **2**
Adam Ant **13**
Adams, Bryan **2**
Adams, Clifford
  See Kool & the Gang
Adams, Donn
  See NRBQ
Adams, John **8**
Adams, Terry
  See NRBQ
Adcock, Eddie
  See Country Gentleman, The
Adler, Steven
  See Guns n' Roses
Aerosmith **3**
Afonso, Marie
  See Zap Mama
AFX
  See Aphex Twin
Ajile
  See Arrested Development
Alabama **1**
Albuquerque, Michael de
  See Electric Light Orchestra
Alexander, Arthur **14**
Alexander, Tim
  See Asleep at the Wheel
Alexander, Tim "Herb"
  See Primus
Ali
  See Tribe Called Quest, A
Alice in Chains **10**
Allcock, Martin
  See Jethro Tull
Allen, Dave
  See Gang of Four
Allen, Debbie **8**
Allen, Duane
  See Oak Ridge Boys, The
Allen, Geri **10**
Allen, Papa Dee
  See War
Allen, Peter **11**

Allen, Red
  See Osborne Brothers, The
Allen, Rick
  See Def Leppard
Allman, Duane
  See Allman Brothers, The
Allman, Gregg
  See Allman Brothers, The
Allman Brothers, The **6**
Allsup, Michael Rand
  See Three Dog Night
Alpert, Herb **11**
Alston, Shirley
  See Shirelles, The
Alvin, Dave
  See X
Ament, Jeff
  See Pearl Jam
Amos, Tori **12**
Anastasio, Trey
  See Phish
Anderson, Al
  See NRBQ
Anderson, Emma
  See Lush
Anderson, Ian
  See Jethro Tull
Anderson, John **5**
Anderson, Jon
  See Yes
Anderson, Laurie **1**
Anderson, Marian **8**
Anderson, Ray **7**
Anderson, Signe
  See Jefferson Airplane
Andersson, Benny
  See Abba
Andrews, Barry
  See XTC
Andrews, Julie **4**
Andrews, Laverne
  See Andrews Sisters, The
Andrews, Maxene
  See Andrews Sisters, The
Andrews, Patty
  See Andrews Sisters, The
Andrews Sisters, The **9**
Anger, Darol
  See Turtle Island String Quartet
Anka, Paul **2**
Anselmo, Philip
  See Pantera
Ant, Adam
  See Adam Ant
Anthony, Michael
  See Van Halen

Anthrax **11**
Anton, Alan
  See Cowboy Junkies, The
Antunes, Michael
  See Beaver Brown Band, The
Aphex Twin **14**
Appice, Vinnie
  See Black Sabbath
Araya, Tom
  See Slayer
Ardolino, Tom
  See NRBQ
Armatrading, Joan **4**
Armstrong, Louis **4**
Arnaz, Desi **8**
Arnold, Eddy **10**
Arnold, Kristine
  See Sweethearts of the Rodeo
Arrau, Claudio **1**
Arrested Development **14**
Asleep at the Wheel **5**
Astley, Rick **5**
Astro
  See UB40
Asuo, Kwesi
  See Arrested Development
Atkins, Chet **5**
Atkinson, Sweet Pea
  See Was (Not Was)
Auf Der Maur, Melissa
  See Hole
Augustyniak, Jerry
  See 10,000 Maniacs
Auldridge, Mike **4**
    Also see Country Gentlemen, The
    Also see Seldom Scene, The
Autry, Gene **12**
Avalon, Frankie **5**
Avery, Eric
  See Jane's Addiction
Aykroyd, Dan
  See Blues Brothers, The
Babjak, James
  See Smithereens, The
Babyface
  See Edmonds, Kenneth "Babyface"
Bacharach, Burt **1**
Badger, Pat
  See Extreme
Baez, Joan **1**
Bailey, Mildred **13**
Bailey, Pearl **5**
Bailey, Phil
  See Earth, Wind and Fire
Baker, Anita **9**

Cliburn, Van **13**
Cliff, Jimmy **8**
Cline, Patsy **5**
Clinton, George **7**
Clooney, Rosemary **9**
Coasters, The **5**
Cobain, Kurt
  See Nirvana
Cockburn, Bruce **8**
Cocker, Joe **4**
Cocteau Twins, The **12**
Coe, David Allan **4**
Cohen, Jeremy
  See Turtle Island String Quartet
Cohen, Leonard **3**
Cohen, Porky
  See Roomful of Blues
Cole, Lloyd **9**
Cole, Natalie **1**
Cole, Nat King **3**
Coleman, Ornette **5**
Collin, Phil
  See Def Leppard
Collins, Albert **4**
Collins, Allen
  See Lynyrd Skynyrd
Collins, Bootsy **8**
Collins, Judy **4**
Collins, Mark
  See Charlatans, The
Collins, Phil **2**
  Also see Genesis
Collins, Rob
  See Charlatans, The
Collins, William
  See Collins, Bootsy
Colomby, Bobby
  See Blood, Sweat and Tears
Colt, Johnny
  See Black Crowes, The
Coltrane, John **4**
Colvin, Shawn **11**
Comess, Aaron
  See Spin Doctors
Como, Perry **14**
Conneff, Kevin
  See Chieftains, The
Connick, Harry, Jr. **4**
Cooder, Ry **2**
Cook, Jeff
  See Alabama
Cook, Paul
  See Sex Pistols, The
Cooke, Sam **1**
  Also see Soul Stirrers, The
Cooney, Rory **6**
Cooper, Alice **8**
Cooper, Michael
  See Third World
Coore, Stephen
  See Third World
Copeland, Stewart **14**
Copland, Aaron **2**
Copley, Al
  See Roomful of Blues
Corea, Chick **6**

Corgan, Billy
  See Smashing Pumpkins
Cornell, Chris
  See Soundgarden
Cornick, Glenn
  See Jethro Tull
Costello, Elvis **12**
  Earlier sketch in CM **2**
Cotoia, Robert
  See Beaver Brown Band, The
Cotrubas, Ileana **1**
Cotton, Caré
  See Sounds of Blackness
Cougar, John(ny)
  See Mellencamp, John "Cougar"
Country Gentlemen, The **7**
Coverdale, David
  See Whitesnake **5**
Cowan, John
  See New Grass Revival, The
Cowboy Junkies, The **4**
Cox, Andy
  See English Beat, The
Cracker **12**
Crain, S. R.
  See Soul Stirrers, The
Cranberries, The **14**
Crash Test Dummies **14**
Crawford, Ed
  See fIREHOSE
Crawford, Michael **4**
Cray, Robert **8**
Creach, Papa John
  See Jefferson Starship
Cream **9**
Crenshaw, Marshall **5**
Cretu, Michael
  See Enigma
Criss, Peter
  See Kiss
Croce, Jim **3**
Crofts, Dash
  See Seals & Crofts
Cropper, Steve **12**
Crosby, Bing **6**
Crosby, David **3**
  Also see Byrds, The
Crouch, Andraé **9**
Crowded House **12**
Crowe, J. D. **5**
Crowell, Rodney **8**
Cruz, Celia **10**
Cure, The **3**
Curless, Ann
  See Exposé
Currie, Steve
  See T. Rex
Curry, Tim **3**
Curve **13**
Cypress Hill **11**
Cyrus, Billy Ray **11**
Dacus, Donnie
  See Chicago
Dacus, Johnny
  See Osborne Brothers, The
Daddy Mack
  See Kris Kross

Daellenbach, Charles
  See Canadian Brass, The
Dahlheimer, Patrick
  See Live
Daisley, Bob
  See Black Sabbath
Dale, Dick **13**
Daley, Richard
  See Third World
Dall, Bobby
  See Poison
Dalton, Nic
  See Lemonheads, The
Daltrey, Roger **3**
  Also see Who, The
Dando, Evan
  See Lemonheads, The
D'Angelo, Greg
  See Anthrax
Daniels, Charlie **6**
Daniels, Jack
  See Highway 101
Danko, Rick
  See Band, The
Danny Boy
  See House of Pain
Danzig **7**
Danzig, Glenn
  See Danzig
D'Arby, Terence Trent **3**
Darin, Bobby **4**
Darling, Eric
  See Weavers, The
Darvill, Benjamin
  See Crash Test Dummies
Das EFX **14**
Daugherty, Jay Dee
  See Church, The
Daulne, Marie
  See Zap Mama
Dave Clark Five, The **12**
Davenport, N'Dea
  See Brand New Heavies, The
Davidson, Lenny
  See Dave Clark Five, The
Davies, Ray **5**
Davies, Saul
  See James
Davis, Chip **4**
Davis, Clive **14**
Davis, Michael
  See MC5, The
Davis, Miles **1**
Davis, Sammy, Jr. **4**
Dayne, Taylor **4**
Deacon, John
  See Queen
de Albuquerque, Michael
  See Electric Light Orchestra
DeBarge, El **14**
Dee, Mikkey
  See Motörhead
Deee-lite **9**
Deep Purple **11**
Def Leppard **3**
DeGarmo, Chris
  See Queensryche

Eldridge, Ben
  See Seldom Scene, The
Eldridge, Roy **9**
Electric Light Orchestra **7**
Elfman, Danny **9**
Elias, Manny
  See Tears for Fears
Ellefson, Dave
  See Megadeth
Ellington, Duke **2**
Elliot, Cass **5**
Elliot, Joe
  See Def Leppard
Ellis, Terry
  See En Vogue
ELO
  See Electric Light Orchestra
Ely, John
  See Asleep at the Wheel
Emerson, Bill
  See Country Gentlemen, The
Emerson, Keith
  See Emerson, Lake & Palmer/Powell
Emerson, Lake & Palmer/Powell **5**
Emery, Jill
  See Hole
English Beat, The **9**
Enigma **14**
Eno, Brian **8**
Enos, Bob
  See Roomful of Blues
Enright, Pat
  See Nashville Bluegrass Band
Entwistle, John
  See Who, The
En Vogue **10**
Enya **6**
EPMD **10**
Erasure **11**
Eric B.
  See Eric B. and Rakim
Eric B. and Rakim **9**
Erlandson, Eric
  See Hole
Ertegun, Ahmet **10**
Eshe, Montsho
  See Arrested Development
Estefan, Gloria **2**
Estrada, Roy
  See Little Feat
Etheridge, Melissa **4**
Eurythmics **6**
Evan, John
  See Jethro Tull
Evans, Dick
  See U2
Evans, Mark
  See AC/DC
Everlast
  See House of Pain
Everly, Don
  See Everly Brothers, The
Everly, Phil
  See Everly Brothers, The
Everly Brothers, The **2**
Everman, Jason
  See Soundgarden

Ewen, Alvin
  See Steel Pulse
Exkano, Paul
  See Five Blind Boys of Alabama
Exposé **4**
Extreme **10**
Fabian **5**
Fabulous Thunderbirds, The **1**
Fadden, Jimmie
  See Nitty Gritty Dirt Band, The
Fagan, Don
  See Steely Dan
Faithfull, Marianne **14**
Faith No More **7**
Fakir, Abdul "Duke"
  See Four Tops, The
Falconer, Earl
  See UB40
Fall, The **12**
Fallon, David
  See Chieftains, The
Fältskog, Agnetha
  See Abba
Farley, J. J.
  See Soul Stirrers, The
Farndon, Pete
  See Pretenders, The
Farrell, Perry
  See Jane's Addiction
Farris, Dionne
  See Arrested Development
Farriss, Andrew
  See INXS
Farriss, Jon
  See INXS
Farriss, Tim
  See INXS
Fay, Martin
  See Chieftains, The
Fearnley, James
  See Pogues, The
Feinstein, Michael **6**
Fela
  See Kuti, Fela
Felder, Don
  See Eagles, The
Feliciano, José **10**
Fender, Freddy
  See Texas Tornados, The
Fender, Leo **10**
Ferguson, Keith
  See Fabulous Thunderbirds, The
Ferguson, Maynard **7**
Ferguson, Steve
  See NRBQ
Ferry, Bryan **1**
Fiedler, Arthur **6**
Fielder, Jim
  See Blood, Sweat and Tears
Fields, Johnny
  See Five Blind Boys of Alabama
Finch, Jennifer
  See L7
Finer, Jem
  See Pogues, The
Finn, Micky
  See T. Rex

Finn, Neil
  See Crowded House
Finn, Tim
  See Crowded House
fIREHOSE **11**
Fishbone **7**
Fisher, Eddie **12**
Fisher, Jerry
  See Blood, Sweat and Tears
Fisher, John "Norwood"
  See Fishbone
Fisher, Phillip "Fish"
  See Fishbone
Fisher, Roger
  See Heart
Fishman, Jon
  See Phish
Fitzgerald, Ella **1**
Five Blind Boys of Alabama **12**
Flack, Roberta **5**
Flansburgh, John
  See They Might Be Giants
Flatt, Lester **3**
Flavor Flav
  See Public Enemy
Flea
  See Red Hot Chili Peppers, The
Fleck, Bela **8**
  Also see New Grass Revival, The
Fleetwood, Mick
  See Fleetwood Mac
Fleetwood Mac **5**
Flemons, Wade
  See Earth, Wind and Fire
Fletcher, Andy
  See Depeche Mode
Flür, Wolfgang
  See Kraftwerk
Flynn, Pat
  See New Grass Revival, The
Fogelberg, Dan **4**
Fogerty, John **2**
Foley
  See Arrested Development
Ford, Lita **9**
Ford, Mark
  See Black Crowes, The
Ford, Tennessee Ernie **3**
Fortune, Jimmy
  See Statler Brothers, The
Fossen, Steve
  See Heart
Foster, David **13**
Foster, Malcolm
  See Pretenders, The
Foster, Paul
  See Soul Stirrers, The
Fountain, Clarence
  See Five Blind Boys of Alabama
Fountain, Pete **7**
Four Tops, The **11**
Fox, Lucas
  See Motörhead
Fox, Oz
  See Stryper
Fox, Samantha **3**
Frampton, Peter **3**

Green, Grant **14**
Green, Karl Anthony
  See Herman's Hermits
Green, Peter
  See Fleetwood Mac
Green, Susaye
  See Supremes, The
Green, Willie
  See Neville Brothers, The
Greenspoon, Jimmy
  See Three Dog Night
Greenwood, Lee **12**
Gregg, Paul
  See Restless Heart
Gregory, Dave
  See XTC
Griffin, Bob
  See BoDeans, The
Griffith, Nanci **3**
Grohl, Dave
  See Nirvana
Groucutt, Kelly
  See Electric Light Orchestra
Grove, George
  See Kingston Trio, The
Grusin, Dave **7**
Guaraldi, Vince **3**
Guard, Dave
  See Kingston Trio, The
Gudmundsdottir, Björk
  See Sugarcubes, The
Guerin, John
  See Byrds, The
Guest, Christopher
  See Spinal Tap
Guns n' Roses **2**
Gunther, Cornell
  See Coasters, The
Guru
  See Gang Starr
Guss, Randy
  See Toad the Wet Sprocket
Gustafson, Steve
  See 10,000 Maniacs
Gut, Grudrun
  See Einstürzende Neubauten
Guthrie, Arlo **6**
Guthrie, Robin
  See Cocteau Twins, The
Guthrie, Woodie **2**
Guy, Billy
  See Coasters, The
Guy, Buddy **4**
Gwar **13**
Hacke, Alexander
  See Einstürzende Neubauten
Hackett, Steve
  See Genesis
Haden, Charlie **12**
Hagar, Sammy
  See Van Halen
Haggard, Merle **2**
Haley, Bill **6**
Halford, Rob
  See Judas Priest
Hall, Daryl
  See Hall & Oates

Hall, Randall
  See Lynyrd Skynyrd
Hall, Tom T. **4**
Hall, Tony
  See Neville Brothers, The
Hall & Oates **6**
Halliday, Toni
  See Curve
Hamilton, Frank
  See Weavers, The
Hamilton, Milton
  See Third World
Hamilton, Tom
  See Aerosmith
Hamlisch, Marvin **1**
Hammer, M.C. **5**
Hammerstein, Oscar
  See Rodgers, Richard
Hammett, Kirk
  See Metallica
Hammon, Ron
  See War
Hammond, John **6**
Hammond-Hammond, Jeffrey
  See Jethro Tull
Hampson, Sharon
  See Sharon, Lois & Bram
Hampson, Thomas **12**
Hampton, Lionel **6**
Hancock, Herbie **8**
Handy, W. C. **7**
Hanley, Steve
  See Fall, The
Hanna, Jeff
  See Nitty Gritty Dirt Band, The
Hanneman, Jeff
  See Slayer
Harding, John Wesley **6**
Harley, Bill **7**
Harrell, Lynn **3**
Harrington, Carrie
  See Sounds of Blackness
Harrington, David
  See Kronos Quartet
Harris, Addie "Micki"
  See Shirelles, The
Harris, Damon Otis
  See Temptations, The
Harris, Emmylou **4**
Harris, Evelyn
  See Sweet Honey in the Rock
Harris, Gerard
  See Kool & the Gang
Harris, R. H.
  See Soul Stirrers, The
Harris, Steve
  See Iron Maiden
Harrison, George **2**
  Also see Beatles, The
Harrison, Jerry
  See Talking Heads
Harrison, Nigel
  See Blondie
Harry, Deborah **4**
  Also see Blondie
Hart, Lorenz
  See Rodgers, Richard

Hart, Mark
  See Crowded House
Hart, Mickey
  See Grateful Dead, The
Hartford, John **1**
Hartke, Stephen **5**
Hartman, Bob
  See Petra
Hartman, John
  See Doobie Brothers, The
Harvey, Polly Jean **11**
Hashian
  See Boston
Haslinger, Paul
  See Tangerine Dream
Hassan, Norman
  See UB40
Hatfield, Juliana **12**
  Also see Lemonheads, The
Hauser, Tim
  See Manhattan Transfer, The
Havens, Richie **11**
Hawkins, Coleman **11**
Hawkins, Screamin' Jay **8**
Hay, George D. **3**
Hayes, Isaac **10**
Hayes, Roland **13**
Haynes, Warren
  See Allman Brothers, The
Hays, Lee
  See Weavers, The
Hayward, Richard
  See Little Feat
Headliner
  See Arrested Development
Headon, Topper
  See Clash, The
Healey, Jeff **4**
Heart **1**
Heavy D **10**
Hedges, Michael **3**
Heggie, Will
  See Cocteau Twins, The
Hellerman, Fred
  See Weavers, The
Helm, Levon
  See Band, The
  Also see Nitty Gritty Dirt Band, The
Henderson, Joe **14**
Hendricks, Barbara **10**
Hendrix, Jimi **2**
Henley, Don **3**
  Also see Eagles, The
Herman, Woody **12**
Herman's Hermits **5**
Herndon, Mark
  See Alabama
Herrmann, Bernard **14**
Herron, Cindy
  See En Vogue
Hester, Paul
  See Crowded House
Hetfield, James
  See Metallica
Hewson, Paul
  See U2
Hiatt, John **8**

Jagger, Mick **7**
    Also see Rolling Stones, The
Jairo T.
    See Sepultura
Jam, Jimmy
    See Jam, Jimmy, and Terry Lewis
Jam, Jimmy, and Terry Lewis **11**
Jam Master Jay
    See Run-D.M.C.
James **12**
James, Andrew "Bear"
    See Midnight Oil
James, Cheryl
    See Salt-N-Pepa
James, Doug
    See Roomful of Blues
James, Elmore **8**
James, Etta **6**
James, Harry **11**
James, Richard
    See Aphex Twin
James, Rick **2**
Jane's Addiction **6**
Jardine, Al
    See Beach Boys, The
Jarobi
    See Tribe Called Quest, A
Jarre, Jean-Michel **2**
Jarreau, Al **1**
Jarrett, Irwin
    See Third World
Jarrett, Keith **1**
Jasper, Chris
    See Isley Brothers, The
Jay, Miles
    See Village People, The
Jeanrenaud, Joan Dutcher
    See Kronos Quartet
Jefferson Airplane **5**
Jefferson Starship
    See Jefferson Airplane
Jennings, Greg
    See Restless Heart
Jennings, Waylon **4**
Jessie, Young
    See Coasters, The
Jesus and Mary Chain, The **10**
Jethro Tull **8**
Jett, Joan **3**
Jimenez, Flaco
    See Texas Tornados, The
Jobson, Edwin
    See Jethro Tull
Jodeci **13**
Joel, Billy **12**
    Earlier sketch in CM **2**
Johansen, David **7**
Johanson, Jai Johanny
    See Allman Brothers, The
John, Elton **3**
Johnson, Brian
    See AC/DC
Johnson, Courtney
    See New Grass Revival, The
Johnson, Daryl
    See Neville Brothers, The

Johnson, Gene
    See Diamond Rio
Johnson, Gerry
    See Steel Pulse
Johnson, Mike
    See Dinosaur Jr.
Johnson, Ralph
    See Earth, Wind and Fire
Johnson, Robert **6**
Johnson, Shirley Childres
    See Sweet Honey in the Rock
Johnson, Tamara "Taj"
    See SWV
Johnston, Bruce
    See Beach Boys, The
Johnston, Tom
    See Doobie Brothers, The
JoJo
    See Jodeci
Jolson, Al **10**
Jones, Booker T. **8**
Jones, Brian
    See Rolling Stones, The
Jones, Busta
    See Gang of Four
Jones, Davy
    See Monkees, The
Jones, Elvin **9**
Jones, Geoffrey
    See Sounds of Blackness
Jones, George **4**
Jones, Grace **9**
Jones, John Paul
    See Led Zeppelin
Jones, Kendall
    See Fishbone
Jones, Kenny
    See Who, The
Jones, Maxine
    See En Vogue
Jones, Michael
    See Kronos Quartet
Jones, Mick
    See Clash, The
Jones, Quincy **2**
Jones, Rickie Lee **4**
Jones, Sandra "Puma"
    See Black Uhuru
Jones, Spike **5**
Jones, Steve
    See Sex Pistols, The
Jones, Tom **11**
Jones, Will "Dub"
    See Coasters, The
Joplin, Janis **3**
Joplin, Scott **10**
Jordan, Lonnie
    See War
Jordan, Louis **11**
Jordan, Stanley **1**
Jorgensor, John
    See Desert Rose Band, The
Jourgensen, Al
    See Ministry
Joyce, Mike
    See Buzzcocks, The

    Also see Smiths, The
Judas Priest **10**
Judd, Naomi
    See Judds, The
Judd, Wynonna
    See Judds, The
    Also see Wynonna
Judds, The **2**
Jukebox
    See Geto Boys, The
Jungle DJ "Towa" Towa
    See Deee-lite
Jurado, Jeanette
    See Exposé
Kabongo, Sabine
    See Zap Mama
Kahlil, Aisha
    See Sweet Honey in the Rock
Kakoulli, Harry
    See Squeeze
Kalligan, Dick
    See Blood, Sweat and Tears
Kaminski, Mik
    See Electric Light Orchestra
Kanawa, Kiri Te
    See Te Kanawa, Kiri
Kane, Big Daddy **7**
Kannberg, Scott
    See Pavement
Kanter, Paul
    See Jefferson Airplane
Karajan, Herbert von
    See von Karajan, Herbert
Kath, Terry
    See Chicago
Katz, Steve
    See Blood, Sweat and Tears
Kaukonen, Jorma
    See Jefferson Airplane
Kaye, Tony
    See Yes
Kay Gee
    See Naughty by Nature
K-Ci
    See Jodeci
Keane, Sean
    See Chieftains, The
Kelly, Kevin
    See Byrds, The
Kendrick, David
    See Devo
Kendricks, Eddie
    See Temptations, The
Kennedy, Nigel **8**
Kenner, Doris
    See Shirelles, The
Kenny G **14**
Kentucky Headhunters, The **5**
Kern, Jerome **13**
Ketchum, Hal **14**
Khan, Chaka **9**
Khan, Nusrat Fateh Ali **13**
Kibble, Mark
    See Take 6
Kibby, Walter
    See Fishbone

Levy, Ron
    See Roomful of Blues
Lewis, Huey **9**
Lewis, Jerry Lee **2**
Lewis, Otis
    See Fabulous Thunderbirds, The
Lewis, Peter
    See Moby Grape
Lewis, Ramsey **14**
Lewis, Roy
    See Kronos Quartet
Lewis, Samuel K.
    See Five Blind Boys of Alabama
Lewis, Terry
    See Jam, Jimmy, and Terry Lewis
Libbea, Gene
    See Nashville Bluegrass Band
Liberace **9**
Lifeson, Alex
    See Rush
Lightfoot, Gordon **3**
Lilienstein, Lois
    See Sharon, Lois & Bram
Lilker, Dan
    See Anthrax
Lillywhite, Steve **13**
Lincoln, Abbey **9**
Lindley, David **2**
Linnell, John
    See They Might Be Giants
Lipsius, Fred
    See Blood, Sweat and Tears
Little, Keith
    See Country Gentlemen, The
Little Feat **4**
Little Richard **1**
Little Texas **14**
Little Walter **14**
Live **14**
Living Colour **7**
Llanas, Sammy
    See BoDeans, The
L.L. Cool J. **5**
Lloyd Webber, Andrew **6**
Lockwood, Robert, Jr. **10**
Loewe, Frederick
    See Lerner and Loewe
Loggins, Kenny **3**
Lombardo, Dave
    See Slayer
Lopez, Israel "Cachao" **14**
Lord, Jon
    See Deep Purple
Los Lobos **2**
Los Reyes
    See Gipsy Kings, The
Loughnane, Lee
    See Chicago
Louvin, Charlie
    See Louvin Brothers, The
Louvin, Ira
    See Louvin Brothers, The
Louvin Brothers, The **12**
Lovano, Joe **13**
Love, Courtney
    See Hole

Love, Gerry
    See Teenage Fanclub
Love, Mike
    See Beach Boys, The
Loveless, Patty **5**
Lovering, David
    See Cracker
Lovett, Lyle **5**
Lowe, Chris
    See Pet Shop Boys
Lowe, Nick **6**
Lowery, David
    See Cracker
Lozano, Conrad
    See Los Lobos
L7 **12**
Lucia, Paco de
    See de Lucia, Paco
Luke
    See Campbell, Luther
Lupo, Pat
    See Beaver Brown Band, The
LuPone, Patti **8**
Lush **13**
Lydon, John **9**
    Also see Sex Pistols, The
Lyngstad, Anni-Frid
    See Abba
Lynn, Loretta **2**
Lynne, Jeff **5**
    Also see Electric Light Orchestra
Lynne, Shelby **5**
Lynott, Phil
    See Thin Lizzy
Lynyrd Skynyrd **9**
Lyons, Leanne "Lelee"
    See SWV
Ma, Yo-Yo **2**
MacColl, Kirsty **12**
MacGowan, Shane
    See Pogues, The
MacKaye, Ian
    See Fugazi
Mack Daddy
    See Kris Kross
Madonna **4**
Magoogan, Wesley
    See English Beat, The
Maher, John
    See Buzzcocks, The
Makeba, Miriam **8**
Malkmus, Stephen
    See Pavement
Malone, Tom
    See Blood, Sweat and Tears
Mancini, Henry **1**
Mandrell, Barbara **4**
Maness, J. D.
    See Desert Rose Band, The
Manhattan Transfer, The **8**
Manilow, Barry **2**
Manuel, Richard
    See Band, The
Manzarek, Ray
    See Doors, The
Marie, Buffy Sainte
    See Sainte-Marie, Buffy

Marini, Lou, Jr.
    See Blood, Sweat and Tears
Marley, Bob **3**
Marley, Rita **10**
Marley, Ziggy **3**
Marr, Johnny
    See Smiths, The
Marriner, Neville
Mars, Chris
    See Replacements, The
Mars, Mick
    See Mötley Crüe
Marsalis, Branford **10**
Marsalis, Ellis **13**
Marsalis, Wynton **6**
Marshal, Cornel
    See Third World
Martin, Barbara
    See Supremes, The
Martin, Christopher
    See Kid 'n Play
Martin, Dean **1**
Martin, George **6**
Martin, Greg
    See Kentucky Headhunters, The
Martin, Jim
    See Faith No More
Martin, Jimmy **5**
    Also See Osborne Brothers, The
Martin, Phonso
    See Steel Pulse
Martin, Sennie
    See Kool & the Gang
Martin, Tony
    See Black Sabbath
Marx, Richard **3**
Mascis, J
    See Dinosaur Jr.
Masdea, Jim
    See Boston
Masekela, Hugh **7**
Maseo, Baby Huey
    See De La Soul
Mason, Nick
    See Pink Floyd
Masse, Laurel
    See Manhattan Transfer, The
Massey, Bobby
    See O'Jays, The
Masur, Kurt **11**
Material
    See Laswell, Bill
Mathis, Johnny **2**
Matlock, Glen
    See Sex Pistols, The
Mattea, Kathy **5**
May, Brian
    See Queen
Mayall, John **7**
Mayfield, Curtis **8**
Mays, Odeen, Jr.
    See Kool & the Gang
Mazibuko, Abednigo
    See Ladysmith Black Mambazo
Mazibuko, Albert
    See Ladysmith Black Mambazo

Monkees, The **7**
Monroe, Bill **1**
Montand, Yves **12**
Montgomery, John Michael **14**
Montgomery, Wes **3**
Monti, Steve
  See Curve
Moon, Keith
  See Who, The
Moore, Alan
  See Judas Priest
Moore, Angelo
  See Fishbone
Moore, Melba **7**
Moore, Sam
  See Sam and Dave
Moore, Thurston
  See Sonic Youth
Moraz, Patrick
  See Yes
Morgan, Frank **9**
Morgan, Lorrie **10**
Morley, Pat
  See Soul Asylum
Morris, Kenny
  See Siouxsie and the Banshees
Morris, Stephen
  See New Order
Morrison, Bram
  See Sharon, Lois & Bram
Morrison, Jim **3**
  Also see Doors, The
Morrison, Sterling
  See Velvet Underground, The
Morrison, Van **3**
Morrissey **10**
  Also see Smiths, The
Morrissey, Bill **12**
Morrissey, Steven Patrick
  See Morrissey
Morton, Everett
  See English Beat, The
Morton, Jelly Roll **7**
Morvan, Fab
  See Milli Vanilli
Mosely, Chuck
  See Faith No More
Moser, Scott "Cactus"
  See Highway 101
Mosley, Bob
  See Moby Grape
Mothersbaugh, Bob
  See Devo
Mothersbaugh, Mark
  See Devo
Mötley Crüe **1**
Motörhead **10**
Motta, Danny
  See Roomful of Blues
Mould, Bob **10**
Moulding, Colin
  See XTC
Mouskouri, Nana **12**
Moyet, Alison **12**
Mr. Dalvin
  See Jodeci

Mueller, Karl
  See Soul Asylum
Mullen, Larry, Jr.
  See U2
Murph
  See Dinosaur Jr.
Murphey, Michael Martin **9**
Murphy, Dan
  See Soul Asylum
Murray, Anne **4**
Murray, Dave
  See Iron Maiden
Musselwhite, Charlie **13**
Mustaine, Dave
  See Megadeth
  Also see Metallica
Mwelase, Jabulane
  See Ladysmith Black Mambazo
Mydland, Brent
  See Grateful Dead, The
Myers, Alan
  See Devo
Myles, Alannah **4**
Nadirah
  See Arrested Development
Nagler, Eric **8**
Nakamura, Tetsuya "Tex"
  See War
Nakatami, Michie
  See Shonen Knife
Nascimento, Milton **6**
Nashville Bluegrass Band **14**
Nastanovich, Bob
  See Pavement
Naughty by Nature **11**
Navarro, David
  See Jane's Addiction
Nawasadio, Sylvie
  See Zap Mama
N'Dour, Youssou **6**
Near, Holly **1**
Neel, Johnny
  See Allman Brothers, The
Negron, Chuck
  See Three Dog Night
Neil, Vince
  See Mötley Crüe
Nelson, Errol
  See Black Uhuru
Nelson, Rick **2**
Nelson, Willie **11**
  Earlier sketch in CM **1**
Nesmith, Mike
  See Monkees, The
Neville, Aaron **5**
  Also see Neville Brothers, The
Neville, Art
  See Meters, The
  Also see Neville Brothers, The
Neville, Charles
  See Neville Brothers, The
Neville, Cyril
  See Meters, The
  Also see Neville Brothers, The
Neville Brothers, The **4**
New Grass Revival, The **4**

New Kids on the Block **3**
Newman, Randy **4**
Newmann, Kurt
  See BoDeans, The
New Order **11**
New Rhythm and Blues Quartet
  See NRBQ
Newton, Wayne **2**
Newton-John, Olivia **8**
Nicholls, Geoff
  See Black Sabbath
Nichols, Todd
  See Toad the Wet Sprocket
Nicks, Stevie **2**
  Also see Fleetwood Mac
Nico
  See Velvet Underground, The
Nielsen, Rick
  See Cheap Trick
Nilsson **10**
Nilsson, Harry
  See Nilsson
Nirvana **8**
Nisbett, Steve "Grizzly"
  See Steel Pulse
Nitty Gritty Dirt Band, The **6**
Nocentelli, Leo
  See Meters, The
Noone, Peter
  See Herman's Hermits
Norica, Sugar Ray
  See Roomful of Blues
Norman, Jessye **7**
Norman, Jimmy
  See Coasters, The
Norvo, Red **12**
Novoselic, Chris
  See Nirvana
NRBQ **12**
Nugent, Ted **2**
Nunn, Bobby
  See Coasters, The
N.W.A. **6**
Nyolo, Sally
  See Zap Mama
Nyro, Laura **12**
Oakley, Berry
  See Allman Brothers, The
Oak Ridge Boys, The **7**
Oates, John
  See Hall & Oates
O'Brien, Dwayne
  See Little Texas
O'Bryant, Alan
  See Nashville Bluegrass Band
Ocasek, Ric **5**
Ocean, Billy **4**
Oceans, Lucky
  See Asleep at the Wheel
Ochs, Phil **7**
O'Connell, Chris
  See Asleep at the Wheel
O'Connor, Billy
  See Blondie
O'Connor, Daniel
  See House of Pain

Poindexter, Buster
 See Johansen, David
Pointer, Anita
 See Pointer Sisters, The
Pointer, Bonnie
 See Pointer Sisters, The
Pointer, June
 See Pointer Sisters, The
Pointer, Ruth
 See Pointer Sisters, The
Pointer Sisters, The **9**
Poison **11**
Poland, Chris
 See Megadeth
Polygon Window
 See Aphex Twin
Pomus, Doc
 See Doc Pomus
Ponty, Jean-Luc **8**
Pop, Iggy **1**
Porter, Cole **10**
Porter, George, Jr.
 See Meters, The
Porter, Tiran
 See Doobie Brothers, The
Posdnuos
 See De La Soul
Potts, Sean
 See Chieftains, The
Powell, Billy
 See Lynyrd Skynyrd
Powell, Cozy
 See Emerson, Lake & Palmer/Powell
Powell, William
 See O'Jays, The
Prater, Dave
 See Sam and Dave
Presley, Elvis **1**
Pretenders, The **8**
Price, Leontyne **6**
Price, Louis
 See Temptations, The
Price, Ray **11**
Price, Rick
 See Electric Light Orchestra
Pride, Charley **4**
Primal Scream **14**
Primettes, The
 See Supremes, The
Primus **11**
Prince **14**
 Earlier sketch in CM **1**
Prince Be
 See P.M. Dawn
Prine, John **7**
Proclaimers, The **13**
Professor Longhair **6**
Propes, Duane
 See Little Texas
Prout, Brian
 See Diamond Rio
Public Enemy **4**
Puente, Tito **14**
Pusey, Clifford "Moonie"
 See Steel Pulse
Pyle, Artemis
 See Lynyrd Skynyrd

Q-Tip
 See Tribe Called Quest, A
Queen **6**
Queen Ida **9**
Queen Latifah **6**
Queensrÿche **8**
Querfurth, Carl
 See Roomful of Blues
Rabbitt, Eddie **5**
Rabin, Trevor
 See Yes
Raffi **8**
Raheem
 See Geto Boys, The
Raitt, Bonnie **3**
Rakim
 See Eric B. and Rakim
Ramone, C. J.
 See Ramones, The
Ramone, Dee Dee
 See Ramones, The
Ramone, Joey
 See Ramones, The
Ramone, Johnny
 See Ramones, The
Ramone, Marky
 See Ramones, The
Ramone, Ritchie
 See Ramones, The
Ramone, Tommy
 See Ramones, The
Ramones, The **9**
Rampal, Jean-Pierre **6**
Ranaldo, Lee
 See Sonic Youth
Randall, Bobby
 See Sawyer Brown
Ranken, Andrew
 See Pogues, The
Ranking Roger
 See English Beat, The
Rarebell, Herman
 See Scorpions, The
Ray, Amy
 See Indigo Girls
Raymonde, Simon
 See Cocteau Twins, The
Rea, Chris **12**
Reagon, Bernice Johnson
 See Sweet Honey in the Rock
Redding, Otis **5**
Reddy, Helen **9**
Red Hot Chili Peppers, The **7**
Redman, Joshua **12**
Redpath, Jean **1**
Reed, Lou **1**
 Also see Velvet Underground, The
Reese, Della **13**
Reeves, Jim **10**
Reeves, Martha **4**
Reich, Steve **8**
Reid, Charlie
 See Proclaimers, The
Reid, Christopher
 See Kid 'n Play
Reid, Craig
 See Proclaimers, The

Reid, Delroy "Junior"
 See Black Uhuru
Reid, Don
 See Statler Brothers, The
Reid, Ellen Lorraine
 See Crash Test Dummies
Reid, Harold
 See Statler Brothers, The
Reid, Janet
 See Black Uhuru
Reid, Jim
 See Jesus and Mary Chain, The
Reid, Vernon **2**
 Also see Living Colour
Reid, William
 See Jesus and Mary Chain, The
Reinhardt, Django **7**
Relf, Keith
 See Yardbirds, The
R.E.M. **5**
Reno, Ronnie
 See Osborne Brothers, The
Replacements, The **7**
Residents, The **14**
Restless Heart **12**
Rex
 See Pantera
Reyes, Andre
 See Gipsy Kings, The
Reyes, Canut
 See Gipsy Kings, The
Reyes, Nicolas
 See Gipsy Kings, The
Reynolds, Nick
 See Kingston Trio, The
Reynolds, Sheldon
 See Earth, Wind and Fire
Reznor, Trent **13**
Rhodes, Nick
 See Duran Duran
Rhone, Sylvia **13**
Rich, Buddy **13**
Rich, Charlie **3**
Richard, Cliff **14**
Richard, Keith
 See Richards, Keith
Richard, Zachary **9**
Richards, Keith **11**
 Also see Rolling Stones, The
Richie, Lionel **2**
Richman, Jonathan **12**
Rieckermann, Ralph
 See Scorpions, The
Rieflin, William
 See Ministry
Riley, Teddy **14**
Riley, Timothy Christian
 See Tony! Toni! Toné!
Rippon, Steve
 See Lush
Ritchie, Brian
 See Violent Femmes
Ritchie, Jean **4**
Ritenour, Lee **7**
Roach, Max **12**
Robbins, Marty **9**

Schuman, William **10**
Schuur, Diane **6**
Scofield, John **7**
Scorpions, The **12**
Scott, Ronald Belford "Bon"
    See AC/DC
Scott, George
    See Five Blind Boys of Alabama
Scott, Howard
    See War
Scott, Jimmy **14**
Scott, Sherry
    See Earth, Wind and Fire
Scott-Heron, Gil **13**
Scruggs, Earl **3**
Seal **14**
Seals, Brady
    See Little Texas
Seals, Dan **9**
Seals, Jim
    See Seals & Crofts
Seals & Crofts **3**
Sears, Pete
    See Jefferson Starship
Secada, Jon **13**
Sedaka, Neil **4**
    Seeger, Pete **4**
        Also see Weavers, The
Segovia, Andres **6**
Seldom Scene, The **4**
Sen Dog
    See Cypress Hill
Sepultura **12**
Seraphine, Daniel
    See Chicago
Sermon, Erick
    See EPMD
Setzer, Brian
    See Stray Cats, The
Severin, Steven
    See Siouxsie and the Banshees
Severinsen, Doc **1**
Sex Pistols, The **5**
Seymour, Neil
    See Crowded House
Shabalala, Ben
    See Ladysmith Black Mambazo
Shabalala, Headman
    See Ladysmith Black Mambazo
Shabalala, Jockey
    See Ladysmith Black Mambazo
Shabalala, Joseph
    See Ladysmith Black Mambazo
Shaffer, Paul **13**
Shakespeare, Robbie
    See Sly and Robbie
Shallenberger, James
    See Kronos Quartet
Shane, Bob
    See Kingston Trio, The
Shanice **14**
Shankar, Ravi **9**
Shannon, Del **10**
Shanté **10**
Shanté, Roxanne
    See Shanté

Sharon, Lois & Bram **6**
Shaw, Artie **8**
Shearer, Harry
    See Spinal Tap
Sheehan, Fran
    See Boston
Sheila E. **3**
Shelley, Peter
    See Buzzcocks, The
Shelley, Steve
    See Sonic Youth
Sherba, John
    See Kronos Quartet
Sherman, Jack
    See Red Hot Chili Peppers, The
Shines, Johnny **14**
Shirelles, The **11**
Shocked, Michelle **4**
Shock G
    See Digital Underground
Shogren, Dave
    See Doobie Brothers, The
Shonen Knife **13**
Shontz, Bill
    See Rosenshontz
Shorter, Wayne **5**
Siberry, Jane **6**
Siegal, Janis
    See Manhattan Transfer, The
Sikes, C. David
    See Boston
Sills, Beverly **5**
Silva, Kenny Jo
    See Beaver Brown Band, The
Simien, Terrance **12**
Simmons, Gene
    See Kiss
Simmons, Joe "Run"
    See Run-D.M.C.
Simmons, Patrick
    See Doobie Brothers, The
Simmons, Russell **7**
Simon, Carly **4**
Simon, Paul **1**
Simone, Nina **11**
Simonon, Paul
    See Clash, The
Simpson, Derrick "Duckie"
    See Black Uhuru
Simpson, Ray
    See Village People, The
Sinatra, Frank **1**
Singer, Eric
    See Black Sabbath
Sioux, Siouxsie
    See Siouxsie and the Banshees
Siouxsie and the Banshees **8**
Sir Mix-A-Lot **14**
Sir Rap-A-Lot
    See Geto Boys, The
Sixx, Nikki
    See Mötley Crüe
Skaggs, Ricky **5**
    Also see Country Gentlemen, The
Skillings, Muzz
    See Living Colour

Skoob
    See Das EFX
Slash
    See Guns n' Roses
Slayer **10**
Sledd, Dale
    See Osborne Brothers, The
Slick, Grace
    See Jefferson Airplane
Slovak, Hillel
    See Red Hot Chili Peppers, The
Sly and Robbie **13**
Smalls, Derek
    See Spinal Tap
Smashing Pumpkins **13**
Smith, Adrian
    See Iron Maiden
Smith, Bessie **3**
Smith, Chad
    See Red Hot Chili Peppers, The
Smith, Charles
    See Kool & the Gang
Smith, Curt
    See Tears for Fears
Smith, Debbie
    See Curve
Smith, Fred
    See Blondie
Smith, Fred
    See MC5, The
Smith, Garth
    See Buzzcocks, The
Smith, Mark E.
    See Fall, The
Smith, Michael W. **11**
Smith, Mike
    See Dave Clark Five, The
Smith, Parrish
    See EPMD
Smith, Patti **1**
Smith, Robert
    See Cure, The
    Also see Siouxsie and the
        Banshees
Smith, Smitty
    See Three Dog Night
Smith, Tweed
    See War
Smith, Willard
    See DJ Jazzy Jeff and the Fresh
        Prince
Smithereens, The **14**
Smiths, The **3**
Smyth, Joe
    See Sawyer Brown
Sneed, Floyd Chester
    See Three Dog Night
Snow, Don
    See Squeeze
Snow, Phoebe **4**
Solal, Martial **4**
Soloff, Lew
    See Blood, Sweat and Tears
Solti, Georg **13**
Sondheim, Stephen **8**
Sonic Youth **9**

Willson-Piper, Marty
  See Church, The
Wilton, Michael
  See Queensryche
Wimpfheimer, Jimmy
  See Roomful of Blues
Winans, Carvin
  See Winans, The
Winans, Marvin
  See Winans, The
Winans, Michael
  See Winans, The
Winans, Ronald
  See Winans, The
Winans, The 12
Winfield, Chuck
  See Blood, Sweat and Tears
Winston, George 9
Winter, Johnny 5
Winter, Paul 10
Winwood, Steve 2
Wolstencraft, Simon
  See Fall, The
Womack, Bobby 5
Wonder, Stevie 2
Wood, Danny
  See New Kids on the Block
Wood, Ron
  See Rolling Stones, The
Wood, Roy
  See Electric Light Orchestra
Woods, Terry
  See Pogues, The
Woodson, Ollie
  See Temptations, The
Woody, Allen
  See Allman Brothers, The
Woolfolk, Andrew
  See Earth, Wind and Fire
Worrell, Bernie 11

Wreede, Katrina
  See Turtle Island String Quartet
Wretzky, D'Arcy
  See Smashing Pumpkins
Wright, David "Blockhead"
  See English Beat, The
Wright, Jimmy
  See Sounds of Blackness
Wright, Norman
  See Country Gentlemen, The
Wright, Rick
  See Pink Floyd
Wright, Simon
  See AC/DC
Wurzel
  See Motörhead
Wyman, Bill
  See Rolling Stones, The
Wynette, Tammy 2
Wynonna 11
    Also see Judds, The
X 11
XTC 10
Ya Kid K
  See Technotronic
Yamamoto, Hiro
  See Soundgarden
Yamano, Atsuko
  See Shonen Knife
Yamano, Naoko
  See Shonen Knife
Yamashita, Kazuhito 4
Yankovic, "Weird Al" 7
Yanni 11
Yardbirds, The 10
Yarrow, Peter
  See Peter, Paul & Mary
Yates, Bill
  See Country Gentlemen, The
Yauch, Adam
  See Beastie Boys, The

Yearwood, Trisha 10
Yella
  See N.W.A.
Yes 8
Yoakam, Dwight 1
York, John
  See Byrds, The
Young, Angus
  See AC/DC
Young, Faron 7
Young, Fred
  See Kentucky Headhunters, The
Young, Gary
  See Pavement
Young, Grant
  See Soul Asylum
Young, Jeff
  See Megadeth
Young, Lester 14
Young, Malcolm
  See AC/DC
Young, Neil 2
Young, Richard
  See Kentucky Headhunters, The
Young, Robert "Throbert"
  See Primal Scream
Young M.C. 4
Yo Yo 9
Yule, Doug
  See Velvet Underground, The
Zander, Robin
  See Cheap Trick
Zap Mama 14
Zappa, Frank 1
Zevon, Warren 9
Zimmerman, Udo 5
Zoom, Billy
  See X
Zukerman, Pinchas 4
ZZ Top 2